Change and Stability

Change and Stability

A Cross-National Analysis of Social Structure and Personality

Melvin L. Kohn

Paradigm Publishers
Boulder•London

Copyright © 2006 Paradigm Publishers

Published in the United States by Paradigm Publishers, 3360 Mitchell Lane Suite E, Boulder, CO 80301 USA.

Paradigm Publishers is the trade name of Birkenkamp & Company, LLC, Dean Birkenkamp, President and Publisher.

ISBN 1-59451-175-6 (cloth)

Library of Congress Cataloging-in-Publication Data

Kohn, Melvin L., 1928–
    Change and stability : a cross-national analysis of social structure
and personality / Melvin L. Kohn.
      p. cm.
    Includes bibliographical references and index.
    ISBN 1-59451-175-6 (hc)
    1. Social structure—Psychological aspects—Cross-cultural studies.
    2. Social stability—Psychological aspects—Cross-cultural studies.
    3. Social change—Psychological aspects—Cross-cultural studies.
    4. Personality and situation—Cross-cultural studies.   5. Personality
and culture—Cross-cultural studies.   I. Title.
HM706.K64 2005
155.9′2—dc22

2005015681

Designed and typeset by Straight Creek Bookmakers.

10 09 08 07 06 5 4 3 2 1

To Janet,
My partner in life for more than half a century, 'til her death did us part.

Contents

List of Tables and Figures   ix

Preface   xiii

Acknowledgments   xix

1. Social Structure and Personality under Conditions of Apparent
   Social Stability: The United States, Japan, and Poland   1

2. Doing Social Research under Conditions of Radical
   Social Change: The Biography of an Ongoing Research Project   53

3. Rationale and Research Design for the Comparative Study
   of Poland and Ukraine under Conditions of Radical Social Change   77

4. Class, Stratification, and Personality under Conditions of Radical
   Social Change: A Comparative Analysis of Poland and Ukraine   91

5. Extending the Analysis to the Nonemployed: Part 1. Complexity of
   Activities and Personality under Conditions of Radical Social Change   125

6. Extending the Analysis to the Nonemployed: Part 2. Structural Location
   and Personality during the Transformation of Poland and Ukraine   151

7. Social Structure and Personality during the Process of
   Radical Social Change: A Study of Ukraine in Transition   175

8. Reflections   219

Appendix: My Two Visits to My Mother's Village:
    A Glimpse at Social Change in Rural Ukraine   239

References   245

Index   253

About the Author   267

Tables and Figures

Tables

Table 1.1   Measurement Models of Social-Stratificational Position, for
U.S. Men (1964 to 1974), Japanese Men (1979), and Polish
Men (1978).   15

Table 1.2   Relationship of Social Class to Social Stratification, for U.S.
Men (1974), Japanese Men (1979), and Polish Men (1978).   17

Table 1.3   Measurement Models of Parental Valuation of Self-Direction
vs. Conformity to External Authority, for U.S. Fathers (1964
to 1974), Japanese Fathers (1979), and Polish Fathers (1978).   20

Table 1.4   Measurement Models of Intellectual Flexibility, for U.S. Men
(1964 to 1974), Japanese Men (1979), and Polish Men (1978).   21

Table 1.5   Measurement Models of Orientations to Self and Society, for
U.S. Men (1964 to 1974), Japanese Men (1979), and Polish
Men (1978).   25

Table 1.6   Relationships of Social Class with Parental Valuation of Self-
Direction, Self-Directedness of Orientation, Distress, and
Intellectual Flexibility, for U.S. Men (1964 and 1974),
Japanese Men (1979), and Polish Men (1978).   31

Table 1.7   (Multiple-) Partial Correlations of Social Stratification and of
Social Class with Personality, for U.S. Men (1974), Japanese
Men (1979), and Polish Men (1978).   34

Table 1.8   Measurement Models of Occupational Self-Direction, for
U.S. Men (1964 to 1974), Japanese Men (1979), and Polish
Men (1978).   37

Table 1.9   Relationships of Class and Stratification with Occupational Self-
Direction, for U.S. Men (1974), Japanese Men (1979), and
Polish Men (1978).   38

Table 1.10   Effects on Class Correlations of Statistically Controlling Occupational Self-Direction, Social Characteristics, and Social Stratification, for U.S. Men (1974), Japanese Men (1979), and Polish Men (1978).   41

Table 1.11   The Reciprocal Effects of Occupational Self-Direction and Personality, for U.S. Men (1964 and 1974), Japanese Men (1979), and Polish Men (1978).   45

Table 4.1   Measurement Models of First-Order Dimensions of Orientation to Self and Society, for Poland (1992) and Ukraine (1992–1993).   96

Table 4.2   "Second-Order" Measurement Models of Orientation, for Poland (1992) and Ukraine (1992–1993).   99

Table 4.3   Measurement Models of Intellectual Flexibility, for Poland (1992) and Ukraine (1992–1993).   101

Table 4.4   Measurement Models of Social-Stratificational Position, for Poland (1992) and Ukraine (1992–1993).   104

Table 4.5   Class, Stratification, and Personality, for Poland (1992) and Ukraine (1992–1993).   106

Table 4.6   Measurement Models of the Job Conditions That Facilitate or Limit the Exercise of Occupational Self-Direction, for Poland (1992) and Ukraine (1992–1993).   111

Table 4.7   The Relationships of Social Class and Social Stratification with the Job Conditions That Facilitate or Limit the Exercise of Occupational Self-Direction, for Poland (1992) and Ukraine (1992–1993).   112

Table 4.8   (Multiple-) Partial Correlations: Class and Stratification with Personality, Statistically Controlling the Substantive Complexity of Work, Closeness of Supervision, and Routinization, for Poland (1992) and Ukraine (1992–1993).   114

Table 4.9   Zero-Order Correlations of the Substantive Complexity of Work, Closeness of Supervision, and Routinization with Personality, for Poland (1992) and Ukraine (1992–1993).   116

Table 5.1   Measurement Models of Complexity of Activities, for Unemployed and Pensioned Polish Men and Women (1992).   137

Table 5.2   Measurement Models of Complexity of Household Work, for Polish Housewives (1992) and Ukrainian Housewives (1992–1993).   140

Table 5.3   Correlations of Several Measures of Complexity of Activities with Personality, by Country and Gender: U.S. Men (1974), Polish Men (1978), Polish Men and Women (1992), and Ukrainian Men and Women (1992–1993).   142

Table 5.4   Partial Correlations of Complexity of Activities with Personality, Statistically Controlling Educational Attainment and the Substantive Complexity of Past Jobs: Poland (1992) and Ukraine (1992–1993).   146

Table 6.1   Structural Location and Personality, by Country and Gender:
             Poland (1992) and Ukraine (1992–1993).   157
Table 6.2   Structural Location and Personality—Statistically Controlling
             Age and Educational Attainment, by Country and Gender:
             Poland (1992) and Ukraine (1992–1993).   160
Table 6.3   Measurement Models of Perceived Economic Well-Being,
             for Poland (1992) and Ukraine (1992–1993).   166
Table 6.4   Structural Location and Distress—Statistically Controlling
             Perceived Economic Well-Being, by Country and Gender:
             Poland (1992) and Ukraine (1992–1993).   167
Table 6.5   Measurement Model of Complexity of Activities—Estimated
             for Employed, Unemployed, and Pensioned Polish Adults as a
             Single Population (1992).   169
Table 6.6   Structural Location and Personality—Statistically Controlling
             Complexity of Activities: Limited to Polish Employed,
             Unemployed (Other than Unemployed Housewives), and
             Pensioners (1992).   170
Table 7.1   Longitudinal Measurement Model of Authoritarian
             Conservatism, Ukraine (1992–1993 to 1996).   181
Table 7.2   Over-time Correlations of First-Order Dimensions of
             Orientation, Ukrainian Men and Women (1992–1993 to 1996),
             U.S. Men (1964 to 1974), and Polish Men and Women
             (1992 to 1996).   183
Table 7.3   "Second-Order" Longitudinal Measurement Model of
             Orientation, Ukraine (1992–1993 to 1996).   185
Table 7.4   Longitudinal Measurement Model of Intellectual Flexibility,
             Ukraine (1992–1993 to 1996).   187
Table 7.5   Structural Location and Personality, Ukraine (1992–1993 and
             1996).   191
Table 7.6   Longitudinal Measurement Model of Social-Stratificational
             Position, Ukraine (1992–1993 to 1996).   194
Table 7.7   Social-Stratificational Position and Personality, Ukraine
             (1992–1993 and 1996).   196
Table 7.8   Movement to and from the Ranks of the Employed and
             Change in Personality, Ukraine, from 1992–1993 to 1996.   198
Table 7.9   Longitudinal Measurement Model of the Substantive
             Complexity of Work in Paid Employment, Ukraine
             (1992–1993 to 1996).   203
Table 7.10   Social Structure and the Substantive Complexity of Work
             in Paid Employment for Ukrainian Men and Women
             Employed Both in 1992–1993 and in 1996.   205
Table 7.11   The Degree to Which the Relationships of Social Class and
             Social Stratification with Personality Are Attributable to the
             Substantive Complexity of Work, Ukraine (1992–1993 and
             1996).   207

Table 7.12   Longitudinal Measurement Model of Perceived Economic
              Well-Being, Ukraine (1992–1993 to 1996).   212
Table 7.13   Correlations of the Substantive Complexity of Work and of
              Perceived Economic Well-Being or Duress with Feelings of
              Distress, Ukraine (1992–1993 and 1996).   213
Table 7.14   Structural Location and Distress—Unadjusted and Statistically
              Controlling Perceived Economic Well-Being, for Ukrainian
              Men and Women in 1996.   214

Figures

Figure 1.1   Schematic Outline of U.S. Class Categories.   8
Figure 1.2   Schematic Outline of Polish Class Categories.   13
Figure 1.3   Prototypic Model: The Reciprocal Effects of Occupational
              Self-Direction and Personality.   44
Figure 7.1   The Reciprocal Effects of the Substantive Complexity of Work
              and Intellectual Flexibility: U.S. Men (1964 and 1974),
              Ukrainian Men (1992–1993 and 1996), and Ukrainian
              Women (1992–1993 and 1996).   209

Preface

None of my books started out to be a book, this one least of all. In each instance, I started with a theoretical or empirical problem, did research directed to solving that problem, moved along from the initial problem to others that came to the fore as each in turn was addressed, published articles about my empirical studies of these problems, and only gradually over the years, as the articles formed larger intellectual entities, felt compelled to bring them all together to elucidate those entities and draw out their implications in what I intended to be comprehensive and coherent volumes.

Class and Conformity: A Study in Values (a double misnomer, for it would have been more accurate, if less alliterative, to call the main title, *Social Stratification and Self-direction*) was my first such venture. Some reviewers of my later books say that this one established "the paradigm," while the subsequent books were "normal science," but I see a rather more gradual development of the thesis throughout a long series of articles and books. The core idea was set forth, even if the nomenclature was as yet imprecise, in a speculative paper called "Social Class and Parent-Child Relationships: An Interpretation," published in 1963. This paper was incorporated into *Class and Conformity,* which set forth a somewhat more precise but still incomplete statement of the central thesis and tested it about as well as was possible with only cross-sectional data based primarily on a survey of employed men in a single country, using the statistical methods available forty-some years ago.

That thesis, familiar to anyone who has read any of my writings, is that position in the larger social structure affects (and is affected by) personality primarily because of the strong linkages of social-structural position to more proximate conditions of life, and of the linkages of these conditions of life to individual personality. When one focuses on *class* and *stratification* as the dimensions of social structure under investigation, as I generally do, these proximate conditions of life are necessarily mainly occupational, particularly (but not only) the occupational conditions that facilitate or impede the exercise of self-direction in work—first and foremost, the substantive complexity of that work, but also how closely the work is supervised and how routinized it is. This thesis has stood the test of repeated replication, its validity and its power having been assessed in a host of studies in many countries (see the reviews in Kohn and Schooler 1983, Chapter 12; and Kohn and Słomczynski 1990, Chapter 9, especially pp. 251–259).

In the second book, *Work and Personality: An Inquiry into the Impact of Social Stratification* (coauthored with Carmi Schooler), the principal concepts were refined and the empirical analyses broadened in many ways: (1) by distinguishing between *social stratification* and *social class* and by developing a conceptualization of social class more consonant with my treatment of occupational conditions than the previous conceptualizations on which I built; (2) by examining the relationships of job conditions to personality for women as well as for men, even though we did not yet have a sample fully representative of all employed women;[1] (3) by considerably enlarging the range of job conditions studied, to encompass not only the conditions that facilitate or impede the exercise of occupational self-direction, but all the conditions of work that we termed "structural imperatives of the job"; (4) by assessing the psychological effects, not only of the work done in paid employment but also of the work done in housework; (5) by examining not only the subjective phenomena we call personality but also (reported) behavior; and (6)—crucially—by using the newly invented statistical techniques of confirmatory factor analysis and linear structural-equations modeling, applied to longitudinal data, to deal frontally with the central interpretive issue in the study of social structure and personality ever since Weber—*the direction of effects.* Do social-structural position and its attendant job conditions *affect* or only *reflect* personality? Schooler's and my (I think, definitive) answer to this long-standing question was that the relationship of social structure and personality is *quintessentially reciprocal.* I would now add: *at least under conditions of social stability.*

This might have been the end of my saga were it not for my exceptionally good fortune (described in Chapter 2 of the present book) of Włodzimierz Wesołowski's proposing and then sponsoring a replication of our principal survey in Poland to see whether the findings and interpretations of our U.S. research obtained in that socialist society. I had already had a small taste of cross-national research in

---

1. At the time of the original survey, we did not have the financial resources for a survey of representative samples of both employed men and employed women sufficiently large for the types of multivariate analysis feasible at that time. We therefore limited the initial study to employed men, intending to do a comparable study of employed women when we had the financial resources to do so, and when we had figured out how to deal with the frequent pattern of women leaving and later reentering the labor force with the birth and maturation of their children. But, soon after our initial survey, funds for social research were preempted by the government's giving priority to the Vietnam War. When we at last were able to do a study of women (in conjunction with a ten-year follow-up survey of a subsample of the men in the original study), we elected to base that study on the wives of those men, rather than on a sample fully representative of all employed women, to make possible analyses of parental influences on offspring's personalities (K. Miller, Kohn, and Schooler 1985; 1986) and of the *transmission of values* in the family (Kohn, Słomczynski, and Schoenbach 1986; Kohn and Słomczynski 1990, Chapter 7).

my limited participation in Leonard Pearlin's replication and extension in Turin, Italy, of an early study of mine done in Washington, D.C., and the promise of a full-scale study, testing the heart of my thesis in socialist Poland, was extremely appealing. The idea that a comparative analysis of Poland and the United States might eventuate in a book was the furthest thing from my mind; but here, again, as the analyses progressed and the papers cumulated, my principal collaborator, Kazimierz Słomczynski, and I produced, initially, a book in Polish (Słomczynski and Kohn 1988), and later a more fully developed version of that book in English, which we called *Social Structure and Self-Direction: A Comparative Analysis of the United States and Poland* (Kohn and Słomczynski 1990).

We characterized the latter book as both the third volume in a trilogy and a new venture, the new venture being to test whether the findings and interpretation of the U.S. research applied as well to a socialist society. In that book, we also incorporated a conceptualization of social class for Poland's socialist society that Słomczynski had developed, which we used in comparative analyses of social class and personality in the United States and Poland. Again in parallel for the two countries, we traced the consequences of social structure and attendant job conditions, not only for parents' values for their offspring, but continuing on to the carryover of parents' values to the offspring's own values.

I would say, and I hope that the reader of the first chapter of the present book (which summarizes and extends the central findings of that study, together with those of a parallel study of Japan that Carmi Schooler and Atsushi Naoi had conducted) would agree, that the central thesis held up extraordinarily well, albeit with some fascinating cross-national discrepancies, which we thought of as variations on theme. In some respects, though, the cross-national inconsistencies are even more intriguing than the consistencies that supported the generalizability of the interpretation. These inconsistencies became all the more intriguing as we were able to see whether they persisted as Poland was transformed from a socialist to a nascent capitalist society.

With the publication of the third volume in the trilogy, together with the one article (now incorporated into Chapter 1 of this book) that systematically compared the capitalist United States to socialist Poland, and both Poland and the United States to non-Western, capitalist Japan, I thought that my collaborators and I had answered the most important questions about the generalizability of the thesis across the principal boundaries of culture and sociopolitical system. And then the variant of the socialist system characteristic of the Soviet Union and Eastern Europe was overthrown, with Polish workers leading the way. I thought the challenge of finding out whether the core of the thesis applied even under the conditions of radical social change attendant on the transformation of Eastern Europe and the former Soviet Union irresistible.

Here I have an admission to make. When I wrote an initial draft of a grant proposal to do a comparative study of Poland and Ukraine in transition from socialism to nascent capitalism, I said that I expected our findings and interpretation to hold even under the extreme conditions of radical social change attendant on that transformation. In critiquing that draft for me, Carmi Schooler asked forthrightly, "If you are so sure that you will get the same findings as in all your past studies, why should any funding agency think it worthwhile to support the study?" As I spelled out for him, and later for the funding agencies, all the reasons why the past findings might very well *not* apply under these conditions, my expectations changed almost completely, and I came to expect that one or more of my alternative hypotheses would actually turn out to be valid.

I went into the new research with all the excitement of discoveries to be made, and with all the enthusiasm of venturing into new theoretical issues—a crucial one being whether the interpretive scheme applied not only to the employed but also to the nonemployed segments of the populations of the countries of Eastern Europe and the former Soviet Union. My collaborators and I published a series of papers, systematically assessing all the interpretive issues we had set out to study. Each paper, however, was self-contained, and the papers appeared in diverse journals: nobody was likely to see them all, or to do the integrative job of putting them all together. A familiar pattern had repeated itself: Here were all the ingredients for turning a set of separate, even if interconnected, papers into an integrated whole.

Still, despite my successful experiences in converting sets of papers into books, I was ambivalent about converting this particular set of papers into a book. This was partly because I wasn't quite sure until I got deeply into the analysis of longitudinal Ukrainian data (Chapter 7 of this book) that the findings of that analysis would actually turn out to be the climax, and not the anticlimax, of such a book: For a long while, I was dumbfounded by the unexpected discovery of extreme instability of personality in Ukraine during the early stages of the transition. Could longitudinal analyses of such data possibly yield conclusive findings about the relationships of social structure and personality? I wasn't at all certain that they could. And, partly, perhaps even mainly, I was hung up by the thought that a fourth volume might be one too many for a trilogy. Was there really enough new material here to justify a book? It was only as the analyses of the longitudinal data gelled that I was confident that the papers did form a coherent whole, that the whole was greater than the sum of its parts, and that there was an important story to be told.

I was reassured in this belief by a proposal from the Chinese Academy of Social Sciences that they translate and publish in Chinese *both* this book and its predecessor. Their proposal helped change my own conception of the book from "fourth in a trilogy" to a more feasible "second in a pair" (and, in all likelihood, "last in a series"). The first pair of books, though addressed to a thesis that was intended to apply to industrialized societies everywhere, was based primarily on studies carried out in the United States. The second pair of books is the fruit of my long-term venture into cross-national research, the first book in this pair about cross-national research done under conditions of social stability, the second—this one—about cross-national research done under conditions of radical social change.

The first chapter of this book, based on rigorously comparable studies of the United States, socialist Poland, and Japan, depicts the relationships of social structure and personality during times of apparent social stability; it is the baseline for all that follows. The following two chapters tell the personal story (mine and my collaborators') leading to our study of how these relationships were affected by the transition of Poland and Ukraine from socialism to nascent capitalism; and they present the theoretical rationale and research design of our comparative study of Poland and Ukraine. Next comes the comparative analysis of social structure and personality for the *employed segments* of the Polish and Ukrainian urban populations, which is followed by two chapters that extend the analyses of social structure and personality to the *nonemployed* segments of these populations. I then take advantage of the wonderful opportunity provided by my Ukrainian collaborators' follow-up survey, to assess the ongoing processes with fully longitudinal data. In the last chapter, I offer some reflections on the theoretical and methodological significance of the mode of cross-national research that the analyses of this book (building on its predecessors) have made. As a tidbit, almost a tease, I offer in an appendix a brief account (I think of it as amateur ethnography) of what I learned about radical social change in *rural* Ukraine from two visits to the village where my mother was born. It is a revealing tale.

Acknowledgments

I gratefully acknowledge that this book is based on research conducted with the full and invaluable collaboration of my friends:

Krystyna Janicka
Valeriy Khmelko
Bogdan W. Mach
Atsushi Naoi
Vladimir Paniotto
Carrie Schoenbach
Carmi Schooler
Kazimierz M. Słomczynski
and
Wojciech Zaborowski

It will become ever more evident as the book proceeds that I have been hugely dependent on my collaborators in all the research that I present in this book. And yet the book lists me as sole author. This was not the case in any of the original articles on which most of the chapters are based, which listed as coauthors all the collaborators who had made significant contributions to the formulation of the theoretical issues, the design of the research, the conduct of the surveys, or the analyses of the data on which the particular paper was based. I could not do the same for a book, if only because a set of nearly a dozen coauthors would appear to be a committee report rather than a book. When I initially thought of turning the articles into a book, I intended to use a device that I had employed in two previous books ("with the collaboration of..."). My publisher suggested that it would be more accurate to say, "with the *research* collaboration of ...," since I had done the actual writing of the earlier papers and would certainly do the actual writing in converting the papers into chapters of the book. That made sense to me, and in an e-mail to my Polish and Ukrainian collaborators I asked their permission to list them as research collaborators.

My long-standing Polish collaborator, Kazimierz Słomczynski, immediately counterproposed, first in a Thanksgiving-Day phone call, then in an e-mail to me and our Polish and Ukrainian collaborators, that a book is different from articles, with the writing counting for more, and that I should be listed as the sole author of a book in which I would integrate the several papers in the context of my general interpretation. My collaborators quickly agreed to this. I was, and remain, grateful to them for their generosity of spirit, even though I still preferred my original proposal.

I consulted my even longer-term U.S. collaborator, Carmi Schooler, who saw merit in Słomczynski's arguments, and agreed with his suggestions that I list my collaborators on a page other than the title page of the book, and describe their contributions to the research, although not necessarily in a single introductory essay, as Słomczynski had proposed. I have instead placed the detailed description of my collaborators' roles in prefatory notes to almost all of the chapters, so that I could tie the descriptions of their roles to the arenas in which they played those roles. I must admit, though, that I did find (rather to my surprise) that being listed as the sole author made it easier for me in writing this book to differentiate between what we (collectively) had done and what I (singularly) put forth as my own beliefs.

I (as a statement of individual belief) declare now, at the beginning of this book, that although I have put the words to paper, there would have been no words were it not for my having been blessed with marvelous collaborators. As you will see in the prefatory notes to the chapters of this book, and elsewhere throughout the text, I am immensely indebted to my invaluable collaborators in the research on which this book is based. Without their efforts, this research could not possibly have been done and there would have been no book to write. In the concluding chapter of the book, I will discuss in larger scope the particular mode of collaborative, cross-national research that we have together developed, its merits and its limitations—both for the research and for those whose lives are caught up in doing such research.

In the same prefatory notes in which I describe my collaborators' roles in the research on which each particular chapter is based, I also thank many of the people who helped us in the research described in that chapter or who critiqued one version or another of the paper that was predecessor to that particular chapter. Here, though, I want to thank a few people and institutions whose contributions extended more generally throughout the research on which this book is based.

Although I had left the National Institute of Mental Health before the publication of any of the papers on which this book is directly based, I remain indebted to the two long-term leaders of the Intramural Research Program of that Institute, John C. Eberhart and Robert A. Cohen. They provided both administrative and emotional support to me and my collaborators in the U.S., Polish, and Japanese studies underlying Chapter 1 and referred to in subsequent chapters.

Three eminent scholars and wonderful colleagues played remarkable roles in making possible the research in Poland, Japan, and Ukraine by their initiative, by their intellectual and emotional commitment to the research and to my collaborators and me personally, and by staking their own formidable scientific and scholarly credentials in sponsoring our research: Włodzimierz Wesołowski of Poland, Ken'ichi Tominaga of Japan, and Vladimir Yadov of Russia (and the former Soviet Union).

For sharing their technical expertise, I am also indebted to Ronald Schoenberg, who gave me valuable advice on many issues of data analysis and whose computer program I used for creating factor scores, a program that not only employs a sophisticated method of dealing with missing values but also provides the correlation between true scores and factor scores, which is invaluable for correcting unreliability in the factor scores; to Andrzej Wejland and Pawel Daniłowicz for their immense help in pretesting surveys in both Poland and Ukraine; and to Carmi Schooler and Mesfin Mulatu for advice about statistical problems I encountered in data-analysis at several junctures.

The comparative study of Poland and Ukraine in transition was financially supported (as described in Chapter 2) by institutions in three countries: the National Science Foundation (Grants #SES9107584 and #SRB-9728374) and the National Council for Soviet and East European Research (now the National Council for Eurasian and East European Research) in the United States; the State Committee for Scientific Research (KBN) in Poland; and the State Committee for Science and Technology in Ukraine.

The American Sociological Association has granted permission to use materials from two papers published in the *American Sociological Review* (Kohn 1987; Kohn et al. 1997) and three papers published in the *Social Psychology Quarterly* (Kohn 1993; Kohn et al. 2000; 2002). The University of Chicago Press has similarly permitted me to use materials published in the *American Journal of Sociology* (Kohn et al. 1990); and *Koninklijke Brill NV* (Brill Academic Publishers) has permitted me to use materials published in *Comparative Sociology* (Kohn et al. 2004). These organizations of course retain copyright to the original publications.

Chapter 1

Social Structure and Personality under Conditions of Apparent Social Stability

The United States, Japan, and Poland

This chapter is a substantial revision and extension of a paper coauthored with Atsushi Naoi, Carrie Schoenbach, Carmi Schooler, and Kazimierz Słomczynski and published in *The American Journal of Sociology* (*AJS*) (Kohn, Naoi, et al. 1990), with some text, tables, and two figures added from Kohn and Słomczynski (1990), other text added from Kohn (1987), and measurement models taken from several of the sources noted below. The *AJS* paper, and this chapter, build on prior published analyses: for the United States, from Kohn and Schoenbach (1983); for Poland, from Słomczynski, J. Miller, and Kohn (1981 and 1987), Słomczynski and Kohn (1988), and Kohn and Słomczynski (1990); and for Japan, from Naoi and Schooler (1985) and Schooler and Naoi (1988).

I developed the conceptualization of social class for the United States and other advanced capitalist societies; Schoenbach and I developed the criteria for differentiating the social classes for the United States; Naoi, Schooler, and Słomczynski developed the conceptualization of social class and the criteria for differentiating the social classes for Japan; and Słomczynski developed the conceptualization of social class and the criteria for differentiating the social classes for Poland. I did new causal analyses for all three countries, with considerable help from Schoenbach and with considerable reliance on earlier published analyses by all of my collaborators in the publications noted above. I also wrote most of the text,

1

with valuable editing by Schoenbach and with critical commentaries by my collaborators in the research.

I am indebted also to Karl Alexander, Andrew Cherlin, William Form, Alejandro Portes, Erik Olin Wright, and the *AJS* referees for critical readings of earlier drafts of the *AJS* paper.

In this chapter, I examine the relationship between social structure and personality in three diverse nations—the United States, Japan, and Poland when it was socialist—all of these countries appearing to be relatively stable at the time my collaborators and I studied them. Our intent was to ascertain whether position in the social structure[1] has similar or dissimilar psychological effects in capitalist and socialist industrialized societies, and in Western and non-Western industrialized societies. My intent in using these analyses as the introductory chapter in the present book is to establish a baseline for comparison to later analyses of the relationship between social structure and personality in nations undergoing radical social change.

In comparing the United States to Japan and to socialist Poland, my collaborators and I did not claim that the United States was typical of Western capitalist countries, Japan of non-Western capitalist countries, or Poland of socialist countries. Our rationale, instead, was that, if we found cross-national similarities in the psychological effects of class and stratification in these three countries, we could have considerable confidence that the findings have generality—not only beyond the boundaries of any one of these three nations, but also beyond any one *type* of society. If we found cross-national differences in the psychological effects of class and stratification, the deliberate choice of such diverse societies would help us to establish the limits of generality of the findings and perhaps even to understand whatever differences we found (see the extended discussion of these issues in Kohn [1987, pp. 716–724]).

This inquiry subsumes four specific questions: First, is it possible to conceptualize and to index social class in common terms in three such diverse societies? By

? #1

---

1. My definition of "social structure" is borrowed from House's (1981, p. 542) historical and analytic review of the field of social structure and personality: "A *social structure* is a *persisting* and bounded *pattern* of social relationships (or patterns of behavioral interaction) among the units (that is, persons or positions) in a social system." As I trust will be evident in my treatment of *social structure* throughout this book, my ideas are heavily influenced by Robin Williams's (1951, pp. 20–21) statement: "To demonstrate structure one need only show a recurrence of elements related in definite ways. In the interests of realism it is best to speak of the structure of social phenomena only where there is an *important* degree of continuity—where human activities are so patterned (recurrent) that we can observe a group standardization persisting, although changing, over a considerable time. Human beings in society do exhibit complexes of action, thought, and emotion (1) shared by many individuals, (2) repeated in many successive situations, (3) definitely related to *other* patterns in the same social aggregate. This is essentially all that is here meant by 'structure', an appreciable degree of regularity and relationship. There is thus nothing obscure or mystical about the concept, and the question of how definite and enduring the structure is in any particular case is left open for empirical study." My interest in this book is focused on the structure of the society as a whole, particularly the fundamental lines of organization and cleavage characteristic of that society.

social classes, I mean groups defined in terms of their relationship to ownership and control of the means of production, and of their control over the labor power of others. I deliberately distinguish social class from social stratification—the hierarchical ordering of society as indexed by educational attainment, occupational status, and job income. There is considerable evidence that social stratification is a quite general phenomenon and that one can index social stratification in much the same way in all industrialized nations (Treiman 1977). The question in this inquiry is whether it is meaningful to employ the concept, *social class,* not only in a Western, capitalist society, but also in a non-Western society and in a socialist society. Furthermore, can we develop indices of social class that not only are valid for all three countries, each with its own distinctive history, culture, and political-economic system, but also are comparable from country to country?

Second, is social class not only conceptually but also empirically distinct from social stratification? I see class and stratification as alternative conceptualizations of social structure, both conceptualizations theoretically useful, albeit not necessarily for answering the same questions. Class is the more fundamental concept, for it addresses the political and economic organization of the society. Yet, classes are internally heterogenous, each one encompassing a wide spectrum of occupations. In terms of the relationship of social structure to personality, class produces the basic map, but stratification affords a more fine-grained basis of differentiation. In this sense, the conceptualizations are not so much alternatives as they are complementary. Nonetheless, we must ask whether class and stratification are sufficiently distinct empirically that, in actual analysis, there is any utility in differentiating them. My concern here is not with testing the theoretical claims of either the proponents of class or the proponents of stratification, but only with ensuring that what we conclude from these analyses about the psychological effects of social class is not merely a reflection of the psychological effects of social stratification, or the reverse.

Third, does social class position have similar psychological effects in all three of these nations? I hypothesize that it does: I expect members of more "advantaged" social classes to be more intellectually flexible, to value self-direction more highly for their children, and to have more self-directed orientations to self and society than do members of less advantaged social classes in all three countries. By "advantaged," I do *not* mean higher in social-stratificational position, but rather advantaged in terms of the very definition of social class: having greater control over the means of production and greater control over the labor power of others.

Since social class is a multidimensional typology rather than a unidimensional rank-ordering, this hypothesis does not imply a single rank-ordering but rather a complex set of comparisons. In terms of *ownership* of the means of production, for example, employers (even small employers) and the self-employed are more advantaged than are *any* employees (even executives of multinational corporations). In terms of *control* over the means of production, managers are more advantaged than are many small employers. And in terms of *control over people,* managers and even some first-line supervisors are more advantaged than are small employers and the self-employed. I would expect employers and managers, who generally have greatest control over the means of production and the labor power of others, to value self-direction most highly and manual workers, who have least control over the means of production and the labor power of others, to value self-direction least highly. Similarly, I would expect employers and managers to have the most self-directed orientations and to be the most intellectually flexible of all the social classes, and manual workers to be at the other extreme. But, since the other social classes are advantaged in some respects and disadvantaged in other respects, I have no *a priori* basis for predicting their relative ranking with respect to their values, orientations, or intellectual functioning. Moreover, I have no basis for expecting either cross-national similarity or dissimilarity in the relationships between social class and the sense of well-being or of distress.

P # 4   Fourth, what explains the psychological effects of social class? I think that the explanation will be much the same as the explanation for the psychological effects of social stratification. In all three countries, the cross-nationally consistent relationships of social stratification with parental valuation of self-direction, self-directedness of orientation, and intellectual flexibility result, in large part, from the job conditions associated with social-stratification position: People of higher position enjoy greater opportunity to be self-directed in their work; the experience of occupational self-direction, in turn, has a profound effect on people's values, orientations, and cognitive functioning (for the United States, see Kohn and Schoenbach 1983; for Poland, see Słomczynski, Miller, and Kohn 1981 or 1987, and Kohn and Słomczynski 1990; for Japan, see Naoi and Schooler 1985). I hypothesize that social class will affect people's values, self-directedness of orientation, and intellectual flexibility for much the same reason: because those who are more advantageously located in the class structure have greater opportunity to be self-directed in their work.

This is a very strong hypothesis. I *define* social class in terms of ownership and control over the means of production and control over the labor power of others; but I hypothesize that the reason *why* social class affects personality is because class position is determinative of how much control one has over the conditions of one's *own* work. There is nothing in the classic definition of social class, nor in the criteria I employ to index social class, that speaks directly to the issue of control over the conditions of one's own occupational life. Yet, on the basis of Schooler's and my analyses of job conditions and personality (Kohn and Schooler 1983, particularly Chapter 6), I believe that what is psychologically crucial about control in the workplace is not control over others, but control over the conditions of one's own life—*occupational self-direction.* I therefore hypothesize that what is psychologically important about having an advantaged class position is not the power over others that it affords, nor even the socioeconomic rewards that it confers, but the opportunity it provides to be self-directed in one's own occupational life. Conversely, the psychological importance of a disadvantaged class position lies primarily in the limits it imposes on the opportunity to be self-directed in one's occupational life.

My belief that position in the class structure has generally similar psychological effects in the United States, Japan, and Poland, and for essentially the same reasons, in no way denies that class structure differs in different economic and political systems. Nor do I dispute that the contemporary class structure of any particular country has been shaped by the history and culture of that country. Quite the contrary: I believe that it is necessary to develop indices of social class that are attuned to the particular history, culture, and political and economic systems of each country, and my collaborators and I have done so. Nonetheless, I hypothesize that the psychological effects of social class, and the explanation of these effects, will be generally similar in all industrial societies—capitalist and socialist, Western and non-Western.

Samples and Methods of Data Collection

The analyses of this chapter are based on three studies, the original study done in the United States, with replications in Japan and Poland. These analyses are limited to men, since the data for women are not sufficiently comprehensive for class analysis.

The original U.S. survey was based on interviews conducted for Carmi Schooler and me by the National Opinion Research Center in 1964, based on a representative sample of 3,101 men, 16 years old or older, employed in civilian occupations throughout the contiguous states. The sample, methods of data-collection, and other pertinent information are described in detail in Kohn (1969, particularly in Appendix C). Ten years later, in 1974, a representative subsample of 687 of those men in the original survey who were then 65 or younger was re-interviewed (for details, see Kohn and Schooler 1983, Appendix A). In the analyses of this chapter, I focus on the 687 men included in both the baseline and follow-up surveys, utilizing data from both.   (-) much later

The Japanese survey, carried out in the summer of 1979, was based on a random probability sample of 629 men, 26 to 65 years old, employed in civilian occupations in the Kanto plain of Japan. This area, which includes Tokyo and six other prefectures in north central Japan, is a mix of urban, suburban, and rural locales. The Japanese interview schedule consists primarily of questions translated from the U.S. interview schedule. Extensive pretesting was carried out to ensure the meaningfulness and cultural appropriateness of the questions (Naoi and Schooler 1985).

The Polish survey was conducted in 1978 under the auspices of the Polish Academy of Sciences. The probability sample of 1,557 men was designed to be representative of men aged 19 to 65 living in urban areas and employed full-time in *only* civilian occupations (for further information about sampling procedures and quality *urban* control of the interview data, see Słomczynski et al. 1981 or Kohn and Słomczynski 1990, particularly Chapter 2). The study was designed to be an exact replication of the main parts of the U.S. study. Questions about occupational self-direction and personality were adopted from the Kohn-Schooler interview schedule. The measures of social stratification came from previous Polish studies (Daniłowicz and Sztabinski 1977; Słomczynski and Kacprowicz 1979), where they had been intensively tested.

Great care was taken to assure comparability of meaning and measurement of the Polish and U.S. surveys (see Kohn and Słomczynski 1990, Chapter 2).

Conceptualizing and Indexing Social Class

My intent is to *conceptualize* social class on the same theoretical basis for all three countries, but to *index* social class in ways specifically appropriate to the particular historical, cultural, economic, and political circumstances of each of the three countries. In this way, I hope to achieve meaningful rather than merely mechanical comparability.

Social Classes in the United States

The classic bourgeoisie-proletariat distinction is generally recognized to be insufficient as a depiction of the class structure of a modern capitalist society. The question is, What further distinctions should be drawn? In postulating a petty bourgeoisie, which like the true bourgeoisie owns the means of production, but which like the proletariat performs labor rather than controlling the labor power of others, Marx proposed both an important distinction and a rationale for making further distinctions. Nearly all subsequent theorists have followed Marx's example, making distinctions that attempt to "disaggregate" the two large composites, owners and workers, into a greater number of more homogeneous categories. I do the same, borrowing from Erik Wright (1976; 1978), Robinson and Kelley (1979), Gagliani (1981), and Mach and Wesołowski (1986).

In his provocative analyses of the class structure of American society, Wright argued that in the United States and other advanced capitalist societies three basic class locations exist—a bourgeoisie, whose members control investments and the accumulation process, the physical means of production, and the labor power of others; a petty bourgeoisie, whose members control investment and the means of production, but not the labor power of others; and a proletariat, whose members control none of these essential elements of production. Wright argued that there are, in addition, groups who occupy "contradictory locations." The contradictory location between the proletariat and the bourgeoisie is management, which does not *own* the means of production but certainly *controls* both the means of production and the labor power of others. Between the proletariat and the petty bourgeoisie is a group he termed "semi-autonomous employees," mainly nonmanual technical employees and certain highly skilled craftsmen, who have control over how they do their work and have at least some control over what they produce, but who do not enjoy the degree of autonomy of the self-employed. The contradictory location between the petty bourgeoisie and the bourgeoisie is composed of small employers, a group of considerable importance to our analyses, since almost all employers interviewed in any representative survey of the population have only a small number of employees.

The evidence is considerable that this conceptualization is empirically potent (Wright and Perrone 1977; Kalleberg and Griffin 1980; Robinson and Kelley

1979). For my purposes, however, Wright's schema requires some modification. I find problematic his use of "autonomy" (which is similar to my "occupational self-direction") as the criterion for distinguishing semiautonomous employees from the proletariat. In my view, autonomy, although closely linked to the job's location in the class structure, is not itself definitional of class. The fact of being subject to the supervisory authority of an employer or his agent may be determined by one's class position, but the degree of autonomy allowed by the supervisory authorities depends on a particular job situation rather than being an invariant concomitant of class. (In later work, Wright [1985, pp. 53–55] comes to a similar conclusion.) Moreover, if I were to use autonomy as a criterion for indexing social class, it would be logically inconsistent to then ask whether the psychological effects of social class are attributable to occupational self-direction. I therefore do not employ Wright's distinction between the proletariat and semiautonomous workers.

I do, however, accept Wright's argument that control over the work of others is a valid criterion of class. Here I also follow the logic of Robinson and Kelley (1979), who would merge Marx and Ralph Dahrendorf to define classes in terms both of control over the means of production and of control over subordinates. The major import of their argument for present purposes is that the principal distinction among employees would be in terms of their control over other persons. I find this argument compelling; moreover, there is no logical contradiction between using authority over others as a criterion of class and then asking whether the psychological effect of class is attributable, in part, to control over *one's own* work activities.

Unless I employ some substitute for Wright's distinction between the proletariat and semiautonomous workers, though, I will treat as a single class category a large and heterogeneous segment of the workforce: all nonsupervisory employees. I therefore follow Gagliani (1981) and Poulantzas (1975) in treating the distinction between manual and nonmanual work as a further criterion of class. This distinction is certainly time-honored, going back to Marx's discussion of the "mental production" of intellectuals and the "physical production" of workers. Gagliani argues that, even in modern capitalist economies, nonmanual workers have conditions of employment sufficiently different from those of manual workers as to make their class situation more akin to that of management than is that of manual workers. The basic situation of nonmanual workers—in terms of job security, employment in an office or commercial setting, payment in the form of salary rather than hourly or piece-work wages, and fringe benefits, as well as the lower incidence of trade union membership among nonmanual workers—is distinctly more akin to that of management, particularly the lower ranks of management, than is that of manual workers. As David Lockwood (1958, p. 208) concluded from his study of British clerks, "As soon as the term 'class situation' is understood to cover not only market situation but also work situation, it is clear that clerk and manual worker do not, in most cases, share the same class situation at all."

With increasing mechanization, standardization, and computerization in offices, and with many service industries blurring the line between manual and nonmanual work, the traditional difference between the work situations of manual and non-manual workers may be diminishing, but the difference still exists and provides

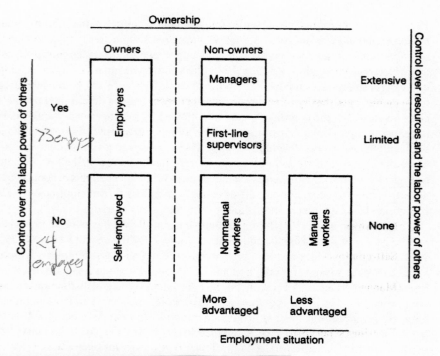

Figure 1.1. Schematic Outline of U.S. Class Categories.

a valid basis for a class distinction. I therefore take as a working hypothesis that nonmanual workers play a role in the productive process sufficiently distinct from that of manual workers that they occupy a separate class position. If nonmanual workers do not constitute a "basic class," then certainly within the Marxist framework they at least constitute a "non-basic class" (Mach and Wesołowski 1986, p. 61) and thus should be separately examined. In any case, I shall repeatedly check to be certain that the conclusions I draw about the psychological effects of social class, and the reasons for these effects, do not result from using the manual/nonmanual distinction as a criterion of class.

On the basis of these considerations, I divide the population of U.S. men employed in civilian occupations into six class categories, distinguished primarily by their differential relationships to ownership and control over the physical resources and the people involved in production, secondarily by their employment situations. This is illustrated in schematic outline in Figure 1.1.

These theoretical considerations do not tell us precisely where to draw the class boundaries. There is, for example, no theoretically compelling basis for deciding what percentage investment in a firm constitutes ownership. To resolve such issues, I turn to the rich descriptive data of the interviews. After detailed examination of the interview reports, Schoenbach and I drew the line between owners and employees at owning 20 percent of the assets of the firm, which seems to differentiate on-the-job roles that are more like those of owners than like those of employed management or first-line supervisors. More problematic: Does having a single employee distinguish a small employer from a petty bourgeois? Two? Three? On the basis of a case-by-case examination of the interview records, we drew the line between three nonfamily employees and four or more. In the United States, having four nonfamily employees seems to differentiate firms where the work role of the owner is more that of supervisor than that of primary producer.

A further problem is that I cannot make all the distinctions I would wish to make (e.g., a distinction between large and small employers), because the sample does not contain sufficient numbers of men in some of the categories. Still, a serviceable classification is possible:

1. Employers: owners who employ four or more nonfamily workers (N = 18 in 1964, 32 in 1974).
2. Self-employed (petty bourgeoisie): owners who employ no more than three nonfamily workers (N = 73, 82).
3. Managers: employees who have less than a 20 percent share in the ownership of the enterprise that employs them and who have at least two hierarchical levels beneath them (N = 37, 65).
4. First-line supervisors (whom I, like Wright, distinguish from managers because first-line supervisors have no real control over the means of production and only severely limited control over the labor power of others): employees who have direct supervisory authority over three or more workers and have only nonsupervisory workers beneath them (N = 120, 122).
5. Nonmanual workers: nonsupervisory employees whose work is predominantly nonmanual in character (N = 138, 106).
6. Manual workers: nonsupervisory employees whose work is predominantly manual in character (N = 301, 219).

Social Classes in Japan

In conceptualizing and indexing social class for Japan, my collaborators and I attempted to take account not only of those general considerations that would apply to any highly industrialized capitalist nation, but also of the particular historical circumstances of Japan. Our schema incorporates class divisions proposed both in the Marxist literature (Ohashi 1971; see also Mizuno 1974; Steven 1983; Hashimoto 1986) and in the non-Marxist literature (e.g., Cummings 1980, pp. 41–52; Naoi 1972). Some features of the dual economy (Lockwood 1968; Taira 1970) and of the modernized occupational structure of Japan (Cole and Tominaga 1976; Naoi 1970) are implicitly included. The resultant set of class categories is generally similar to the one I use for the United States (and the conceptualization illustrated in Figure 1.1 is equally applicable to Japan), but the precise criteria for defining membership in each of the classes is tailored to Japanese social and economic structures. The intent is to assure cross-national comparability in the conceptualization of social class, while at the same time developing precise criteria of classification that are true to the realities of class structure in each nation.

Steven (1983) has shown how various forms of private ownership shape the Japanese capitalist class. Our approach is narrower: We simply apply the classic criterion of class, owners versus nonowners, to identify those members of the labor force who work for profit rather than for wages or salaries. This approach is consistent with the Japanese sociological tradition (Ohashi 1971) as well as with Japanese statistical usage (Japanese Bureau of Statistics 1970).

One of the most striking features of modern Japan's development has been the emergence of a dual economy, with a primary (or central) sector characterized by capital-intensive operations and a secondary (or peripheral) sector characterized by labor-intensive operations (Cummings and Naoi 1974). In our sample, almost all the owners are part of the secondary (or peripheral) sector of the economy; they do not represent "big capital" but rather small, entrepreneurial business.

A further distinction, in Japan as in the United States, is between employers and the self-employed. For the United States, I designated as employers those owners who employ four or more nonfamily workers. In Japan, however, where it is common for small enterprises to employ several family members, employing even a single nonfamily member creates so wide a gulf as to embody a class distinction. Thus I separate the self-employed from small employers in Japan on the basis of employing even one nonfamily member. To see whether there is any real difference in personality between the smallest employers (those who employ only one to four nonfamily workers) and those who employ a larger workforce, I shall examine them separately, even though I do not regard them as distinct social classes. The first group is essentially a "petty bourgeoisie," the second, "small capitalists" (Steven 1983, p. 71).

The classification of Japanese employees is intended to parallel that used for the United States, but my collaborators and I do not believe that the precise criteria for differentiating managers from first-line supervisors in the United States would be appropriate for Japan. Instead, I classify as "managers" those top officials who in Japan are called "executives," that is, high-ranking governmental officials or presidents or directors of private companies employing at least five persons, as well as all other officials of private and public organizations who supervise twenty-five or more workers. In differentiating first-line supervisors from nonsupervisory employees, I again make a slightly different distinction from the one that I make for the United States. For the United States, the descriptive data suggest that the point of differentiation between first-line supervisors and nonsupervisory employees is supervising three or more workers; for Japan, this point of differentiation appears to be four or more workers. I thus treat as first-line supervisors only those foremen and their functional equivalents who control the work of at least four people.

As in other industrial countries, one of the key distinctions in Japanese society is that between nonmanual and manual workers (see Cole 1971, pp. 142–145; Cummings 1980, pp. 46–52). Before the Second World War the distinction between these two groups, known as *shokuin* and *kain,* was quite pronounced. In the postwar period, the status gap between the two groups narrowed, but the gap in objective conditions of life still remained substantial. In some descriptions of Japanese society, nonmanual workers have been treated as a new middle class (see Kishimoto 1962; Vogel 1963; Odaka 1966) and manual workers as a working class (Horie 1962). In my analyses, I make the distinction between nonmanual and manual workers on the basis of the respondents' detailed occupational titles, using a schema developed for the Social Mobility Survey (Naoi 1979).

The resulting set of class categories for Japan is thus:

1. Employers: owners who employ at least one worker in addition to members of their own families (N = 99).
   1a. Owners who employ five or more nonfamily workers (N = 40).
   1b. Owners who employ one to four nonfamily workers (N = 59).
2. Self-employed: owners who do not employ paid labor other than family members (N = 122).
3. Managers: employees who have positions at the top of the organizational hierarchy or who supervise 25 or more workers (N = 43).
4. First-line supervisors: employees who directly supervise 4 to 24 workers (N = 86).
5. Nonmanual workers: nonsupervisory employees whose work is predominantly nonmanual in character (N = 135).
6. Manual workers: nonsupervisory employees whose work is predominantly manual in character (N = 144).

Social Classes in Socialist Poland

Many conceptualizations of social class in socialist Poland (Wesołowski 1979; Ladosz 1977; Widerszpil 1978; Hryniewicz 1983; Drazkiewicz 1980) share the premise that, in the transition from a capitalist to a socialist society, the class structure is to some extent inherited from the previous formation. My collaborators' and my approach is rather different. We believe that classes in a socialist society should be distinguished solely on the basis of features characteristic of this type of society—central planning and state control of the economy. We consider these criteria to be appropriate to class divisions in socialist Poland:

1. *Control over the means of production,* which was a crucial class criterion in the nationalized and centralized economy of Poland. Managers form the most influential and decisive group in the process of economic planning; they are an extension of the state power apparatus. Managers in socialist countries implement ideological goals and cannot subject such goals to a technical or economic rationale. The importance of political goals in administering the economic system affects the class interests of managers and their relation to other classes.
2. *The direct control over labor,* which separates supervisors not only from their supervisees, but also from higher management. In socialist enterprises,

perhaps even more than in capitalist enterprises, the coordination of work is delegated to first-line supervisors, but they are given very limited authority.

3. *Manual versus nonmanual work,* which is a basic distinction even in a nationalized economy. This distinction is deeply rooted in Polish history. Describing the class situation of Poland before the Second World War, a prominent sociologist wrote, "Nowhere is the social distance between nonmanual work, be it of the most inferior kind, and manual work, even though it is constructive, so clearly defined as in Poland" (Rychlinski 1938, p. 180). Nor has the manual/nonmanual distinction diminished in importance in postwar Poland.

4. *Location in the centralized economy,* which divides all manual workers of the nationalized economy into two classes: those who are employed in the large-scale manufacturing and extractive enterprises of the centralized economy—in steel mills, ship-building, auto manufacture, coal mining—and those who are employed in secondary and supportive industries and in service—in transportation, food-processing, and repair. The former, whom I call *production workers,* constitute the core of the working class; the latter, whom I call *nonproduction workers,* constitute the periphery. In the nationalized economy of Poland in 1978, this distinction was not only descriptive of labor-market segmentation, but also constituted a true class distinction. Production workers had been the main force in the immediate bargaining process with the government. Economically, production workers had been pivotal to socialist industrialization; this has been treated by the government as a factor legitimizing the privileges given to these workers.

5. *Ownership of the means of production,* which is the basic category of Marx's theory of social classes in so-called antagonistic formations but not a major basis of differentiation in the urban, socialized economy of Poland. The self-employed, or petty bourgeoisie, must nevertheless be included in the class schema. However, it must be remembered that in Poland the intervention of the state into small business limited owners' independence in planning work and in making other economic decisions.

The resulting set of class categories (see Figure 1.2) is generally similar to the one I use for the United States and Japan, the major differences being that there was no employer class in socialist Poland and that I distinguish two classes of manual workers. Although the class categories are conceptually similar, the precise criteria I use for defining membership in each of the classes is tailored to Polish social and economic structures. My intent, for Poland as for Japan, is to assure cross-national comparability in the conceptualization of social class, while at the same time developing precise criteria of classification that are true to the realities of class structure in each nation.

For socialist Poland, just as for the capitalist United States and Japan, the criteria for distinguishing among classes are based on a close analysis of the actual interview data. Thus, for example, the criteria for what constitutes a "manager" are

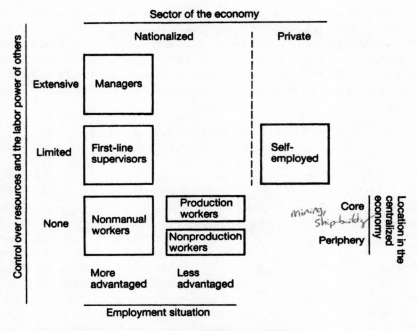

Figure 1.2. Schematic Outline of Polish Class Categories.

tailored to the particulars of the economic structure of socialist Poland; similarly for first-line supervisors. The six classes thus distinguished are:

1. Managers: employees in top decision-making positions in state and cooperative enterprises; employees who have the formal title of supervisor and who have supervisory authority over 25 or more people; employees who have supervisory authority over 50 or more subordinates, whether or not they have the formal title of supervisor; and employees who have supervisory authority over two or more levels of subordinates (N = 62).
2. First-line supervisors: employees who have direct supervisory authority over 2 to 24 workers, none of whom is himself a supervisor (N = 302).
3. Nonmanual workers: the core of what in socialist Poland were called the intelligentsia, consisting of professionals, technicians, and office workers (N = 266).
4. Production workers: nonsupervisory employees whose work is predominantly manual in character and who are employed in the large-scale manufacturing and extractive enterprises of the centralized economy (N = 526).
5. Nonproduction workers: nonsupervisory employees whose work is predominantly manual in character and who are employed in secondary and supportive industries and in service industries (N = 327).
6. Self-employed: owners of the means of production and members of the owners' families employed in those enterprises (N = 73).

P#1

yes

I conclude this portion of the analysis, then, with an affirmative answer to the question, Is it possible to conceptualize social class in common terms in such diverse countries as the United States, Japan, and socialist Poland? My collaborators and I have developed indices of social class that are broadly comparable for the three nations, yet each was developed with due attention to the particular historical, cultural, and political circumstances of the country to which it applies.

The Relationship between Social Class and Social Stratification

P#2

Is social class, as I have measured it, both conceptually and empirically distinct from social stratification? I measure social stratification—the hierarchical ordering of the society—by second-order confirmatory factor analyses,[2] in which the first-order factors are occupational status, job income, and educational attainment (see Table 1.1). The indices of job income and educational attainment are single-indicator measures of these concepts. The measurement models of occupational status all use Donald Treiman's (1977) International Prestige Scale as one indicator; for each nation, I also use measures of occupational status developed for that particular country as indicators.[3] In this way, I attempt to achieve cross-national comparability without losing intercountry variations. The models fit the data well, by the best criterion available at the time we did these analyses, the ratio of chi-square to degrees of freedom.[4]

From these measurement models, I created factor scores, both for the first-order factors and for the second-order factors.[5]

---

2. A second-order factor analysis is essentially a factor analysis of a factor analysis, in which one asks what are the fundamental dimensions underlying a set of factors inferred in analyses of measured indicators. In such an analysis, the first-order factors serve as "indicators" of the second-order factors.

3. For the United States, I use the Hollingshead occupational classification (Hollingshead and Redlich 1958, pp. 387–397; for the detailed occupational classification, see Bonjean et al. 1967, pp. 441–448) and later indices developed by Duncan (1961) and by Hodge, Siegel, and Rossi (1964; Siegel 1971). For Poland, I use the Polish Prestige Score (Słomczynski and Kacprowicz 1979). For Japan, my source is Naoi and Suzuki (1977); see also Naoi (1979) .

4. The chi-square for a LISREL measurement model is an assessment of how well the variance-covariance matrix implied by a model fits the actual variance-covariance matrix of the measured indicators. Although chi-square is highly sensitive to the number of cases on which the model is based, the ratio of chi-square to degrees of freedom has long been employed as a very useful way of comparing the fit of models based on similar numbers of cases. As a rule of thumb, when judging models based on the numbers of cases in our analyses, a ratio of less than 5.0 is generally deemed a good fit; somewhat higher ratios are quite acceptable.

5. These and all other factor scores used in this book are based on the LISREL output for the measurement models, using a computer program called FSCORE developed by Ronald Schoenberg. This program not only utilizes a sophisticated procedure for estimating missing data, but also provides the correlation between true scores and factor scores, information that is invaluable for correcting correlations of these factor scores with other variables, taking into account unreliability in the factor scores.

Table 1.1. Measurement Models of Social-Stratificational Position, for U.S. Men (1964 to 1974), Japanese Men (1979), and Polish Men (1978).

Concepts and Indicators	U.S. Men		Japanese Men	Polish Men
	1964	1974	1979	1978
	Standardized Paths, Concepts to Indicators			
Educational Attainment				
Years of Schooling	1.00	1.00	1.00	.95*
Educational level	—	—	—	.95*
Job Income				
Earnings, main job	1.00	1.00	1.00	.94*
Total job income	—	—	—	.95*
Family income	—	—	—	—
Occupational Status				
Treiman (International) Scale	.94*	.94*	.86*	.97*
Hollingshead Index of Occupational Status	.93*	.95*	.94*	.90*
Duncan SEI (Socio-economic Index)	.88*	.84*	—	—
Siegel Index	.93*	.92*	—	—
Polish Prestige Scale	—	—	—	.90*
Japanese Prestige Scale	—	—	.81*	—
Social-Stratificational Position	Standardized Paths, Social-Stratificational Position to Its First-Order Dimensions			
Educational attainment	.83*	.81*	.55*	.77*
Job income	.48*	.49*	.50*	.41*
Occupational status	.86*	.88*	.99*	.97*
Ratio of chi-square to degrees of freedom	2.66	6.57	0.61	—
Number of cases	687	629	1557	—

*p < .05.

Sources: The U.S. model is based on Kohn and Schoenbach (1983, Figure 7.1, p. 157). I developed the Japanese model for Kohn, Naoi, et al. 1990, but the model was not presented in that paper. The Polish model is based on Kohn and Słomczynski (1990, Figure 3.3, p. 46).

Descriptive statistics demonstrate the validity of the argument of class theorists that, even though social class and social stratification have much in common, they are far from identical (see Table 1.2). In particular, the relationships of social class with social stratification and with the components of social stratification are not linear or even ordinal. For example, in neither the United States nor Japan do employers rank highest in overall social stratification position; in all three countries, managers do. Managers rank especially high in educational attainment, with nonmanual workers—a class that includes professionals—outdistancing both employers and the self-employed. But employers do rank very high in job income (more so in the United States than in Japan). Manual workers rank lowest on all components of social stratification in all three countries, but by a wider margin for occupational status than for income and education. In all three countries, first-line supervisors rank lower than nonmanual workers in education; and in the United States and Poland, in occupational status; but in all three countries they rank higher in income. In short, these descriptive data justify the contention that social classes are discrete categories, not a single socioeconomic continuum. Class is a nominal, not an interval or even an ordinal, variable.

There is an apparent—but only apparent—contradiction between my speaking of social classes as being more or less advantaged and my treating social class as a nominal, rather than an ordinal, variable. The explanation is that there are *multiple* dimensions of advantage to the class structure: ownership of the means of production, control over the means of production, control over the labor power of others, and a more or less advantaged employment situation. A particular social class can be more advantaged than some other social class on one dimension, less advantaged on another. As a result, the six social classes do not comprise a single rank-ordering and must be treated as nominal categories.

Nonetheless, the correlations between social class and social stratification—expressed in terms of *eta,* a correlation coefficient appropriate to the nonordinal classification of social class[6]—are very substantial: 0.72 for the United States, 0.75 for Japan, and 0.82 for Poland. Although these correlations are a good deal less than unity, there is no gainsaying that social class and social stratification have a great deal in common. Similarly for the correlations (*etas*) of social class with the components of social stratification, particularly with occupational status: the correlations are substantial, albeit well below unity.[7]

The sharp differences in the social-stratification positions of manual workers and nonmanual workers, in all three countries, suggest that my treating manual and non-

---

6. *Eta* is directly analogous to the product-moment correlation coefficient in that it represents the square root of the proportion of the variance in a dependent variable that can be attributed to the independent variable(s). All *etas* presented in tables and text throughout this book have been corrected for unreliability due to measurement error in the factor scores.

7. The data presented for the United States in Table 1.2 are from the follow-up survey of 1974; the patterns of means are exactly the same, and the *etas* nearly identical, for the baseline survey of 1964.

Table 1.2. Relationship of Social Class to Social Stratification, for U.S. Men (1974), Japanese Men (1979), and Polish Men (1978).

	N	Standardized Differences from the Mean for Employed Men of the Particular Country			
		Social Stratification	Education	Job Income	Occupational Status
U.S. Men (1974):					
Employers	32	.70	.45	1.27	.76
Self-employed	82	.14	-.11	.22	.34
Managers	65	.80	.67	.81	.78
First-line supervisors	122	.12	.03	-.04	.18
Nonmanual workers	106	.78	.71	-.12	.72
Manual workers	219	-.83	-.58	-.42	-.92
Correlation (eta)[a]		.72*	.51*	.47*	.71*
Correlation, combining manual and nonmanual workers		.41*	.28*	.39*	.44*
Japanese Men (1979):					
Employers: 5+ employees	40	.99	.36	.66	.99
Employers: 1–4 employees	59	.22	-.20	.16	.23
Self-employed	122	-.22	-.37	-.31	-.19
Managers	43	1.11	.62	.95	1.09
First-line supervisors	86	.54	.38	.33	.53
Nonmanual workers	135	.31	.54	-.08	.30
Manual workers	144	-1.13	-.62	-.38	-1.14
Correlation (eta)[a]		.75*	.49*	.40*	.75*
Correlation, combining manual and nonmanual workers		.55*	.29*	.39*	.55*
Polish Men (1978):					
Managers	62	1.89	1.40	1.30	1.88
First-line supervisors	302	.66	.51	.42	.66
Nonmanual workers	266	.89	.94	-.01	.85
Production workers	526	-.62	-.55	-.16	-.60
Nonproduction workers	327	-.74	-.57	-.50	-.73
Self-employed	73	.15	-.16	.60	.20
Correlation (eta)[a]		.82*	.69*	.43*	.78*
Correlation, combining manual and nonmanual workers		.57*	.41*	.40*	.55*

[a]Corrected for unreliability of measurement.

*$p < .05$.

17

manual workers as distinct social classes contributes to, and might even explain, the correlations between social class and social stratification. Indeed, the manual versus nonmanual distinction does contribute to the magnitudes of these correlations, but even if I combine all nonsupervisory employees into a single social class, the proletariat, the correlations between social class and social stratification remain substantial (again see Table 1.2). The relationship between social class and social stratification is not only a function of the nonmanual versus manual distinction but also results from the differential statuses, incomes, and educational levels of men who stand in different positions with respect to ownership and control of the means of production and control over the labor power of others. Thus, in all three countries social class is highly correlated with, yet distinct from, social stratification.

Class, Stratification, and Personality

Our surveys contain information about many facets of men's personality: their valuation of self-direction *versus* conformity to external authority; their cognitive functioning; and several dimensions of their orientations to self and society.[8] I hypothesize that all these facets of personality are meaningfully related to social class. Yet, an analysis of the relationships between social class and all these facets of personality for these three countries would be presentationally unwieldy. Fortunately, detailed analyses show that nothing of importance is lost by dealing instead with four basic concepts: valuation of self-direction; intellectual flexibility; self-directedness of orientation; and a sense of well-being or of distress.

Indices of Personality

Parental valuation of self-direction versus conformity to external authority. By parental values, I mean those standards of desirability that parents would most like to see embodied in their children's behavior (Kohn 1969, pp. 18–20). To assess parental values, all three surveys asked fathers to partially rank the desirability of a standard list of 13 characteristics for a boy or girl the same age as a randomly selected child of their own. Extensive pretests verified that the 13 characteristics used in the U.S. survey are also appropriate to Japanese and Polish fathers. Exploratory factor analyses also showed that for Japan (but not for the U.S. or Poland) the factorial structures of parental values for boys and for girls are sufficiently

---

8. In choosing which dimensions of personality to index in the U.S. survey (on which the Polish and Japanese surveys are based), Schooler and I did not intend to provide a comprehensive assessment of personality, but to index those dimensions of personality that we hypothesized might affect or be affected by position in the social-stratificational hierarchy or by job conditions. (For pertinent discussions of our rationale in the selection of these dimensions of personality, see Kohn 1969, particularly Chapter 5 and Appendix D; Kohn 1990; Kohn and Schooler 1983, particularly Chapters 3 and 6; and Kohn and Słomczynski 1990, particularly Chapter 4.)

different that it is useful to develop separate measurement models of values for the two sexes.

The U.S. confirmatory factor-analytic model (see Table 1.3) is longitudinal, the children being 3 to 15 years old at the time of the baseline interview in 1964 and 13 to 25 years old at the time of the follow-up interview ten years later. The Japanese and Polish models (again see Table 1.3) are cross-sectional analogues to the longitudinal U.S. model, the children in both surveys being 3 to 15 years old at the time of the interviews. All of the models clearly portray a dimension, where one pole is valuation of self-direction; the other pole the valuation of conformity to external authority.

Intellectual flexibility. To measure intellectual flexibility, I rely on a variety of indicators—including the respondents' answers to seemingly simple but highly revealing cognitive problems, their handling of perceptual and projective tests, their propensity to agree when asked agree-disagree questions, and the interviewers' appraisals of their intelligence after a long session that required a great deal of thought and reflection by the respondents. I do not assume that any of these indicators is entirely valid; but I do assume that all the indicators reflect, to some substantial degree, the respondents' flexibility in attempting to cope with the intellectual demands of complex tasks.

My Polish collaborators had to make appropriate modifications in the cognitive questions asked in the United States to make them suitable to socialist Poland,[9] but, aside from that, the models are essentially the same for all three countries (see Table 1.4). All the models show two underlying dimensions to intellectual flexibility, one ideational, the other perceptual. Since my analytic interest is in ideational flexibility, I shall henceforth use the more general term, intellectual flexibility, to refer to its ideational component.

Although these models are based on only a few indicators, these indicators reflect people's actual intellectual functioning in a situation that seemed to elicit considerable intellectual effort from nearly all the respondents. Schooler, Mulatu, and Oates (1999) have recently shown that the U.S. measure of intellectual flexibility, on which the measures employed for all three countries are based, correlates highly (0.87) with more traditional measures of effective intellectual functioning.

---

9. For the U.S. and Japanese measurement models, we rated the adequacy of the respondents' answers to two questions: "Suppose you wanted to open a hamburger stand and there were two locations available. What questions would you consider in deciding which of the two locations offers a better business opportunity?" and "What are all the arguments you can think of for and against allowing cigarette commercials on TV?" Since there were no hamburger stands in Poland at that time, "kiosk" (newsstand) was substituted for "hamburger stand." Similarly, *allowing* the "advertisement of goods" on TV in socialist Poland was substituted as a debatable issue equivalent to *banning* "cigarette commercials" on U.S. TV. The pilot study, the field work, and confirmatory factor analyses all indicated that Polish men responded to the modified questions much as their U.S. and Japanese counterparts did to the original questions.

Table 1.3. Measurement Models of Parental Valuation of Self-Direction *vs.* Conformity to External Authority, for U.S. Fathers (1964 to 1974), Japanese Fathers (1979), and Polish Fathers (1978).

Concepts and Indicators	U.S. Fathers (1964) Children Aged 3–15	U.S. Fathers (1974) Children Aged 13–25	Japanese Fathers (1979) Children Aged 3–15 Boys	Japanese Fathers (1979) Children Aged 3–15 Girls	Polish Fathers (1978) Children Aged 3–15
		Standardized Paths, Concepts to Indicators			
Valuation of Self-Direction vs. Conformity to External Authority					
Responsible	+.50	+.45	—	—	—
Interested in how and why things happen	+.45	—	+.31	—	+.19
Considerate of others	+.36	+.31	+.32	+.59	—
Good sense and sound judgment	+.17	+.23	+.61	—	+.37
Self-control	—	—	—	+.26	+.27
Neat and clean	−.41	−.42	—	−.32	—
Obedient to parents	−.37	−.41	−.29	−.27	−.39
Good manners	−.45	—	—	—	—
Acts like a boy/girl (man/woman) should	—	−.28	—	—	−.16
Good student	—	—	−.25	−.46	−.45
Honest	—	—	−.53	—	—
Valuation of Success					
Tries hard to succeed	+1.00	+1.00	+1.00	+1.00	+1.00
Considerate	−.29	−.26	−.16	−.28	—
Responsible	−.26	−.28	—	—	—
Interested in how and why things happen	−.18	—	—	—	—
Good sense and sound judgment	—	−.18	—	—	—
Gets along well with others	—	—	—	—	−.14
Honest	—	—	—	—	−.19
Ratio of chi-square to degrees of freedom	2.18		0.63	1.46	7.22
Number of cases	399		111	114	660

All paths shown are statistically significant, $p < .05$. Where no path is shown, the characteristic may have been left out of the model to avoid problems of linear dependency in a forced-choice index (see the discussion in Kohn and Schoenbach 1993, pp. 133–134). A positive sign indicates that a father's considering the characteristic to be highly desirable for someone of the same age and sex as a randomly selected child of his own is indicative of high valuation of that dimension of parental values.

Sources: The U.S. model is based on Kohn and Schooler 1983 (Figure C.1, p. 330). I developed the Japanese model for Kohn, Naoi, et al. 1990, but the model was not presented in that paper. I later published it in Kohn and Schoenbach 1993 (Figure C.1, p. 68). The Polish model is based on Kohn and Słomczynski 1990 (Figure 4.1, p. 68).

Table 1.4. Measurement Models of Intellectual Flexibility, for U.S. Men (1964 to 1974), Japanese Men (1979), and Polish Men (1978).

	U.S. Men		Japanese Men	Polish Men
	1964	1974	1979	1978
	Standardized Paths, Concepts to Indicators			
Concepts and Indicators				
Ideational Flexibility				
"Agree" Score	-.44*	-.57*	-.34*	-.35*
"Commercials" Questions	.40*	.38*	.31*	.32*
"Hamburger Stand" or "Kiosk" Question	.26*	.36*	.33*	.29*
Interviewer's Appraisal of Respondent's Intelligence	.65*	.71*	.49*	.62*
Embedded Figures Test	.40*	.47*	.71*	.54*
Perceptual Flexibility				
Good Enough Estimate of Intelligence	.82*	.76*	.83*	.98*
Witkin Summary of Draw-a-Person Test	.68*	.52*	.94*	.91*
Embedded Figures Test	.21*	.24*	—	.21*
Ratio of Chi-Square to Degrees of Freedom	1.17		1.39	1.99
Number of Cases	687		629	1557

*p < .05

Sources: The U.S. model is based on Kohn and Schooler 1983 (Figure 5.3, p. 113). The Japanese model is based on Naoi and Schooler 1985 (Figure 2, p. 736). The Polish model is based on Kohn and Słomczynski 1990 (Figure 4.2, p. 71).

Orientations to Self and Society

My collaborators and I have measured several distinct dimensions of orientation to self and society and have developed rigorous procedures for establishing that our indices measure truly equivalent concepts for the United States, Poland, and Japan (see Słomczynski et al. 1981 or 1987; Kohn and Słomczynski 1990; Naoi and Schooler 1985). These dimensions are:

Authoritarian conservatism. Conceptions of what is socially acceptable—at one extreme, rigid conformance to the dictates of authority and intolerance of nonconformity; at the other extreme, open-mindedness.

Personally responsible standards of morality. A continuum of moral positions, from believing that morality consists of strict adherence to the letter of the law and keeping out of trouble, to defining and maintaining one's own moral standards.

Trustfulness. The degree to which one believes that other people can be trusted.

Self-confidence. The positive component of self-esteem—the degree to which one has confidence in one's own capacities.

Self-deprecation. The self-critical component of self-esteem—the degree to which one disparages oneself.

Anxiety. The intensity of consciously felt psychic discomfort.

Fatalism. The sense of being controlled by outside forces, or at the other extreme, of having some control over one's fate.

Idea-conformity. The degree to which one believes that his ideas mirror those of the social entities to which he belongs.

Using LISREL 8, we have developed confirmatory factor-analytic measurement models for all these dimensions of orientation (see the first section of of Table 1.5). Wherever possible, we used the same set of items for the United States, Japan, and Poland. Where this proved not to be feasible, we used greatly overlapping sets of items. We estimated the actual measurement models, though, entirely independently for the three countries, deliberately making no attempt to pool the data. This follows from the general logic of analysis in which countries are used as context for parallel analyses of the relationship between social structure and personality (see Kohn 1987). Nor did we deem it either necessary or appropriate to allow the same correlations of residuals of indicators for the three countries, since shared error variance might well be idiosyncratic to country. This follows from the general logic of confirmatory factor analysis as applied to cross-national research (see Kohn and Słomczynski 1990, pp. 44–45).

The model for U.S. men is longitudinal, the models for Japanese and Polish men are cross-sectional. As is shown in the table, all the models fit the data well, the criterion again being the ratio of the chi-square divided by the degrees of freedom. The table provides the actual question wording, in English, for each of the indicators. The Japanese and Polish questions were as close translations as we could meaningfully develop in the languages and cultures of those countries.

Building on analyses that my collaborators and I had done for U.S. men, women, and children (Kohn and Schooler 1982; 1983, Chapter 6; K. Miller, Kohn, and Schooler 1986), my collaborators and I believed that, in Japan and Poland as well there would be two principal dimensions underlying the several facets of orientation to self and society that we have measured: *self-directedness of orientation versus conformity to external authority,* and *a sense of distress versus a sense of well-being.* Self-directedness of orientation implies the beliefs that one has the capacity to take responsibility for one's actions and that society is so constituted as to make self-direction possible; the opposite pole of this concept is conformity to external authority. The second dimension, distress versus a sense of well-being, focuses on people's general feelings of psychic comfort or pain. Self-directedness and conformity may each have distinct psychic costs and rewards.

To index these underlying dimensions of orientation, we used "second-order" confirmatory factor analyses[10] of the dimensions of orientation discussed above (see the second section of Table 1.5). The measurement model for U.S. men shows that self-directedness of orientation is reflected in not having authoritarian conservative beliefs, and in having personally responsible standards of morality, being trustful of others, not being self-deprecatory, not being fatalistic, and not being conformist in one's ideas—all of which accords with our premises. Distress is reflected in anxiety, self-deprecation, lack of self-confidence, nonconformity in one's ideas, and distrust—which certainly appears valid. The measurement models for Japanese and Polish men are cross-sectional analogues to the U.S. model, but are entirely consonant with the U.S. model in what they tell us about the relationships between the first-order factors and the underlying second-order factors. All three models fit the data well.

The three models differ decidedly, though, in what they tell us about the relationship between self-directedness of orientation and distress (again see the second part of Table 1.5): For U.S. men, this relationship is negative; for Japanese men, there is almost no relationship; and for Polish men, the relationship is positive.

It would therefore appear that there is a fundamental cross-national difference in personality structure: U.S. men who are self-directed in their orientations tend also to have a sense of personal well-being; Japanese men who are self-directed in their orientations are neither more nor less distressed than are Japanese men who are conformist; Polish men who are self-directed in their orientations tend also to have a sense of personal distress. I believe, though, that what here appear to be cross-national differences in the *structure of personality* can better be understood as cross-national differences in how *social structures affect personality* in the three countries. I shall therefore search for the explanation of these apparent cross-national

---

10. Since there were several first-order dimensions of orientation, measured for the U.S. men at two times, based on a large set of measured indicators, a true (full-information) second-order confirmatory factor analysis that simultaneously estimated both the paths from first-order factors to their indicators and the paths from second-order factors to first-order factors was too formidable to test all at once. We therefore used the correlations of factor scores based on the first-order factors as the input to a confirmatory factor analysis that treated these factor scores as if they were measured variables. I put quotation marks around "second-order" in text and tables to signify that this is not a true second-order model but an approximation thereto.

differences in personality structure in corresponding cross-national differences in the relationships of social structure and personality.

In the analyses that follow, I shall present findings for the two "second-order" dimensions of orientation: self-directedness of orientation and distress. More detailed analyses consistently show that the findings for self-directedness also apply to the first-order dimensions of orientation that most strongly and unambiguously reflect this underlying dimension of orientation, namely open-mindedness (the opposite pole of authoritarian conservatism), trustfulness, and personally responsible standards of morality. The findings for distress also apply to the first-order dimensions of orientation that most strongly and unambiguously reflect distress, namely anxiety and self-deprecation. Whenever I speak of "orientation," without specifying a particular dimension or dimensions of orientation, I mean not only self-directedness of orientation and distress, but also the first-order dimensions of orientation that reflect these underlying dimensions.

Social Class Position and Personality

I deal first with the relationships of social class position to parental valuation of self-direction, intellectual flexibility, and self-directedness of orientation, leaving distress for later discussion. As hypothesized, in all three countries these relationships are meaningful and the correlations (*etas*) are substantial (see Table 1.6).

Consider the U.S. findings. The correlation (*eta*) between social class position and parental valuation of self-direction was 0.38 in 1964, when the children were 3–15 years old, and increased to 0.47 ten years later, when the children were 13–25 years old. The pattern is the same at both times, with managers and employers valuing self-direction most highly, followed by nonmanual workers, first-line supervisors and the self-employed, and finally—the most decidedly conformist in their values—manual workers. The correlation (*eta*) between social class position and intellectual flexibility is even higher, at 0.58, with the rank-order of social classes exactly the same. (Except for parental values, not only the patterns of means but even the *etas* are essentially the same for 1964 and 1974. To simplify the tables, I present further data only for 1974.) The correlation (*eta*) between social-class position and self-directedness of orientation is 0.43, with employers ranking highest, managers and nonmanual workers next, and manual workers lowest.

For Japan, too, social class is consistently and meaningfully related to parental valuation of self-direction, intellectual flexibility, and self-directedness of orientation. The magnitudes of the correlations (*etas* of 0.28, 0.48, and 0.28) may be somewhat lower than for the United States.[11] Nonetheless, the patterns of class

---

11. I may be understating the magnitude of the correlation between social class and Japanese fathers' values for their children. Since the exclusion of non-fathers from this analysis reduces the already small numbers of cases in each class category, I have had to combine larger and smaller employers and, probably of greater import, I have had to combine managers with first-line supervisors. Moreover, because of the relatively small numbers of cases even then, I have had to combine (standardized) factor scores for boys and for girls.

Table 1.5. Measurement Models of Orientations to Self and Society, for U.S. Men (1964 to 1974), Japanese Men (1979), and Polish Men (1978).

	U.S. Men 1964	U.S. Men 1974	Japanese Men 1979	Polish Men 1978
First-Order Dimensions of Orientation		Standardized Paths, Concepts to Indicators		
Authoritarian Conservatism				
The most important thing to teach children is absolute obedience to their parents.	.61*	.68*	.51*	.73*
In this complicated world, the only way to know what to do is to rely on leaders and experts.	.58*	.54*	.39*	.53*
It's wrong to do things differently from the way our forefathers did.	.45*	.52*	.58*	.40*
Any good leader should be strict with people under him in order to gain their respect.	.41*	.54*	.45*	.53*
No decent man can respect a woman who has had sex relations before marriage.	.43*	.51*	.40*	.42*
Prison is too good for sex criminals; they should be publicly whipped or worse.	.46*	.50*	.39*	—
Young people should not be allowed to read books that are likely to confuse them.	.50*	.46*	—	—
There are two kinds of people in the world: the weak and the strong.	.57*	.62*	—	—
People who question the old and accepted ways of doing things usually just end up causing trouble.	.51*	.47*	.37*	.62*
One should always show respect to those in authority.	—	—	.53*	.50*
You should obey your superiors whether or not you think they're right.	—	—	—	—
Do you believe that it's all right to do whatever the law allows, or are there some things that are wrong even if they are legal?	—	—	—	.42*
It generally works out best to keep on doing things the way they have been done before.	—	—	.60*	—
Ratio of chi-square to degrees of freedom		1.09	0.64	0.72
Personally Responsible Standards of Morality				
It's all right to do anything you want as long as you stay out of trouble.	-.59*	-.64*	-.41*	-.70*
If something works, it doesn't matter whether it's right or wrong.	-.44*	-.30*	-.49*	-.38*
It's all right to get around the law as long as you don't actually break it.	-.58*	-.61*	-.52*	-.30*
Do you believe that it's all right to do whatever the law allows, or are there some things that are wrong even if they are legal?	-.33*	-.26*	-.18*	—
Ratio of chi-square to degrees of freedom	0.86		0.08	0.0

Table 1.5. (continued)

	U.S. Men		Japanese Men	Polish Men
	1964	1974	1979	1978
Trustfulness				
Do you think that most people can be trusted?	.51*	.53*	1.00*	.31*
If you don't watch out, people will take advantage of you.	-.52*	-.61*	-.16*	-.33*
Human nature is really cooperative.	.20*	.11*	.04	.31*
When you get right down to it, no one cares much what happens to you.	—	—	—	-.35*
Ratio of chi-square to degrees of freedom	1.06		1.17	0.99
Self-Esteem (Two-Concept Model)				
Self-Confidence				
I take a positive attitude toward myself.	.60*	.71*	.39*	.39*
I feel that I'm a person of worth, at least on an equal plane with others.	.47*	.45*	.62*	.58*
I am able to do most things as well as other people can.	.43*	.34*	.64*	.53*
I generally have confidence that when I make plans I will be able to carry them out.	.54*	.45*	.47*	—
Once I have made up my mind, I seldom change it.	—	—	—	.41*
Self-Deprecation				
I feel useless at times.	.43*	.40*	.58*	.53*
At times I think I am no good at all.	.49*	.51*	.64*	.71*
There are very few things about which I'm absolutely certain.	.29*	.43*	.50*	.29*
I wish I could be as happy as others seem to be.	.58*	.59*	—	—
I wish I could have more respect for myself.	.76*	.71*	—	—
When you get right down to it, no one cares much what happens to you.	—	—	.26*	—
Correlation, Self-Confidence and Self-Deprecation	-.29*	-.28*	-.49*	-.27*
Ratio of chi-square to degrees of freedom[e]	1.49		1.18	0.60

26

Table 1.5. *(continued)*

| | U.S. Men | | Japanese Men | Polish Men |
	1964	1974	1979	1978
Anxiety				
How often do you feel that you are about to go to pieces?	.55*	.58*	.65*	.53*
How often do you feel downcast and dejected?	.68*	.68*	.66*	.60*
How frequently do you find yourself anxious and worrying about something?	.49*	.47*	.60*	.54*
How often do you feel uneasy about something without knowing why?	.45*	.50*	.55*	.58*
How often do you feel so restless that you cannot sit still?	.47*	.39*	.36*	.48*
How often do you find that you can't get rid of some thought or idea that keeps running through your mind?	.41*	.44*	.55*	.47*
How often do you feel bored with everything?	.58*	.57*	.53*	.41*
How often do you feel powerless to get what you want out of life?	.54*	.52*	.51*	.42*
How often do you feel guilty for having done something wrong?	.36*	.36*	.40*	—
How often do you feel that the world just isn't very understandable?	.48*	.44*	.39*	—
How often do you feel that there isn't much purpose to being alive?	.45*	.37*	.45*	—
Ratio of chi-square to degrees of freedom		1.35	0.86	1.22
Idea-Conformity				
According to your general impression, how often do your ideas and opinions about important matters differ from those of your relatives?	-.69*	-.64*	-.68*	-.41*
How often do your ideas and opinions differ from those of your friends?	-.63*	-.51*	-.72*	-.55*
How about from those of other people with your religious background?	-.50*	-.44*	-.57*	-.58*
Those of most people in the country?	-.68*	-.35*	-.49*	-.63*
Ratio of chi-square to degrees of freedom		1.19	0.18	0.0
Fatalism				
When things go wrong for you, how often would you say it is your own fault?	-.65*	-.57*	-.42*	—
To what extent would you say you are to blame for the problems you have—would you say that you are mostly to blame, partly to blame, or hardly at all to blame?	-.59*	-.70*	-.59*	—

27

Table 1.5. (continued)

	U.S. Men		Japanese Men	Polish Men
	1964	1974	1979	1978
Do you feel that most of the things that happen to you are the result of your own decisions or of things over which you have no control?	-.37*	-.38*	-.54*	—
Ratio of chi-square to degrees of freedom	0.43		0.0	—
Second-Order Dimensions of Orientation	Standardized Paths, Second-Order Concepts to First-Order Concepts			
Self-Directedness of Orientation				
Authoritarian Conservatism	-.91*	-.85*	-.50*	-.99*
Personally Responsible Standards of Morality	.66*	.73*	.56*	.54*
Trustfulness	.55*	.70*	.79*	.47*
Fatalism	-.31*	-.34*	-.41*	—
Self-Deprecation	-.41*	-.51*	-.38*	-.44*
Idea-conformity	-.37*	-.24*	-.15*	—
Distress				
Trustfulness	-.32*	-.20*	-.36*	-.47*
Self-confidence	-.33*	-.33*	-.34*	-.42*
Self-deprecation	.63*	.61*	.68*	.85*
Anxiety	.83*	.84*	.81*	.59*
Idea-conformity	-.32*	-.26*	-.54*	-.37*
Correlation between Self-Directedness of Orientation and Distress	-.19*	-.35*	-.03	+.43*
Ratio of chi-square to degrees of freedom (Second-Order model)	2.43		6.59	7.05
Number of cases	687		629	1557

[a]A high score on the indicator generally implies agreement or frequent occurrence; where alternatives are posed, the first alternative is scored high.
[b]Correlations between residuals not shown.

Table 1.5. (*continued*)

---

[a]The chi-square of the two–concept model of self-esteem refers to the entire model.

*p < .05

Sources: The U.S. models for the first-order dimensions of orientation are based on Kohn and Schooler 1983 (Table C.1, pp. 327–328); for the second-order dimensions of orientation, the U.S. models are based on Kohn and Schooler 1983 (Figure 6.3, p. 147). Atsushi Naoi and Carmi Schooler developed the Japanese models for Kohn, Naoi, et al. 1990, but the models were not presented in that paper nor in any of their other published papers. I developed the second-order measurement model for the Japanese data. The Polish models for the first-order dimensions of orientation are based on Kohn and Slomczynski 1990 (Table 4.3, Column 3, pp. 78–83); for the Polish-language version of the questions, see Slomczynski and Kohn 1988 (Appendix D, pp. 213–219). The Polish model for the second-order dimensions of orientation is based on Kohn and Slomczynski 1990 (Figure 4.3, p. 87).

rankings are generally similar for the two countries, with the contrast between managers and manual workers again marked—managers being decidedly more self-directed in values and orientation, and more intellectually flexible, than manual workers. Employers, though, do not rank as high in intellectual flexibility in Japan as they do in the United States.

The distinction between larger and smaller Japanese employers does not have any great importance for these facets of personality; combining larger and smaller employers into a single category would have virtually no effect on the magnitudes of the *etas*.

Aside from there being no "employer" class in socialist Poland, the findings for Poland are very similar to those for the United States and Japan. Even the magnitudes of correlation are quite similar for socialist Poland and the capitalist United States. The relative positions of the classes, too, are remarkably consistent with those for the capitalist countries. Consider, for example, Polish fathers' valuation of self-direction: Managers value self-direction most highly, and by a wide margin; then follow first-line supervisors and nonmanual workers follow; the self-employed are in the middle; at the other extreme, valuing conformity to external authority most highly, are production and nonproduction workers, who are virtually identical in their values. This pattern is essentially repeated for intellectual flexibility and for self-directedness of orientation.

Since there are sizeable differences between nonmanual and manual workers in all three countries, one must wonder whether my building this distinction into the index of social class has produced exaggerated correlations between social class and personality. The question is easily answered: If I combine nonmanual and manual workers into a single category—the proletariat—the correlations between social class and these facets of personality are reduced in magnitude but remain substantial (again see Table 1.6).

I have thus confirmed that in all three countries members of more advantaged social classes are more intellectually flexible, value self-direction for their children more highly, and have more self-directed orientations to self and society than do members of less advantaged social classes. As will shortly be seen in the first column of Table 1.7, the findings are similar for social stratification: higher stratification position is positively correlated with intellectual flexibility, with valuing self-direction for one's offspring, and with a self-directed orientation to self and society.

Distress. The correlations of social class with distress are smaller than those with other facets of personality and *the patterns are cross-nationally inconsistent.* For the United States, the correlation (*eta*) between social class and distress, at 0.18, is much smaller than that between social class and other facets of personality, but the pattern parallels that for other facets of personality: Employers (followed closely by managers and first-line supervisors) are at one extreme—the least distressed;

(note 11 continued from page 24) More detailed analyses suggest, though, that the correlation (*eta*) of social class with paternal valuation of self-direction is somewhat higher for Japanese fathers' values for boys (*eta* = .40) than for girls (*eta* = .28).

Table 1.6. Relationships of Social Class with Parental Valuation of Self-Direction, Self-Directedness of Orientation, Distress, and Intellectual Flexibility, for U.S. Men (1964 and 1974), Japanese Men (1979), and Polish Men (1978).

U.S. Men:

| | Parental Valuation of Self-Direction (1964/1974) | | | | Intellectual Flexibility (1974) | | Self-Directedness of Orientation (1974) | | Distress (1974) | |
	Children Aged 3–15 (1964)		Children Aged 13–25 (1974)							
	Mean	N	Mean	N	Mean	N	Mean	N	Mean	N
Employers	.57	15	.39	20	.58	32	.52	32	−.20	32
Self-employed	−.01	45	.06	47	.01	82	−.04	82	−.08	82
Managers	.60	26	.42	40	.59	65	.41	65	−.16	65
First-line supervisors	.01	77	.14	72	.23	122	.12	122	−.16	122
Nonmanual workers	.26	66	.24	60	.44	106	.41	106	.04	106
Manual workers	−.26	160	−.41	128	−.61	219	−.45	219	.18	219
Correlation (eta)[a]	.38*		.47*		.58*		.43*		.18*	
Correlation, combining manual and nonmanual workers	.27*		.34*		.38*		.26*		.17*	

Japanese Men:

	Parental Valuation of Self-Direction (1979) Boys and Girls Combined (Aged 3–15)		Intellectual Flexibility (1979)		Self-Directedness of Orientation (1979)		Distress (1979)	
	Mean	N	Mean	N	Mean	N	Mean	N
Employers (large and small)	.19	44						
Employers with 5+ employees			.10	40	.22	40	−.15	40
Employers with 1–4 employees			.02	59	−.01	59	−.05	59
Self-employed	−.18	25	−.35	122	−.05	122	−.13	122
Managers and first-line supervisors	.13	59						
Managers			.27	43	.24	43	−.24	43
First-line supervisors			.34	86	.16	86	−.13	86
Nonmanual workers	.14	47	.44	135	.15	135	.33	135
Manual workers	−.36	50	−.44	144	−.32	144	.01	144

Table 1.6. (continued)

	Parental Valuation of Self-Direction (1979) Boys and Girls Combined (Aged 3–15)		Intellectual Flexibility (1979)		Self-Directedness of Orientation (1979)		Distress (1979)	
	Mean	N	Mean	N	Mean	N	Mean	N
Correlation (eta)[a]	.28*		.48*		.28*		.22*	
Correlation, combining manual and nonmanual workers	.18*		.28*		.17*		.18*	

	Parental Valuation of Self-Direction (1978) (Children Aged 3–15)		Intellectual Flexibility (1978)		Self-Directedness of Orientation (1978)		Distress (1978)	
	Mean	N	Mean	N	Mean	N	Mean	N
Polish Men:								
Managers	.45	29	.92	62	.77	62	.10	62
First-line supervisors	.26	136	.41	302	.30	302	.05	302
Nonmanual workers	.24	108	.56	266	.50	266	.19	266
Production workers	-.22	219	-.36	526	-.28	526	-.09	526
Nonproduction workers	-.19	138	-.41	327	-.35	327	-.04	327
Self-employed	-.01	30	-.05	73	-.14	73	-.17	73
Correlation (eta)[a]	.36*		.55*		.42*.		.14*	
Correlation, combining manual and nonmanual workers	.27*		.36*		.26*		.06	

Note. Means are expressed as standardized differences from grand mean for the country.
[a]Corrected for unreliability of measurement.
*p < .05.
The correlations of *social stratification* and personality are given in the first column of Table 1.7.

32

manual workers are at the other extreme—the most distressed. In Japan, as in the United States, managers and employers have a strong sense of well-being (in Japan, managers even more than employers), but in Japan *non*manual workers surpass manual workers in their degree of distress. The Polish pattern is still different: As in Japan (and, to a lesser degree, the United States), Polish nonmanual workers stand out for their relatively high level of distress; but the self-employed in Poland have a relatively stronger sense of well-being than do their counterparts in the capitalist countries. Where the Polish pattern differs most decidedly from those for the capitalist countries, though, is that Polish managers stand out for their relatively *high* level of distress; moreover, Polish production and nonproduction workers are *less* distressed than are members of most other social classes, quite in contrast to what we have seen for manual workers in the capitalist countries. The findings for social stratification parallel those for social class, with the correlation between social stratification and distress significantly negative for the United States, nearly zero for Japan, and significantly positive for Poland.

The Independent Effects of Social Class and Social Stratification

Might the relationships between social class and personality result from the close relationship between social class and social stratification? Conversely, might the relationships between social stratification and personality result from that same close relationship between social class and social stratification? To test these possibilities, I examine the correlations of social stratification with personality, statistically controlling social class, and the correlations of social class with personality, statistically controlling social stratification. I must emphasize that this heuristic exercise in no way tests the validity of either my conceptualization of social class or my conceptualization of social stratification. Not only do I not deal with that facet of subjective experience of greatest concern to class theorists—class consciousness—but I in no way evaluate the long-term historical consequences of either class structure or the stratification order. What this analysis does tell us—and this is precisely why I engage in such an exercise—is whether social stratification has an *independent* effect on personality, even if I arbitrarily assign all shared variance to social class, and whether social class has an *independent* effect on personality, even if I arbitrarily assign all shared variance to social stratification.

I find (see Table 1.7) that the correlations of social stratification with parental valuation of self-direction, intellectual flexibility, and self-directedness of orientation are somewhat reduced when social class is statistically controlled, but that these correlations remain statistically significant, cross-nationally consistent, and substantial in magnitude. The correlations between social stratification and distress (like those between social class and distress) were neither substantial nor cross-nationally consistent even before social class was statistically controlled; controlling social class does not change that situation. Thus, the effects of social stratification on personality cannot by any stretch of imagination be attributed to social class.

Table 1.7. (Multiple-) Partial Correlations of Social Stratification and of Social Class with Personality, for U.S. Men (1974), Japanese Men (1979), and Polish Men (1978).

	Zero-Order Correlation with Social Stratification	Partial Correlation, Controlling Social Class	Multiple Correlation with Social Class	Multiple-Partial Correlation, Controlling Social Stratification
U.S. men (1974)				
Parental valuation of self-direction	.66*	.54*	.47*	.14*
Intellectual flexibility	.85*	.77*	.58*	.23*
Self-directedness of orientation	.70*	.63*	.43*	.19*
Distress	–.18*	–.13*	(–).18*	(–).12*
Japanese men (1979)				
Parental valuation of self-direction	.34*	.24*	.28*	.08
Intellectual flexibility	.48*	.33*	.48*	.32*
Self-directedness of orientation	.36*	.25*	.28*	.07
Distress	–.01	.01	(–).22*	(–).21*
Polish men (1978)				
Parental valuation of self-direction	.44*	.28*	.36*	.09*
Intellectual flexibility	.69*	.50*	.55*	.10*
Self-directedness of orientation	.50*	.31*	.42*	.08*
Distress	.15*	.10*	.14*	.09*

Note: The multiple and multiple-partial correlations for social class use dummy variables for all but one class category. I have added minus signs in parentheses for those multiple correlations where the *betas* for the most advantaged social classes are negative (in all cases, for the relationships of class with distress).
*p < .05.

34

The correlations of social class with parental valuation of self-direction, intellectual flexibility, and self-directedness of orientation—which are smaller than those for social stratification to begin with—are markedly reduced when social stratification is statistically controlled. Nevertheless, most of these correlations remain statistically significant and nontrivial in magnitude. (For distress, of course, the relationships with social class were small and cross-nationally inconsistent to begin with.) At minimum, social class has some, in a few instances substantial, psychological effect entirely above and beyond that of social stratification.

The Role of Occupational Self-Direction in Explaining the Relationships of Social Class with Valuation of Self-Direction, Intellectual Flexibility, and Self-Directedness of Orientation

My preferred hypothesis to explain the cross-nationally consistent relationships of social class with valuation of self-direction, intellectual flexibility, and self-directedness of orientation is that these relationships are largely attributable to the differential opportunities for occupational self-direction available to members of the several social classes.

P #4

Conceptualization and Measurement of Occupational Self-direction

By *occupational self-direction,* I mean the use of initiative, thought, and independent judgment in work. I see three job conditions as crucial in facilitating or impeding the exercise of occupational self-direction: the substantive complexity of the work, closeness of supervision, and routinization. By *the substantive complexity of work,* I mean the degree to which performance of the work requires thought and independent judgment. Substantively complex work by its very nature requires making many decisions that must take into account ill-defined or apparently conflicting contingencies. I measure the substantive complexity of work on the basis of our appraisals of the complexity of each man's work with data, with people, and with things; our appraisal of the overall complexity of his work; and his estimates of the number of hours he spends each week working at each of the three types of activity. *Closeness of supervision* is measured by a worker's subjective appraisals of his freedom to disagree with his supervisor, how closely he is supervised, the extent to which his supervisor tells him what to do rather than discussing it with him, and the importance in his job of doing what one is told to do.[12] *Routinization*

---

12. We faced a dilemma in deciding how to evaluate closeness of supervision for employers and the self-employed. We could not ask them our standard interview questions about how closely they are supervised, since they have no formal supervisor. We might, nonetheless, have placed them in the least closely supervised category, on the rationale that, having no supervisors, they could not be closely supervised. To do so, however, would have confounded social class and occupational self-direction. This would favor our principal hypothesis, that the psychological effects of social class will be greatly reduced when

is measured by a single indicator, combining the respondent's view of the repetitiveness and predictability of his job.

In second-order confirmatory factor-analytic measurement models, I infer the higher-order concept, occupational self-direction, from the three job conditions that enhance or diminish the opportunity, even necessity, of exercising self-direction in one's work (see Table 1.8). The parameters of the models are similar in the three countries, with the substantive complexity of work by far the most important determinant of occupational self-direction, albeit not by as wide a margin for Japan as for the United States or Poland.

Class, Stratification, and Occupational Self-direction

The hypothesis that occupational self-direction will provide the key to explaining the relationships of social class and of social stratification with personality will prove to be valid if, and only if, there are differential opportunities for occupational self-direction available to people differentially situated in the class structure and the stratification hierarchy. I find, in fact, that the relationship between social class and occupational self-direction is very strong in all three countries (Table 1.9). Even the correlations of social class with the job conditions that facilitate or interfere with occupational self-direction are moderate-to-strong, those with the substantive complexity of work especially strong. (Here, too, the findings are essential paralleled for social stratification.)

In all three countries, managers are the most self-directed in their work of any social class. In Japan, employers who have five or more employees rank a very close second; in the United States, employers (all of whom have at least four non-family employees) rank fairly high. In all three countries, nonmanual workers rank substantially above the mean in occupational self-direction, as do first-line supervisors. The self-employed rank relatively low, and manual workers lowest of all. (In Poland, the difference between production and nonproduction workers is minimal.) These patterns hold not only for occupational self-direction taken in toto, but also, with only minor variations, for the substantive complexity of the work, closeness of supervision, and routinization. Clearly, social class is strongly and meaningfully related to occupational self-direction.

Clearly, too, the strong relationship between class and occupational self-direction results in part, but only in part, from manual workers being, on the average, less occupationally self-directed than are nonmanual workers. Still, if I combine manual and nonmanual workers into a single social class, the correlations (*etas*) between class and occupational self-direction remain strong, even if not as strong as when

(*note 12 continued*) occupational self-direction is statistically controlled. The alternative procedure, which we followed, is to risk understating the relationship between social class and occupational self-direction by treating closeness of supervision as "missing data" for employers and the self-employed. Reanalyses of our data, treating employers and the self-employed as being in the least closely supervised category, yield essentially the same substantive conclusions as do those presented in this chapter.

Table 1.8. Measurement Models of Occupational Self-Direction, for U.S. Men (1964 to 1974), Japanese Men (1979), and Polish Men (1978).

Concepts and Indicators	U.S. Men 1964	U.S. Men 1974	Japanese Men 1979	Polish Men 1978
	Standardized Paths, Concepts to Indicators			
Substantive Complexity of Work				
Complexity of work with data	.86*	.75*	.85*	.89*
Complexity of work with things	.24*	.05*	.39*	.23*
Complexity of work with people	.77*	.63*	.80*	.89*
Hours of work with data	.59*	.53*	.47*	.61*
Hours of work with things	−.59*	−.57*	−.60*	−.67*
Hours of work with people	.50*	.40*	.29*	.26*
Overall complexity	.79*	.66*	.93*	.86*
Closeness of Supervision				
Freedom to disagree with supervisor	−.42*	−.45*	−.69*	−.24*
Respondent's assessment of how closely he (she) is supervised	.77*	.64*	.70*	.56*
Extent to which supervisor tells respondent what to do	.64*	.68*	.70*	.53*
Importance of doing what one is told	.68*	.31*	—	.39*
Routinization				
Variability of tasks	1.00	1.00	1.00	1.00
Ratio of chi-square to degrees of freedom		2.40	1.19	6.56
	Standardized Paths, Occupational Self-Direction to Its First-Order Dimensions			
Occupational Self-Direction				
Substantive Complexity of Work	.93*	.89*	.99*	.98*
Closeness of Supervision	−.74*	−.69*	−.19*	−.68*
Routinization	−.24*	−.21*	−.20*	−.34*
Ratio of chi-square to degrees of freedom		2.37	2.25	6.56
Number of cases		687	629	1557

*p < .05.

Sources: The U.S. model is based on Kohn and Schooler 1983 (Figures 6.1, p. 128, and C.4, p. 335). The Japanese measurement model of the first-order dimensions of occupational self-direction is derived from Naoi and Schooler 1985 (Figure 1). I developed the second-order Japanese model for Kohn, Naoi, et al. 1990, but the model was not presented in that paper. The Polish model is based on Kohn and Słomczynski 1990 (Figure 5.2, p. 112).

Table 1.9. Relationships of Class and Stratification with Occupational Self-Direction, for U.S. Men (1974), Japanese Men (1979), and Polish Men (1978).

	N	Mean[a]			
		Occupational Self-Direction	Substantive Complexity of Work	Closeness of Supervision	Routinization
A. Social Class					
U.S. men (1974)					
Employers	32	.41	.67	...[b]	-.25
Self-employed	82	-.01	-.02	...[b]	-.13
Managers	65	.91	.88	-.54	-.34
First-line supervisors	122	.34	.29	-.21	-.07
Nonmanual workers	106	.56	.65	-.23	.01
Manual workers	219	-.79	-.83	.39	.22
Correlation (eta)[c]		.74*	.74*	.41*	.19*
Correlation, combining manual and nonmanual workers		.50*	.48*	.34*	.17*
Partial correlation, controlling social stratification		.47*	.43*	.27*	.13*
Japanese men (1979)					
Employers: 5+ employees	40	.93	.95	...[b]	.01
Employers: 1–4 employees	59	.05	.16	...[b]	.18
Self-employed	122	-.26	-.53	...[b]	.18
Managers	43	.98	1.06	-.38	-.48
First-line supervisors	86	.52	.61	-.39	-.05
Nonmanual workers	135	.35	.41	-.02	-.16
Manual workers	144	-1.00	-.94	.33	.10
Correlation (eta)[c]		.90*	.70*	.40*	.18*

Table 1.9. (continued)

	N				
Correlation, combining manual and nonmanual workers		.65*	.53*	.38*	.16*
Partial correlation, controlling social stratification		.94*d	.35*	.26*	.15*
Polish men (1978)					
Managers	62	1.70	1.64	-.63	-.51
First-line supervisors	302	.74	.71	-.49	-.28
Nonmanual workers	266	.98	.94	-.50	-.28
Production workers	526	-.65	-.62	.41	.19
Nonproduction workers	327	-.71	-.71	.32	.34
Self-employed	73	-.16	-.05	...b	-.25
Correlation (eta)c		.83*	.78*	.57*	.28*
Correlation, combining manual and nonmanual workers		.53*	.52*	.40*	.20*
Partial correlation, controlling social stratification		.29*	.25*	.27*	.08*
B. Social Stratification					
Correlations for:					
U.S. Men (1974)	687	.90*	.95*	-.52*	-.29*
Japanese Men (1979)	629	.97*	.86*	-.45*	-.18*
Polish Men (1978)	1557	.91*	.89*	-.64*	-.34*

a Expressed as standardized differences from grand mean for the particular country.
b Treated as "missing data."
c Corrected for unreliability of measurement
d Combines large and small owners, and also combines managers and first-line supervisors; unless this is done, the multiple correlation of occupational self-direction with class and stratification is greater than 1.0, and a partial correlation cannot be calculated.
*p < .05.

I differentiate between manual and nonmanual workers (again see Table 1.9). Even if I statistically control social stratification, thereby attributing all shared variance to it, the correlations between social class and occupational self-direction remain substantial in all three countries.

Social Class, Occupational Self-Direction, and Personality

It is, then, an entirely plausible hypothesis that position in the class structure affects personality mainly because of the differential opportunities for occupational self-direction afforded to men variously located in the class structure. To test this hypothesis, I statistically control the substantive complexity of work, closeness of supervision, and routinization. Insofar as the correlations between social class and personality are thereby reduced, we can tentatively infer that social class affects personality because of the differential opportunities for occupational self-direction available to members of the several social classes. (I shall examine the issue of directionality of effects shortly.) These analyses demonstrate that, for all three countries, the magnitudes of the correlations of social class with parental valuation of self-direction, intellectual flexibility, and self-directedness of orientation are markedly reduced (see Table 1.10), albeit not by quite as much for Japan as for the United States and Poland. Although the opportunity to exercise occupational self-direction does not *completely* explain the effect of class on these facets of personality, it does provide a cross-nationally consistent explanation of the lion's share of the psychological effects of social class. Occupational self-direction similarly explains a large portion of the psychological effects of social stratification.

An obvious alternative hypothesis is that social class is related to these facets of personality, not because of differential opportunities for occupational self-direction, but because of the social compositions of the several social classes—the varying proportions of people from higher and lower socioeconomic backgrounds, rural or urban origins, and the like. To test this possibility, I statistically control all pertinent social characteristics about which we have information (listed in Table 1.10). For all three countries, the proportional reductions in the correlations between social class and these facets of personality are decidedly smaller when the pertinent social characteristics are statistically controlled than when the job conditions determinative of occupational self-direction are statistically controlled. Moreover, controlling *both* the social characteristics of the class members *and* their opportunities for occupational self-direction generally does not reduce the class correlations any more than does controlling only the job conditions determinative of occupational self-direction. The explanation of the relationship between social class and these facets of personality does not rest in the social composition of the classes. Instead, the explanation would seem to be that social class position markedly affects men's opportunities to exercise occupational self-direction; and that the exercise of occupational self-direction in turn markedly affects these pivotal facets of personality.

Once again we must reckon with social stratification, this time with the possibility that it is not occupational self-direction but social stratification that accounts for the relationships between social class and personality. To test this possibility,

Table 1.10. Effects on Class Correlations of Statistically Controlling Occupational Self-Direction, Social Characteristics, and Social Stratification, for U.S. Men (1974), Japanese Men (1979), and Polish Men (1978).

	U.S. Men (1974)	Japanese Men (1979)	Polish Men (1978)
Parental valuation of self-direction			
Correlation (*eta*) with social class	.47	.28	.36
Proportional reduction, statistically controlling:			
Occupational self-direction (%)	78	70	79
Social characteristics (%)*	10	14	0
Both occupational self-direction and social characteristics (%)	65	53	68
Both occupational self-direction and social stratification (%)	56	61	78
Intellectual flexibility			
Correlation (*eta*) with social class	.57	.48	.55
Proportional reduction, statistically controlling:			
Occupational self-direction (%)	87	46	83
Social characteristics (%)*	3	16	0
Both occupational self-direction and social characteristics (%)	75	66	78
Both occupational self-direction and social stratification (%)	76	56	95
Self-directedness of orientation			
Correlation (*eta*) with social class	.43	.27	.42
Proportional reduction, statistically controlling:			
Occupational self-direction (%)	70	59	77
Social characteristics (%)*	13	16	4
Both occupational self-direction and social characteristics (%)	67	55	74
Both occupational self-direction and social stratification (%)	78	54	79
Distress			
Correlation (*eta*) with social class	.18	.22	.14
Proportional reduction, statistically controlling:			
Occupational self-direction (%)	35	12	38
Social characteristics (%)*	7	24	10
Both occupational self-direction and social characteristics (%)	31	34	44
Both occupational self-direction and social stratification (%)	36	23	59

*For the United States, the pertinent social characteristics are age, race, national background, religious background, mother's and father's education, father's occupational status, maternal and paternal grandfathers' occupational statuses, urbanness and region of the country of the principal place where respondent was raised, and the number of brothers and sisters; for parental values, also child's age and sex. For Japan, the pertinent social characteristics are age (except vis-à-vis parental values, because father's and child's ages are too highly correlated for both to be in the equation), father's and mother's education, father's occupational status, urbanness of principal place raised, and number of children in parental family; for parental values, also child's age (sex being controlled in process of index construction). For Poland, the pertinent social characteristics are year of birth, urbanness of principal place raised, and father's education and occupational status; for parental values, also child's age and sex.

I statistically control not only the job conditions determinative of occupational self-direction but also social-stratificational position. Doing so (again see Table 1.10) explains, at most, only a slightly greater portion of the correlations between social class and personality than does controlling only the opportunity to exercise occupational self-direction. Moreover, the standardized regression coefficients for the substantive complexity of work, or for closeness of supervision, or for both remain statistically significant and nontrivial in magnitude. In short, the contribution of occupational self-direction to explaining the psychological effects of social class is not merely a reflection of the close relationship between occupational self-direction and social stratification.

Issues of Causal Directionality in the Interrelationships of Class Position, Occupational Self-Direction, and Personality

I have to this point assumed that social class actually does affect occupational self-direction, and that occupational self-direction actually does affect parental valuation of self-direction, intellectual flexibility, and self-directedness of orientation. It could be argued, though, that the process is not one of class affecting personality, but of personality affecting attained class position. I see three interrelated issues: the relationship between social class and occupational self-direction; the relationship between occupational self-direction and personality; and the possibility that personality could affect class placement through processes *other than* its effect on the exercise of occupational self-direction.

Social class and occupational self-direction. In my collaborators' and my research on the relationship between *social stratification* and occupational self-direction, we have been able to assess the reciprocal effects between two of the three component dimensions of social stratification (occupational status and job income) and occupational self-direction (Słomczynski et al. 1981 and 1987; Kohn and Schoenbach 1983, Fig. 7.2, p. 163), finding strong effects in both directions. This type of statistical analysis is not possible for *social class,* because class is a nominal variable. I can, however, treat two of the two principal criteria of class—ownership and hierarchical position—as ordinal variables, and Schooler and I have in fact done so in a longitudinal analysis, for the United States, of job structure (Kohn and Schooler 1983, Table 6.1, pp. 134–35). This analysis shows modest reciprocal effects of ownership on the substantive complexity of work and of the substantive complexity of work on ownership; it also shows much more substantial reciprocal effects of hierarchical position on substantive complexity and of substantive complexity on hierarchical position, as well as substantial unidirectional effects of hierarchical position on closeness of supervision and on routinization. All this suggests reciprocal effects of social class and occupational self-direction, with the predominant direction of effect being *from* social class *to* occupational self-direction. An analysis of retrospective job-history information (using the models presented in Schooler and Naoi 1988) yields entirely consonant conclusions for Japan. For

Poland, we do not have sufficiently comprehensive data about past job conditions to carry out similar analyses.

Occupational self-direction and personality. Here we deal with ordinal variables, hence we can employ linear structural-equations modeling of what on *a priori* grounds may well be reciprocal effects. The prototypic model is presented in Figure 1.3, which is modified from a longitudinal model developed for the United States (Kohn and Schoenbach 1983, Figure 7.4 and Table 7.4, pp. 172–174), the Polish and Japanese models being cross-sectional equivalents thereto.[13] In these models, occupational self-direction in the baseline (earlier) job is permitted to affect occupational self-direction in the job held at the time of the follow-up study (the "later" job), and the particular facet of personality measured at the earlier time is permitted to affect that facet of personality measured at the later time. Cross-lagged effects (i.e., the effects of earlier occupational self-direction on later personality, and of earlier personality on later occupational self-direction), however, are fixed at zero—they are used as instruments. As a result, what appear in the models to be *contemporaneous* effects of occupational self-direction on personality and of personality on occupational self-direction are actually *total* effects, the additive effects of the lagged and the contemporaneous. (I shall discuss this further in Chapter 8.)

Since most U.S. men had completed their formal education before the time of the baseline interviews, education is modeled as having unidirectional effects on both occupational self-direction and personality. This may exaggerate the effects of *education* on personality, since at even earlier times in the men's lives personality must also have affected their educational attainment; but for assessing the

---

13. The Japanese and Polish models build on earlier models presented in Naoi and Schooler 1985 and Słomczynski et al. 1981 and 1987. The models I now use are cross-sectional analogues to a prototypic longitudinal model; the rationale for these models is presented in detail in Kohn, Słomczynski, and Schoenbach 1986 and in Kohn and Słomczynski 1990, pp. 159–162, 194–196. Essentially, we use actual (retrospective) data for information about earlier job conditions, but in the absence of any information about earlier personality we have to introduce a hypothetical construct, e.g., "earlier intellectual flexibility." This requires that we estimate the correlations between this hypothetical construct and other exogenous variables, i.e., social characteristics and earlier occupational self-direction. This we do by extrapolating from the correlations of these same variables with current intellectual flexibility, adjusting those correlations to take account of over-time changes as inferred from the longitudinal data for U.S. men. We initially estimate the path from earlier to later intellectual flexibility to be the same as we find it to be for U.S. men. Then, in "sensitivity analyses," we systematically assess the robustness of the models by modifying these estimates. All the models for Poland prove to be highly robust, the conclusions we draw being changed to only a minor degree when the estimated stability of personality and the estimated correlations are increased or decreased by even as much as 25 percent. For Japan, the models for parental valuation of self-direction and (crucially) for distress are equally robust; those for intellectual flexibility and for self-directedness of orientation are not quite this robust, but even these are relatively insensitive to changes of plus or minus 10 percent in the estimated stability of personality and the estimated correlations of earlier personality with other variables.

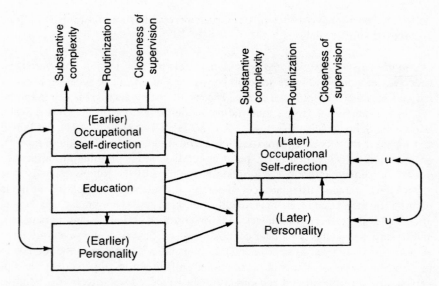

Figure 1.3. Prototypic Model: The Reciprocal Effects of Occupational Self-Direction and Personality.

effects of *occupational self-direction* on personality it is a conservative assumption. (For Poland, where in the post–World War II years many men had continued their educations well into their occupational careers, we modify the models accordingly.) In the longitudinal U.S. model, education directly affects occupational self-direction at both the earlier and later times, but directly affects personality only at the earlier time, thus affecting later personality only indirectly through its effects on occupational self-direction and on personality at an earlier time. If we were to allow direct effects of education on later personality, these effects would mainly be inconsistent in sign with the zero-order correlations, and as a consequence would exaggerate the effects of occupational self-direction on personality. For Japan and Poland, where the analyses are cross-sectional analogues to the longitudinal U.S. model, it is possible, even necessary, to allow direct effects of education on later personality.

The models also permit pertinent social characteristics (the same as those listed in Table 1.10) to affect both earlier and later personality, as well as earlier occupational self-direction; those social characteristics that might be seen by an employer as credentials for a job are also permitted to affect later occupational self-direction.

I find (see Table 1.11) that, in all three countries, occupational self-direction has appreciable, statistically significant effects on parental valuation of self-direction, intellectual flexibility, and self-directedness of orientation. In most cases, there are reciprocal effects of personality on occupational self-direction as well. Thus, the assumption that occupational self-direction actually does affect these facets of personality is impressively borne out by these analyses.

Table 1.11. The Reciprocal Effects of Occupational Self-Direction and Personality, for U.S. Men (1964 and 1974), Japanese Men (1979), and Polish Men (1978).

	Standardized Path Coefficients		
	Occupational Self-Direction to Personality	Personality to Occupational Self-Direction	Education to Personality[a]
Parental valuation of self-direction			
U.S. men	.41*	.13*	.47*
Japanese men	.46*	.31*	−.18
Polish men	.30*	.29*	.00
Intellectual flexibility			
U.S. men	.27*	.63*	.64*
Japanese men	.37*	.31*	−.14
Polish men	.26*	.11*	−.01
Self-directedness of orientation			
U.S. men	.43*	.28*	.53*
Japanese men	.29*	.06	−.02
Polish men	.31*	.07*	.00
Distress			
U.S. men	−.21*	−.04	−.06
Japanese men	−.38*	.01	.29*
Polish men	.00	.00	.19*

[a]For the United States, where the data are longitudinal, path is from education to baseline personality; for Japan and Poland, where the data are cross-sectional, path is from education to current personality.
*$p < .05$.

Personality and class placement. Personality might affect class placement not only by affecting occupational self-direction, but also by other selection processes; more intellectually flexible men might, for example, be promoted into jobs with more supervisory or administrative responsibility, or might open their own businesses. Here, again, the nominal nature of social class prevents linear structural-equations modeling of the relationship between social class position and personality, but there is nothing to prevent us from examining the over-time effects of personality on ownership and hierarchical position. Since the issue is whether there are additional effects of personality on ownership and hierarchical position above and beyond those that occur because these facets of personality affect occupational self-direction, it is essential that occupational self-direction be statistically controlled. Schooler and I have done such analyses for intellectual flexibility and for self-directedness of orientation (Kohn and Schooler 1983, Table 6.4, p. 149); the smaller number of fathers makes it impractical to do a similar analysis for parental values. Since this type of analysis requires truly longitudinal data, we can do it only for the United States. Still, for the United States the results are unequivocal: Although we find a statistically significant effect of intellectual flexibility (at the time of the baseline interview) on ownership (at the time of the follow-up interview), this effect is quite small (0.06), and there is no statistically significant effect of intellectual flexibility on hierarchical position, nor of self-directedness of orientation on either owner-ship or hierarchical position. The direct effects of intellectual flexibility and of self-directedness of orientation on ownership and hierarchical position, hence on position in the class structure, are dwarfed by their indirect effects via occupational self-direction.

The analyses thus demonstrate that there are important effects both of personality on class position and of class position on personality. They also demonstrate that occupational self-direction plays the pivotal role in explaining both. Position in the class structure affects men's values, intellectual flexibility, and self-directedness of orientation primarily because class position affects occupational self-direction and occupational self-direction, in turn, affects these facets of personality. These facets of personality affect men's positions in the class structure, in turn, mainly because they affect occupational self-direction.

Explaining the Cross-National Differences in the Relationships of Social Class and Social Stratification with Distress

Distress has all along been the exception to an otherwise-consistent cross-national pattern. As we have seen, the correlation (*eta*) of social class with distress is not very large in any of the three countries; nor is the nature of the relationship consistent from country to country. The correlations of social stratification and distress are also weak and cross-nationally inconsistent (Table 1.6). This means that I have to explain, not only what accounts for the cross-national differences in the relationships of class and stratification with distress, but also—and perhaps as important—why the magnitudes of these relationships are so much smaller than are those of class and stratification with other facets of personality.

Part of the explanation for the relationships' being weak and cross-nationally inconsistent—and also part of the interpretive problem—is that occupational self-direction, although strongly and consistently related to social class, fails to have strong, cross-nationally consistent effects on distress (again see Table 1.11). Although occupational self-direction has a statistically significant (negative) effect on the sense of distress for the United States and Japan, it has no effect at all for Poland.

If occupational self-direction does not provide a cross-nationally consistent explanation of the relationships of class and stratification with distress, might such an explanation lie in the social composition of the classes? For the United States and Poland, statistically controlling the pertinent social characteristics (once again, see Table 1.10) has only a small effect on the magnitudes of the class-distress relationships. For Japan, though, the social composition of the classes does seem to be pertinent: Younger Japanese workers tend to be more distressed than older workers and younger workers are disproportionately nonmanual. Men whose fathers enjoyed high occupational status tend to be less distressed than others, and such men tend to be disproportionately employers and managers. Also, men from urban backgrounds tend to be more distressed than men from rural backgrounds, and men of urban background tend to belong to the social classes that evidence the greatest distress. Still, these social characteristics account for only one-fourth of the class-distress correlation. Even for Japan, an adequate explanation of the class-distress relationship cannot be limited to occupational self-direction and social background.

In our earlier U.S. research, Schooler and I had found that job conditions other than those directly involved in occupational self-direction are more important for distress than for other facets of personality (Kohn and Schooler 1983, Chapter 6). This suggested that the effects of some of these other job conditions on distress might be at odds with those of occupational self-direction. There is some pertinent, albeit limited, evidence that lends credence to this possibility.

In the United States, job protections (such as seniority provisions in union contracts) ameliorate distress. Nonetheless, the very people who at the time of our interviews enjoyed the greatest job protections—manual workers—were also the most distressed. Manual workers were distressed *because* they lacked opportunities for occupational self-direction and *despite* the job protections that many of them—particularly union members—enjoyed. Were it not for these job protections, manual workers would be even more distressed than they are. Occupational self-direction and job protections have countervailing effects, which accounts for the relatively modest relationship of social class with distress, even for the United States.

For Japan, we do not have a good index of job protections. We do find, however, that two job conditions positively related to occupational self-direction—namely, believing that one works under considerable time pressure, and believing that people in one's occupation may be held responsible for things outside of their control—are also positively related to distress. Although these findings may reflect a propensity for distressed people to overestimate the pressures and uncertainties of their jobs, it is at least plausible that these job conditions do increase distress, thus counteracting the ameliorative effects of occupational self-direction. Moreover, our linear structural-effects model of the reciprocal effects of occupational self-direction and distress (again see Table 1.11) suggests that either education itself, or other job conditions related to education, increase distress. The countervailing effects of occupational self-direction, which decreases distress, and of education or of job conditions associated with greater educational attainment that increase distress, may help explain not only why the overall relationship of class to distress for Japan is modest, but also why nonmanual workers are more distressed than manual workers are.

In socialist Poland at the time of the 1978 survey, *all* employees of the nationalized sector of the economy—production workers, nonproduction workers, nonmanual workers, first-line supervisors, and managers alike—by law enjoyed employment security, sick leave, guaranteed vacations, and other job protections akin to those of unionized workers in the United States. Since manual workers enjoyed the same job protections as all other employees of the nationalized sector of the economy, their having such protections does not in itself explain why production and nonproduction workers were the least distressed of all employee classes. Their having such protections, though, represented a substantial, if gradual, improvement over their past situation, for it was only during the late 1960s and early 1970s that Polish labor law had been changed to give them the job protections that previously had been enjoyed only by nonmanual workers. The full implementation of those laws took place in the early 1970s, approximately five years before our survey. Thus, Polish manual workers enjoyed a degree and range of job protections and job benefits that constituted a decided improvement over those that they had had in the past. I believe that this helps explain why production workers and nonproduction workers were the least distressed of employee social classes.

Moreover, manual workers, particularly production workers, enjoyed the further job security attendant on a labor market in which they were in especially great demand. And both production and nonproduction workers enjoyed other protections and benefits by virtue of their class positions in the Polish socialist society—such as preferential access to housing, the provision of health care through their place of employment, and preferential access to higher education for their children. These, too, may have contributed to manual workers' being the least distressed of all employee classes.

As for the Polish managers, whom we have seen to be more distressed than members of any other social class except nonmanual workers (quite in contrast to the situation of managers in the United States and Japan): We have one fascinating bit of information that may help explain what it is about the conditions of life experienced by Polish managers that made them so distressed. One segment of the Polish managerial class was particularly distressed—namely, those Polish managers who were *not* members of the Polish United Workers' (Communist) Party. Although there are too few non-Party managers for this finding to be definitive (N = 13), it is nonetheless impressive that the non-Party managers had decidedly higher levels of distress, compared not only to managers who were members of the Party, but compared to members of any other social class whether they were Party members or not. Moreover, Party membership *per se* is not related to distress; it is only the non-Party *managers* who were particularly distressed.

The implications of these findings, I think, are that being a non-Party manager in the Polish system of centralized planning (circa 1978) entailed uncertainties, risks, and insecurities—greater than those experienced by managers who were members of the Party, and greater than those experienced by managers in the less centralized systems of capitalist countries. The Polish system may have held these managers responsible for accomplishments they had neither the leeway nor the resources to achieve.

The evidence, admittedly incomplete, thus suggests that not only does occupational self-direction fail to have the cross-nationally consistent effect on distress that it has on other facets of personality, but also that other job conditions—job uncertainties and insecurities, and protections from those uncertainties and insecurities—may have countervailing effects. It is these countervailing effects that seem to explain—at least in part—the striking cross-national difference in the relationships of social structure and distress. To adequately explain the relationships of social structure to job conditions to distress, we must enlarge the range of job conditions beyond those directly involved in occupational self-direction. A model that appears to be sufficient for other dimensions of personality does not adequately account for distress.[14]

Later in this book, we will see what happened to the cross-nationally idiosyncratic findings of the Polish manual workers having a strong sense of well-being and the managers being distressed once Poland began its transition from socialism to nascent capitalism.

Conclusion

Poland considered Western?

My collaborators and I have conceptualized and indexed social class for three disparate countries: a Western capitalist country (the United States), a non-Western capitalist country (Japan), and a socialist country (Poland). For all three countries, we have adapted the same basic idea—that social classes are to be distinguished primarily in terms of ownership and control of the means of production and control over the labor power of others—to the historical, cultural, economic, and political circumstances of the particular country. We have also shown that, even though social class and social stratification are closely linked empirically, social class is both conceptually and empirically distinct from social stratification in all three countries.

Q#1

I hypothesized that men who are more advantageously located in the class structure of their society would be more likely to value self-direction for their children, to be intellectually flexible, and to be self-directed in their orientations than men who are less advantageously located in the class structure. This expectation was strikingly confirmed for all three countries. Thus, the effect of social class on these pivotal facets of personality is not limited to Western, capitalist society, but would seem to be much the same for Western and non-Western, capitalist and socialist, industrialized societies.[15] Moreover, these cross-nationally consistent relationships of social class with personality are not merely the result of our having used the manual-nonmanual distinction as a secondary criterion of class, nor even of the close relationship between social class and social stratification. Class and stratification both have cross-nationally consistent effects on these facets of personality.

Q#2

I also hypothesized that in all three countries occupational self-direction would play a crucial role in explaining the psychological effects of class and stratification. This hypothesis, too, was strikingly confirmed. The effects of social class on parental valuation of self-direction, on self-directedness of orientation, and on intellectual

Q#3 + 4

---

14. See also the extended discussion in Kohn 1987, pp. 721–724 of other possible ways of interpreting cross-national differences in the relationships of social structure and distress.

15. There has been one study of a less industrialized society using methods and indices designed to be precisely comparable to those of the studies discussed in this chapter, a study of Bogota, Colombia (Gutierrez 1995). Although the N is relatively small, circa 200, Roberto Gutierrez effectively demonstrates that the relationships of social class and social stratification with these facets of personality are very similar in that less industrialized country to what we have found them to be for more industrialized countries, and furthermore that the relationships are substantially the same for the regulated and unregulated segments of the Colombian economy.

flexibility prove to be in very substantial degree a function of the varying oppor-tunities for occupational self-direction enjoyed by men at various locations in the class structure.[16] Here, again, the findings do not simply reflect my having used the manual-nonmanual distinction as one of the criteria of social class, nor the close association between occupational self-direction and social stratification.

Moreover, these analyses show that the interrelationship of social class, occupa-tional self-direction, and personality does not result solely, or even primarily, from selective processes by which self-directed, intellectually flexible men attain jobs that afford greater opportunity for occupational self-direction and more advantaged class position. Although these processes do occur, the evidence is clear that class position has a powerful effect on opportunities to exercise occupational self-direction, and that occupational self-direction has decided, cross-nationally consistent effects on intellectual flexibility, valuation of self-direction, and self-directedness of orienta-tion. Occupational self-direction thus plays a major part in explaining the effect of social class on these facets of personality. Admittedly, this might not be the case for facets of personality that I have not examined in these analyses. However, for the broad spectrum encompassed in our indices of values, self-directedness of ori-entation, and cognitive functioning, social class affects personality mainly because class is so closely related to occupational self-direction.

There is one apparent anomaly in the findings, the cross-national difference in the relationships of social class and of social stratification with distress. I had no firm basis for anticipating what would be the relationships of class and stratification with a sense of distress. The pattern is cross-nationally inconsistent: In the United States, managers have a strong sense of well-being and manual workers are distressed; in Poland, just the opposite; and in Japan, managers have a strong sense of well-being, but it is the nonmanual workers, not the manual workers, who are most distressed. Part of the explanation for the cross-national difference in the relationships between social class and distress is that occupational self-direction does not have the cross-nationally consistent effect on distress that it has on other facets of personality. In addition, other job conditions, which may be differentially related to social class in the three countries, have effects countervailing to those of occupational self-direction.

Even in the cross-nationally inconsistent relationships of class and stratifica-tion with distress, however, we have further evidence of the great importance of

16. The Polish-U.S. comparative analyses provide many additional examples of cross-national similarity. My collaborators and I have found, for example, that in both Poland and the United States, occupational self-direction not only affects intellective process, but does so consistently for younger, middle-aged, and older workers (J. Miller, Słomczynski, and Kohn 1985). We have further found that, in both the United States and Poland, the social-stratificational position of the parental family has a considerable effect on the values of its adolescent and young-adult offspring (Kohn, Słomczynski, and Schoenbach 1986; Kohn and Słomczynski 1990, Chapter 7). The family's stratification position affects both father's and mother's occupational self-direction; each parent's occupational self-direction affects that parent's values; the parents' values affect their offspring's values. The processes by which social stratification affects values and orientations—even unto the next generation—are essentially the same for a socialist and a capitalist society.

occupational self-direction as a principal vehicle by which social structure affects personality. The analyses demonstrate that wherever occupational self-direction has cross-nationally consistent effects on personality, so too do social class and social stratification. The converse is also true. Wherever occupational self-direction fails to have cross-nationally consistent psychological effects, class and stratification fail to have cross-nationally consistent effects.

The implications of these findings are considerable. Social stratification is defined in terms of a hierarchy of power, privilege, and prestige; it is indexed in terms of occupational status, educational attainment, and income. Social class is defined and indexed primarily in terms of ownership and control over the means of production and control over the labor power of others, secondarily in terms of the employment situation. Neither stratification nor class is defined or indexed in terms of *control over the conditions of one's own work.* Nevertheless, Schooler's and my prior U.S. research has found that social stratification affects personality not because of the status the job confers, nor because of the income that it affords, but because higher stratification position provides greater opportunities for occupational self-direction (Kohn and Schooler 1983). From the analyses of this chapter, I can add that position in the class structure affects personality, not because of ownership or control over resources, or control over other people, or the employment situation, but primarily because class position affects opportunities for occupational self-direction.

The analyses of this chapter strongly support the interpretation that occupational self-direction provides a powerful, albeit incomplete, explanation of the psychological effects of a fundamental facet of social structure, whether that facet is conceptualized as social class or as social stratification. These analyses have also strengthened the basic premise on which all of my collaborators' and my analyses of social structure and personality are predicated: that social structure affects individual personality mainly by affecting the proximate conditions of people's own lives.

I said earlier that I see class and stratification as alternative conceptualizations of social structure—both conceptualizations theoretically useful, albeit not necessarily for answering the same questions. The analyses of this chapter demonstrate that class and stratification have independent, albeit overlapping, and altogether parallel psychological effects. This "parallelism" is more than coincidental. It happens for essentially the same reason—because both higher stratification position and more advantaged class position afford greater opportunity for occupational self-direction. This, at any rate, is what I find in studies conducted under conditions of apparent social stability.

Chapter 2

Doing Social Research under Conditions of Radical Social Change

The Biography of an Ongoing Research Project

This chapter is based on a paper that I presented at the annual convention of the American Sociological Association in Pittsburgh, August 24, 1992, as the 1992 Cooley-Mead Address and subsequently published as Kohn 1993. I include this account of the history of my Polish and Ukrainian research because I think it enriches the reader's understanding of the research to know something of its development and of the intimate relationship between the conceptualization of the research and the lives of the people who did the research—not only my life, but also the lives of my collaborators in the research on which this book is based. I deliberately present the essay virtually unchanged from its original publication (aside from a few changes of tense, some after-the-fact clarifications, and the deletion of a couple of footnotes about the prior research that add nothing to what the reader of this book already knows from Chapter 1), because I do not want to change the sense of how my collaborators and I viewed the research on radical social change at its inception, and in context of our past experiences. As you will shortly see, the timing of my writing the essay, and even the very fact of my ever having written such an essay, was fortuitous, but also (I now think) very fortunate: This is how the research appeared as we experienced the beginning of the process of radical social change, before we had a single finding to guide us, but not before we had ample opportunity to observe and to think about what Poland and Ukraine were experiencing through the lens of what we ourselves were experiencing in trying to study the process. I leave for the following chapter a more formal statement of the hypotheses and research design we formulated, and for all the rest of the book (save a short, personal appendix) the results of the research and its theoretical implications.

I am indebted to Marta Elliott, Roberto Gutierrez, Krystyna Janicka, Valeriy Khmelko, Elliot Liebow, Bogdan Mach, Vladimir Paniotto, Carrie Schoenbach, Carmi Schooler, Kazimierz Słomczynski, Katherine Verdery, and Wojciech Zaborowski for their suggestions for correcting and improving earlier versions of the text.

Introduction

In February 1992, while I was in Warsaw working with my collaborators on our study of social structure and personality under conditions of radical social change, I received word that I had been designated this year's Cooley-Mead awardee. The award was conditional on my giving an address that had not already been committed for publication. But a paper embodying the conceptualization and design of the research had already been so committed (Kohn et al. 1992a), and the research had not proceeded nearly far enough to have produced any substantive findings that could provide the basis for an address. Lamenting this state of affairs, I commented to my Hopkins colleague and friend, the anthropologist of Romania, Katherine Verdery, that the only conclusion I could thus far draw from my efforts was that it is damned near impossible to do research under conditions of radical social change. Katherine properly retorted, "*Your* kind of research. Not ethnographic research." She was of course right, and her remark stimulated me to write a quasi-ethnographic account of the project itself.

If there is a rationale for this essay above and beyond its providing an excuse for my telling some of my favorite anecdotes, it is simply this: One can learn a great deal about social and psychological phenomena by examining the problems one encounters in trying to study them.[1] Our problems have resulted mainly, albeit not entirely, from the research infrastructures of Poland and Ukraine falling into disarray. But why should *research* infrastructures *not* fall into disarray when *all* the institutional structures of Eastern European societies are disintegrating, as these countries make their uncertain transitions from centralized political and economic systems to whatever will be?

I have not the slightest doubt that each of my collaborators—Krystyna Janicka, Valeriy Khmelko, Bogdan Mach, Vladimir Paniotto, Kazimierz Słomczynski, and

---

1. For a fascinating demonstration of the validity of this observation, see William Form's (1976, pp. 277–299) depiction of what he learned about labor-management relations in the automobile industries of four countries in the course of attempting to gain access to auto workers in those countries.

Wojciech Zaborowski, all of them deeply involved in the project—would tell a rather different, although consonant, history of the research. This is one participant's account, based, in the main, on extensive field notes and innumerable memoranda written very shortly after the events described here.[2]

Pre-history of the Project

The start of it all is an event that marked the beginning of my awareness of those remarkable Poles. It took place at a world congress of the International Sociological Association (ISA) in Varna, Bulgaria, in September 1970. The program listed a session organized by the Soviet Sociological Association on social stratification in socialist society. That session turned out to be a sparring match between Soviets and Poles, with Hungarians joining in support of the Poles and East Germans in subservience to the Soviets—almost all of it in English, as if for my benefit.

This was a time of imposed orthodoxy in Eastern Europe, and the head of the Soviet delegation, a commissar named M. N. Rutkevich, was an especially severe imposer. The Soviet line—I will caricature it, but only slightly—was: "Yes, we do have some occupational *differentiation* in socialist societies, but certainly not social *stratification*; that's impossible under socialism." The Polish response, put forth by their leading Marxist scholar, Włodzimierz Wesołowski, was, in essence: "We've read our Marx, too, but we've also done surveys, and our findings come out remarkably similar to those of the West Europeans and the Americans. In socialist Poland, we certainly do have social stratification, and our system of social stratification is not much different from that of capitalist societies." This response infuriated Rutkevich and his followers, which seemed to spur Wesołowski and his compatriots to the energetic pursuit of what I only later learned was the Poles' favorite indoor game, baiting the Soviets.

Who are these incredible people? I had to find out. Under the constrained circumstances of the Varna congress, the best I could do was to move to where the Poles were sitting and exchange what Americans call "business cards" and Japanese more appropriately call "name cards." This was followed in later weeks and months by exchanges of books and reprints.

Four years later, at an ISA congress held in Toronto, I attended a similar session, this time co-chaired by Rutkevich and Wesołowski. Although the session was called "Transformations of Social Structure in the U.S.S.R. and Poland," it dealt with much the same issues, and the exchange was just as spirited. On this occasion, though, I received news from Wesołowski: I was on a list of people who would be invited to visit Poland, though the time of the visit was indefinite ("Ours is a planned society, so everything has to be worked out well in advance. . . .") The invitation actually came only a few months later, and I visited Poland soon thereafter.

---

2. Having once upon a time been trained by Bill Whyte in the fine art of taking field notes, and being compulsive, I have several hundred pages of notes—raw materials enough for such an endeavor.

I will compress the most fascinating week of my professional life into one brief meeting, the climax of the week, on its penultimate day. I had begun the day with an intensive three-hour discussion with Stefan Nowak, the leading *non*-Marxist Polish sociologist. He then took me to visit Wesołowski at the third of Wesołowski's three of-fices, the first two being at the academy (where he did his research) and the university (where he taught his students). The third was at the Institute for the Study of Fundamental Problems in Marxism-Leninism of the Polish United Workers' (Communist) Party, where Wesołowski was officially second, and operationally first, in command.

In his office at the Party Institute, with a large picture of Karl Marx looking down on us (and an empty hook from which I supposed Vladimir Illich Lenin was also supposed to look down on us), Wesołowski put his proposition to me: "We have enjoyed your lectures and we have enjoyed having you in Poland. Now let us talk business." For a moment, I thought that Karl winked at me; I certainly looked up at him in some disbelief, hearing these words in that setting. The proposal, though, was simple and compelling. Wesołowski wanted to replicate my research in Poland, the aim of the inquiry being to learn whether my findings and interpre-tations about social stratification, job conditions, and personality would apply in a socialist society.[3] What could please me more? Of course I wanted to cooperate in such an endeavor.

Wesołowski went on: The study was to be theirs, paid for by them. They would own the data. As he put it, they had had too much experience with Big Brother to want any other arrangement. He asked me to be a technical consultant to the study, "and let's see how things develop from there." His proposal was to become a model—I came to think of it as the "Wesołowski model"—that I would follow in all my cross-national research.

Wesołowski proposed that his protégé, Kazimierz Słomczynski, come to spend a month at the National Institute of Mental Health (NIMH), where I was then employed, to translate Carmi Schooler's and my interview schedule into Polish, discussing that translation with me as he worked. Nowak said, "Mel, you're lucky. He's the best sociologist of his generation we have." I was delighted. Costs? "Since Słomczynski is a Polish citizen, we can pay his airfare to New York on LOT (the Polish airline) in *złotys*. But he'd need transportation from New York to Washington, and he'd need living expenses in Washington." No problem; even if NIMH should balk at this minor expense, I could pay for a rail ticket and he would in any case live with my wife and me.

Thus began more than a decade and a half of close collaboration with Słomczynski, who spent long periods of time working with me at NIMH and later at Hopkins. I, in turn, visited Poland regularly. The project culminated in Słomczynski's and my publishing one book in Polish (Słomczynski and Kohn 1988) and another in English (Kohn and Słomczynski 1990), the latter dedicated to Wesołowski in these words: "To

---

3. The evening before, he had shown me a passage in his just-published book (Wesołowski 1975), where he had written of my *Class and Conformity* (as he roughly trans-lated on the spot): "This controversial book cries out ... to be tested in a socialist society ... to see how universal are its conclusions."

Włodzimierz Wesołowski, whose idea it was." We had found that—with the major and intriguing exception of the relationship of social structure and distress—the U.S. findings and interpretation did apply to then-socialist Poland.

During those years, there were many important events that bear upon the current research, prominent among them the advent of *Solidarnosc,* the imposition of martial law, and Wesołowski's dramatic resignation from the Party when it invoked martial law; he was reportedly the highest official of the Party to do so. On a bureaucratic pretext, he was dismissed from the university—where he could contaminate students—but not from the academy. He had long since left the Party Institute.

Origins of the Soviet Connection

Concurrently, almost by happenstance, I was involved in re-establishing relations between the American and Soviet Sociological Associations, relations that had withered with the end of the *relative* freedom of the Khrushchev regime and the re-imposition of orthodoxy under Brezhnev.

My involvement had begun at dinner one evening in December 1983 in Barcelona, during a meeting of the ISA Executive and Publications Committees. The official translator for Khatchik Momdjan, the Soviet member of those committees, told me, "Professor Momdjan would like to discuss possibilities for improving relations between Soviet and American sociologists." I readily agreed, on the rationale that it might not do much good—this was pre-Gorbachev—but at any rate couldn't *hurt* world peace. So, at dinner the next evening, the three of us sat aside from the others and talked.

The conversation began slowly, painfully so. Momdjan said something in Russian, which was translated as "Professor Momdjan says that it would be desirable to have more contacts between American and Soviet sociologists." I replied in kind, raising the ante just a bit. We went on in this manner for three or four interchanges, barely beginning to approach anything concrete, when I decided to speed up the process with a proposal for making a first small step toward meeting Momdjan's worthy objective. To my astonishment, the "translator" accepted my proposal and made a further, more substantial one of his own. I pointed to Momdjan, who had understood neither what I had said nor his "translator's" reply. The translator, who of course had caught my intent, said, "This is taking too long; I'll tell him later." So Momdjan—who at the time was president of the Soviet Sociological Association—was not a free agent, not that I had thought he was.

The three of us in time worked out arrangements for a delegation from the Soviet Sociological Association to come to the 1985 ASA convention and present a set of papers about Soviet research on the sociology of work, the theme of that year's convention.[4] It wasn't a great set of papers, although the papers and the ensuing

---

4. That session, which I chaired, was my last public appearance as a staff member of NIMH, for I had earlier decided that the U.S. government was not large enough for both Ronald Reagan and me, and it was evident that he would have the votes to be re-elected. I also supposed—

discussion revealed quite a lot, perhaps more than the presenters intended. Of far greater import than the session itself, the Soviet presentations led to the establishment of a series of joint U.S.–U.S.S.R. symposia in sociology and—with the advent of the Gorbachev era—to such other innovations as Soviet students coming to do graduate work in U.S. Departments of Sociology, several U.S. sociologists—I among them—giving lectures in the Soviet Union, several Soviet sociologists lecturing in the United States, and expanded exchange programs for mid-career sociologists.

At the first of the U.S.–U.S.S.R. symposia, held in Vilnius, Lithuania, in July 1987, I met Vladimir Yadov, the preeminent Soviet social psychologist and sociologist of work. I had been exchanging books and papers with Yadov for several years, but I had never met him in person; he hadn't been allowed out. Yadov and I explored the possibilities of his replicating my research in the Soviet Union. He could see no way to do it, though, because he was in disfavor with the authorities, with few resources for any research and none at all for research on so ideologically sensitive a topic as social structure and personality.

I next saw Yadov in October 1988, at the second of the U.S.–U.S.S.R. symposia, one that he and I co-organized at a conference center near Baltimore. The U.S. participants were greeted with startling news: The Central Committee of the Soviet Communist Party had legitimized sociology. One of their first acts had been to re-name an Institute of the Soviet Academy of Sciences that had masqueraded under several other names, at long last giving it its proper name: the Institute of Sociology. More startling still, Yadov—who had been expelled from the Leningrad branch of an earlier incarnation of that institute—had been named director. He would now have authority and resources. All he would lack was time to do research.

With that in mind, Yadov had included as part of the Soviet delegation two Ukrainian sociologists, Valeriy Khmelko and Vladimir Paniotto, both of whom he greatly respected. With Yadov's encouragement, Khmelko and I had some exploratory discussions. (Paniotto, the methodologist, gave the lead to Khmelko, the social psychologist.) We spoke not so much about a research project *per se* as about the possibility of his spending two or three months with me at Hopkins (where I was now employed) if he could get a fellowship. All of this was exceedingly tentative, but nonetheless encouraging. The interest was there on both sides, but it wasn't at all clear how we could do it.

The Beginnings of the Actual Project

The next major steps towards a Ukrainian study occurred in December 1989. I spent three weeks in the Soviet Union in a complicated mixture of activities,

---

correctly, as it turns out—that I would have a better shot at getting research funds from the U.S. government by applying for grants through a university than as an employee of NIMH. That, however, lay in the future—farther in the future than I imagined at the time.

among them attending the third of the Soviet–U.S. symposia. This one was on public opinion research.

The morning after my arrival in Moscow, Yadov told me that I was to divide my time between Moscow and Kiev, attending the symposium in Moscow, lecturing in both places, and discussing research with Khmelko and Paniotto in Kiev. And so, immediately after the symposium, my wife and I were off by the night train for four days in Kiev.

Our discussions about the possibilities for collaborative research were held in Khmelko's office at the Ukrainian branch of the Marxism-Leninism Institute of the Communist Party of the Soviet Union. The institute was analogous to the one where Wesołowski had proposed the Polish study a decade and a half before. Khmelko told me that he had proposed, and his colleagues and chief had approved, a survey on social-psychological factors that might facilitate or interfere with the development of "self-regulation"—a term approximately equivalent to my "self-direction." This was not the way I would have preferred to state the issue. To my mind, Soviet sociologists were too disposed to treat psychological variables as independent variables in causal analyses, social-structural as dependent.[5] I would have preferred to talk about the reciprocal relationship between social structure and personality. But, since both the social-structural and the psychological variables were to be included in the same survey, there would be a basis for data analysis.

I was of course concerned about potential bias to people's answers in a survey done under the Party's auspices. This concern was at least partly mitigated when I learned that the survey was to be carried out by the Ukrainian branch of Tat'iana Zaslavskaya's Public Opinion Center, as "progressive" an institution as could be found in this highly politicized society. My principal remaining concern was with the content of the interview schedule.

Khmelko's colleagues and chief had approved the inclusion of many of the psychological variables from my surveys, and had also agreed to measure both social stratification and social class as I measure them. The latter would have been unthinkable a couple of years before. At the Vilnius conference, my paper on class position and psychological functioning (later published as Kohn et al. 1990) had been roundly attacked for its attempt to conceptualize and index social class in socialist Poland. To many Soviet social scientists, the very idea of there being social classes in a socialist society implied the Stalinist formulation: two classes,

---

5. This had become especially apparent in a debate among the Soviet participants in the Baltimore symposium, in the discussion of my own paper (later published as Kohn 1989a), a critique of *American* sociologists' failure to take social structure sufficiently into account in their social-psychological inquiries. One of the Soviet participants—Ovsei Shkaratan—thought the criticism applied at least as much to Soviet as to U.S. sociologists, and as the debate went on I came to agree with him. In my subsequent public lectures in Moscow and Kiev, I had even taken to criticizing Soviet sociologists for not taking Marx seriously, because many of them knew only a politicized Marx, seen through the writings of Lenin and Stalin.

one stratum.[6] But no longer; now it was possible for a Party institute to accept the reality of social classes in the Soviet Union.

Khmelko asked what else I would be interested in including. I replied that job conditions were crucial—they were the heart of my theoretical model of how social-structural position affects and is affected by personality. Khmelko told me that he *hoped*—but had no assurances—that he would be able to include my questions about the most important facet of occupational self-direction, the substantive complexity of work. He did not have the resources to include questions about the other major facets of occupational self-direction—closeness of supervision and routinization—or about other job conditions. He asked, instead, "Do you want to pay for those questions?"

Even with the foreknowledge of the *ad hoc* ways that Soviet research institutions were having to fund their studies, I wasn't quite prepared for the possibility that a Party institute would be seeking outside funds. The idea of my applying for research funds in the United States to support a survey being conducted under the auspices of the Ukrainian Communist Party was too ludicrous to try to explain. Moreover, it was altogether inconsistent with the Wesołowski model.

My answer must have come as a shock to Khmelko: "Not on your life! If the Party Institute wants a study, they should pay for it. There is no way that I can get a grant to buy a few questions in a survey whose quality I don't control." I counter-proposed: "I am available as a consultant and possible collaborator in the data-analysis. My price is that the study has to interest me ... and unless the study includes the crucial job conditions, it has zero interest for me." Khmelko accepted all this with remarkably good grace, and we moved quickly to technical questions of translation and implementation.

As we left the institute, I made the lame joke that the last time a Communist Party Institute had sponsored a replication of my research, the research had prospered but the Party (the Polish Communist Party) had gone under. It did not seem remotely possible that the same fate could be in store for the Communist Party of the second most populous republic of the Soviet Union.

Back to Moscow, where there were three events of note for the study, two of them happy and one dismal. The first was Yadov's telling me that it was likely that his institute could fund the proposed study. The second was a telephone call from Paniotto, telling me that he had just received word from the International Research and Exchanges Board (IREX) that he was invited to visit Columbia University from mid-January to mid-February. We decided that I would try to get IREX to extend his stay, with a modest increase in stipend, so that he could work with me at Hopkins on a Russian translation of Schooler's and my interview schedule. The third event—the dismal one—was startling in its implications for a possible Ukrainian survey.

---

6. In that formulation, although "theoretically" there could be only one true social class in socialist society—the working class—there still remained as a historical anachronism a second class, the peasantry; and within the working class, the intelligentsia constituted a distinct stratum.

At dinner one night, Boris Grushin—a particularly well-informed Soviet sociologist—told me that the American participants at the recent public-opinion conference had been shown a "Potemkin Village." The Soviet participants had implied that they do surveys much as we do them in the West. Grushin told me, though, that few Soviet surveys were based on face-to-face personal interviews. The usual procedures are to send out mail questionnaires, or to distribute paper-and-pencil questionnaires at places of work, or to have a so-called interviewer watch the respondent fill out a questionnaire. This last alternative at least assures that the person who fills it out is the designated respondent, but in no sense is it an interview. With few exceptions, the only interviewing done is in telephone surveys. In a country where few people have private telephones, though, the sampling is necessarily abysmal. The news did not bode well for a Ukrainian study.

The next major event was Paniotto's month-long visit to Hopkins. I had managed to get IREX to arrange for an extension of time, and to give him an additional thousand dollars stipend, most of which he invested in a computer. Although I didn't realize it at the time, that computer made our future research possible.

What I had learned in Moscow about Soviet methods of survey research made me eager to learn precisely how surveys are done in Ukraine. To my dismay, Paniotto told me that Ukrainian surveys were a variant of the general Soviet pattern: An untrained, underpaid woman delivers a paper-and-pencil questionnaire to the home of the respondent and returns a day or two later to pick it up. Her only substantive role is to make certain that the respondent has answered all the questions. I contended that this method could not possibly give the detailed information we would require. After two weeks of often spirited and sometimes strained discussion, Paniotto agreed that it would not be sensible to compare data from Ukraine collected by self-administered questionnaires to data from the United States and Poland collected by interviews. The clear implication was that my Ukrainian collaborators would have to learn how to conduct an interview-based survey and I would have to help them learn.

The next issue was language. Ukrainian practice had been to conduct all surveys in Russian. Knowing Paniotto's role as an advisor to the Ukrainian nationalist movement, Rukh, I was surprised that he followed this practice. The possibility that Ukrainians might resist or resent being interviewed in Russian seemed to be one of those things that are more apparent to outsiders than even to engaged insiders. When I suggested giving the respondents a choice of being interviewed in Russian or in Ukrainian, Paniotto agreed—and did not think that it would be difficult to develop linguistically equivalent interview schedules. (Only two-and-a-half years later, it had become standard operating procedure in Ukraine to conduct surveys in both languages.)

Finally, we turned to the painstaking work of translating. It was a repeat of Słomczynski's efforts of a decade and a half earlier, when Słomczynski had translated the U.S. interview schedule into Polish. The one major difference was that Paniotto understands both English and Polish, so he was able to make use of both versions of the interview schedule in preparing the Russian translation. To my delight, he has an uncanny gift with language. Not only did he raise perceptive questions about the meaning of the English-language version of the questions, but whenever he discerned a difference in nuance between the English-language and Polish-language versions of a question, the two versions almost invariably had proved to be less than fully equivalent in our measurement models.

By the time Paniotto left, I was still not certain that there would be a Ukrainian study. I was dismayed at how much work lay ahead before Paniotto and Khmelko would be able to do a high-quality interview-based survey. I was reassured, however, that my Ukrainian collaborators would be able to produce an interview schedule fully comparable in meaning to the U.S. and Polish versions.

I asked Paniotto to carry back to Khmelko a long letter, in which I broached the question of interviews *versus* questionnaires and raised any number of other technical issues. I also suggested:

> Both the US and Polish studies were done at times of *relative* social stability. . . . The Ukrainian study will be done at a time of great social change. In some respects, this makes planning and executing a Ukrainian study much more difficult. But it also represents a potentially huge advantage, if you can somehow study the process of change. . . . This is a large question for extended discussion.

That extended discussion was to take place the following June.

Planning in Earnest

When I returned to Kiev in June 1990, my goal was to see if it were possible to make the Ukrainian study into something real and substantial. From there I was to go to Warsaw to see if there were any prospects for a new Polish study.

Officially I was in Kiev to represent IREX in establishing relations with the Ukrainian Academy of Sciences. This official role got me a room in the Communist Party's hotel, with an assured source of food, not too easy to come by in Ukraine at that time. My IREX role also provided access to officials of the academy, which gave me a first-hand picture of the academy's being run by officials whose academy and Party roles could hardly be differentiated.

My colleagues' situations had greatly changed since my earlier visit. Khmelko had authored a "Democratic Platform" for the Ukrainian Communist Party, a call for the transformation of the Party into a democratic socialist party, whereupon he was given an ultimatum by the Party Committee of the Institute: either withdraw from the Democratic-Platform faction of the Party or leave the Party Institute. He left the Institute. He had also become more and more heavily involved in intra-Party politics; he was even elected to the first (and last) partly democratically elected Party Congress.

Meantime, the sociologists of Ukraine had created an independent sociological organization, the Sociological Association of Ukraine. Khmelko was elected first vice president and Paniotto vice president for international relations. The association created a research center, to be financed by contracts with government agencies and foreign customers. Khmelko had been appointed its director, so he had a job—albeit one with no certainty of salary or longevity. Paniotto remained for the time being at the Ukrainian Academy of Sciences, but would also work closely with Khmelko in developing the research center.

For our study—if there was to be a study—these changes had several major implications. Any survey we did would no longer be part of a larger Party-Institute survey. This meant that we would no longer have to compress our questions into a composite interview schedule, and I would no longer have to be concerned about how Party sponsorship of the survey might affect people's answers to our questions. But it also meant that there was no longer an assured source of funding for the field work. Moreover, and perhaps more important, Khmelko and Paniotto would now be creating a field operation from scratch. This would be a formidable undertaking, but also an opportunity to create something that hardly existed in the Soviet Union—a research center that could carry out surveys based on face-to-face personal interviews. It was very exciting, and a bit intimidating as well.

Khmelko, Paniotto, and I had ten days of discussion, with interruptions for my meetings with officials of the academy, our meeting with the officers of the Sociological Association, my lecturing at the Higher Party School (where I was astonished to be questioned by several anxious members of the audience of mid-career Party officials about the future of that Party), and Khmelko's several Party meetings.[7] Despite these distractions, we worked out a plan for research. The study was to be essentially a replication of the surveys that my collaborators and I had conducted in the United States and Poland, and that Naoi and Schooler had conducted in Japan. The main focus would be on whether our findings and inter-pretations applied to a portion of the Soviet Union—Ukraine—in its "processes of democratization" and its transition from a centrally planned and administered economy to "a market economy." We had considerable discussion about which questions to include in the survey, what new questions had to be invented, and how to achieve comparability between the Russian-language and Ukrainian-language versions of their interview schedule.

We also decided that Khmelko and Paniotto would attempt to secure funds for fieldwork from Soviet and Ukrainian sources—the "Wesołowski model." We were confident that Yadov would try to provide as much support as possible from the Soviet Academy of Sciences, but we were not at all certain that he would suc-ceed. We were far less confident that we could count on the assurances of support we were given by officials of the Ukrainian academy, mainly Communist Party functionaries. We also explored other possibilities. Our estimates of financial need were modest—too modest, for they were based on previous Ukrainian experience in conducting surveys and did not take full account of how much more expensive an interviewer-based survey would be.

---

7. One other interruption, not mentioned in my address to ASA or in the original pub-lication of this essay, was the first of "my two visits to my mother's village," the subject of the appendix to this book. What I now treat as a fascinating opportunity for the observation of social change in rural Ukraine, I then saw as a day off from work to satisfy my curiosity about my mother's origins.

I committed myself to applying to U.S. sources for financial support of those portions of the data analysis that would be carried out in the United States. These costs would include both Khmelko's and Paniotto's coming to Johns Hopkins for extended periods, when I would give them intensive training in confirmatory factor analysis and linear structural-equation modeling (LISREL) and we would analyze the data collaboratively. We even signed a formal agreement, which they thought might be useful in applying for Soviet and Ukrainian funds.

As I looked at this agreement in 1992, only two years later, it already seemed quaintly dated: The aim of the research is stated as "collecting and analyzing data that are necessary for assessing and forecasting the mutual influence of social structure and personality during *perestroika.*" That formulation, which now included the notion of reciprocal effects, was deliberately put in terms of the buzzword that then seemed most likely to elicit Soviet support, *perestroika.* In fact, the agreement called mainly for extending the comparative studies of the United States, Poland, and Japan to Ukraine. But the term, *perestroika,* did signify a new emphasis on social change.

During this time, I was further developing what was then still only the germ of an idea: Everything we had done in our U.S., Polish, and Japanese studies had been done under conditions of relative social stability. Our findings, our conclusions, our interpretation might very well not apply under conditions of radical social change. If so, we could learn some very exciting things, which might lead us to modify our interpretation considerably.

A Comparative Study

Next I traveled directly to Warsaw, where I attended a conference on social change in Eastern Europe and had a series of discussions with Wesołowski, with Słomczynski, and with Bogdan Mach.

Some years back, Wesołowski had enlisted Mach, his next-generation protégé, to translate a set of Carmi Schooler's and my papers into Polish, and from those papers to edit a book (Kohn and Schooler 1986). In working with Mach on that book, I came to recognize him as a first-rate sociologist as well as an extraordinary human being.[8] I was eager to collaborate with him in actual research, but I didn't quite know how to do it.

All three were enthusiastic about the prospect of a Ukrainian study; all three shared my excitement about making radical social change the focus of the study; and all three immediately recognized the central methodological limitation of the planned study: We had no baseline data for Ukraine. Like it or not, the 1978 Polish data would have to stand as a proxy for baseline Ukrainian data. The prospects for a rigorous analysis would be immensely improved if we could do a restudy of

---

8. Just how extraordinary a human being he is was demonstrated dramatically by his underground activities during martial law in Poland. As I had only recently learned—and not from him—he had been responsible for finding safe housing for some of the leaders of the *Solidarnosc* underground and for finding places for the leaders to meet.

Poland, thus making possible a truly comparative study—comparative over time in Poland, as well as cross-nationally comparative.

Who would carry out the new Polish study? I saw two issues as potentially problematic. One was that Słomczynski and his research team (of which Mach was a member) were then planning to do a study of social change in Poland—*not* of the social psychology of social change as I would want to study it, but of changes in Polish social structure as such. Somehow, though—and to this day I am not entirely sure how it happened—the news of the planned Ukrainian study enticed first Słomczynski, then the other members of his research group, into postponing those plans. Instead, they signed on to a replication and major extension of our 1978 study of social structure and personality.

The other problematic issue was that Słomczynski was now teaching at Ohio State and spending much of his time in the United States. He could not play the central role in a new study that he had played in the earlier study. But Mach was eager to participate, as were Krystyna Janicka—who had played a major part in designing and conducting the 1978 survey—and Wojciech Zaborowski, whom I hardly knew at the time, but whom both Słomczynski and Wesołowski held in the highest regard. It seemed then—and still seems—a splendid research team.

As I wrote in a memo to myself while in Warsaw, "I think that the pieces have come together, at least potentially: a *comparative* study of Poland and Ukraine, focusing on social change. We already have a comparative study of the U.S., Poland, and Japan under conditions of apparent stability; what happens under conditions of radical social change? It's a very exciting prospect!"

What about funding? Fieldwork would now be much more expensive in Poland than it had been in 1978 or would be in Ukraine. Not only were Polish prices rising more and more to meet the level of world prices, but Polish interviewers had long been underpaid and were now catching up. Of even greater concern, the traditional method of funding research in the Polish Academy of Sciences—direct allocations from the academy—was ending and it wasn't clear what method, if any, would replace it. That problem was to haunt us in the ensuing months. Still, from the beginning, we all thought the Wesołowski model best: Our aim should be to secure Polish funding for the fieldwork and to obtain U.S. funding to bring Polish collaborators to Johns Hopkins for collaborative analysis and (except for Słomczynski, who was already expert) for training in LISREL.

From Warsaw, I went to Madrid for a meeting of the ISA Executive Committee and the World Congress of Sociology. It was a ghastly two weeks: The tone was set when I was mugged by three men on my first day in Madrid. The Executive Committee meetings were even worse. But there were two happier events in Madrid that are directly pertinent to this story.

I introduced Słomczynski to Paniotto. All three of us were very much aware, and somewhat amused, that an American was bringing Polish and Ukrainian sociologists together in a collaborative endeavor. Paniotto readily grasped the advantages of a Polish-Ukrainian comparative study; he and Khmelko had all along intended to compare their Ukrainian data with the 1978 Polish data, and a new Polish study fit into their plans.

The second event was Yadov's assuring me of full financial support for the Ukrainian survey. Even though subsequent circumstances prevented hm from making good on that promise, his endorsement of our research proved invaluable.

Fund-Raising and Interviewer Training

The major activities of the next several months—both mine and my collaborators'—were devoted to raising funds for the research from U.S., Polish, and Soviet sources. Our three efforts were intimately interrelated. Not only did *we* see all three as essential to the overall project, but each of the funding agencies sought validation in the actions of institutions in the other countries.

The National Science Foundation (NSF) and the National Council for Soviet and East European Research (NCSEER) were greatly impressed that our research had the endorsement of the Polish Academy of Sciences, the Soviet and Ukrainian Academies of Sciences, the Polish Sociological Association, and the Sociological Association of Ukraine. These endorsements demonstrated that the proposed research was of potential value to the relevant scientific institutions in the host countries, not only to U.S. sociologists. Moreover, both NSF and NCSEER were well aware of the virtues of the Wesołowski model in terms of the quality of the data that would likely be secured: This was to be the very antithesis of "dollars for data." The Polish and Ukrainian authorities, in turn, were greatly impressed at the scientific imprimatur of the National Science Foundation and the National Council for Soviet and East European Research. But I am running ahead of my story; many events occurred and we experienced many anxieties before we put it all together.

In July 1990, soon after I returned home, I read an article in *ASA Footnotes* about NSF's interest in supporting collaborative research in Eastern Europe. It seemed made to order, as indeed it was. As I settled in to work on a proposal, though, I got scared about the size of the budget: I was asking for funds for coding and quality control for both surveys; for bringing two Ukrainians and two Poles to Hopkins for a semester each; for computers for Kiev, Warsaw, and Hopkins; for salaries for research assistants; for travel; and astronomical amounts for overhead. These items added up to so much that I was afraid the very act of asking for this much would ruin my chances of getting any funds at all. On the advice of Murray Webster, the director of NSF's sociology program, I did propose a full budget of all necessary expenses. Eventually the project was approved and NSF gave me nearly half of what I had asked for. Certainly there was enough to begin the study and to convince the Polish and Ukrainian authorities that the project met NSF's scientific standards. The rub was that I now had to submit a new budget, in the amount actually granted, explaining how I could do the research at that reduced cost "without sacrificing either scope or quality." As my wife put it, I had to prove that I had been a liar when I originally told NSF that it would cost twice as much to do the job.

To make the task even more intricate, I had learned meantime from Bob Randolph, the executive eirector of NCSEER, that the council would be willing to supplement a partial grant from NSF if their reviewers thought that the study would contribute significantly to our understanding of Eastern Europe. NCSEER required an application much like NSF's, along with a budget showing precisely what I intended to do with the funds that NSF was providing and what more I would do with the requested supplementary funds. Having explained to NSF how I could do the job perfectly well with the funds that they were able to provide, I now had to explain to NCSEER why these funds were insufficient. I made my proposal and the NCSEER approved it.

Mine was the least difficult part. I was dealing with stable, established institutions with effective and well-understood mechanisms for making decisions. Meanwhile my Polish and Ukrainian collaborators were dealing with institutions in the process of disintegration and new institutions groping to develop rational and effective procedures, or they were inventing their own institutions.

Initially my Polish collaborators had hoped that their fieldwork would be funded by the Polish Academy of Sciences, just as the 1978 survey had been, but this hope quickly dissolved into uncertainty. When I visited Warsaw in January 1991, the director of the Institute of Philosophy and Sociology—where Janicka and Zaborowski were employed and where Słomczynski's research was located administratively—promised administrative support, including support for training the Ukrainians in survey methods. The director of the newly established Institute of Political Studies, where Mach was now employed, also assured us of administrative support. In what amounted to a public endorsement of the study, he even invited me to present a seminar about our proposed research. Whether public endorsement of the research and promises of administrative support would translate into financial support, however, was as uncertain to the institute directors as it was to us. The only certainty was that even administrative support was conditional on my receiving a grant from NSF.

Then the Polish government made a radical change in its mode of supporting research. The government now required scientists employed by the academy to apply for individual grants from a newly created entity, the State Committee for Scientific Research (KBN). It took some time for the state committee to develop application forms and procedures, which delayed our undertaking. My collaborators developed twin proposals—one through each institute—for two separate components of the overall study. In the ensuing competition, peer-review judgments of both projects were extremely favorable. Eventually, the two linked proposals were approved and funded. Even after the awards were announced, though, we suffered horrendously long delays and agonizing frustration. The months had slipped by—months that we had intended to devote to designing new questions to ask in the survey, but which had been devoted instead to administrative matters.

My Ukrainian collaborators faced even more difficult circumstances. The Ukrainian research was initially to have been supported by the Party Institute, but Khmelko had left that institute. In any case, the Party and its institute had ceased to exist. Then the research was to be supported by the Soviet Academy of Sciences, but Yadov's assurance of full financial support was trimmed to token support when Paniotto left the Ukrainian academy to take a position at the University of Kiev and it was no longer possible to fund the research by a transfer of funds from the Soviet academy to the Ukrainian academy. Later, when the Soviet academy was transformed into the Russian academy, even token financial support was no longer possible. The Ukrainian academy showed no interest in supporting my collaborators. All the sources from which we thought we might get financial support for the Ukrainian fieldwork had dried up.

Khmelko and Paniotto, however, are nothing if not inventive. They transformed their newly created Research Center into a thriving survey organization. The center was an enterprise whose primary office was one corner of the Paniottos' bedroom and whose secondary office was one corner of the Khmelkos' living room. Its equipment consisted of the computer that Paniotto bought with the IREX funds he didn't need for subsistence when he was living with my wife and me. Yet, despite the lack of physical resources, Khmelko and Paniotto did surveys for local authorities in Ukraine, for the Research Institute of Radio Liberty, for other Western news organizations, and for the United States Information Agency. The Ukrainian fieldwork was largely supported from the profits that Paniotto and Khmelko made in conducting these client-sponsored surveys. They also received financial support in the form of a grant from the newly created and elegantly named Commission of Scientific and Technological Progress of the Cabinet Ministries of Ukraine. Khmelko and Paniotto husbanded that grant, though, to support a planned, and as it turned out, invaluable, follow-up study.

The client-sponsored surveys provided not only the financial resources for conducting our intended survey, but also extremely valuable experience in conducting surveys. Moreover, by a marvelous stroke of good fortune, they have provided expert interviewer training in the person of Michael Haney of the Research Institute of Radio Liberty. Haney conducted intensive interviewer training sessions (in Russian, which he speaks fluently) in preparation for surveys that the center carried out for Radio Liberty. Later, the center enlisted the aid of that uniquely knowledgeable sociologist and Sovietologist, Michael Swafford, who provided further training in the conduct of academic surveys, again in Russian, which he too spoke fluently. By the time the institute carried out our cross-sectional survey of 1992–1993, it had a trained and experienced field staff and a good system for ensuring that their interviews were of high quality.

We still needed to find some way to train the Ukrainian investigators in methods of intensive pretesting. My hope had been to enlist the help of the Methodology Section of the Institute of Philosophy and Sociology of the Polish Academy of Sciences, which had done an outstanding job in pretesting the 1978 Polish interview schedule. When I was in Warsaw in January 1991, Słomczynski and I appealed to the director of the Institute for the services of Andrzej Wejland, a key member of that section, to help train the Ukrainians in his methods of intensive pretesting. Wejland, who is fluent in Russian, was eager to participate. The director approved his doing so as part of his regular duties. The costs to us would be minimal: perhaps transport from Warsaw to Kiev, perhaps not even that.

In the fiscal crises that befell the institute, however, a new director abolished the methodology section, despite our strong appeals. Wejland and his close associate, Pawel Daniłowicz, were kept on in temporary positions, but found the arrangement unsatisfactory. They resigned and went into business as a private survey firm. We hired them for pretesting, both in Poland (mainly using the Polish grants, supplemented by the quality-control funds in my NSF grant) and in Ukraine (using the NSF funds). In effect, we had to jerry-build our own temporary institutional structure where the existing structure fell apart. For our study, this *ad hoc* solution has proved entirely satisfactory. Whether it would be equally satisfactory for Polish social science was another question altogether.

We also needed office space in both Warsaw and Kiev, quiet places to meet and plan and work. In Warsaw, until the grants were in hand, we met in one or another of the collaborators' apartments or in noisy cafés. The Ukrainians continued to work that way—except that in Kiev it was much more difficult to find even a noisy café; we spent many precious hours looking for a place to meet. The Polish team finally got an office, financed from the overhead on their research grants. In time, the Ukrainians, too, got an office. They at last found a satisfactory institutional home for their research center in the Graduate Department of Sociology of the University "Kiev-Mogila Academia," where both Khmelko and Paniotto were appointed as professors. The Academia is a medieval university, closed in 1815 by the Russian tsar, later converted by the Communist regime into a training school for political officers of the Soviet Navy, and now reconverted into what I like to think of as a new medieval university. Amidst the institutional disarray, some things have turned out quite well.

Even so, dealing with these administrative and organizational problems has interfered greatly with our ability to work on the actual research—not only because so much time was expended on these matters, but also because my collaborators found it exceedingly difficult to invest themselves in issues of research design and question wording when our ability to do the study at all was so problematic. Progress on the research was excruciatingly slow.

The delays certainly have been extremely frustrating. In at least one sense, they also have been costly: The Polish grants are in *złotys,* and there was considerable inflation in Poland. With each passing month, the number of respondents we would be able to interview got smaller. In a strategic sense, however, it was difficult to tell whether we had been *dis*advantaged or conceivably even *advantaged* by falling behind in our time-schedule. Would it have been better to have done the surveys when we originally intended to do so,[9] or was it preferable to wait until the processes of social change progressed further? At what point in the process of radical social change can one best study its psychological ramifications? And how can one tell in advance when that time might be?

---

9. My grant proposal to NSF estimated that we would have the Polish survey in the field in the spring or summer of 1991, the Ukrainian survey "as soon thereafter as feasible." I said then that it was essential that we proceed expeditiously, "since we wish to study the effects of radical social change while it is occurring, rather than afterwards, when new social-structural arrangements may have been stabilized." That may well have happened by the time we were able to conduct the survey in Poland, more than a year later than intended; it certainly had not yet happened in Ukraine.

Research Design as a Reflection of Social Reality

To this point, in my effort to emphasize the research *process* rather than its *content*, I have deliberately touched only lightly on the substance of the planned research. Now, if I am to do justice to the intended theme of this essay—how the problems encountered in the research reflect the very social phenomena that the research attempts to study—I must tell you about some of the changes we have made in research design and in the substance of our inquiry. These changes reflect what had been happening, and what seemed to be impending, in Polish society and increasingly also in Ukrainian society. For the two years that we were planning the research, we were constantly scurrying to keep up with the social and political changes in Poland and Ukraine.

A major strategic issue in planning the Polish portion of the inquiry had been whether it would be preferable to do a follow-up survey of the respondents in the 1978 survey or to do a new cross-sectional survey based on a currently represen-tative sample of Polish adults. Early on, we had decided on a survey of a new cross-sectional sample, on the rationale that, for a study of *social* rather than of *individual* change, it was more important to secure a sample representative of the current Polish population than to have longitudinal data. Still, to establish causal models of change we had planned to re-interview a representative sample of per-haps 500 of the original respondents. This was to have been an important part of Mach's research-grant proposal.

On a visit to Lodz in January 1991, however, we received confirmation of something we had long feared: The names and addresses of the 1978 respondents had been deliberately destroyed during the period of martial law, in what now seemed to have been an overly zealous effort to protect the respondents' anonym-ity. One must remember that this was at a time when the *New York Times* showed photographs of army tanks surrounding the building that houses the Institute of Philosophy and Sociology, and when the police confiscated copies of the institute's journal, *Sisyphus*.

On hearing the disheartening news that a follow-up of the 1978 survey was not possible, Mach and I went for a long walk and a large beer. Two hours later we had a new design, capitalizing on the existence of one especially valuable set of records that fortuitously had *not* been destroyed—the names and addresses of a subsample of 177 of the men, those who in 1978 had one or more children in the 13-to-17 age range. Each man's wife and a randomly selected child had been interviewed about a year and a half after the main survey in a study of the transmission of values in the family. Mach re-interviewed all three members of these triads, using the data for his habilitation dissertation (Mach 1998). We have a long-standing interest in the intergenerational transmission of values (Kohn 1983; Kohn, Słomczynski, and Schoenbach 1986), which Mach was able to study under conditions of radical social change. Thus, an intended but infeasible longitudinal study of Polish men was transformed into a longitudinal study of Polish families.

We have had to make equally great changes in the design of the cross-sectional surveys to keep up with changes in the societies we are trying to study. Initially, we had intended to interview representative samples of employed men and women in both Poland and Ukraine—much as we had done in the earlier Polish, U.S., and Japanese studies, except that this time our primary samples would be fully representative of employed women as well as employed men. To that end, the Poles and I spent a highly pressured month in January 1991 (joined for a week by Paniotto), and again in July (this time joined by both Khmelko and Paniotto), developing new questions that attempted to capture the changing conditions then being experienced, likely to be experienced, hoped for, or feared by employed men and women in Poland and Ukraine. Some of these questions have to do with occupational structure and conditions of employment: ownership and other forms of control over resources and labor power; changes in organizational structure; the changing nature of unions and of workers' relationships with their unions; changes in the bases on which people are paid; and technological developments. Many questions pertain to risks, uncertainties, and job protections—both the reality (including the structural bases of the uncertainties and protections) and perceptions thereof. The risk of unemployment, of course, looms especially large.

During the July 1991 meetings, Słomczynski convinced us that studying only the employed would not do justice to the very people who might be affected most by radical social change. He proposed that we add to the Polish research design special studies of three categories of people that either did not exist under socialism or that had been greatly affected by the ongoing changes: (1) the unemployed (defined as people who have lost their jobs and are now actively seeking new employment)—a new category in a country where unemployment had previously been disguised, and where people were for the first time finding themselves without formal employment or paychecks; (2) employers ("capitalists")—a growing category, whose members would be included in any sample of the employed, but in too small numbers for intensive analysis; and (3) a startling new category in Poland—women who previously had been employed in the state sector of the economy but who now, with the dismantling of child care and other facilities, could no longer afford to be employed and had become housewives. We decided to interview special samples of 500 people in each of these categories. At the time, the Ukrainians deferred any decision about doing the same.

By January 1992, it was apparent to all of us that, with the delays in funding and the postponement of fieldwork, too much time had elapsed for us to employ so complex a research design. We might never get to study the special samples, the very people who might be most affected by social change. Almost as problematic, the delay between our cross-sectional survey of the employed and our special survey of the unemployed might be so prolonged that the two surveys would no longer be comparable. This would be especially troublesome if we found the unemployed to be more distressed than the employed but had no way of knowing whether the employed might have become equally distressed in the interval. Therefore we revised the design of the Polish survey, expanding the sample from employed adults to the entire adult population. Later, I prevailed on the Ukrainians to do the same.

Reluctantly, we dropped the rural segment of the Polish sample (just as in the 1978 study). We did this in part to husband our financial resources for interviewing adequate numbers of urban respondents in each of the employment situations, and in part because we simply did not have time to design questions that would be truly appropriate to rural respondents. On learning this, the Ukrainians decided to drop the rural segment from their survey as well. They did this in part, for the same reasons that we had found compelling for the Polish study; in part because there would no longer be comparability of the rural Ukrainian population to a similar Polish population; and in part because it was becoming increasingly difficult to find transportation in the rural areas of Ukraine, the gasoline shortage being acute and public transport being very limited in those areas. (This is telling evidence that the research infrastructure was certainly not the only infrastructure in disarray.)

We faced three major challenges in expanding the samples to include all adults living in urban areas.[10]

The first was to develop a battery of questions—my Polish collaborators call this the "sorting machine"—to ascertain the respondent's employment situation. This turned out to be a formidable undertaking, requiring weeks of work and a special pretest. The strategy that we developed was to ask a series of questions designed to classify the respondent in the most appropriate employment category, followed by batteries of questions appropriate to people in each of the categories. We begin by asking whether the respondent is employed 15 or more hours per week; if so, we ask about his or her job conditions. If the respondent is not employed 15 hours or more per week, we ask whether he or she is looking for work; if so, we ask questions about job-seeking; if not, we ask whether—in this sequence—she is a housewife, he or she is a full-time student, he or she is a pensioner, and so on. At whatever point we received a positive response, we were to shift to a set of questions appropriate to the respondent's employment situation.[11] The Ukrainian survey does not use so elaborate a procedure for classifying the respondent's employment situation, but relies more on the respondent's self-classification.

A second challenge sounds simple but has proved to be exceedingly complex: How does one decide which is the respondent's principal job? In the Poland of 1978, this question was not especially problematic. Some respondents held more

---

10. In Poland, the term *urban* is a legal designation, rooted in the historical rights given to cities and towns, as revised by the parliament. Several criteria are employed, including not only population size, but also the physical infrastructure—roads, buildings, and the like. For Ukraine, too, the term *urban* is an official designation of parliament. A locality is deemed "urban" if it has a population of at least 2,000 people, the majority of whom are engaged in nonagricultural activities.

11. In one important respect, this design was not followed in the actual survey. In the course of pretesting, my Polish collaborators found it more efficacious to ask the unemployed women who considered themselves to be housewives, as almost all of them did, our detailed questions about housework rather than the more general questions we asked of the unemployed and the pensioners. I assume that the decision was made as a tactical matter—it's generally more fruitful to ask detailed than general questions. Had I been on the scene, though, I would undoubtedly have argued in favor of hewing to a research design that attempted to measure complexity of activities as similarly as possible for all segments of the population (see Chapters 5 and 6).

than one job, but almost always the principal job was the one held in the state sector of the economy, other jobs being decidedly secondary in all respects. In 1992, with their economies in transition, many Poles and Ukrainians held two or even more jobs, and determining which one was primary had become highly problematic. With limited interview time, we could not inquire in detail about all of them. Working out the procedures for determining which is the respondent's principal job has proved to be anything but simple.

Because the heart of the theoretical model is that the lessons learned on the job are generalized to nonoccupational reality (Kohn and Schooler 1983), the prime desideratum in deciding which is the respondent's principal job is what that person actually does in his or her work, not that person's subjective assessment of the work. Thus we use as our principal criterion the amount of time spent on each job, rather than, for example, the respondent's subjective estimate of which job he or she considers to be most important or most satisfying.

The third challenge was the most demanding of all: On a crash basis, we had to develop new batteries of questions for key segments of the population: the unemployed, full-time housewives, students, and pensioners. Our most important objective was to develop questions about the complexity of their principal activities, analogous to those we ask of employed respondents about the substantive complexity of their work in paid employment, it being a theoretical necessity that we have such measures as a likely intervening link between social-structural position and psychological functioning.

We could build on the questions that Carmi Schooler and I had long ago developed in our U.S. research for measuring the complexity of housework, of schooling, and of activities in retirement, but these were only a start. Mach and I sketched out others. Then Janicka, Mach, and Zaborowski did a herculean job of translating and refining those questions and inventing others. My own usefulness decreased precipitously as we moved from English-language formulations to Polish-language implementation.

I spent January through June 1992 (using a blessedly timed sabbatical) shuttling back and forth between Warsaw and Kiev, flying Aeroflot and keeping my fingers crossed that I would arrive in one piece. My principal role during these crucial months was to coordinate the Polish and Ukrainian studies as well as I could, working on research design and question-wording with both research teams and trying to keep each abreast of what the other was doing. I also played an emotionally difficult, quasi-administrative role—pressuring the Poles to speed up their sometimes excruciatingly slow pace in getting interview schedules ready for pretesting, while restraining the Ukrainians, who were eager to begin fieldwork but whose timing was held hostage to the completion of the Polish interview schedules. We all desperately wanted the two surveys to be as comparable as possible, but this was proving very difficult to accomplish. Probably my most useful activities were bringing Wejland and Mach to Kiev to help in the translation of Polish questions into Russian, greatly enlarging the scope and intensity of pretesting in both countries, and facilitating Wejland's full participation in the Ukrainian pretests. In a peculiar way, my frequent presence also provided both my Polish and my Ukrainian collaborators with a useful excuse for putting other responsibilities aside to work concentratedly on our joint endeavor.

By June 1992, pretest versions of both the Polish interview schedule and the Russian-language version of the Ukrainian interview schedule were ready. Intensive pretests were then conducted in both countries—Wejland and Daniłowicz conducted the Polish pretest, and Wejland traveled twice to Kiev to teach his methods of intensive pretesting to the Ukrainians and to assist in the Ukrainian pretest. In mid-July, the Poles and Ukrainians met to discuss the results of those pretests. From what they later told me, the pretests went well in both countries. By early August 1992—when I had to bring my tale to a conclusion, to present it at the ASA convention that month—my collaborators were busily refining their interview schedules. Both surveys were to go into the field in early fall—almost a year and a half behind schedule.

Every aspect of the research—the timing of the surveys, the samples we chose, our conceptualization of what is entailed in radical social change, the very questions we ask our respondents—has been profoundly affected by our own experience of social change. By the same token, every modification we have had to make in our research plans has given us insight into the meaning of radical social change to those whose lives it affects.

Conclusion

Attempting to study the social psychology of radical social change has proved to be exceedingly difficult, sometimes exceedingly frustrating, and, yet, always exceedingly interesting. Our experience in this research—both of having been buffeted about by radical social change and of being forced to cope with such change—helps us to understand the very processes that we are trying to study.

Admittedly, there are obvious and striking differences between the situations we have encountered in attempting to carry out this research and the situations most people in Poland and Ukraine have encountered in their everyday lives. There also are obvious and striking differences between my own situation—operating from a home base in the United States and being subject to the vagaries of radical social change only in my research role—and those of my Polish and Ukrainian collaborators, who have been affected in all aspects of their lives. I am, nonetheless, impressed by how greatly our experiences in attempting to do research reflect those of the people of Eastern Europe in pursuing their lives. I am also impressed by how greatly changes in *research* institutions reflect (and even result from) changes in other social institutions. Research institutions are so integral to the society that they are necessarily affected by any profound changes that occur in that society.

Observing the disintegration of research infrastructures in Poland and Ukraine has provided insight into what is happening to many other institutions as well. From our own experiences in attempting to secure funds and to conduct this research, for example, we have learned how extreme budgetary shortfalls can threaten the very existence of even well-established institutions. From the repeated need to delay our plans so that we could deal with previously unknown obstacles and contingencies, we have learned something about how radical social change prevents people from getting things done in the ways, and on the schedules, that previously were normal and achievable.

Disintegration, though, is only part of what we have witnessed. We have also seen the creation of new research-supporting institutions—the State Committee for Scientific Research in Poland and the Commission of Scientific and Technological Progress of the Cabinet Ministries of Ukraine. These new agencies represent sharp departures from past methods of funding research in Eastern Europe. Rather than following the past practice of allocating research funds to institutions and their component units, they provide grants to individual research projects—the Polish agency even basing its evaluations of those projects on formal peer reviews. These radical departures from past institutional practice embody a major change in the very conceptualization of what constitutes the primary unit of research; such a change clearly reflects a fundamental shift in ideology, affecting all the institutions of Eastern European countries.

We have also witnessed the beginning of a process of transformation of existing research institutions. The Polish Academy of Sciences, to take a notable example, is making strenuous efforts to reorganize itself to meet new and perilous challenges.[12] Perhaps the most radical innovation we have encountered is the resurrection in Ukraine of the Mogila Academy. Reconstituted on a model previously unheard of in the former Soviet Union, this university combines research with teaching. Moreover, it has no ties to the previous regime.

Although we have participated in, fostered to some degree, and directly benefitted from these transformations, I am not at all sure whether they will succeed or, if they do succeed, whether they will be an improvement over previous institutional arrangements. It is too early to tell. It is not too early, though, to observe not only disintegration, but also the creation of new infrastructure and the transformation of the old, based on quite different organizational and ideological principles. There is no question in my mind that the particular developments that we have encountered in conducting this research reflect similar institutional transformations occurring more generally in Poland and Ukraine.

The lessons of our research are not limited to what we have learned from our encounters with formal institutions. We have also learned something about what is happening in the process of radical social change from having had to modify the design and content of our studies. In facing the need to expand our research design to encompass people not currently employed, and to develop new batteries of questions that assess the job-equivalent activities of people in non-job situations, we have gained considerable understanding of the changes now taking place in the class structures of Poland and Ukraine. Even the relatively minor task of identifying

---

12. We have participated in two of these efforts: the beginnings of a reorganization of the Institute of Philosophy and Sociology of the Polish Academy of Sciences, based on research teams (such as ours) rather than on administrative units; and the formalization of the graduate teaching program—in defense against criticisms of the academy for not doing enough teaching.

the respondent's principal job has given us some understanding of changes now occurring in many people's conditions of work.

Finally, we have learned some valuable lessons about the social psychology of radical social change from being forced to cope with such change ourselves. Certainly we have learned more than we cared to experience about how frustrating and discouraging it can be to have one's expectations constantly undermined, and never to know whether yesterday's ground rules apply today or whether today's will apply tomorrow. After living with radical social change for some time, you come to think that no can make commitments, and that no one who does make commitments can fulfill them.

But radical social change also means that new types of initiative are possible. Even the ingenuity that my collaborators have displayed in overcoming the obstacles they have encountered may give us insight into how people are attempting to deal with institutional change. At the extreme, resorting to privatization as a means of supporting research—as Khmelko and Paniotto have done in Ukraine and as Wejland and Daniłowicz have done in Poland—is far from unheard of in Eastern Europe today. And, although few Poles and few Ukrainians enjoy the support of the National Science Foundation and the National Council for Soviet and East European Research, "joint ventures" with foreign capital are the dream of many and are becoming reality for some.

Postscript

I end the history of the research where my essay fortuitously stopped, when the pretesting had been completed and the main surveys were about to be carried out. It's not a bad place to stop for the rest of the story is best told, not in further description of my collaborators' and my lives, nor in how we did the research, but in the research itself—its conceptualization and research design (to be described in the following chapter) and our findings and interpretation (in the rest of the book). I will, however, in the prefatory note to nearly every chapter, describe the roles of my collaborators in the research on which that chapter is based. Although I have composed the text of this entire book, my collaborators not only were partners in the conceptualization and design of the research, and carried out the surveys on which the analyses are based, but also were variously involved in the data analyses; and helped formulate the interpretations of our findings.

Chapter 3

Rationale and Research Design for the Comparative Study of Poland and Ukraine under Conditions of Radical Social Change

The first half of this chapter—which discusses the theoretical rationale and research design of the comparative study of Poland and Ukraine—is mainly based on my research-grant proposal to the National Science Foundation, the text of which was subsequently modified and published in two versions. One (Kohn, Słomczynski, Janicka, Khmelko, Mach, Paniotto, and Zaborowski 1992a), which was intended for an international audience of specialists in cross-national comparative research, emphasizes the cross-national comparative focus of the research; the other (Kohn, Słomczynski, Janicka, Mach, and Zaborowski 1992b), which was intended for a Polish readership, emphasizes the historical comparison of Poland in 1978 and 1992. My grant proposal and both papers grew out of the many planning sessions of the collaborators in the overall project (all the people listed above as coauthors of Kohn et al. 1992a), and benefitted considerably from an incisive critique by Carmi Schooler and from an informal seminar discussion by the graduate students of the Department of Sociology of the Johns Hopkins University. The second half of this chapter—which describes the research design and the practical implementation of this design that my collaborators and I developed in our comparative study of Poland and Ukraine—is based in part on the grant proposal and in part on discussions of these issues in subsequent papers that presented the findings of the cross-sectional analyses (Kohn et al. 1997; 2000; and 2002).

77

Introduction

Our research addresses a central theoretical problem in the relationship between social structure and personality: ascertaining the processes by which position in the structure of the society, in particular, position in the class structure and in the system of social stratification, affects (and is affected by) individual personality and behavior.[1] Most past research addressing this problem, including all of my own, has been done under relatively stable social conditions. In sharp contrast, *this* research is designed to study how radical social change might affect the relationships between social structure and personality. I follow Robin Williams (1970, pp. 620–621) in conceiving *social change* as change in the structure of the society, not merely as an eventful or dramatic period in the life of that society. As Williams puts it, "Change occurs when there is a shift in pattern, when new relationships emerge...." By *radical* social change, I refer not to the pace of change, but to the nature of the change—the transformation of one political and economic system into a different system.

Do generalizations and interpretations that have been developed from studies conducted under conditions of relative stability apply under conditions of radical social change? If so, this would greatly increase the power of those interpretations. If not, how must past interpretations be modified either by delimiting the conditions under which they apply (their scope conditions) or by respecifying the mechanisms through which social structure affects individual personality?

More specifically, our research was designed to test and refine a general interpretation of the relationship between social structure and personality: that social-structural position affects individual personality principally through its profound effects on people's immediately impinging conditions of life. For the dimensions of social structure on which I focus in this book—social class and social stratification—the pertinent conditions of life are likely to be occupational. This interpretation has been elaborated and tested on the basis of cross-national research conducted in a Western capitalist society (the United States), a Western socialist society (Poland, in the late 1970s), and a non-Western capitalist society (Japan)—all studied under conditions of relative social stability (see Chapter 1 and the references cited there). The new research is being conducted in two societies undergoing radical social change—Poland and Ukraine. The principal objective of the research is to use these nations as context for comparative analysis: Poland and Ukraine are chosen for study, not for their own sakes, but because they are strategic choices for the comparative study of social change and its psychological consequences.

A second major objective of the research is to study Poland and Ukraine for their own sakes, or—to put the matter more generally—because we are interested not only in social change as it might occur anywhere in the world, but also in the particular social changes that are occurring in the transformation of Eastern Europe and the former Soviet Union. The research is designed to gain basic knowledge about the

---

1. For pertinent discussions of the theoretical issues basic to research on social structure and personality, see Kohn 1963, 1969, 1989a, 1990; House 1977, 1981; and Spenner 1988.

transformation of Poland and Ukraine from socialist to postsocialist economies. My collaborators' and my intent was to document and interpret the social changes that were occurring in these countries and to trace the consequences of these changes for the lives of the people in these countries. The research is focused on obtaining a fundamental understanding of the very processes of social change, including the psychological consequences of such change, that are essential to an understanding of what has been happening to these two countries—and to all the countries of Eastern Europe and the former Soviet Union—during their transformations.

Theoretical Background

For many years my collaborators and I have been investigating the relationships between social structure and personality in industrialized societies, initially in research based mainly on studies of U.S. men and their wives and offspring, later on cross-national studies, particularly in Poland and Japan. The main theme of our U.S. findings and interpretation is that position in the class structure and the social-stratificational hierarchy affect individual personality mainly by affecting job conditions, particularly those job conditions determinative of one's opportunities to exercise self-direction in work; these job conditions, in turn, profoundly affect personality. A more advantageous class position, or a higher position in the stratification order, affords greater opportunity to be self-directed in one's work, that is, to work at jobs that are substantively complex, that are not subject to close supervision, and that are not routinized. The experience of occupational self-direction, in turn, leads to a higher valuation of self-direction for oneself and for one's children, to greater intellectual flexibility, and to a more self-directed orientation to self and society (Kohn 1969; Kohn and Schooler 1983, particularly Chapters 5–7). Being self-directed in one's work even leads to making more intellectually demanding use of one's leisure time (K. Miller and Kohn 1983).

The effects of occupational self-direction on intellectual functioning are at least as great for older workers as for younger and middle-aged workers (J. Miller, Słomczynski, and Kohn 1985; Schooler, Mulatu, and Oates 1999). And the effects of occupational self-direction on parental values even extend intergenerationally: parents' occupational self-direction affects their own values; their values in turn decidedly affect their children's values (Kohn, Słomczynski, and Schoenbach 1986; Kohn and Słomczynski 1990, Chapter 7). Moreover, self-direction in realms other than paid employment—in particular, in housework (Schooler, Kohn, K. Miller, and J. Miller 1983) and in schoolwork (K. Miller, Kohn, and Schooler 1985, 1986)—affects intellectual flexibility, self-directedness of orientation, and distress in much the same ways as self-direction in paid employment does. The experience of self-direction is of pervasive importance for linking social-structural position and personality.

Many of these findings were initially derived from analyses of cross-sectional surveys conducted in the United States, the principal survey having been conducted in 1964 with a sample representative of all men employed in civilian occupations in the contiguous states (see Kohn 1969; Kohn and Schooler 1983). A ten-year follow-up study made possible longitudinal analyses to assess the directions of effects in the relationships between job conditions and personality. These analyses showed the relationships to be *quintessentially reciprocal*—with job decidedly affecting personality, but with personality also decidedly affecting conditions of work (Kohn and Schooler 1983, Chapters 5–7). The effects of job on personality appear to be ongoing and continuous, those of personality on job more gradual over time—the time it takes to shift from one job to another or to modify one's job conditions to accord with one's values, orientations, and cognitive proclivities. Since all our analyses suggest that the principal psychological process by which job affects personality is one of learning-generalization—that is, of learning from the job and applying those lessons to nonoccupational social reality—this implies that both learning and generalization may be quickly responsive to changed conditions of work.

There have been many replications of this research, both in the United States and in several other industrialized societies; the findings of all of these studies have been generally consonant with those of the original U.S. studies (see the reviews in Kohn and Schooler 1983, Chapter 12, and in Kohn and Słomczynski 1990, Chapter 9). The most systematic replications, and the most rigorous cross-national assessments of the interpretation, have been done in comparative studies carried out by Kazimierz Słomczynski and his associates in Poland in 1978 and by Atsushi Naoi and his associates in Japan in 1979, studies whose design and major findings are summarized in Chapter 1 of this book. The intent of these studies was to determine whether the findings and interpretation developed from the U.S. studies apply as well to an "actually existing socialist society," as Poland then was (see Słomczynski, J. Miller, and Kohn 1981 and 1987; Kohn et al. 1990; and Kohn and Słomczynski 1990) and to a non-Western capitalist society (see Naoi and Schooler 1985; Schooler and Naoi 1988; and Kohn et al. 1990).

I do not mean to imply that the United States in the 1960s and 1970s and Japan in the 1970s were exemplary of some ideal type of capitalist society, nor that in 1978 Poland was exemplary of some ideal type of socialist society (to the contrary, see Wesołowski 1988). Whether the United States and Japan really were capitalist in those years, or some hybrid of capitalism and welfare statism, or whether Poland in 1978 really was socialist or state capitalist or some hybrid of socialism and capitalism, is immaterial. The United States and Japan were different from Poland in the crucial respect of how their economies were organized—the United States and Japan having economies in which market forces predominated, Poland having a centrally planned and administered economy.

Since the findings of the Polish and Japanese studies that are most germane to the central thesis of this book are presented in Chapter 1, I need only summarize them here: In most respects, the findings for Poland and Japan are entirely consistent with those for the United States and support the interpretations we have drawn from the U.S. data—social-structural position greatly affects opportunities, even the necessity, for occupational self-direction; the exercise of self-direction in work, in turn, increases intellectual flexibility, promotes the valuation of self-direction (in contrast to conformity to external authority) by parents for their children, and facilitates a self-directed orientation to self and others. In short, the psychological effects of social-structural position transcend the fundamental differences between capitalist and socialist societies, and between Western and non-Western capitalist societies. Moreover, and even more important, social-structural position has generally similar psychological effects for essentially the same reason. This is because position in the larger social structure profoundly affects people's immediately impinging conditions of life—their job conditions in particular—that affect their values, orientations, and cognitive functioning.

There are also some important cross-national *differences,* the most striking one being in the relationships between social-structural position and a sense of *distress,* in contrast to a sense of well-being. In the United States, managers have a strong sense of well-being and manual workers are the most distressed; in Poland, nearly the opposite; and in Japan, managers have a strong sense of well-being, but it is the nonmanual workers, not the manual workers, who are most distressed. Similarly, in the United States, the correlation between social stratification and distress is negative, in Poland it is positive, and in Japan it is virtually nil. Part of the explanation for these cross-national differences is that occupational self-direction does not have the cross-nationally consistent effect on distress that it has on other facets of personality. A more fundamental reason why the relationships between social-structural position and distress are cross-nationally inconsistent, though, is that job conditions other than those directly involved in occupational self-direction, such as job risks and uncertainties and protections from those risks and uncertainties, have effects countervailing to those of occupational self-direction (see Chapter 1; and, for a more detailed treatment, Kohn and Słomczynski 1990, Chapter 8).

Thus, the cross-national analyses confirm the generality of the U.S.-based interpretation of the relationships between social structure and such important facets of personality as self-directedness of orientation and intellectual flexibility. But these analyses also teach us that a full understanding of the relationship between social structure and distress requires that we enlarge our interpretation to take account of job conditions other than those directly involved in occupational self-direction.

A New Theoretical Context: Radical Social Change

All these findings, and our entire understanding of social structure and personality, are based on studies conducted under relatively stable social conditions. This is true even for the Polish survey, which was carried out two years before the advent of *Solidarnosc,* before there were any decided signs of impending change. The obvious and important question is whether our findings and interpretation apply also in times of radical social change.

The very idea of there being a relationship between social structure and personality implies a dynamic interchange. What we learn about this interchange at times of social stability is a static slice of a dynamic process. Whether what we thereby learn is typical of the more general process, or specific to times of social stability, is at present an open question. Will the thus-far largely consistent findings about the relationships of social structure and personality be confirmed or disconfirmed in societies experiencing radical social change?[2] Does occupational self-direction play the same crucial role in explaining the relationships of class and stratification to self-directedness of orientation and to intellectual flexibility under such circumstances, or do other proximate conditions of life play that role? What more can we learn about the relationship of social structure to people's sense of well-being or distress by studying this relationship under conditions that almost certainly will produce great uncertainty?

The null hypothesis, so to speak, of the planned research is that my general interpretation of the relationships between social structure and personality will prove to be valid even during periods of radical social change. Contrary hypotheses would predict that there are several ways that radical social change might obliterate, or at any rate greatly modify, the relationships between social structure and personality that my collaborators and I have heretofore found:

1. The class and stratification systems of the countries of Eastern Europe and the former Soviet Union are themselves in the process of change. It is an open question as to whether the class structures and the systems of social stratification of these societies will be as completely transformed as their political and economic structures. (After all, our own research and that of many other investigators have shown the class and stratification systems of the two Eastern European countries that have been intensively studied—Poland and Hungary—to be not so very different from those of capitalist societies.) Nevertheless, there is every reason to expect that with marketization and privatization these systems will be substantially reshaped. For example, in Poland there is almost certain to be a considerable expansion and internal diversification of the class of small- to medium-sized employers; in the Soviet Union, where there has been no such class, it is now beginning to emerge (sometimes in the form of "cooperatives"). Almost certainly, everywhere in Eastern Europe the stratification hierarchies will become steeper: inequality will increase. And, of course, with the Communist Party no longer a dominant power, other sources of political power will assume a more important role in shaping the social structure. These and other changes in the class structure and stratification system may be expected to result in corresponding changes in the relationships of these very facets of social structure with personality. It is pertinent to remember that our longitudinal analyses (of U.S. data) imply that changes in social structure may have relatively rapid effects on the personalities of those who are affected.

2. In all our studies, the *invariant* relationship has been between social-structural position and occupational self-direction, a relationship that transcends differences between capitalist and socialist, Western and non-Western societies. (Such cross-

---

2. Contrary to those who see an incompatibility between the concepts of social structure and social change, I think that the concept of structure is entirely consistent with that of change (on this point, see Boskoff 1966). Built into the definition of social structure is the notion of *relatively* enduring patterns of behavior, but certainly not of permanence or nonmodifiability.

national differences as we have found are entirely at the next linkage, that between occupational self-direction and personality.) It is certainly a plausible hypothesis, though, that the relationship of social structure and occupational self-direction may be weakened during periods of transformation from one system to another, when the occupational structure is itself in flux. While I cannot predict the final outcome, it is already clear that as the massive state-run, highly bureaucratized enterprises are dismantled, fewer people will be employed in such enterprises and more people will be employed as entrepreneurs or as employees in small enterprises and in the secondary and informal economies. Many other changes are likely to be introduced in working conditions, including those attendant on the introduction of new technologies—which, as the history of the United States and of Western Europe has shown (Form 1987; Spenner 1983), can have both positive and negative, often unpredictable, implications for workers' opportunities for self-direction in their work. The obvious hypothesis is that the heretofore-invariant relationship between social-structural position and opportunities for occupational self-direction may be weakened or may even disappear under such conditions.

3. The pivotal role of occupational self-direction as an explanatory link between social-structural position and personality may well be challenged under the conditions of change and uncertainty being experienced in Eastern Europe and the former Soviet Union. Job conditions other than those directly involved in occupational self-direction, or conditions of life other than the occupational, may come much more to the fore under such conditions. It is certainly a plausible extrapolation from our past findings vis-à-vis distress that conditions of uncertainty—and not only *job* uncertainty—will have powerful psychological effects. It is a reasonable hypothesis as well that non-job conditions of life may play an important bridging role between social-structural position and personality during a period when occupational conditions are in flux. Church, political organizations, neighborhood, family, friendship networks, and even voluntary organizations may come to play a more important role in shaping, or buffering, the proximate experiences that link position in the social structure to individual personality. Finally, *current* job conditions may play a less crucial role, and people's expectations about their future prospects a more important role, under such conditions.

4. There is also a distinct possibility that the experience of radical social change will itself have such widespread psychological effects as to overwhelm all else. One would certainly expect the uncertainties attendant on radical social change to increase distress. There is reason to expect, as well, that anything that increases distress will also affect the relationships between social-structural position and other facets of personality. *All* the relationships we have studied—those between social-structural position and occupational self-direction; those between occupational self-direction and personality; and—what may be most pertinent here—those between the several dimensions of personality—are reciprocal. In our analyses of U.S. data, for example, Schooler and I (Kohn and Schooler 1983, Chapter 6) found that distress has a dampening effect on self-directedness of orientation, thus also on intellectual flexibility and on occupational self-direction. Might the distress-inducing conditions of life being experienced in Eastern Europe and the former

Soviet Union short-circuit the processes by which advantaged position facilitates a self-directed orientation and intellectual flexibility in more stable times?

5. Finally, even if the interpretation I have drawn from our past research proves to be generally applicable to the changing circumstances of life in Eastern Europe and the former Soviet Union, in many particulars the map of the actual empirical relationships will have to be modified. To take only one striking example: Słomczynski and I (Kohn and Słomczynski 1990, Table 8.3, p. 222) found that in 1978 Polish managers who did *not* belong to the Polish United Workers' (Communist) Party were exceptional in their degree of distress—they were much more distressed than managers who *did* belong to the Party, and also more distressed than members of any other social class. That particular finding cannot be replicated in a Poland where the Party no longer exists. But our more general interpretation—that the non-Party managers were so distressed because their positions entailed uncertainties, risks, and insecurities greater than those experienced by managers who were members of the Party, and greater than those experienced by managers in the less centralized systems of the capitalist countries—can be tested by looking for sources of job insecurities, and job support, in the modified occupational structure of post-socialist Poland. More than that, the changes being experienced in Eastern Europe and the former Soviet Union provide an exceptional opportunity for increasing our understanding of the relationships between social-structurally based uncertainties and the sense of distress.

Research Strategy

How do we learn more about the effects of radical social change on the relationships between social structure and personality? Certainly not by further study of the United States, not at this particular time. Poland is experiencing radical social change, and for my purposes a restudy of Poland is strategically central. The former Soviet Union comes into play for much the same reason that my collaborators and I originally studied Poland and Japan—to differentiate social-structural universals from single-nation particularities (see the discussion of strategies of cross-national research in Kohn 1987 or in Kohn 1989b, Chapter 3). A comparative study of Poland and the former Soviet Union would provide an opportunity to study the effects of social change under contrasting conditions. The political conditions of Poland and the republics of the former Soviet Union are of course quite different; Poland is also much further along in the transition from a socialist to some form of post-socialist society; and we can foresee the eventual outcome of the process with somewhat greater assurance for Poland than for the former Soviet Union. Poland is evidently moving toward some form of capitalist society, the parliament having long since passed all the necessary enabling legislation and the populace being generally in favor of such a transformation, albeit with growing reservations. For the republics of the former Soviet Union, there is considerably greater uncertainty about what form their economies will eventually take.

The former Soviet Union as an entirety, however, is too ethnically and linguistically heterogenous, and too complex politically, for my purposes; a study of one of the larger republics is both more feasible and more strategic. Ukraine is particularly well suited for comparison to Poland, because (in comparison to the other republics) its culture is *relatively* similar to Poland's. By comparing Poland to Ukraine, I can compare two societies that differ less in culture than in political and economic context. This should make it more possible to interpret whatever differences I may find than if I compared societies that differed both in culture and in social-structural context.

The research is thus comparative in three distinct ways: (1) It is comparative over time, in that it compares Poland today, under conditions of radical social change, to the Poland of 1978, a time of relative stability. (2) It compares Poland to Ukraine, a republic of rather similar culture that is also undergoing radical social change but under rather different political and economic circumstances. And (3) it compares both Poland and Ukraine to the United States and Japan, two relatively stable capitalist societies.

Since the primary comparisons will be of *social* rather than of *individual* change, it is more important that the samples be *currently* representative of the populations of Poland and Ukraine than that the data be longitudinal; not that we had much choice (see Chapter 2). The question was in any case moot for Ukraine, for there had been no prior survey. My collaborators therefore conducted new, cross-sectional surveys of Poland and Ukraine.

The 1978 Polish survey had been based on a sample representative of all men living in urban areas and employed in civilian occupations. A year and a half after the survey of these men, the Polish investigators interviewed a representative subsample of their wives and children.[3] In the new surveys we again—reluctantly—limited our samples to urban areas (see Chapter 2). We expanded the scope of the samples, however, to be representative of *all* adults living in urban areas, women as well as men, and whether or not employed.

In the changing conditions that Poland and Ukraine were then experiencing, it was essential that we expand the definition of the pertinent population to include, not only *employed* men and women, but also men and women who were not currently employed. In the process of radical social change, those *not* employed may be the most decidedly, very likely the most adversely, affected. This seemed almost self-evidently the case for those people who had lost their jobs and were actively seeking new employment or were too discouraged to do so. Another segment of the population who may have been decidedly affected by radical social change were the members of a growing social category (in Poland, but not yet in Ukraine) of women who became housewives, either because they lost their jobs and could not find new employment, or because they could no longer afford to be employed as the result of the dismantling of state child care and other facilities. Still another

---

3. In the original U.S., Polish, and Japanese studies, we did not secure representative samples of employed women, but instead interviewed the *wives* of the men in our samples of employed men. We did this to make possible the analysis of the transmission of values in the family (Kohn, Słomczynski, and Schoenbach 1986; Kohn and Słomczynski 1990, Chapter 7), at the price of having to generalize from a sample of employed *wives* to a population of employed *women* in our analyses of the relationships between women's job conditions and personality (J. Miller et al. 1979 or Kohn and Schooler 1983, Chapter 8).

segment who may have been adversely affected were the pensioners whose pensions did not keep up with inflation. The study of social structure and personality could no longer be limited to the employed segments of the population.

Since the nonemployed segments of the population may be greatly affected by social change, we developed multitracked interview schedules, with special batteries of questions designed for the employed (differentiating between the self-employed and employees), the unemployed (those searching for employment), students, housewives, and pensioners. In all of these tracks, the questions attempt to assess the complexity of the respondents' activities. (I shall discuss the mode of inquiry about complexity of activities in realms other than paid employment in Chapters 5 and 6.)

Domains of Inquiry

As in the original U.S., Polish, and Japanese studies, the major domains about which we inquired are social-structural position, other social characteristics, job conditions, and three principal dimensions of personality: intellectual flexibility, self-directedness of orientation, and a sense of well-being or distress. Most of the questions used in the earlier Polish and Japanese surveys had been taken from the original U.S. survey (for the complete interview schedule, see Appendix C of Kohn 1969), albeit with important additions by our Polish and Japanese collaborators—for example, the question about membership in the Polish United Workers' Party that had proved so important for our understanding of the relationship between social structure and distress. We repeated all pertinent questions in the current surveys.

For the present inquiry, we also developed many new questions to be used in both the Polish and the Ukrainian surveys. The most important of these questions concern the changing conditions now being experienced, or likely to be experienced, by the populations of Poland and Ukraine. We also developed questions about the changing social structures of Poland and Ukraine. And we attempted to rectify some of the deficiencies in the questions asked in our past studies.

The new questions fall into five general domains:

1. Questions pertinent to the changing conditions of life in Poland and Ukraine. Some of these have to do with occupational structure and conditions of employment: ownership and other forms of control over resources and labor power; changes in the organizational structure of places of employ; the changing nature of unions and of workers' relationships with their unions; changes in the bases on which people are paid; and technological developments. Many have to do with risks and uncertainties and job protections—both the reality (including the structural bases of the uncertainties and protections) and perceptions thereof. The threat of unemployment, of course, looms especially large in our inquiry.
2. My Polish collaborators—who since 1987 had been studying changes in the social structure of Poland—have developed and tested a number of questions directly pertinent to our present purposes. Some of these are refinements of our

conceptualization and indexing of both social class and social stratification: For measuring social class more precisely, they have developed questions that make distinctions among different types of managers, that differentiate the segments of the private sector of the economy, and that distinguish two distinct types of nonsupervisory, nonmanual workers (on the basis of their educational qualifications and role in the production process). For measuring social stratification more precisely, they have developed questions that make finer distinctions in both level of educational attainment and types of educational institutions, and among sources of income. They have also developed new questions about anticipated career prospects, as well as questions about organizational involvements (particularly in local community organizations), religious beliefs and participation in religious institutions, and beliefs about egalitarianism—all of these matters that are coming more and more to the fore as Poland and Ukraine experience social change and all of which may be pertinent for explaining changes in the relationships between social structure and personality.

3. There are topics that we did ask about in the original U.S. and Polish studies, but about which we did not have enough questions in the U.S. interview schedule to ensure that, if one or two failed of translation, we would still have enough for multiple-indicator measures of the pertinent concept in the Polish and Ukrainian data. A particularly pertinent example is fatalism, for which we had only three indicators. We have added questions wherever the initial battery was too small.[4]

4. There are other questions that were developed for the U.S. studies but not used in the original Polish inquiry—mainly questions about job conditions other than those directly pertinent to occupational self-direction—because the methodologists at the Polish Academy of Sciences thought them too subjective. Their criticism is apt, but the questions—particularly about job uncertainties and job protections—have proved very valuable in the analyses of the U.S. and Japanese data and should be included in the new surveys. We have tried to improve on them, to make them less subjective. There were other questions in the U.S. survey that were not especially pertinent to then-socialist Poland—questions about ownership, for example—that are becoming more important to Poland and Ukraine today.

5. Finally, there are some questions that have never been entirely satisfactory in any of our studies, which we tried to improve on in these studies. One example is our questions about routinization of work, which are too limited in number, too subjective, and which have proved impotent in statistical analysis—leaving us in the quandary of not knowing whether routinization is less important than our theoretical beliefs led us to expect or simply not well enough measured in our studies. Another example is our limited information

---

4. We did, but we didn't always succeed in adding questions that were cross-nationally comparable—those for fatalism being an unfortunate case in point, as will become evident in Chapter 7.

about bureaucratic structure, which nonetheless has proved to be an important dimension of job structure and—if only because of the U.S. finding that bureaucratic employment provides greater job protections than does employment in small, nonbureaucratic firms and organizations (Kohn 1971 or Kohn and Schooler 1983, Chapter 2)—which may prove to be even more important with the radical reorganization of the economies of Poland and Ukraine.[5]

Language

The post–World War II Polish population being largely homogeneous as to ethnicity, the Polish survey could be conducted in one language, Polish. The situation was more complex in Ukraine. In theory, everyone understands Russian and, in practice, until recently Ukrainian surveys have generally been conducted in Russian (see Chapter 2). Given the nationalist sentiments of the country, though, we thought it desirable to give respondents their choice of being interviewed in Russian or in Ukrainian. Fortunately, my Ukrainian collaborators are fluent in both languages, which was a great advantage not only for producing linguistically equivalent interview schedules but also for training bilingual interviewers.

In Chapter 2, I have described the painstaking efforts that Słomczynski made in the original Polish study to capture the intended nuances of meaning of the questions that had been asked in the U.S. survey in his translations into Polish. When he returned to Poland, graduate students of the English Philology Department at the University of Warsaw prepared several versions of each translated question. The alternative versions of the question were judged collectively by a group of linguistic experts, subjected to a pilot study based on interviews with fifty persons selected from the upper and lower ends of the educational and occupational distributions, further revised, and again pretested and revised anew.

Vladimir Paniotto followed a similar procedure for the first step of translating the U.S. (and Polish) questions into Russian (see Chapter 2). We had the advantage, this time, of knowing where Słomczynski's efforts had succeeded and where they had fallen short. We had the further advantage that Paniotto understands both English and Polish, so his translations benefitted from his understanding of not only the English original, but also the Polish equivalent. The translations into Russian were minutely reviewed by two other trilingual colleagues, Andrzej Wejland and Bogdan Mach. Paniotto and Valeriy Khmelko, with the tutelage and assistance of Wejland, then exhaustively pretested the Russian version of these questions. After that, Paniotto and Khmelko translated the entire interview schedule into Ukrainian—our intent being to give the respondents the choice of being interviewed in whichever language they

---

5. As will become evident in the analyses of Chapter 4, we created a more powerful index of routinization by simply using multiple indicators that did little more than ask the same question in slightly different ways. But we failed to come up with a better index of bureaucratization, for the same reason that I had limited my original index to number of levels of supervision (Kohn 1971)—namely, that many respondents are uninformed about other dimensions of bureaucratization in the firm or organization that employs them.

preferred. Russian and Ukrainian being similar, and the Ukrainian investigators being fluent in both, translating the interview schedule into Ukrainian was not nearly so formidable a task as translating from English and Polish into Russian. Still, it took careful work, multiple checking, and an entirely independent pretest.

My collaborators' and my further efforts to assure comparability of meaning and measurement in the several languages involved in our comparative analyses through the use of linear structural-equations (LISREL) measurement models will be described in the chapters that follow.

Sampling and Methods of Data Collection

Our surveys of both Poland and Ukraine were based on face-to-face interviews with representative samples of all men and women living in urban areas of the respective countries. The Polish sample is based on the data of the Ministry of Internal Affairs, which has a complete set of current records of the names and addresses of the entire population organized in a computerized system. Using this information, the ministry's sampling experts provided us a two-stage probability sample, with regions and city districts serving as sampling strata. In the first stage, they drew a representative sample of localities (e.g., districts within cities) in all forty-nine *Voivodships* (regions) in Poland. In the second stage, they drew two representative samples, each composed of people aged 19–65, within those localities officially designated as urban. The first sample was the target sample for interviews. The second was a replacement sample. Whenever an interviewer was unable to interview someone in the target sample, a specific person from the replacement sample—matched with the person originally selected on the basis of sex, age, size of locality, and education—was substituted.

The Ukrainian sample was drawn by Valeriy Khmelko, Leonid Finkel, and Vladimir Paniotto, using a method that they designed to overcome the limitations of past procedures for selecting samples in the former Soviet Union and the poor quality of official statistics in Ukraine. Their method is based on multistage random sampling: the first stage being to sample from several hundred districts, then to successively sample post offices, streets, buildings, and apartments, and finally adult residents (aged 18 or older) living in the selected apartments.

Both surveys were intensively pretested, using similar methods. In conducting the Polish pretests, we relied on the same experts who had proved their worth in the 1978 Polish survey, Andrzej Wejland and Pawel Daniłowicz, who have developed innovative methods for intensive pretesting. Wejland, who is fluent in Russian, went to Kiev to train the Ukrainians in the use of these methods, which they adopted for use in their survey (see Chapter 2).

The Polish survey was conducted by the survey research unit of the Institute of Philosophy and Sociology of the Polish Academy of Science, which maintains a field staff of well-trained and experienced interviewers. As a further guarantee of quality control and of coordination, the Polish investigators trained the supervisors, then the actual interviewers in each region of Poland, in the specifics of this survey with particular emphasis on securing sufficient information for the reliable coding of the substantive complexity of work.

The Ukrainian survey was carried out by the Kiev International Institute of Sociology, a research center that the Ukrainian members of our research team had created in 1990. Although general interviewer training was rigorous (see the discussion in Chapter 2), the Ukrainian investigators were not able to provide their interviewers with intensive verbal instruction about the specific requirements of this study, particularly with respect to the necessity of securing detailed information about the substantive complexity of work, relying instead on very general written instructions.

The Poles successfully interviewed 78 percent of their designated respondents, the Ukrainians 81 percent of theirs. In all, 2,291 people (1,086 men and 1,205 women) were interviewed in the Polish survey, 2,322 people (966 men and 1,356 women) in the Ukrainian survey. The apparent overrepresentation of women in these samples, particularly the Ukrainian sample, largely reflects the demographic compositions of the countries. *interesting*

Chapter 4

Class, Stratification, and Personality under Conditions of Radical Social Change

A Comparative Analysis of Poland and Ukraine

This chapter is based mainly on a paper with a somewhat more encompassing title (namely, "*Social Structure* and Personality under Conditions of Radical Social Change"), coauthored with Kazimierz M. Słomczynski, Krystyna Janicka, Valeriy Khmelko, Bogdan W. Mach, Vladimir Paniotto, Wojciech Zaborowski, Roberto Gutierrez, and Cory Heyman, published in the *American Sociological Review* (*ASR*) (Kohn et al. 1997). I include in this chapter the measurement model for intellectual flexibility that was referred to in that paper but published only later (in Kohn et al. 2000). I have also expanded the tabular presentations and the textual discussion to fully include both social stratification and intellectual flexibility.

The first six coauthors of the published paper cited above played major roles in the conceptualization and design of the research, as described in Chapters 2 and 3. Mach, Zaborowski, Paniotto, and Khmelko also spent extended periods (of several months each) working with me at Johns Hopkins University on the development of measurement models and on the causal analyses described in this chapter. Gutierrez was my research assistant in the earlier phase of the research described in this chapter, and Heyman in the latter phase, both of them contributing far beyond the usual performance of graduate-student research assistants—thus, their being listed as coauthors of the original paper. I want to acknowledge once again my indebtedness to the colleagues noted in Chapter 2 for their roles in the design, pretesting, training of interviewers, and conduct of the surveys—Leonid Finkel, Andrzej Wejland, Pawel Daniłowicz, Roman Lentchovskii, Michael Haney, and Michael Swafford. I am also indebted to Jeylan Mortimer, Carrie Schoenbach, Carmi Schooler, Kenneth Spenner, and the *ASR* editor, Glenn Firebaugh, for their critical readings of early drafts of the paper on which this chapter is primarily based.

I now attempt to make good on the promissory note of Chapter 3 that I would reassess the relationships of social structure and personality under conditions of radical social change. For comparability to the earlier research conducted during times of apparent social stability (and also of nearly full employment), I begin with the *employed segments of the Polish and Ukrainian populations.* In the next two chapters, I shall extend the analysis to include the *nonemployed* segments of these populations.

As formulated in Chapters 1 and 3, my general interpretive model, derived from my collaborators' and my earlier research, is that social-structural position affects personality principally through its profound effects on people's immediately impinging conditions of life. For the dimensions of social structure I consider in this chapter—social class and social stratification—the most pertinent conditions are apt to be occupational. Thus, an advantageous class position or a high position in the social stratification hierarchy affords greater opportunity to be self-directed in one's work, that is, to work at jobs that are substantively complex, not subject to close supervision, and not routinized. The experience of occupational self-direction, in turn, leads to greater intellectual flexibility and to a more self-directed orientation to self and society (see Chapter 1 of this book; see also Kohn 1969, 1977; Kohn and Schooler 1983, Chapters 5–7; Kohn et al. 1990; Kohn and Słomczynski 1990). The effects of class and stratification on the sense of well-being or distress, though, have been cross-nationally inconsistent (Chapter 1), with occupational self-direction not playing the consistent role in mediating the effects of class and stratification on distress that it does for other facets of personality.

The study of Poland and Ukraine during their transition from socialism to nascent capitalism gives us a splendid opportunity to see whether the cross-nationally consistent relationships of class and stratification with occupational self-direction, and of occupational self-direction with intellectual flexibility and self-directedness of orientation, continue to obtain during a period of radical social change. The study also provides a splendid opportunity to see whether the distinctively Polish findings with respect to distress continue to obtain for Poland, and also for Ukraine, during their transition from socialism to nascent capitalism.

A New Theoretical Context: Radical Social Change

The studies on which the interpretive model is based, and the many replications that buttress their conclusions (see the review in Kohn and Słomczynski 1990, Chapter 9) had all been done under conditions of apparent social stability. The obvious and important question is whether the findings and interpretation also apply during times of radical social change.

The null hypothesis is that our general interpretation of the relationships between social structure and personality will prove to be valid even during periods of radical social change. Contrary hypotheses (discussed in Chapter 3 and only summarized here) would predict that radical social change as experienced by the people of Eastern Europe and the former Soviet Union might greatly modify the relationships between social structure and personality for any of several reasons: because the social structures of these countries are themselves in the process of change; because the relationship between position in the larger social structure and the job conditions that enhance or diminish the opportunity to be self-directed in one's work may weaken during periods of transition from one system to another when the occupational structure itself may be in flux; because conditions that facilitate or interfere with the exercise of occupational self-direction may become less important for personality, while conditions that engender risk and uncertainty may become correspondingly more important during such times; or because the uncertainties and fears created by conditions of radical social change may have such wide-ranging psychological consequences as to overwhelm all else.

To assess these possibilities, my Polish and Ukrainian collaborators carried out surveys of representative samples of the adult populations of the urban areas of their countries, as described in Chapters 2 and 3. The Polish survey was conducted in the fall and early winter of 1992, the Ukrainian survey in the winter of 1992–1993.

At the time the surveys were conducted, Poland was moving toward some form of market economy. A vibrant private sector had developed, mainly small enterprises, most of them devoted to import and distribution rather than to production and export—but nonetheless a vibrant private sector. The high inflation rates that had been true of the earliest stages of the transition were coming under control. Nevertheless, for the first time since World War II, there was true unemployment and the specter of much more to come. For Ukraine, there was considerably greater uncertainty about what form the economy would eventually take. The political situation at that time was still indecisive, with the government not yet having made a fundamental decision about what type of economy it envisioned. The private sector was not nearly as developed, and unemployment was a fear rather than a present reality. Inflation was astronomical. The Ukrainian economy might have been better characterized as chaotic than as transitional.

Thus, the people of Poland and Ukraine were experiencing radical social change in very different ways. Poland had passed the most difficult period of transformation and could be relatively confident of the ultimate outcome. Ukraine may have embarked on the same process, but no one could be confident about the ultimate outcome. For the people of Ukraine, social change had to mean great uncertainty. The contrasting situations of the two countries provide two distinct opportunities to assess whether the conditions of radical social change brought about by the transformation of the political and economic systems of Eastern Europe and the former Soviet Union alter the relationships between social structure and personality.

In this chapter, I assess these relationships by considering two dimensions of social structure—social class and social stratification—and three major components of personality—self-directedness of orientation, feelings of well-being or distress, and cognitive functioning.[1] In designing the surveys, my collaborators and I deliberately conceptualized and measured these components of personality in the same way as in the earlier studies of the United States, Poland, and Japan, as described in Chapter 1. We did, however, improve on some of the indices, as described below.

Indices of Orientation to Self and Society

Since the primary samples in the most directly comparable past studies had been limited to men, any comparison of present findings to past findings must be gender-specific. My collaborators and I therefore estimated the parameters of the measurement models separately for men and for women, utilizing the two-population capacity of LISREL to make an overall assessment of the fit of the entire model to the data. We used the same items for men and women, but did not always allow the same correlations of residuals, seeing this as an unnecessary constraint on the models. We constructed measurement models for all except one of the eight first-order dimensions of orientation included in the earlier studies, the exception being idea-conformity, whose face-validity had long seemed to me not to be entirely convincing, and added one that seemed to be especially germane at a time of radical social change—receptiveness to change.

As in the comparison of the measurement models for U.S., Japanese, and Polish men in Chapter 1, wherever possible we used the same set of items for Poland and Ukraine. Where this proved not to be possible, we used greatly overlapping sets of items as will be evident by examination of Table 4.1. The question wording shown in Table 4.1 is not identical to that in Table 1.5, because I now show back-translations from the Polish and Ukrainian versions of the questions. A comparison of the exact question wording in the U.S. interview schedule, as shown in Table 1.5, to the back translations from the Polish and Ukrainian interview schedules, as shown in Table 4.1, indicates the wording changes that we introduced in the Polish and Ukrainian schedules to achieve meaningful rather than literal comparability. There are also a few questions newly added to the battery.

The first part of Table 4.1 presents the confirmatory factor-analytic measurement models that my collaborators and I developed to measure each of the concepts. The table shows the paths from each concept to its indicators (in these models, all such

---

1. As in the earlier studies (see Chapter 1), we also collected data about parents' values for their children, but the numbers of parents in our samples who had children in the specified age-range (ages 3–17) were too small for the intended analyses.

paths are statistically significant); and the fit of model to data, as evaluated by the ratio of chi-square to degrees of freedom and by the Root Mean Square Error of Approximation (RMSEA).[2] All the models fit the data well. These models incorporate correlations of residuals of indicators, as appropriate for gender and country, but to conserve space I do not show these correlations in the table. The models are remarkably similar for Poland and Ukraine, and for men and women, thus giving considerable assurance that we have achieved comparability of measurement.

"Second-Order" Models of Orientation to Self and Society: Self-Directedness of Orientation and Distress

The conceptualization and methods of analysis of the "second-order" models of orientation to self and society are essentially the same as those discussed in Chapter 1 for similar models for the United States, Poland, and Japan during times of apparent social stability. In the models for Poland and Ukraine during their transition to nascent capitalism (see Table 4.2), self-directedness of orientation is reflected primarily in not having authoritarian-conservative beliefs and in being receptive to change, and secondarily in having personally responsible standards of morality, being trustful of others, and not being fatalistic—all of which are in accord with our theoretical premises and with past analyses. Distress is reflected primarily in being self-deprecatory and anxious, secondarily in lacking self-confidence and being distrustful of others—which certainly appears to be face-valid, and which also is in accord with past analyses. The models, which fit the data well, are similar for Poland and Ukraine and for men and women within each country.

These models differ dramatically, though, from the model for Polish men when Poland was socialist (see the second part of Table 1.5), which showed a *positive* correlation between self-directedness of orientation and distress: Self-directed men in the socialist Poland of 1978 tended to be more distressed. In sharp contrast, in the models for both men and women in both Poland and Ukraine in 1992–1993, self-directedness and distress are *negatively* related, just as they are for U.S. men and women. This reversal in the relationship between self-directedness of orientation and distress foreshadows an equally dramatic reversal in the relationship between social structure and distress under the contrasting conditions of apparently stable socialism and radical social change.

Intellectual Flexibility

The logic of my measurement of intellectual flexibility is the same as that followed in the models used in the earlier comparative analyses of the United States,

---

2. The Root Mean Square Error of Approximation (RMSEA) is a recent and thus far the best method for assessing how well models fit data, regardless of the numbers of cases on which the models are based. RMSEA is a measure of the average discrepancy between population covariances and the covariances implied by the model. A RMSEA of less than 0.05, or one of less than 0.08 that is not statistically significant, is generally deemed a good fit.

Table 4.1. Measurement Models of First-Order Dimensions of Orientation to Self and Society, for Poland (1992) and Ukraine (1992–1993).

| | Standardized Paths: Concepts to Indicators | | | |
| | Poland | | Ukraine | |
Concepts and Indicators	Men	Women	Men	Women
Authoritarian Conservatism				
The most important thing to teach children is absolute obedience to their parents.	.64*	.67*	.57*	.63*
It's wrong to do things differently than past generations did.	.50*	.52*	.67*	.71*
Any good manager should be demanding and strict with people under him in order to gain their respect.	.47*	.55*	.46*	.47*
In this complicated world, the only way to know what to do is to rely on specialists.	.43*	.39*	.46*	.51*
No decent man can respect a woman who has engaged in sexual relations before marriage.	.41*	.53*	.47*	.58*
One should always show respect to those in authority.	.49*	.52*	.50*	.49*
You should obey your superiors whether or not you think they're right.	.45*	.55*	.36*	.41*
Young people should not be allowed to read books that are likely to confuse them.	.36*	.40*	.44*	.56*
Ratio of chi-square to degrees of freedom		2.16		3.54
Root mean square error of approximation		.023		.033
Personally Responsible Standards of Morality				
It's all right to do anything you want as long as you don't have problems because of that.	-.56*	-.66*	-.53*	-.52*
If something works, it doesn't matter whether it's morally right or wrong.	-.43*	-.49*	-.56*	-.49*
It's all right to get around the law as long as you don't actually break it.	-.52*	-.44*	-.52*	-.52*
Do you believe that it's all right to do whatever the law allows, or are there some things that are legal yet they are wrong?	-.29*	-.29*	-.31*	-.19*
Ratio of chi-square to degrees of freedom		.72		.45
Root mean square error of approximation		.00		.00
Trustfulness				
Do you think that most people can be trusted?	.42*	.40*	.39*	.32*
If you don't watch out, people will take advantage of you.	-.36*	-.32*	-.27*	-.23*
When you have serious problems, no one cares much what happens to you.	-.35*	-.47*	-.42*	-.44*
How often do you feel absolutely surprised by the behavior of a person you are dealing with?	-.18*	-.21*	—	—

Table 4.1. (continued)

Ratio of chi-square to degrees of freedom		1.14		.00
Root mean square error of approximation		.008		.00

Self-esteem (Two-Concept Model)

Self-Confidence

Usually, I have a positive attitude about myself and my abilities.	.50*	.51*	.42*	.40*
I feel that I'm worth at least as much as others.	.54*	.46*	.58*	.66*
I am able to do most things I care about as well as other people can.	.41*	.47*	.54*	.57*
I generally have confidence that when I make plans I will be able to carry them out.	.62*	.61*	.65*	.69*
Once I have made up my mind, I try very hard not to change it.	.38*	.42*	.47*	.48*

Self-Deprecation

Sometimes I feel I am useless.	.61*	.54*	.63*	.61*
At times I think I am good for nothing.	.73*	.82*	.60*	.69*
There are very few things about which I'm absolutely certain.	.19*	.25*	.21*	.26*
I wish I could have a better opinion about myself.	.24*	.37*	.18*	.24*
Correlation of self-confidence with self-deprecation	−.35*	−.23*	−.55*	−.33*
Ratio of chi-square to degrees of freedom		3.67		4.46
Root mean square error of approximation		.034		.038

Anxiety

How often do you feel so upset that you cannot collect your thoughts?	.63*	.67*	.59*	.63*
How often do you feel downcast?	.62*	.68*	.71*	.67*
How frequently do you find yourself anxious, not knowing the reason.	.62*	.62*	.40*	.45*
How often do you feel uneasy without knowing why?	.64*	.62*	.61*	.59*
How often do you feel so restless that you cannot sit still?	.58*	.62*	.45*	.44*
How often do you have intrusive thoughts?	.49*	.53*	.46*	.47*
How often do you feel bored [with everything]?	.50*	.51*	.57*	.57*
How often do you feel powerless to get what you particularly care about?	.51*	.52*	.61*	.61*
How often do you feel that the world is not very understandable?	.49*	.47*	.53*	.48*
How often do you feel that there isn't much purpose in being alive?	.55*	.48*	.42*	.42*
Ratio of chi-square to degrees of freedom		3.21		3.41
Root mean square error of approximation		.031		.032

Table 4.1. (continued)

Concepts and Indicators	Standardized Paths: Concepts to Indicators			
	Poland		Ukraine	
	Men	Women	Men	Women
Fatalism				
Do you feel that most of the things that happen to you are the result of your own decisions and actions, or are the result of things over which you have no control?	−.34*	−.34*	−.24*	−.11*
If something goes wrong in my life, usually it is my fault rather than that of others or simple misfortune.	−.43*	−.31*	−.40*	−.27*
When things go wrong for you, how often do you consider it to be your own fault?	−.31*	−.33*	−.55*	−.63*
No matter what you do with your life, you will not escape your destiny.	.26*	.31*	—	—
How often do you feel that new situations and events are very exciting for you?	−.24*	−.36*	−.28*	−.16*
When you don't accomplish something, how often is it your own fault?	—	—	−.32*	−.37*
Ratio of chi-square to degrees of freedom		5.16		3.66
Root mean square error of approximation		.043		.034
Receptiveness to Change				
When doing something, it is best to follow proven and common ways.	−.57*	−.68*	−.48*	−.49*
Are you the sort of person who takes life as it comes or are you working toward some definite goal?	−.20*	−.15*	−.27*	−.39*
Usually I am convinced that change is worse than no change.	−.50*	−.47*	−.70*	−.59*
New things more often bring trouble than actually help solve problems.	—	—	—	—
People who don't like the tested [proved] and accepted [well-known] ways of doing things usually end up causing trouble.	−.38*	−.42*	−.37*	−.39*
Ratio of chi-square to degrees of freedom		1.37		2.64
Root mean square error of approximation		.013		.026
Number of cases	1,083	1,205	966	1,356

*p < .05.

Note: A high score on the indicator generally implies agreement or frequent occurrence; when alternatives are posed, the first alternative is scored high. Correlations between residuals are not shown. The chi-square of the two-concept model of self-esteem refers to the entire model.

Table 4.2. "Second-Order" Measurement Models of Orientation, for Poland (1992) and Ukraine (1992–1993).

	Standardized Paths, Second-Order Concepts to First-Order Concepts			
	Poland		Ukraine	
Second-Order and First-Order Concepts:	Men (N = 1083)	Women (N = 1205)	Men (N = 966)	Women (N = 1356)
Self-Directedness of Orientation				
Authoritarian conservatism	-.70	-.76	-.68	-.78
Standards of morality	.45	.62	.21	.25
Trustfulness	.20	.30	.26	.41
Fatalism	-.31	-.33	-.10	-.13
Receptiveness to change	.75	.79	.62	.59
Distress				
Trustfulness	-.22	-.26	-.23	-.18
Self-confidence	-.32	-.23	-.36	-.20
Self-deprecation	.68	.58	.78	.56
Anxiety	.66	.72	.55	.72
Correlation between Self-Directedness of Orientation and Distress	-0.37	-0.33	-0.36	-0.49
Ratio of chi-square to degrees of freedom	4.60		5.40	
Root mean square error of approximation	0.040		0.043	

All paths are statistically significant, $p < 0.05$.

then-socialist Poland, and Japan in Chapter 1—sampling a variety of indicators reflecting the respondent's intellectual performance in the interview itself. The two indicators based on our appraisals of the adequacy of the respondent's answers to apparently simple cognitive problems use the questions earlier developed for socialist Poland: (1) "Let's suppose that you wanted to open a kiosk (a news-paper stand) in a new neighborhood. You have to choose from two locations. What questions would you consider before deciding? What else?" (2) "In your opinion, what arguments can be given for and against (allowing) TV and radio commercials? For? Against?"

A third indicator of intellectual flexibility is the frequency with which the respon-dent agreed when asked the many agree-disagree questions included in the interview. The rationale is that, since some of the questions in our battery are stated positively and other questions of similar import are stated negatively, consistent agreement indicates that the respondent is not thinking carefully about the questions. Because of a relatively high incidence of missing values in the Ukrainian survey, we used the *proportion* of "agree" responses among those agree-disagree questions that the respondent answered, rather than the absolute number. The patterns of missing data suggest that such an index is as valid as an absolute "agree score."

In the Polish model, we again used as a fourth indicator of intellectual flex-ibility the interviewer's appraisal of the respondent's intelligence. Although such appraisals are undoubtedly affected by the content of what the respondent said in the interview and perhaps even by what the interviewer saw in the respondent's home, they represent a competent interviewer's judgment following a long and intellectually demanding interview. Insofar as these appraisals covary with other indicators of intellectual flexibility, there is every reason to employ them. In a rare instance of international misunderstanding, the Ukrainian investigators did not realize that the Polish survey included such an appraisal.

In the earlier Polish inquiry, as in the U.S. studies, the measurement models of intellectual flexibility also included three indicators based on the Draw-a-Person Test and a portion of the Embedded Figures Test (see Chapter 1). Only the last of these reflected the dimension of cognitive functioning that concerns us here, namely ideational (in contrast to perceptual) flexibility. In analyses of those data, Joanne Miller, Kazimierz Słomczynski, and I (J. Miller et al. 1985) found that correlations of factor scores for the ideational dimension of cognitive functioning based on all seven indicators and those based on only the four indicators discussed above were near unity. It thus seemed unnecessary to include the time-consuming Draw-a-Person and Embedded Figures Tests in the current study.

Table 4.3 presents the measurement models of intellectual flexibility for Polish men and women and for Ukrainian men and women. The magnitudes of the paths from concept to indicators are similar but not identical for Polish men and Polish women; I have accordingly created separate factor scores for the two genders. The magnitudes of the paths from concept to indicators are also rather different for Poles and Ukrainians: those for the two cognitive questions are larger for Ukrainians, probably an artifact of our not having the fourth indicator—the interviewer's ap-praisal of the respondent's intelligence—for Ukraine. Perhaps for the same reason,

Table 4.3. Measurement Models of Intellectual Flexibility,
for Poland (1992) and Ukraine (1992–1993)

| | Standardized Paths Concepts to Indicators | | | |
| | Poland | | Ukraine | |
Indicators	Men	Women	Men	Women
"Agree" Score	−.20*	−.40*	−.12*	−.13*
"Commercials" Question	.44*	.44*	.76*	.83*
"Kiosk" Question	.46*	.37*	.33*	.37*
Interviewer's Appraisal of Respondent's Intelligence	.48*	.40*	—	—
Ratio of chi-square to degrees of freedom	.05		3.75	
Root mean square error of approximation	.00		.03	
Number of cases	1,075	1,200	952	1,324

*$p < .05$.
Note: In the Ukrainian model, the unstandardized paths from concepts to indicators are constrained to be the same for men and for women (see text).

I had to constrain the (unstandardized) paths from concept to indicators to be equal for Ukrainian men and women.

Although both the Polish and the Ukrainian models fit the data very well, one must wonder whether the three-indicator model for Ukraine is as powerful a measure of intellectual flexibility as is the four-indicator model for Poland. As a partial test, I developed a model *for Poland* that was limited to the three indicators used in the Ukrainian model, to see whether its correlations with social variables would be smaller than those for the four-indicator model. They were consistently, but not dramatically, smaller. Extrapolating, I infer that the correlations involving intellectual flexibility presented in the following tables underestimate the true correlations for Ukraine by about one-fifth.

Conceptualization and Measurement of Social Class and Social Stratification

The *conceptualization* of social class that I employ for Poland and Ukraine during their transformation from socialism to nascent capitalism is no different from the conceptualization I employed in Chapter 1 for the capitalist United States and Japan, and for socialist Poland, during times of social stability. The precise *categorization* of social classes, however, must certainly be modified to reflect the changing social structures of Poland and Ukraine in transition.

By "social classes" I continue to mean groups defined in terms of their relationship to ownership and control over the means of production, and of their control over the labor power of others. Social classes are distinct groups ("nominal" categories), not a continuum or even a set of categories that can be ranked as higher or lower along some *single* underlying dimension. I think of social stratification, by contrast, as a *single continuum,* an ordinal ranking of social positions.

Because people's class and stratification positions are based on roles in paid employment, *I limit the analyses of class and stratification to men and women who have paid employment of at least 15 hours per week,* whether as employees or as entrepreneurs. (In later chapters, I shall expand the analysis of social structure and personality to include the nonemployed.)

Classification of Social Classes in Transitional Poland and Ukraine

In differentiating the social classes for socialist Poland in Chapter 1, I did not distinguish between those owners who employ significant numbers of employees and those who do not, there having been virtually no private employers with significant numbers of employees in socialist Poland. Under socialism, though, another class distinction had seemed warranted—that between manual workers employed in the large-scale manufacturing and extractive enterprises at the core of the centralized economy, such as steel mills, shipbuilding, auto manufacturing, and coal-mining, and those who were employed in secondary and supportive industries, such as transportation, food-processing, and repair. For Poland and Ukraine in 1992–1993, which were no longer socialist but had not developed the class structures of fully capitalist societies, I no longer distinguish between manual workers in core and secondary sectors of the economy, which was becoming less appropriate to the changing Polish and Ukrainian economies. I continue to distinguish employees from those who own their own enterprises, but by 1992–1993 it was sometimes not entirely clear what constituted ownership. In Ukraine, for example, members of "collectives" were nominally co-owners of the enterprises that employ them, but in many cases this was a formal rather than a real designation. In time, members of collectives may become true owners, perhaps even a distinguishable social class, but for Ukraine in late 1992 and early 1993 it seemed more appropriate to classify them as employees.

Two further distinctions highlight the transformation of the Polish and Ukrainian economies: With an emerging class of employers, it was now possible to differentiate employers from other owners who have few or no nonfamily employees, whom I term the *self-employed.* Employers are distinguished by having three or more nonfamily employees. Even using so small a number of employees as the criterion, I find relatively few employers in our samples, particularly in Ukraine. It is nevertheless desirable to differentiate a social class that may play an important part in the transformation and that will undoubtedly grow in numbers and importance.

I also differentiate "experts"—professionals whose work is based on control over knowledge—from other nonmanual, nonsupervisory employees. Słomczynski and I (Kohn and Słomczynski 1990) did not treat professionals as a distinct social class in our analysis of socialist Poland, considering the distinction between the "intelligentsia" and other nonmanual employees at that time to be more a difference in status than a true class distinction. In the transitional period, though, the experts have a distinctly different employment situation from that of other nonmanual workers, one with greater responsibility but also greater control over the conditions of their own occupational lives. Many experts have attained or retained crucial positions in major economic and social organizations where they are playing a pivotal role in the transformation of the economy (Wesołowski 1994). It is because of this important role that I focus attention on them.

I also modified the criteria for those class categories that are carried over from the earlier classification for socialist Poland to fit the changing realities of the economic and social structures of Poland and Ukraine in late 1992 and early 1993. Of particular importance, I use more restrictive criteria for managers, thereby differentiating true managers from supervisors who may oversee relatively large numbers of employees but who do not perform high-level managerial functions. I correspondingly enlarged the category of supervisors, no longer limiting it to first-line supervisors but now also including those second-line supervisors who do not perform truly managerial functions.

Using this schema, I employ for the analyses of Poland and Ukraine in transition a classification of social class that has seven class categories:

1. *Managers:* Employees who direct and control the operation of a firm, organization, or major governmental unit or large subdivision thereof, as well as other employees in appropriate occupational categories who directly or indirectly supervise the activities of more than 50 people, some of whom themselves are supervisors.
2. *Supervisors:* All other employees who supervise at least two people.
3. *Nonmanual workers:* All nonsupervisory employees whose work includes a substantial nonmanual component, other than those classified as experts.
4. *Experts:* Nonsupervisory employees who work in professional occupations that usually require university or polytechnic institute education.
5. *Manual workers:* Nonsupervisory employees whose work is predominantly manual in character.
6. *Self-employed:* Owners of the means of production who have no more than two nonfamily employees, and members of the owners' families who are employed in such enterprises.
7. *Employers:* Owners of the means of production who have at least three nonfamily employees.

I apply this categorization to women as well as to men, basing the categorization of women's class positions on *their own* employment situations, not on those of their husbands, fathers, or other male members of their families. As one would expect, the class distributions are different for men and for women, particularly in Ukraine, with women in decidedly less advantaged class positions (see the N's in Table 4.5).

Conceptualization and Measurement of Social Stratification

There being no reason to believe that the *structure* of the social stratification system has been greatly affected by radical social change, I rely on the conceptualization I

Table 4.4. Measurement Models of Social-Stratificational Position, for Poland (1992) and Ukraine (1992–1993).

	Poland		Ukraine	
Concepts and Indicators	Men	Women	Men	Women
	Standardized Paths, Concepts to Indicators			
Educational Attainment				
Years of schooling	.99*	.99*	.98*	.99*
Educational level	.97*	.96*	.99*	.99*
Job Income				
Earnings, main job	1.00	1.00	—	—
Job income (log)	—	—	.69*	.78*
Family income (log)	—	—	.79*	.42*
Occupational Status				
Treiman (international) scale	.96*	.97*	.97*	.95*
Polish (Ukrainian) prestige scale	.89*	.92*	.89*	.95*
	Standardized Paths, Social-Stratificational Position to Its First-Order Dimensions			
Social-Stratificational Position				
Educational attainment	.84*	.87*	.75*	.86*
Job income	.45*	.44*	.14*	.35*
Occupational status	.81*	.88*	.84*	.83*
Ratio of chi-square to degrees of freedom	2.58		3.93	
Root mean square error of approximation	.033		.051	
Number of cases	792	658	557	583

*$p < .05$.

employed in Chapter 1 (see also Kohn and Słomczynski 1990, p. 42 and Figure 3.3 for Poland under socialism). I again define social stratification as the hierarchical ordering of society, a single dimension inferred from the covariation of educational attainment, occupational status, and job income. The measurement models are presented in Table 4.4. These models are similar but not identical for Poland and Ukraine.

For Polish men and women in 1992, educational attainment and occupational status reflect social-stratificational position equally strongly, with income of lesser importance. Although the measurement models for Ukrainian men and women in 1992–1993 are similar to those for Polish men and women, income is a decidedly less important component of social stratification in the Ukrainian model, especially for men. (Detailed surveys of household income suggest that reported income was not an accurate measure of true income in the chaotic economy of Ukraine, because many people depended on part-time employment and the produce they raised for themselves for much of their sustenance.) Still, the overall models for the two countries are sufficiently similar for comparative analysis.

Class, Stratification, and Personality ~~Results~~

Social Class

Self-directedness of orientation. Under conditions of relative social stability, whether in Poland under socialism or in the United States and Japan under capitalism, the consistent finding had been that members of more advantaged social classes have more self-directed orientations (see Chapter 1; see also Kohn et al. 1990, Table 2; Kohn and Słomczynski 1990, Table 4.4, pp. 94–95). The general pattern had been that managers (and, in the capitalist countries, employers) had the most self-directed orientations, followed by nonmanual workers and supervisors, then the self-employed, with manual workers (in Poland, both those in the core and those in the secondary sectors of the economy) consistently ranking lowest of all. Leaving aside the small numbers of women managers and employers in both Poland and Ukraine in 1992–1993, and the small number of Ukrainians, men or women, who were employers—too few for statistical analysis—we again find this same general pattern, consistently for Poles and Ukrainians, and for men and women (see Part A of Table 4.5). With the changing class structures of Poland and Ukraine, two new features have emerged: Employers outrank the self-employed in self-directedness of orientation, and experts outrank even the managers.

Moreover, the *magnitude* of the relationship between social class and self-directedness of orientation (as assessed by a correlation statistic, *eta,* that is appropriate to a relationship in which one of the variables is nominal—see Chapter 1) is nearly as large for Polish men in 1992 as it had been in 1978 (0.35 as compared to 0.42) and a bit larger for Polish women (0.44).[3] For Ukrainians, however, the magnitudes of relationship between social class and self-directedness of orientation are distinctly smaller than they are for Poles of the same gender. Interpreting the implications of the cross-national differences in magnitudes of relationship becomes a major challenge.

Sense of distress versus well-being. What made the relationships between social class and distress interesting in the original U.S.-Polish-Japanese comparisons was not the magnitudes of the relationships, which were only modest, but the difference in *patterns* for the three countries. For the United States, managers were the least distressed social class and manual workers were the most distressed. For Poland, nearly the opposite. For Japan, an intermediate pattern, with managers the least

---

3. To assess the possibility that the magnitudes of the relationships between social class and self-directedness of orientation may unduly reflect the extreme position of experts, I recalculated the correlations (*etas*), combining experts and other nonmanual employees into one social class (thus making the classification more comparable to that for the socialist Poland of 1978). The correlations are reduced by only a minor extent.

Table 4.5. Class, Stratification, and Personality, for Poland (1992) and Ukraine (1992–1993).

		Standardized Differences from Mean for Employed People of the Particular Country and Gender		
	(Ṅ)	Self-Directedness of Orientation	Distress	Intellectual Flexibility
A. Social Class				
Polish Men				
Managers	(31)	.38	−.44	.78
Supervisors	(126)	.15	−.26	.09
Nonmanual workers	(54)	.26	−.15	.41
Experts	(43)	.87	−.21	.77
Manual workers	(385)	−.26	.16	−.28
Self-employed	(120)	.10	.01	.11
Employers	(24)	.29	.09	.28
Correlation (*eta*) =		0.35*	0.23*	0.50*
Correlation, combining experts and nonmanual workers		0.32*	0.23*	0.49*
Polish Women				
Managers	(7)	—	—	—
Supervisors	(67)	.35	−.25	.21
Nonmanual workers	(224)	.17	−.09	.17
Experts	(77)	.66	−.32	.78
Manual workers	(227)	−.52	.29	−.56
Self-employed	(45)	−.02	−.04	.16
Employers	(6)	—	—	—
Correlation (*eta*) =		0.44*	0.28*	0.70*
Correlation, combining experts and nonmanual workers		0.41*	0.27*	0.63*
Ukrainian Men				
Managers	(21)	.59	−.09	.47
Supervisors	(116)	.01	−.16	.02
Nonmanual workers	(19)	.30	−.02	.26
Experts	(31)	.62	−.27	.36
Manual workers	(319)	−.13	.09	−.10
Self-employed	(15)	.08	.05	−.24
Employers	(6)	—	—	—
Correlation (*eta*) =		0.26*	0.15	0.24*
Correlation, combining experts and nonmanual workers		0.25*	0.15	0.23*
Ukrainian Women				
Managers	(1)	—	—	—
Supervisors	(102)	.09	−.11	.04
Nonmanual workers	(130)	.00	−.07	.06
Experts	(74)	.50	−.06	.45
Manual workers	(234)	−.20	.10	−.19

Table 4.5. *(continued)*

| | (N) | Standardized Differences from Mean for Employed People of the Particular Country and Gender | | |
		Self-Directedness of Orientation	Distress	Intellectual Flexibility
Self-employed	(10)	.13	.02	−.17
Employers	(2)	—	—	—
Correlation (*eta*) =		0.25*	0.14	0.26*
Correlation, combining experts and nonmanual workers		0.20*	0.14	0.22*

B. Social Stratification (Correlations with Personality)

		Self-Directedness of Orientation	Distress	Intellectual Flexibility
Polish men		0.50*	−0.23*	0.65*
Polish women		0.51*	−0.31*	0.78*
Ukrainian men		0.25*	−0.08	0.26*
Ukrainian women		0.33*	−0.17*	0.21*

*$p < .05$.

distressed social class, but manual workers at about the mean level of distress for employed men.

For Polish men in 1992, the *magnitude* of relationship between social class and distress is still only modest, albeit somewhat stronger than in 1978 (an *eta* of 0.23 now as compared to 0.14 then). The *pattern* of relationship, though, is nearly a complete reversal from what it had been under socialism: Manual workers are now the most distressed social class and managers the least distressed.[4] For Polish women, too, manual workers are by far the most distressed social class; there are too few female managers to judge reliably just how distressed they are.[5] The one respect in which the new Polish pattern differs from the U.S. pattern is that current Polish *employers* (nearly all of them male) are nearly as distressed as are the manual workers, which may reflect their precarious situation in the early stages of the transformation of the economy. This important difference aside, what is most striking about the patterns for Polish men and women in 1992 is that they are so similar to the capitalist pattern and so dissimilar from the socialist pattern that had been found earlier. For the manual workers of a country to be transformed in

---

4. To be certain that this complete reversal in managers' sense of well-being or distress does not result from my having narrowed the criteria for managers, I reclassified as managers all those who would have qualified by the looser criteria employed in the 1978 analyses and computed their mean score for distress. Even by these criteria, the managers of 1992 are the least distressed social class.

5. By the looser criteria of the 1978 classification there would be many more female managers. For this larger category, it is unequivocal that female managers—like male managers, albeit not to as great a degree—are less distressed than are other employed women.

just a few years from the least distressed to the most distressed social class, and for managers to move from being decidedly distressed to having a strong sense of well-being means that the psychological effects of the transformation have been not only dramatic, but astonishingly rapid.

Another dramatic manifestation of radical social change is provided by a change in the sense of well-being or distress of the intelligentsia. In a reanalysis of the 1978 Polish data, I find that the men we would now classify as experts were even more distressed than were the managers. In socialist Poland, the situation of such people was akin to that of the non-Party managers in that they had considerable responsibility but their positions entailed great insecurity. The finding that the experts (male and female) of transitional Poland are among the less distressed social classes accords nicely with a decided improvement in their circumstances.

For Ukrainians, the magnitudes of relationship between social class and distress are smaller than they are for Poles—the *etas* are only 0.15 for Ukrainian men and 0.14 for Ukrainian women, neither of them statistically significant. I am nevertheless impressed that the *patterns* of relationships are much more similar to those for Poles in 1992 than for Polish men in 1978. Ukrainian managers, for example, are less distressed than are most other employed Ukrainian men, and Ukrainian manual workers (of both genders) are, admittedly by only a modest margin, the most distressed of all the social classes in their country.

Intellectual flexibility. The *pattern* of relationships of class and intellectual flexibility is much the same as the pattern for class and self-directedness of orientation. For Poland, the *magnitudes* of relationship are substantially greater for intellectual flexibility than for self-directedness of orientation, especially for women. For Ukraine, the magnitudes are no greater for intellectual flexibility than for self-directedness of orientation, but this may well be because (as discussed above) the 3-indicator Ukrainian measurement model of intellectual flexibility underestimates the magnitudes of its correlations with other variables.

In sum, the patterns of relationship of social class with *self-directedness of orientation* and with *intellectual flexibility* are much the same under the emerging class structures of Poland and Ukraine in transition as they were under the class structures of Poland under socialism and the United States and Japan under capitalism, although the magnitudes of relationships are not as great for Ukraine. The relationships between social class and *distress,* particularly for Poland, are distinctly different from what they had been for Poland under socialism—they are much more like that of the capitalist United States. The *patterns* of relationships are much the same for Ukraine as for Poland, but the *magnitudes* of relationships are again smaller for Ukraine.

Social Stratification

The relationships between *social stratification* and personality precisely parallel those between *social class* and personality (see Part B of Table 4.5).[6] For both

___
6. As a heuristic exercise, to demonstrate that social class and social stratification are not

Poles and Ukrainians, men and women, the correlations of social stratification with self-directedness of orientation and intellectual flexibility are *positive*—the higher people's social stratification positions, the more self-directed their orientations and the more intellectually flexible they are—just as had been found for Polish men under socialism and for U.S. and Japanese men under capitalism. For both Poles and Ukrainians, both men and women, the correlations between social stratification and *distress* are now *negative*—the higher people's social stratification positions, the less their feelings of distress—unlike what had been found for Polish men under socialism, but very much like what had been found for U.S. men under capitalism. All these correlations, though, are smaller in magnitude for Ukrainians than for Poles.

The Role of Occupational Self-Direction in Explaining the Relationships between Social Structure and Personality

Why is position in the social structure related to personality? I hypothesize that—just as under conditions of social stability (as shown in Chapter 1)—the occupational conditions that facilitate or limit the exercise of self-direction in one's work are of major importance for explaining the relationships of social structure with self-directedness of orientation and with intellectual flexibility. However, it is possible that they are not of as great importance for explaining the relationships between social structure and distress. Especially for the latter, I shall also look to other (occupational and nonoccupational) conditions of life, particularly to the conditions of risk, uncertainty, and economic insecurity attendant on radical social change.

Conceptualization and Measurement of Occupational Self-Direction

There is no reason to modify either the conceptualization or the strategy of measurement for occupational self-direction from those presented in Chapter 1 for the United States, Poland, and Japan under conditions of apparent social stability. By occupational self-direction, I continue to mean the use of initiative, thought, and independent judgment in work. I see three job conditions as crucial in facilitating or limiting the exercise of occupational self-direction: the substantive complexity of the work, closeness of supervision, and routinization—defined exactly as in Chapter 1. Doing substantively complex work (i.e., work that requires thought and independent judgment) facilitates, even requires, the exercise of occupational self-direction; being closely supervised and doing routinized work limit opportunities for occupational self-direction.

---

only analytically but also empirically distinguishable, I assessed the magnitudes of the relationships between social class and personality when social stratification is statistically controlled, and between social stratification and personality when social class is statistically controlled. All the relationships are of course substantially reduced in magnitude, but they remain nontrivial.

The measurement models of occupational self-direction and of the job conditions from which we infer occupational self-direction (see Table 4.6) are in most respects similar to those presented in Chapter 1, the exception being that my collaborators and I have improved our measurement of routinization by adding indicators. As a result, routinization is now a stronger indicator of occupational self-direction than it had appeared to be when measured by a single indicator. I doubt that this has any substantive importance, although it certainly is evidence for the methodological value of multiple-indicator measurement.

The models are quite similar for Poland and Ukraine and for men and women within each country. The models for both countries fit the data reasonably well.

The Relationships of Social Class and Social Stratification with Occupational Self-Direction

I had speculated in Chapter 3 that the heretofore invariant relationship between social-structural position and the job conditions that facilitate or limit the exercise of occupational self-direction might be weakened during periods of transition from one system to another. Contrary to these speculations, the relationships between social class and the job conditions determinative of occupational self-direction remain invariant even under conditions of radical social change (see Part A of Table 4.7). The patterns of relationship are not only much the same for Polish men, Polish women, Ukrainian men, and Ukrainian women, but also much the same as they had been for Polish men under socialism and for U.S. and Japanese men under capitalism. Managers (along with experts) have the greatest opportunity to be self-directed in their work, manual workers have by far the least opportunity. Moreover, the magnitudes of relationship are uniformly strong, especially for the relationships between social class and the substantive complexity of work.

Thus, the relationships between social class and the job conditions determinative of occupational self-direction are as robust for Poland and Ukraine in transition as for any society previously studied. Here again our conclusion for social class is buttressed by parallel analyses for social stratification (see Part B of Table 4.7), which show the relationships between social stratification and the substantive complexity of work, routinization, and closeness of supervision to be as strong for Polish and Ukrainian men and women as for any populations previously studied.

The obvious next question is whether these strong relationships between social structure and occupational self-direction help to explain the relationships between social structure and personality.

Occupational Self-Direction and the Relationships of Social Class and Social Stratification with Personality

To test the hypothesis that the relationships between social structure and personality may be explained, at least in substantial part, by the differential opportunities for

Table 4.6. Measurement Models of the Job Conditions That Facilitate or Limit the Exercise of Occupational Self-Direction, for Poland (1992) and Ukraine (1992–1993).

Concepts and Indicators	Poland		Ukraine	
	Men	Women	Men	Women
	Standardized Paths, Concepts to Indicators			
Substantive Complexity of Work				
Complexity of work with data	.91*	.85*	.91*	.91*
Complexity of work with things	.11*	.38*	.32*	.36*
Complexity of work with people	.90*	.85*	.81*	.75*
Hours of work with data	.52*	.34*	.60*	.51*
Hours of work with things	-.61*	-.46*	-.68*	-.60*
Hours of work with people	.30*	.26*	.40*	.32*
Overall complexity	.78*	.94*	.80*	.85*
Ratio of chi-square to degrees of freedom	5.19		2.07	
Root mean square error of approximation	.054		.030	
Closeness of Supervision				
Freedom to disagree with supervisor	-.48*	-.39*	-.25*	-.21*
Respondent's assessment of how closely he (she) is supervised	.50*	.63*	.45*	.34*
Extent to which supervisor tells respondent what to do	.40*	.50*	—	—
Importance of doing what one is told	—	—	.51*	.60*
Freedom to take time from work for personal matters	-.62*	-.33*	-.53*	-.28*
Proportion of time that supervisor oversees respondent	—	—	.41*	.36*
Ratio of chi-square to degrees of freedom	2.50		2.51	
Root mean square error of approximation	.032		.036	
Routinization				
Do same thing over and over	.71*	.69*	.58*	.77*
Know exactly what to do	.64*	.80*	.62*	.63*
Follow procedures exactly	.50*	.59*	.71*	.73*
Ratio of chi-square to degrees of freedom	0.0		0.0	
Number of cases	792	658	557	583

*p < .05.

111

Table 4.7. The Relationships of Social Class and Social Stratification with the Job Conditions That Facilitate or Limit the Exercise of Occupational Self-Direction, for Poland (1992) and Ukraine (1992–1993).

| | (N) | Standardized Differences from Mean for Employed People of the Particular Country and Gender | | |
		Substantive Complexity of Work	Routiniz- ation	Closeness of Supervision
A. Social Class				
Polish Men				
Managers	(29)	1.66	−.70	−1.12
Supervisors	(123)	.72	−.15	−.53
Nonmanual workers	(52)	.46	−.16	−.47
Experts	(42)	1.60	−.64	−.80
Manual workers	(386)	−.65	.24	.41
Self-employed	(118)	.08	−.13	—
Employers	(24)	.62	−.02	—
Correlation (*eta*) =		0.77*	0.34*	0.67*
Polish Women				
Managers	(5)	—	—	—
Supervisors	(65)	.77	−.26	−.53
Nonmanual workers	(216)	.16	−.07	−.17
Experts	(74)	1.43	−.63	−.47
Manual workers	(224)	−.94	.39	.49
Self-employed	(45)	.23	.05	—
Employers	(6)	—	—	—
Correlation (*eta*) =		0.83*	0.40*	0.54*
Ukrainian Men				
Managers	(20)	1.67	−.79	−.75
Supervisors	(105)	.78	−.13	−.29
Nonmanual workers	(16)	.41	−.20	−.02
Experts	(25)	1.38	−.71	−.70
Manual workers	(313)	−.51	.21	.22
Self-employed	(13)	−.26	−.39	—
Employers	(6)	—	—	—
Correlation (*eta*) =		0.77*	0.39*	0.44*
Ukrainian Women				
Managers	(1)	—	—	—
Supervisors	(91)	.71	−.27	−.02
Nonmanual workers	(121)	.38	−.04	.00
Experts	(68)	1.08	−.70	−.43
Manual workers	(221)	−.85	.36	.13
Self-employed	(7)	—	—	—
Employers	(2)	—	—	—
Correlation (*eta*) =		0.82*	0.44*	0.26*
B. Social Stratification (Correlations)				
Polish Men		0.78*	−0.45*	−0.67*
Polish Women		0.88*	−0.48*	−0.56*
Ukrainian Men		0.81*	−0.42*	−0.49*
Ukrainian Women		0.82*	−0.50*	−0.30*

*$p < .05$.

occupational self-direction enjoyed by people of more advantaged social-structural position, I systematically control the substantive complexity of work, closeness of supervision, and routinization, to assess the degree to which this reduces the correlations of social class and social stratification with the three dimensions of personality.[7] I do this separately for Polish men, Polish women, Ukrainian men, and Ukrainian women. This procedure assumes that occupational self-direction affects, and does not merely reflect, personality. Although there is no compelling *a priori* basis for this assumption, past analyses of longitudinal data for the United States, and simulated longitudinal analyses using cross-sectional data for socialist Poland and for Japan, demonstrate that a substantial portion of the relationships between occupational self-direction and personality results from occupational self-direction affecting personality, at least during times of apparent social stability (see Kohn and Schooler 1983; Kohn and Słomczynski 1990; and Chapter 1 of this book). I shall return to this issue in Chapter 7, using longitudinal data for Ukraine under conditions of radical social change.

The findings are generally consistent for social class and for social stratification, for Poles and for Ukrainians, for men and for women in each country, and for all three dimensions of personality: Statistically controlling the substantive complexity of work, closeness of supervision, and routinization markedly reduces the correlations between social structure and personality, whether we focus on social class or on social stratification, whichever country and gender we consider, and whichever dimension of personality we examine (see Table 4.8). The substantive complexity of work is the pivotal job condition: Statistically controlling the substantive complexity of work generally accounts for nearly as much of the relationship between social structure and personality as does controlling all three job conditions. Thus, the hypothesis that the job conditions determinative of occupational self-direction, particularly the substantive complexity of work, contribute substantially to the relationships of social class and social stratification with personality is decisively confirmed.

There are, however, cross-national differences in the *degree to which* statistically controlling these job conditions reduces the magnitudes of correlation, with the proportional reductions generally smaller for Ukraine than for Poland. The heart of the matter, once again, is the substantive complexity of work: An extreme example is that statistically controlling the substantive complexity of work explains at least two-thirds of the relationships between social class and self-directedness of orientation for Polish men and women, but less than one-half of that relationship

---

7. For the analyses involving social class, one cannot use ordinary partial-correlation techniques, because social class is a nominal variable. Instead, I use multiple-partial correlations. A multiple-partial correlation is analogous to a partial correlation except that instead of a single independent variable one uses a set of independent variables, in this case dummy variables for all but one of the class categories, the omitted category serving as a reference. To make these analyses consonant with the earlier analyses of the magnitudes of the relationships between social class and personality, I corrected the correlation matrix used as input for the multiple-regression analyses to take account of unreliability in the factor scores for the job conditions and the three dimensions of personality.

Table 4.8. (Multiple-)Partial Correlations: Class and Stratification with Personality, Statistically Controlling the Substantive Complexity of Work, Closeness of Supervision, and Routinization, for Poland (1992) and Ukraine (1992–1993).

	Self-Directedness of Orientation		Distress		Intellectual Flexibility	
	Men	Women	Men	Women	Men	Women
A. Social Class						
Poland						
(a) Multiple correlation with social class	.35*	.44*	.23*	.28*	.50*	.69*
(b) Proportional reduction, controlling:						
(1) substantive complexity of work	63%	76%	54%	72%	53%	60%
(2) closeness of supervision	46%	38%	66%	38%	45%	16%
(3) routinization	28%	23%	18%	0%	14%	9%
(4) all three job conditions (or least collinear subset thereof)	65%	80%	73%	77%	54%	59%
Ukraine						
(a) Multiple correlation with social class	.26*	.25*	.15	.14	.23*	.23*
(b) Proportional reduction, controlling:						
(1) substantive complexity of work	34%	45%	62%	26%	36%	43%
(2) closeness of supervision	18%	29%	0%	0%	21%	4%
(3) routinization	31%	57%	31%	21%	13%	14%
(4) all three job conditions (or least collinear subset thereof)	41%	69%	62%	26%	37%	46%
B. Social Stratification						
Poland						
(a) Correlation with social stratification	.49*	.51*	-.23*	-.31*	.65*	.78*
(b) Proportional reduction, controlling:						
(1) substantive complexity of work	48%	58%	68%	73%	60%	45%
(2) closeness of supervision	45%	29%	70%	35%	39%	12%
(3) routinization	24%	22%	28%	0%	11%	8%
(4) all three job conditions (or least collinear subset thereof)	65%	64%	92%	73%	72%	48%

Table 4.8. (continued)

	Self-Directedness of Orientation		Distress		Intellectual Flexibility	
	Men	Women	Men	Women	Men	Women
Ukraine						
(a) Correlation with social stratification	.26*	.32*	-.12*	-.15*	.26*	.21*
(b) Proportional reduction, controlling:						
(1) substantive complexity of work	39%	55%	72%	27%	29%	57%
(2) closeness of supervision	22%	25%	0%	0%	56%	4%
(3) routinization	38%	55%	71%	69%	13%	17%
(4) all three job conditions (or least collinear subset thereof)	46%	86%	85%	56%	55%	63%

*$p < .05$.

Table 4.9. Zero-Order Correlations of the Substantive Complexity of Work, Closeness of Supervision, and Routinization with Personality, for Poland (1992) and Ukraine (1992–1993).

	Self-Directedness of Orientation	Distress	Intellectual Flexibility
Polish Men			
Substantive Complexity of Work	.45*	−.23*	.67*
Closeness of Supervision	−.47*	.27*	−.62*
Routinization	−.41*	.19*	−.37*
Polish Women			
Substantive Complexity of Work	.48*	−.31*	.72*
Closeness of Supervision	−.43*	.26*	−.53*
Routinization	−.40*	.04	−.47*
Ukrainian Men			
Substantive Complexity of Work	.19*	−.17*	.19*
Closeness of Supervision	−.17*	−.01	−.34*
Routinization	−.29*	.19*	−.13*
Ukrainian Women			
Substantive Complexity of Work	.30*	−.12	.26*
Closeness of Supervision	−.36*	−.04	−.12*
Routinization	−.42*	.23*	−.17*

$*p < .05$.
Note: The correlations have been adjusted to take account of unreliability in the factor scores both for job conditions and for personality.

for Ukrainian men and women. Underlying these cross-national differences is the simple fact that the zero-order correlations between the substantive complexity of work and all three dimensions of personality are stronger for Polish men than for Ukrainian men, and for Polish women than for Ukrainian women (see Table 4.9). By implication, if the relationships between the substantive complexity of work and personality were as strong for Ukrainians as they are for Poles, all the relationships between social structure and personality would very likely be strengthened. The same may be true, albeit to a lesser extent, for closeness of supervision and routinization.

I do not believe that the explanation of the weaker correlations between the substantive complexity of work and personality in Ukraine is an artifact of the Polish interviewers having had special training in probing for detailed information about the complexity of the respondents' work, while the Ukrainian interviewers had only general, written instructions (see Chapter 3). If that were the explanation, the Ukrainian measurement models for the substantive complexity of work would not have been as convincing as they are, and the correlations of class and stratification with the substantive complexity of work would not be as strong for Ukrainian men and women as they are for Polish men and women. Nor are the weaker relationships of the substantive complexity of work with personality for Ukrainian men and women than for Polish men and women merely a statistical artifact: The variances of the substantive complexity of work and of the three dimensions of personality are of approximately the same magnitude for Ukrainian men as for Polish men, and for Ukrainian women as for Polish women.

A strong hint of what may really be at issue is that the correlations are much higher for men living in the easternmost region of Ukraine than for men living in any of the other four regions of the country. This region is highly industrialized and has the second highest proportion of people who identify themselves as ethnically Russian. Because the correlation is nearly as high for those men in this region who identify themselves as Ukrainian as for those who identify themselves as Russian, it would seem that industrialization, not ethnicity, is the pivotal variable.

The cross-national differences in *magnitudes of correlation* of the substantive complexity of work (and also, of closeness of supervision and routinization) with personality, and the resulting cross-national differences in the *degree to which* the correlations of social structure and personality, can be attributed to these job conditions. However, the principal conclusion of these analyses must be the consistent finding, across nation and gender, that the substantive complexity of work plays a pivotal part in explaining the relationships of social structure and personality for the employed segments of the Polish and Ukrainian populations, even during a period of radical social change.

The Possible Relevance of Other Conditions of Life for Explaining the Relationships of Social Structure and Personality

My collaborators and I had hypothesized that, under conditions of radical social change, a number of other conditions of life—in addition to, or perhaps instead of, those determinative of occupational self-direction—might be important in explaining the relationships, or lack thereof, between social class and personality, particularly the relationship between class and distress. To pursue these hypotheses, we asked about respondents' social characteristics (potentially of much greater importance for Ukraine than for Poland because Ukraine is much more heterogeneous with respect to language, ethnicity, and religion), their job conditions other than those directly involved in occupational self-direction, and their job context (the size of the firm or organization in which the person works—here treated as a proxy for bureaucratization, and—for employees—whether the job is located in the state sector or the private sector of the economy). We also asked about a number of conditions and concerns attendant on the transformation of Poland and Ukraine from socialism to nascent capitalism: fear of unemployment, perceived economic duress, and the direct experience of change in the workplace—privatization and significant alterations in technology, organizational structure, or administration.

For Poland, we also asked about respondents' past and present involvement in organizations and institutions that advocate one type or another of social change, such as *Solidarnosc*-affiliated unions, "populist" political parties, and the Catholic Church. For Ukraine, we asked instead about whether respondents experienced either of two alleged features of the former political and economic system that many

Ukrainians thought were still pervasive—a marked disparity between educational credentials and the actual educational requirements of the job, and the system's rewarding workers for their relationships with their supervisors rather than for their efforts at work.

The interpretive issues are somewhat different for Poland and Ukraine. For Poland, we already have a compelling explanation of the relationships between social structure and personality: They are largely explained by the characteristically greater opportunities for occupational self-direction available to people of more advantaged class position or stratificational level. The remaining issue is whether any other social conditions or experiences add to the explanatory power of occupational self-direction, or perhaps provide alternative explanations. For Ukraine, much more remains to be explained—including why the relationships of social structure with personality, particularly with distress, are not more powerful than we find them to be. The mode of analysis, though, is much the same for Poland and Ukraine. I assess the degree to which the relationships between social structure and personality are reduced when one or another, or a meaningful set, of these variables is statistically controlled (just as was done for the substantive complexity of work, closeness of supervision, and routinization).[8] I also assess whether statistically controlling *both* the job conditions determinative of occupational self-direction *and* these "other conditions" explains any more of the relationships of social structure and personality than does controlling only the job conditions directly involved in occupational self-direction.

A large body of analyses can be readily summarized. Many of these conditions—notably those stemming from the experience of social change attendant

---

8. I deliberately do not include the respondent's own educational attainment as one of the conditions to be statistically controlled in attempting to explain the relationships of *social class* with personality. If educational attainment is thought of as a major component of stratification, to do so would be to overcontrol, this time not as a heuristic exercise. If education is considered in its own right, to do so would be tantamount to assuming that the causal sequence is from class position to educational attainment to personality. Not even in immediate post–World War II Poland, when some adults returned to school to obtain educational credentials for their jobs (Kohn and Słomczynski 1990), was this the modal pattern. It seems more reasonable to treat the causal sequence as one of educational attainment affecting job placement and class position, with job conditions serving as an intervening link helping to explain the effects of educational attainment on personality. Because educational attainment and occupational self-direction are highly correlated, the specification of the appropriate sequence is crucial in determining the outcome of the analyses. If we statistically control educational attainment in attempting to explain the relationships between social class and personality, we find that doing so reduces the magnitudes of the relationships of class with self-directedness of orientation and with intellectual flexibility (but not with distress) to about the same extent as does controlling occupational self-direction. If, by contrast, we statistically control the substantive complexity of work, closeness of supervision, and routinization when attempting to explain the relationships between educational attainment and orientation, we find that doing so greatly reduces the correlations between education and personality, particularly for Poland.

on the transformation of the Polish and Ukrainian economies, such as perceived economic duress and the direct experience of change in the workplace—are related to personality, particularly to the sense of distress. But because people throughout the social structure experienced these conditions, none of them contributes much to explaining the relationships between *social structure* and personality. Moreover, these conditions, even those most directly related to the experience of radical social change, add little or nothing to the explanatory power of the job conditions determinative of opportunities for occupational self-direction.

We are left, then, with occupational self-direction providing the best explanation of the relationships between social structure and personality. For Poland, this is a powerful explanation, for Ukraine much less so. In answer to the question, why are the relationships weaker for Ukraine than for Poland? we have found only one answer: Because the substantive complexity of work (and perhaps also because closeness of supervision) is less strongly related to personality for Ukrainians than for Poles. Why? On this crucial matter, I can only speculate, as I shall do in the concluding section of this chapter and again (armed with intriguing further evidence) later in this book.

Discussion

My strategy of analysis has been comparative, a complex strategy because I am making several comparisons at once: I compare Poles to Ukrainians, I compare men to women in both countries, and at the heart of the entire analysis, I compare the findings for Poland and Ukraine during a period of radical social change to those for Poland under socialism in 1978 and for the United States and Japan under capitalism.

Polish Men under Socialism and under Conditions of Radical Social Change

Insofar as the original findings for Polish men under socialism were similar to those for U.S. and Japanese men under capitalism, nothing has changed: For Polish men in 1992, the relationships of social class and social stratification with *self-directedness of orientation* remain as strong and as meaningful as they had been, as do the relationships of class and stratification with occupational self-direction. As before, occupational self-direction largely explains the relationships of social class and social stratification with self-directedness of orientation. In all these respects, radical social change has had no effect at all.

I also find that the relationships of class and stratification with *intellectual flexibility,* which also had been much the same for socialist Poland as for the capitalist United States and Japan, precisely parallel those for self-directedness of orientation for transitional Poland. Occupational self-direction again provides the explanatory key. Here, too, a cross-nationally consistent relationship between social structure and a major facet of personality is not affected by radical social change.

But, insofar as the original findings for Polish men under socialism differed from those for U.S. and Japanese men—that is, in the relationships of class and stratification with *distress*—there has been great change indeed. Now the pattern for Polish men is much the same as that for U.S. and Japanese men, with managers (who under socialism were the most distressed social class) and the experts (not then considered to be a distinct social class, but certainly highly distressed) now having a strong sense of well-being, and manual workers (who had been among the least distressed of all social classes) now being the most distressed of all social classes. Similarly, there has been a reversal in the relationship between social stratification and distress: Whereas high social-stratificational positions were earlier associated with a sense of distress, now these positions are associated with a sense of well-being.

Moreover, while occupational self-direction played little or no role in explaining the relationships between social structure and distress for Polish men under socialism, it now is of decisive importance, and the other conditions of life that we measured play a decidedly less important role. In this respect, radical social change has had a very great effect indeed. Occupational self-direction has assumed even greater importance in transitional Poland than it has in the capitalist United States. Conditions of uncertainty, which had been important for distress both in the United States and in socialist Poland, and which I thought might become even more important in mediating the relationships between social structure and distress during the transitional period in Poland, have declined in importance to virtual irrelevance.

Gender in Poland in 1992

Because women had decidedly different positions from men's in the class structure of transitional Poland, some comparisons are not possible: There were too few women in the most privileged positions—managers, for example, and employers—for confident assessment. But, insofar as direct comparisons are possible, the relationships between social structure and occupational self-direction, and between occupational self-direction and personality, are strikingly similar for Polish women and Polish men. Even the magnitudes of relationship are as large, or larger, for Polish women as for Polish men. The findings for Polish women thus strongly reinforce those for Polish men.

Cross-National Similarities and Differences

My collaborators and I studied Poland in transition to see whether the relationships between social structure and personality that obtained under socialism remained the same or became different under conditions of radical social change. We studied Ukraine to differentiate what is idiosyncratic to Poland with its particular history and culture from what is more generally characteristic of the countries of Eastern Europe and the former Soviet Union undergoing radical social change. The major limitation of this comparative analysis, aside from our having data for only two of the several countries undergoing radical social change, is that we do not have "baseline" data for Ukraine under socialism. This limitation notwithstanding,

Ukraine does provide a splendid basis for seeing whether the findings for Poland are idiosyncratic or also apply to at least one country experiencing radical social change under quite different circumstances. This analysis has shown:

1. Basic to all other comparisons, our conceptualization and measurement of the principal concepts appear to be equally applicable to Poland and Ukraine. Our conceptualization of social class during the transitional period applies to both countries, notwithstanding that the class structure of Ukraine in 1992–1993 had not been as greatly transformed as had the class structure of Poland. Moreover, the measurement models of personality, social stratification, and occupational self-direction are strikingly similar for the two countries. Thus, in this domain, we find nothing but similarities.

2. The *pattern* of relationships between social class and self-directedness of orientation is much the same for Ukraine as it is for Poland. The same is true for intellectual flexibility. There is even substantial similarity in the relationships between social class and distress. But the *magnitudes* of relationship, both for social class and for social stratification, are distinctly smaller for Ukraine.

3. Another major substantive similarity is the strong relationship of social class and social stratification to the job conditions that facilitate or impede the exercise of occupational self-direction. Moreover, occupational self-direction plays an important role in explaining the relationships of class and stratification with personality for both countries. But, here again, there is a difference in magnitude: Occupational self-direction is not nearly as important in explaining the relationships of class and stratification to self-directedness of orientation or to intellectual flexibility for Ukrainian men as for Polish men, or for explaining the relationships of class and stratification to distress for Ukrainian women as for Polish women.

4. The magnitudes of the correlations of the substantive complexity of work and of closeness of supervision with personality are smaller for Ukrainians than they are for Poles. This, presumably, underlies the smaller correlations of class and stratification with personality for Ukraine than for Poland.

5. For both Poland and Ukraine, conditions of uncertainty attendant on radical social change are distinctly less important in explaining the relationships between social structure and personality than are the job conditions determinative of occupational self-direction. Radical social change undoubtedly increases the risks and uncertainties of life, but (unlike what Słomczynski and I [Kohn and Słomczynski 1990] found for Poland and the United States under more stable social conditions), I find little evidence that these risks and uncertainties mediate the relationships of class and stratification with personality, not even with distress.

The cross-national similarities buttress the conclusions drawn from the analyses of Poland and in this sense are not problematic. The cross-national differences require explanation. The most gnawing question, which appears to be at the heart of all the cross-national differences, is why the substantive complexity of work and closeness of supervision are less strongly related to personality for Ukrainian men and women than they are for Polish men and women.

Because there are some differences in the ways the Polish and Ukrainian surveys were done, we must consider the possibility of methodological artifact (Kohn 1987). The procedures for differentiating the working from the nonworking portions of the Polish and Ukrainian samples were somewhat different, but it is difficult to see how this could account for the particular substantive differences that we found.[9] It is possible, of course, that despite all our efforts there may be differences in the Polish, Ukrainian, and Russian variants of our interview schedules in the meaning of some of the questions. The cross-national and cross-language similarity of measurement models reassure us on this issue. Of continuing concern, though, is that the Ukrainian interviewers did not receive the special training in eliciting information about job complexity that was given to the Polish interviewers, and thus they might not have secured information as complete as we would wish. Still, the Ukrainian procedures for coding job complexity were closely tailored to the Polish procedures. Moreover, the Ukrainian measurement models for the substantive complexity of work are very similar to the Polish models, and the cross-nationally similar relationships of social class and social stratification with the substantive complexity of work attest to the robustness of the Ukrainian index of substantive complexity. Although one can never rule out the possibility that cross-national differences in findings are somehow an artifact of differences in method, I doubt that the differences I found result from differences in the methods employed in the Polish and Ukrainian surveys.

I believe, instead, that the Polish-Ukrainian differences are real and that they may have important implications for our interpretation. In particular, they bear on the third of the four alternatives to the "null" hypothesis (Chapter 3)—namely, that under conditions of radical social change the pivotal role of occupational self-direction as an explanatory link between social-structural position and personality may well be challenged. The rub is that there are at least two possible explanations of why the job conditions determinative of occupational self-direction appear to be less strongly related to personality for Ukraine than for Poland.

One possible explanation is that the Ukrainian pattern is a carryover from Ukraine's history as part of the Soviet Union: As a result of the chaotic organization of production characteristic of Soviet economic enterprise, the relationship between work and personality may always have been weaker in the Soviet Union than in Poland or the capitalist countries. With the transformation of economic enterprise still only nascent in the Ukraine of 1992–1993, the weaker relationships of the substantive complexity of work and closeness of supervision with personality may have been a legacy of the former system in Ukraine rather than a product of ongoing social change.

A diametrically opposite possibility is that, although the process of transformation was undoubtedly less far along in Ukraine than in Poland at the time of our

---

9. In the Polish survey, we asked respondents whether they are employed 15 or more hours per week. If so, we classified them as employed, whether or not they were also formally retired, or housewives, or in another category. For Ukraine, we asked respondents to choose whether their main activity was working, looking for a job, keeping house, learning (as students), being retired, or doing something else. We classified as employed those who said they were working and that they worked at least 15 hours per week.

surveys, the economic situation in Ukraine in 1992–1993 was so chaotic that job conditions, although strongly related to social class position, had less effect on personality than they did in more stable times. If so, then the *process* of social change had greater effects on the relationships between social structure and personality in Ukraine than in Poland, precisely because the emotional consequences of such change were greater under the conditions of uncertainty that Ukraine was then experiencing than they were under the conditions of more orderly transformation that Poland was experiencing.

There is also a third possibility, one that didn't become apparent to me until the longitudinal analyses three chapters (and several years of data analysis) hence. I shall bring that possibility into play when the unfolding evidence makes it plausible.

I cannot choose between these explanations with the data of the cross-sectional surveys of 1992–1993. It is important to remember, though, that whichever explanation of the weaker findings for Ukraine is correct, the findings for Ukraine differ from those for Poland, not in kind, but only in degree.

Conclusion

The "null" hypothesis—that my general interpretation of the relationship between class structure and personality is valid even under conditions of radical social change—is largely confirmed, strongly so for Poland, less strongly but unambiguously for Ukraine. Consider what we have learned about the alternative possibilities (spelled out in Chapter 3) motivating this research:

1. Although the class structure of Poland has changed considerably, the relationship between social structure and personality has been modified only in that it is now closer to that of capitalist societies. And, although the magnitudes of relationship are not as strong for Ukraine as they are for Poland, Ukraine, too, shows a pattern more like that of capitalist countries than like that of Poland under socialism.

2. The heretofore invariant relationships of class and stratification to occupational self-direction have not weakened in the slightest.

3. Occupational self-direction is even more important in explaining the relationships between social structure and personality for Poland in transition in 1992 than for the socialist Poland of 1978. And, although occupational self-direction is less important in explaining these relationships for Ukraine than it is for Poland, occupational self-direction is of decided import even for Ukraine. Risk and uncertainty, and in particular fear of unemployment—which I thought might have displaced occupational self-direction under conditions of radical social change—are of distinctly secondary importance for explaining the relationships between social structure and personality for both countries.

4. The experience of radical social change does not have such wide-ranging psychological consequences as to overwhelm all else. (I must alert the reader, though, that the longitudinal analyses of Ukrainian data in Chapter 7 raise some question as to whether this conclusion is entirely valid.)

In short, the hypothesis that the *process* of radical social change might undermine the relationships between social structure and personality found earlier in countries enjoying apparently stable social conditions is not borne out. Instead, radical social change seems to affect the relationships between social structure and personality primarily in that social structures in transition come to exhibit patterns characteristic of the type of society they are in the process of becoming. By late 1992, Poland already exhibited the capitalist pattern, a surprisingly rapid transformation. As of late 1992 and early 1993, Ukraine seemed to be following a similar trajectory, although at a slower pace and perhaps from a starting point further back.

Do remember, though, that the analyses have thus far been limited to the employed. We have not yet considered how the transition from socialism to nascent capitalism affected the relationships between social structure and personality for that growing proportion of the population who was not formally employed.

Chapter 5

Extending the Analysis to the Nonemployed

Part 1. Complexity of Activities and Personality under Conditions of Radical Social Change

This chapter is based primarily on a paper coauthored with Wojciech Zaborowski, Krystyna Janicka, Bogdan W. Mach, Valeriy Khmelko, Kazimierz Słomczynski, Cory Heyman, and Bruce Podobnik, published in the *Social Psychology Quarterly* (*SPQ*) (Kohn et al. 2000). I am also including a more extended history of the concept, the substantive complexity of work, that I wrote for an earlier version of the paper but removed from the paper for reasons of space and the journal coeditor's preference. She thought the paper more effective when leaner, and I reluctantly concluded that—as a stand-alone article in a journal—she was probably right. For this book, however, I do think that the history of a key concept, which has played a crucial role in past chapters and which I will utilize again in the following chapters for further analyses of the nonemployed, should be of interest to readers.

The first five coauthors of the paper cited above played major roles in the conceptualization and design of the research, as did Vladimir Paniotto, who elected not to be a coauthor of the paper. Zaborowski, Mach, and Khmelko spent prolonged periods working with me at Johns Hopkins University on the development of measurement models and on the causal analyses described in this chapter. Heyman was my research assistant in the earlier phase of the research described in this chapter, and Podobnik in the latter phase, both of them providing far beyond the usual contribution of graduate-student research assistants.

In addition to the people I thanked in previous chapters for their help in the conduct of the surveys, I want to thank Agnieszka Kalbarczyk and Joanna Czarnota-Bojarska for developing the coding scheme for complexity of job-search activities for the Polish unemployed and for coding those materials; Bonnie Erickson for suggesting that I write the paper and for valuable suggestions for its development; and the coeditor of *SPQ*, Linda Molm, and three anonymous referees for valuable suggestions for revision of an early draft of the paper.

Any reader will be aware of my immense debt to Carmi Schooler, whose insightful analyses of the complexity of environments and psychological functioning inspired the hypotheses I formulate and test here, and whose critical reading of an early version of the paper contributed to my formulation of the issues.

I begin the analysis of the nonemployed by adapting what has in all our analyses of the employed been a key concept for linking position in the larger social structure to individual personality—the substantive complexity of work—to the situation of the nonemployed. I hypothesize that *complexity of activities* plays an analogous role for the nonemployed in linking position in the larger social structure to personality. I shall begin the chapter by reviewing the evidence that complexity of work in paid employment profoundly affects personality, and also the more limited evidence that complexity of work in realms other than paid employment—namely housework and schoolwork—has similar psychological effects. Then I shall extend the analysis from complexity of *work* to complexity of *activities,* even in realms of life not ordinarily thought of as work. *My fundamental hypothesis is that the complexity of people's activities in any important realm of life profoundly affects, and in all likelihood is also profoundly affected by, their personalities.*[1] I shall test this hypothesis under extremely stringent conditions—the conditions of life that people experience during a period of radical social change.

Theoretical Background

"Complexedness [from complex]: Complication; involution of many particular parts in one integral; contrariety to simplicity; compound state or nature."
            —from Samuel Johnson's (1755) *Dictionary of the English Language*

---

1. Although this extension of the formulation from the complexity of *work* to the complexity of *activities* may seem audacious, it pales by comparison to Schooler's (1984) intriguing hypothesis that complex *environments* affect the intellectual functioning and self-directedness of orientation of adults, children, the aged, and even of animals, in ways consonant with the effects of the substantive complexity of work on employed adults' personalities. Extrapolating from a wide-ranging review of a vast and disparate literature, Schooler finds considerable support for his hypothesis.

The Substantive Complexity of Work in Paid Employment

Development of the concept in research on employed U.S. men. As indicated in the definition of "complexedness" given by Samuel Johnson in 1755, the idea of "complexity" is very old indeed. For present purposes, it is sufficient to trace the much more recent development of the concept, the "substantive complexity of work," for it is that usage that I wish to expand, to incorporate the complexity of activities in other realms of life.

The forerunner of the concept appeared in my 1963 speculative essay, "Social Class and Parent-Child Relations: An Interpretation," in which I sought the explanation of class differences in parents' values for their children in their own immediately impinging conditions of life. I speculated that a crucial difference is "that middle-class occupations deal more with the manipulation of interpersonal relations, ideas, and symbols, while working-class occupations deal more with the manipulation of things" (Kohn 1963, p. 476). In an empirical test of this incompletely formulated hypothesis in a study of Turin, Italy, Leonard Pearlin and I (1966; Kohn 1969, Chapter 9; Pearlin 1971) found that working primarily with ideas or people is associated with valuing self-direction for one's children, while working primarily with things is associated with valuing conformity to external authority.

By 1969, in my *Class and Conformity* and in Schooler's and my "Class, Occupation, and Orientation" (Kohn and Schooler 1969), we had shifted from assuming that work with data or people is necessarily more complex than work with things, to assessing the complexity of work within each of the three domains.[2] As I later put it (1980, p. 197),

> Although, in general, work with data or with people is likely to be more complex than work with things, this is not always the case.... Work with things can vary in complexity from ditch-digging to sculpting; similarly, work with people can vary in complexity from receiving simple instructions or orders to giving legal advice; and work with data can vary from reading instructions to synthesizing abstract conceptual systems.

In detailed analyses of a large, representative sample of U.S. men employed in civilian occupations, I found (Kohn 1969, pp. 155–158) that doing complex work in *any* of the three domains—even in work with things—is associated with valuing self-direction for children. In further analyses, treating the complexity of work with

---

2. The full scales for rating the complexity of work with things, with data, and with people, which were modeled on those of the *Dictionary of Occupational Titles* (U.S. Employment Service 1965), are presented in Kohn 1969, Appendix E, pp. 271–276. While the *Dictionary*'s ratings are averages for entire occupations, Schooler's and my ratings are specific to the respondent's own job. We also added a crucial fourth rating of our own—the highest level of complexity at which the respondent ordinarily works, regardless of whether that work is with data, with people, or with things. This rating is based on the coder's evaluation of *all* the information provided in the interview about the respondent's work.

things, with data, and with people as independent variables in multiple regressions, Schooler and I (Kohn and Schooler 1969; Kohn 1969, Chapters 9 and 10) found the "substance of the work," thus appraised, to be significantly related to parental valuation of self-direction, men's valuation of self-direction for themselves, and several dimensions of orientation to self and society.

It was not until my 1971 paper, "Bureaucratic Man," that I coined the term, "substantive complexity of work," thereby emphasizing that what mattered for personality was not whether the work was primarily with things, with data, or with people, but the complexity of that work, in whatever domain it was performed.[3] In that paper, I used a single index of substantive complexity, described (in footnote 15, p. 469) as "a linear combination of seven constituent indices, which measure the complexity of the man's work with data, with things, and with people, the overall complexity of his job, and the amount of time he spends working with data, with things, and with people."

I did not, however, explain how I combined the seven elements. That came in "Occupational Experience and Psychological Functioning" (Kohn and Schooler 1973), which said (p. 104) that the index was based on a factor analysis (what would now be called an exploratory factor analysis) of the seven elements—*thus providing the first solid evidence of a single dimension of complexity pervading all three domains of work.* Using factor scores based on this analysis, we found statistically significant, nontrivial associations between the substantive complexity of work and job satisfaction, occupational commitment, parental valuation of self-direction, valuation of self-direction for oneself, nine distinct facets of orientation to self and society, intellectual flexibility, and even the intellectual demandingness of leisure-time activities. Moreover, using two-stage least squares as our statistical tool for the analysis of reciprocal effects, we found that the substantive complexity of work does affect each of these facets of psychological functioning. However, we recognized that these cross-sectional analyses could not be definitive: Using retrospective accounts of past jobs, it was possible to statistically control the substantive complexity of those jobs in assessing the effects of psychological functioning on current substantive complexity, but there was no way to assess and thereby to statistically control "earlier" levels of personality in assessing the effects of the substantive complexity of work on current personality.[4]

---

3. By contrast, Rose Coser (1975), employing Robert K. Merton's concept of role-sets, interpreted Schooler's and my findings as meaning that the complexity of role-sets is fundamental to why complexity affects personality. Her thoughtful analysis elucidates the meaning of complexity in work with people. But, since her evidence comes entirely from our analyses, which provide no evidence that complexity of work with people is of any greater importance for personality than is complexity of work with data or the overall complexity of the job, there is no reason to accord complexity of work with people, or complexity of role-sets, a more fundamental role than complexity of work with data or the overall complexity of the work.

4. Robert M. Hauser later suggested an intriguing method for stretching the cross-sectional data to take "earlier" personality into account—synthetic cohort analysis (see the

The next, and decisive, step came in Schooler's and my *longitudinal* assessment of the reciprocal relationship between the substantive complexity of work and intellectual flexibility, based on a ten-year follow-up of a representative subsample of the men in the original study (Kohn and Schooler 1978). For this assessment, we developed confirmatory factor-analytic measurement models of both the substantive complexity of work and intellectual flexibility. These models explicitly take measurement error and, crucially, over-time correlations of measurement error into account. The measurement model for the substantive complexity of work demonstrates that conceptualizing complexity as a single dimension that pervades all three domains of work fits the data better than does any sensible alternative conceptualization. And the model for intellectual flexibility shows that the dimension of cognitive functioning that concerns us here—ideational flexibility—is remarkably stable, the ten-year over-time correlation being 0.93. Using indices based on these models, we assessed the effects of the substantive complexity of work on this exceptionally stable facet of personality (statistically controlling the men's ten-year earlier levels of intellectual flexibility), while simultaneously assessing the effects of intellectual flexibility on the substantive complexity of work (statistically controlling the substantive complexity of the jobs the men had held ten years before). Our conclusion, to use a phrase that thereafter occurs repeatedly in our writings, was that the relationship between the substantive complexity of work and intellectual flexibility is "quintessentially reciprocal."

In a logical extension, we used the same longitudinal data set to assess the reciprocal relationships between the substantive complexity of work and several dimensions of orientation to self and society (Kohn and Schooler 1982). These analyses demonstrated that the substantive complexity of work affects such important dimensions of orientation as authoritarian conservatism, personally responsible standards of morality, self-deprecation, and fatalism, even with other "structural imperatives of the job" statistically controlled. Moreover, the substantive complexity of work is positively related to self-directedness of orientation (as it should be), and—even with other job conditions held constant—substantially and significantly affects this underlying dimension of orientation. The substantive complexity of work is negatively related to a sense of distress (as it should be), but the relationship, although statistically significant, is only modest in magnitude. In a model that includes other job conditions, the substantive complexity of work does not significantly affect distress; its effect is surpassed by those of such other job conditions as closeness of supervision and lack of job protections. (As is evidenced in earlier chapters of this book, I have returned repeatedly to the perplexing relationship between the complexity of work and distress.)

Extending the longitudinal analyses from intrapsychic phenomena to (reported) behavior, Karen Miller and I (1983) showed that the substantive complexity of

---

discussion in note 18 on p. 78 of Kohn and Schooler 1983). Synthetic cohort analyses lent plausibility to the two-stage least squares models that we had created, which was the best we could do until LISREL provided more powerful methods of statistical analysis than those available at the time of the original analysis.

work strongly affects (and is in turn significantly, albeit less strongly, affected by) the intellectual demandingness of leisure-time activities.

In a test of whether the substantive complexity of work continues to have psychological effects throughout men's careers, J. Miller et al. (1985) demonstrated that the effects of the substantive complexity of work on intellectual flexibility and authoritarian conservatism are at least as great for the oldest cohort of the work force as for the youngest and intermediate cohorts. Carmi Schooler, Mesfin Mulatu, and Gary Oates (1999) have recently found that, when one extends the longitudinal analysis twenty years further, the effects of the substantive complexity of work on intellectual flexibility are even greater for the very old (but still employed) than for younger cohorts.

Finally, and crucially, the substantive complexity of work plays a decisive role in explaining the relationships of social class and social stratification with personality: It is largely because position in the class structure and in the social-stratification hierarchy is closely linked to the substantive complexity of men's work that these fundamental facets of social structure affect personality (Kohn and Schoenbach 1983).

Why is the substantive complexity of work of such pivotal importance, not only in its strong effects on personality, but also for explaining the effects of occupational structure, of social stratification, and of social class on personality? Schooler's and my interpretation is simple and straightforward. As I put it in a 1980 paper (Kohn 1980, p. 205), "[I]n an industrial society, where work is central to people's lives, what people do in their work directly affects their values, their conceptions of self, and their orientation to the world around them—'I do, therefore I am.' Hence, doing substantively complex work tends to increase one's respect for one's own capacities, one's valuation of self-direction, one's intellectuality (even in leisure-time pursuits), and one's sense that the problems one encounters in the world are manageable." Note that this formulation applies not only to intellectual flexibility and to self-directedness of orientation (and its component dimensions), but also to the underlying dimension of orientation that has been most problematic in past research: the sense of well-being or distress. Doing substantively complex work should enhance one's sense of well-being, because of the sense of accomplishment it provides and the assurance that the "problems one encounters in the world are manageable."

Generalizability to employed U.S. women. Schooler's and my initial survey was limited to men. In our ten-year follow-up study, we interviewed the men's wives to make possible a study of the transmission of values in the family. Thus, analyses of women's job conditions and personality are based on a sample of employed wives, with attendant limitations of generalizability. Still, the relationships of the substantive complexity of work with intellectual flexibility, the intellectual demandingness of leisure time, and several distinct dimensions of orientation to self and society are remarkably consistent for employed men and women (J. Miller et al. 1979). Moreover, these relationships are as strong for employed women as they are for employed men. Since the data for women are cross-sectional, longitudinal analyses of the reciprocal effects of the substantive complexity of work and personality are not possible. Simulated longitudinal analyses, similar to those described in Chapter 1, however, show that the substantive complexity of work affects intellectual flexibility (J. Miller et al. 1979) and the intellectual demandingness of leisure-time activities (K. Miller and Kohn 1983). Moreover, Schooler et al. (1999) have recently found, in fully longitudinal analyses based on a further follow-up study twenty years later, that the substantive complexity of work affects not only intellectual flexibility, as my colleagues and I have measured it, but also more traditional measures of effective intellectual functioning.

Younger workers in the United States. Other studies done in the United States, notably those by Jeylan Mortimer and her collaborators of men early in their careers (Mortimer et al. 1986) and of high school students working part-time (Mortimer et al. 1996) reinforce and extend the findings, albeit for subjective analogues to actual work conditions.

Generalizability to employed men and women in other countries. Studies done in several other countries similarly confirm the findings of the U.S. studies, albeit in many of the studies using indices that only approximate those used in the U.S. research (see the discussions of this research in Kohn and Schooler 1983, Chapter 12, and in Kohn and Słomczynski 1990, Chapter 9).

Five studies conducted in other countries, though, use methods of inquiry and indices precisely comparable to those developed in Kohn and Schooler's U.S. study: the studies of Poland and Japan under conditions of apparent social stability described in Chapter 1 of this book; the studies of the employed segments of the Polish and Ukrainian populations under conditions of radical social change described in Chapter 4; and a Colombian study, designed to see whether the U.S. findings apply to a partially industrialized society and to both the regulated and unregulated sectors of that country's economy (Gutierrez 1995). With one striking exception, the findings of all these studies are remarkably consonant with those for the United States. All of these studies find essentially the same relationships of the substantive complexity of work with parental valuation of self-direction, intellectual flexibility, and several dimensions of orientation, including the underlying dimension, self-directedness of orientation, as do the U.S. study. Since the data for these studies are cross-sectional, the analyses of the reciprocal effects of the substantive complexity of work and these dimensions of personality are, as with analyses of employed U.S. wives, simulated rather than actual longitudinal analyses. Moreover, the samples of women in the original Polish and Japanese studies are again limited to wives. The number of cases in the Colombian study is small (the total N being 180), particularly when the analyses are done separately for the regulated and unregulated segments of the economy. But the findings of all these studies are so similar to those for the United States as to greatly extend the generalizability of the U.S. findings.

The exception to the general pattern of cross-national similarity of findings is, not surprisingly, in the relationship between the substantive complexity of work and a sense of distress versus a sense of well-being. In the Colombian study, as in

distress except

the U.S. study, substantively complex work is *negatively* correlated with distress: people who do complex work are less likely to be distressed than are those whose work is not as complex. This is equally true for people in the regulated and unregulated sectors of the economy. In the Japanese study, as we have seen, the correlation between the substantive complexity of work and distress is nearly zero, dwarfed by the correlation between closeness of supervision and distress. In the study of socialist Poland, the substantive complexity of work is *positively* (and significantly, albeit modestly) related to a sense of distress.

Even in the U.S. study, the *effect* of the substantive complexity of work on distress is overshadowed by that of other job conditions, and further analyses (Kohn and Słomczynski 1990, Chapter 8) show that there are countervailing effects of the substantive complexity of work, which enhances a sense of well-being, and conditions of risk and uncertainty and lack of protections from these risks and uncertainties, which are conducive to feelings of distress. Słomczynski and I argued (Kohn and Słomczynski 1990, Chapter 7) that, under the conditions prevalent in Poland under socialism, the protections from job insecurity enjoyed by workers so enhanced their sense of well-being as to overwhelm the negative effect that their lack of opportunity to engage in substantively complex work might otherwise have had. The sharp turnaround in the relationship between the substantive complexity of work and distress in transitional Poland (Chapter 4 of this book) buttresses that interpretation.

Notwithstanding the important and problematic exception of the sense of well-being or distress, the relationships between the substantive complexity of work in paid employment and other major facets of personality appear to be consistent across gender and nation, and to obtain under conditions of radical social change as well as during times of apparent social stability.

Extrapolating from the Substantive Complexity of Work in Paid Employment to the Complexity of Housework and Schoolwork

Although the concept of the substantive complexity of work originated in an effort to explain the relationships of *employed* people's social-stratificational positions with their personalities, Schooler and I hypothesized that the complexity of work in institutional contexts *other* than paid employment would have similar effects on personality. To test this hypothesis, we included a battery of questions about housework in our ten-year follow-up study of employed men and their wives, and a battery of questions about schoolwork in our study of these people's offspring. The rationale was that housework is in crucial respects comparable to work in paid employment, particularly for women, and perhaps especially for women who do not have paid employment; and that schoolwork is in many respects the analogue to paid employment for children and many young adults.

Housework. The findings are quite different for women than for men (Schooler et al. 1983). For women, multiple-regression analyses (which assume uni-directionality of effect) show that the substantive complexity of housework significantly affects intellectual flexibility, self-directedness of orientation, and distress. Moreover, these "effects" are much the same for women who are employed outside the home and for full-time housewives. Schooler et al. recognized that the issue of direction of effects is even more crucial for housework than for paid employment, because the constraining conditions are less pronounced: Although many of the tasks in housework have to be done, there may be much more leeway in *how* these tasks are done in one's own household than in paid employment. They attempted to deal with this issue by simulated longitudinal analyses, which—although hardly definitive because of a lack of information about either complexity of housework or personality at some earlier time—lend support to the conclusion that, in women's housework as in their paid employment, the complexity of work does affect personality.

For men, though, the complexity of housework seems to have little or no effect on personality. This may be because few men do much housework and even those who do mainly carry out delineated "projects" rather than the everyday activities of running a household. It would seem that not all work outside the realm of paid employment, but only work that assumes some considerable importance in the lives of the people concerned has the hypothesized psychological effects.

Schoolwork. The questions about schoolwork were asked of those randomly selected offspring who were still in school, whether in high school or college. Miller, Schooler, and I (K. Miller et al. 1985; 1986) used these data to develop a confirmatory factor-analytic measurement model of the complexity of schoolwork, which we employed in assessments of the reciprocal effects of educational conditions and personality. These assessments could not take account of "earlier" personality or of the complexity of schoolwork at some specified earlier time. The models did, however, statistically control the pertinent dimensions of the *parents'* personalities, as measured with data from the parents' own interviews, thus taking into account family-experiential and genetic determinants of personality. These analyses showed that the substantive complexity of schoolwork affects (and is affected by) not only students' intellectual flexibility (K. Miller et al. 1985) but also their self-directedness of orientation and distress (K. Miller et al. 1986). Separate analyses of high school and college students show that these findings apply to both.

The exception for men's performance (or nonperformance) of housework notwithstanding, the evidence for housework and schoolwork strongly suggests that the complexity of work in contexts other than paid employment bears much the same reciprocal relationships with personality as does the substantive complexity of work in paid employment. One necessarily wonders whether the findings are generalizable to countries other than the United States. One also necessarily wonders how far beyond "work" and worklike activities it is possible to extend the generalizations. Does complexity of activities in important *non*work realms of life have similar effects on personality?

Proposed Extension and Tests of the Hypothesis

I now propose to extend the hypothesis that the complexity of *work* profoundly affects (and is affected by) personality to encompass the complexity of *activities* in any realm of life that is psychologically salient and to which the individual devotes substantial time, regardless of whether those activities are thought of as work. My rationale for so doing is much the same as Schooler's and my original rationale for interpreting the relationships between the substantive complexity of work in paid employment and personality, namely, that people learn from their jobs and apply those lessons to outside-the-job realities—a straightforward process of learning and generalization.

Although I do not question the psychological centrality of *work,* I hypothesize that complexity of *activities* in realms other than paid employment should be similarly related to personality. *As I would now put it, engaging in complex activities—in work or in any other important realm of life—should increase one's intellectuality, one's self-directedness of orientation, and one's sense that the problems one encounters in the world are manageable.* I even hypothesize that "complexity" is of such pervasive importance that the *magnitudes* of relationship between the complexity of nonwork activities and personality will be nearly as great as the magnitudes of comparable relationships between the substantive complexity of work in paid employment and the same dimensions of personality. And I hypothesize that these relationships do not merely reflect the propensity of more highly educated people to engage in more complex activities, or of a carryover from the complexity of people's past jobs to their present personalities. *The central hypothesis is that the complexity of people's current activities will be significantly, even substantially, related to their personalities, regardless of their educational attainment and regardless of the complexity of their work in their prior employment.*

I put this hypothesis to an extremely demanding test: that these relationships obtain even under conditions of radical social change. During a period of radical social change, economic duress, uncertainty, and insecurity might so unsettle people's lives that conditions of life that ordinarily have profound importance for personality—even the complexity of their activities—might become much less important than in more stable times. (Think of the firsthand account in Chapter 2 of how the experience of radical social change unsettles even the conditions under which research can be conducted.) Nevertheless, I hypothesize that the effects of complexity of activities on personality are so pervasive that the relationships between complexity of activities and personality will be robust for people in all segments of the population, even under conditions of radical social change.[5]

---

5. Since the data are cross-sectional, I cannot do truly longitudinal analyses that would permit me to assess empirically the directionality of effects. Nor can I do simulated longitudinal analyses, because the very fact of radical social change precludes me from extrapolating from what we have learned about rates of individual change from longitudinal analyses done in more stable times. It might be argued that, under the unstable conditions of radical social change, any relationships we might find between complexity of activity and personality would reflect, not

Segments of the Population

For these analyses, I will consider five major segments of the population: those men and women who were employed, either as employees or self-employed, for at least 15 hours per week; those who were out of work and seeking employment (i.e., the *un*employed); those who were pensioners, whether because they had retired for reasons of age, had taken early retirement willingly or otherwise, or had suffered some disability; housewives; and students.[6] Taking cognizance of a rapid increase in the number of housewives, many of whom were seeking employment, my Polish collaborators made an additional distinction between housewives who were seeking employment ("unemployed housewives") and those who were not ("pure housewives"). This distinction would not have made sense for Ukraine at that time because Ukrainian women were not then under pressure to leave their jobs. The Ukrainian inquiry, however, distinguished a separate category of women who were on maternity or child-care leave from their regular jobs—women whose circumstances were distinctly different from those of either the employed or the housewives.[7]

---

reciprocity of effects, but solely the propensity of intellectually flexible, self-directed people who have a strong sense of well-being to take advantage of new opportunities to engage in complex activities. My rationale for believing otherwise is that, if we find patterns of relationship between complexity of activity and personality similar to those previously found in truly longitudinal and in simulated longitudinal analyses, much the same processes—processes that produce *reciprocal* effects—would account for the relationships. I recognize, though, that the effects of personality on complexity of activity may be relatively stronger in non-work activities, where there is more latitude for discretionary activity than in paid employment, and also that, even for work in paid employment, the effects of personality on complexity of activity might be stronger during times of radical social change. These are profoundly important issues to which I shall return after I present the empirical findings.

6. In the original paper on which this chapter is based (Kohn et al. 2000), we called these five segments of the population *structural locations,* but I now prefer to reserve that term for a more encompassing classification that differentiates the employed segment of the population into its component social classes and adds the four segments of the nonemployed. This classification will be discussed anew in Chapter 6 and utilized in Chapter 7.

7. The two surveys used somewhat different methods for distinguishing which respondents belonged in each of the segments. The Polish survey asked respondents whether they were employed 15 or more hours per week, whether as employees, as self-employed, or in some combination of the two. If they were, we classified them as employed. The interviewers asked men who were not employed 15 or more hours per week whether they were looking for work. If so, we classified them as unemployed. Women who were not employed 15 or more hours per week were asked whether they considered themselves to be housewives. If so, they were asked whether they were looking for work, so that we could distinguish between "pure" and "unemployed" housewives. Those men who were not looking for work, and those women who were not looking for work and did not consider themselves to be housewives, were asked whether (depending on their age) they were attending school full-time or were pensioners. There were very few people who did not fit into one of our categories.

Dimensions of Personality

In this assessment of the relationships between complexity of activities and personality, I am deliberately focusing on the same dimensions of personality that I measured in the analyses of the relationships of class and stratification with personality for the employed segments of the Polish and Ukrainian populations in the preceding chapter. Additionally, my collaborators and I deliberately included both the employed and the nonemployed in the *same measurement models of these dimensions of personality,* the measurement models presented in Chapter 4.

Measures of Complexity of Activities

My intent was to assess the complexity of activities carried out by people in all major segments of the population. To this end, my collaborators and I asked diverse questions; some were quite general, while others were tailored to activities characteristic of a particular segment of the population. We succeeded to varying degrees (more so for Poland than for Ukraine) for people in all segments of the population except students. Although we collected information about Polish students' schoolwork, the number of students in our (adult) sample was too small for reliable indices.

The Substantive Complexity of Work in Paid Employment

For the analyses of the substantive complexity of work in paid employment, I use the data and measurement models in Chapter 4. But, since I am using the employed segment of the population as a baseline against which to compare the complexity of activities of other segments of the population, I shall now treat all the employed as a single category, rather than dividing them (as I did in Chapter 4) into several social classes.

The Complexity of Activities of the Unemployed and of Pensioners

A general index of complexity of activities. The Polish survey asked the unemployed men, those unemployed women who did not consider themselves to be housewives, and the pensioners (both men and women) very general questions about their activities in dealing with things, with data, and with people. In approximate translation:

(note 7 continued) For Ukraine, which in late 1992 and early 1993 had not yet experienced any substantial amount of formal unemployment, the interviewers simply asked the respondents whether they were working, looking for a job, keeping house, learning (as students), retired, or doing something else. We classified as employed only those who said that they were working and that they worked at least 15 hours per week in any one of their jobs. If they said they were employed but were not working at least 15 hours per week, they were asked whether they were on leave from their jobs. For the other categories, we relied entirely on self-designation.

I would like to discuss your time allocation in detail—what you do during an average day. We are interested in both any intellectual work—such as reading and writing—and manual labor. Let's start with activities involving the use of hands, regardless of whether they are simple tasks or ones that involve the use of tools and devices. We mean any kind of work that requires the use of your hands, for example: use of an electric drill, mechanical saw, computer, or cooking, painting, or playing piano. What do you do most often that requires manual labor?

On the average, how many hours per week do you work using your hands?

And now let's talk about reading and writing. Please take into consideration letters, notes, books, newspapers, and any other written material. How many hours per week do you spend on those activities?

What do you do during this time? What do you read? If you write, what is it?

How many hours per week do you interact with people?

What do those interactions consist of? What's the subject matter of the contacts with people other than your family?

Using this information, survey specialists who were well versed in our measurement of the substantive complexity of work in paid employment rated the complexity of each respondent's activities in dealing with things, with data, and with people. They also appraised the overall complexity of that person's activities, using rating scales closely modeled on those for rating the substantive complexity of work in paid employment (for those scales, see Kohn and Schooler 1983, Appendix B).

From these ratings of complexity, together with the respondents' estimates of the amount of time they spend dealing with things, with data, and with people, we constructed confirmatory factor-analytic measurement models of the complexity of the activities of the unemployed and the pensioners (Table 5.1). Since the mode of inquiry and the coding were similar for the unemployed and for the pensioners, we

Table 5.1. Measurement Models of Complexity of Activities, for Unemployed and Pensioned Polish Men and Women (1992).

Concept and Indicators	Standardized Paths: Concept to Indicators	
	Unemployed	Pensioners
Complexity of Activities		
Complexity of activities with data	.77*	.86*
Complexity of activities with things	.49*	.23*
Complexity of activities with people	.13	.07
Hours of activities with data	.36*	.44*
Hours of activities with things	.20	−.09
Hours of activities with people	.17	−.03
Overall complexity	.69*	.65*
Ratio of chi-square to degrees of freedom	1.88	
Root mean square error of approximation	.05	
Number of cases	98	205

*p < .05.

estimated a two-population model. But because the parameters were significantly different for the unemployed and for the pensioners, we did not constrain them to be the same for the two populations. And because only those few unemployed women who did not consider themselves to be housewives were asked the pertinent questions, and our sample contains relatively few female pensioners, we did not attempt to estimate separate models for men and for women.

The model fits the data well. The paths from concept to indicators are generally similar to those for the substantive complexity of work in paid employment (compare Table 5.1 to Table 4.6 [p. 111]). The greatest difference is that complexity of activities with people is not statistically significant, perhaps reflecting a lack of clarity about what constitutes meaningful activity with people outside the realm of paid employment. Nevertheless, the paths from concepts to indicators are sufficiently similar to those for the substantive complexity of work in paid employment to provide assurance that we are measuring the same phenomenon albeit in very different realms.

We did not secure similar information for Ukraine.

Complexity of job-search activities. In questioning the unemployed, including unemployed women who considered themselves to be housewives, we also attempted to assess something akin to the complexity of their activities in searching for jobs. This was an exploratory effort based on our asking the respondents whether they had engaged in each of the following job-seeking activities: visiting an employment office or agency; answering an advertisement; placing an advertisement; visiting companies and organizations that might have job openings; asking their families and acquaintances for information about job openings; taking continuing education classes; or trying to start their own businesses.

Using this information, two occupational psychologists who were thoroughly knowledgeable about the Polish employment situation at that time attempted to assess the degree of complexity implied in the *patterns* of job-search activities. Their algorithm ranks these activities in the following order of increasing complexity:

1. Relying solely on friends and family for information about job openings.
2. Going to an employment office.
3. Answering an ad.
4. Placing an ad and/or going to various companies and institutions and/or taking a continuing education course.
5. Starting own business or taking a continuing education course *and* any four of the other five job-search activities.

The same questions were asked of the unemployed in Ukraine, but because Ukraine had not yet developed several of the mechanisms for seeking employment used in Poland, few people pursued most of these job-search activities. The algorithm therefore proved to be meaningless for Ukraine. Instead, I employ a measure based on the one mechanism that was most effective in Ukraine at that time: going to a state employment office to seek information about job openings.[8]

Complexity of Work in Housework

Both the Polish and the Ukrainian surveys asked housewives a set of detailed questions, twenty-three in all. I present an illustrative few—those concerning cooking:

> Do you cook dinner every day, almost every day, 3–4 times a week, 1–2 times a week, less than once a week, almost never, or never?
> When cooking dinner do you use only fully processed or semi-processed products; mainly processed products, but sometimes raw ingredients; mainly raw ingredients, but sometimes processed products; or only raw ingredients?
> Do you use cookbooks or recipes: once in a week or more often; 2–3 times in a month; on average once in a month; or seldom or never?
> For everyday cooking do you use: the nearly newest and newest recipes and/or ingredients; or do you prefer to make dishes that have proven to be successful?
> Do you sometimes use a food processor or other multipurpose appliance of this type?
> Do you use a mixer?

From this information my collaborators evaluated the complexity of each housewife's cooking; and from similar information evaluated the complexity of her other activities in doing household work. We then used these ratings as the indicators of two of the first-order factors, the complexity of household work with data and with things (Table 5.2). For assessing the complexity of work with data, the indicators are our ratings of the complexity of whatever the respondents read about housework, the complexity of what they write in doing their housework, the amount of time they spend reading materials pertinent to housework, and (for Poland) one additional indicator, the preparation of new dishes. For complexity of work with things, the indicators are the complexity of cooking, laundry, and sewing. Paths from both concepts to their indicators are of roughly similar magnitude for Polish and Ukrainian housewives.

We had great difficulty finding satisfactory indicators of the complexity of interacting with people in household work. This, too, may reflect ambiguity about what constitutes work with people outside the context of paid employment. I decided to use the number of household members as the single indicator of the complexity of work with people, on the rationale that the number of people in the household serves

---

8. My index is a three-category classification: not utilizing the state employment office, using such an office but also relying on friends and relatives for information, and using such an office exclusively. The rationale for this ordering is that exclusive reliance on state employment offices, in Ukraine in 1992–1993, was the most effective way to search for a job. A simple dichotomy, using or not using the state employment office, correlates nearly as well with all three dimensions of personality as does the three-category classification.

Table 5.2. Measurement Models of Complexity of Household Work, for Polish Housewives (1992) and Ukrainian Housewives (1992–1993).

Concepts and Indicators	Polish Housewives	Ukrainian Housewives
	Standardized Paths: First-Order Concepts to Indicators	
Complexity of Work with Data		
Reading	.81*	.94*
Writing	.58*	.63*
Time spent reading	.42*	.42*
New dishes	.36*	—
Complexity of Work with Things		
Cooking	.59*	.54*
Laundry	.42*	.28*
Sewing	.21*	.45*
Complexity of Work with People		
Number of Persons in Household	1.00	1.00
	Standardized Paths: Complexity of Household Work to First-Order Concepts	
Complexity of Household Work		
Complexity of work with data	.47*	.56*
Complexity of work with things	.82*	.96*
Complexity of work with people	.34*	.15
Ratio of chi-square to degrees of freedom	2.17	1.17
Root mean square error of approximation	.049	.034
Number of cases	490	148

$*p < .05.$

as a rough proxy for Coser's (1975) concept of complexity of role-sets, which may be fundamental to the complexity of one's dealing with people.

The three first-order factors—complexity of work with data, with things, and with people—serve as the "indicators" of the second-order concept, the complexity of housework. The second-order portions of the models are similar for the two countries: The complexity of work with things is the strongest indicator of the complexity of household work and (not surprisingly) the complexity of work with people—based on a single indicator of questionable validity—is the weakest. The models for both Polish and Ukrainian housewives fit the data well.

Complexity of Activities and Personality

Using these context-sensitive measures of the complexity of activities, I can now assess whether the complexity of people's activities bears much the same relationship to personality for people in all segments of the population. I expect all the correlations to be nontrivial; the magnitude of correlations for the employed, I believe, will be roughly similar to those for employed men studied during more stable times; and those for the nonemployed will be nearly as large as those for the employed.

Correlations between Complexity of Activities and Personality under Conditions of Radical Social Change[9]

Employed men and women in Poland and Ukraine. The correlations of the substantive complexity of work with personality are taken from Table 4.6 in Chapter 4. I repeat them here, in a different theoretical context, to establish a baseline against which to assess correlations for complexity of activities in nonwork realms. As shown in Table 5.3, the correlations of the complexity of work with self-directedness of orientation and with intellectual flexibility are very similar for employed Polish men under conditions of radical social change attendant on the transition of Poland from socialism to nascent capitalism to what they had been under the apparently more stable conditions of the socialist era. The correlation of the substantive complexity of work with distress for Polish men during the transition, however, is opposite in sign from that for socialist Poland—but it is the same in sign and nearly equal in magnitude to that for the United States. The one respect in which Poland had differed from the United States in earlier research can now be attributed to the conditions of life in Poland under socialism (see the discussion in Chapter 4).

The correlations between the substantive complexity of work and personality are slightly *stronger* for employed Polish women than for employed Polish men. All the correlations, however, are distinctly *weaker* for employed Ukrainians than for Poles of the same gender. Still, even under the extremely uncertain conditions of life then obtaining in Ukraine, all six of the correlations were of appropriate sign and nontrivial in magnitude, with five of the six statistically significant.

The unemployed. The evidence for unemployed Polish men is entirely consistent with my hypothesis: The (positive) correlations of the complexity of their activities with self-directedness of orientation and with intellectual flexibility are nearly as

---

9. To compute the correlations presented in this chapter, I created factor scores based on the measurement models presented above or in the preceding chapter using a computer program called FSCORE developed by Ronald Schoenberg. This program not only utilizes a sophisticated procedure for estimating missing data, but also provides the correlation between true scores and factor scores; this information is invaluable for correcting correlations of these factor scores with other variables to take account of unreliability of factor scores. All correlations presented here have been corrected for such unreliability.

Table 5.3. Correlations of Several Measures of Complexity of Activities with Personality, by Country and Gender: U.S. Men (1974), Polish Men (1978), Polish Men and Women (1992), and Ukrainian Men and Women (1992–1993).

	(N)	Self-Directedness of Orientation	Distress	Intellectual Flexibility
U.S. Men (1974)				
Employed: Substantive				
Complexity of Work	(687)	.64*	−.24*	.77*
Polish Men (1978)				
Employed: Substantive				
Complexity of Work	(1,557)	.48*	.17*	.65*
Polish Men (1992)				
Employed: Substantive				
Complexity of Work	(769)	.45*	−.23*	.67*
Unemployed: Complexity				
of Activities	(84)	.43*	−.27*	.53*
Complexity of				
Job Search	(84)	.30*	−.29*	.57*
Pensioners: Complexity				
of Activities	(165)	.29*	−.09	.42*
Polish Women (1992)				
Employed: Substantive				
Complexity of Work	(632)	.48*	−.31*	.72*
Unemployed:				
Complexity of				
Job Search	(144)	.14	.00	.14
Pensioners: Complexity				
of Activities	(27)	.23	−.31	.73*
Housewives: Complexity				
of Household Work				
All Housewives	(475)	.43*	−.43*	.67*
"Pure Housewives"	(341)	.47*	−.54*	.73*
"Unemployed Housewives"	(134)	.36*	−.23*	.51*
Ukrainian Men (1992–1993)				
Employed: Substantive				
Complexity of Work	(495)	.19*	−.17*	.19*
Unemployed: Job-Search				
Index	(37)	.29	−.24	.21
Ukrainian Women (1992–1993)				
Employed: Substantive				
Complexity of Work	(492)	.30*	−.12	.26*
Unemployed: Job-Search				
Index	(31)	.07	−.23	.22
Housewives: Complexity of				
Household Work	(138)	.42*	−.26*	.38*

*$p < .05$.

strong as the corresponding correlations of the substantive complexity of work with these facets of personality for employed Polish men, and the (negative) correlation with distress is slightly stronger. Moreover, the complexity of job-search activities also correlates positively with self-directedness of orientation and with intellectual flexibility, and negatively with distress. Here, too, the correlations with distress are stronger than for the substantive complexity of employed men's paid work.

For unemployed Polish women, we have the measure of the complexity of activities only for the ten women who did not consider themselves to be housewives, too small a number for reliable correlations. For *all* unemployed Polish women, though, we do have the measure of complexity of job search. This does *not* correlate strongly or significantly with any of the three dimensions of personality. A likely explanation is suggested by the finding that the unemployed Polish women who considered themselves to be housewives—and who constitute most of the unemployed—spent little time in actively seeking employment. The complexity of their job-search activities probably does not fully reflect the overall complexity of their activities.

We have no information about the general activities of the Ukrainian unemployed, nor is the index of the complexity of job-search activities that was developed for Poland meaningful for Ukraine. Moreover, since formal unemployment was still rare in Ukraine at the time of our survey, the numbers of unemployed men and women in the Ukrainian sample are too small to yield statistically significant findings for any but massive correlations. Even so, my simple measure of reliance on the state employment offices yields what appear to be meaningful findings. Reliance on the state employment office correlates at least as strongly with all three facets of personality for unemployed Ukrainian men as does the substantive complexity of their work for employed Ukrainian men. And, although this measure of job-search activity correlates only weakly with unemployed Ukrainian women's self-directedness of orientation, it correlates nearly as strongly with their intellectual flexibility as does the substantive complexity of work for employed Ukrainian women, and more strongly with their sense of well-being or distress. All the correlations are of the expected sign. Thus the findings for the Ukrainian unemployed, although not statistically significant, are consonant with my thesis.

Pensioners. The evidence for Polish pensioners is equivocal: For male Polish pensioners, the correlations of complexity of activities with self-directedness of orientation and with intellectual flexibility, although distinctly smaller than the corresponding correlations for employed Polish men, are moderately strong and statistically significant. The correlation with distress, though, is small ($r = -.09$) and nonsignificant. Here a detailed examination of the first-order dimensions of orientation yields information not obtainable from the analyses of the second-order dimensions. Although the complexity of male Polish pensioners' activities is not significantly related to either self-deprecation or anxiety, it is significantly (and substantially) related to self-confidence, to receptivity to change, to not being fatalistic, and to having personally responsible standards of morality. This set of dimensions would seem to connote a sense of being in control of one's life, which is certainly in keeping with my interpretation.

The Polish sample contains only twenty-seven female pensioners. The correlations of the complexity of their activities with self-directedness of orientation and with distress, although substantial (the latter being as strong as the corresponding correlation for the employed), are not strong enough to be statistically significant on so small an N. The correlation with intellectual flexibility, which (at $r = .73$) is truly massive, *is* statistically significant. Thus, the evidence for the female pensioners is entirely consistent with my hypothesis, although hardly definitive.

We have no data about the complexity of activities of the Ukrainian pensioners.

Housewives. The evidence for both Poland and Ukraine is entirely consistent with my overriding hypothesis. All of the correlations of the complexity of housework with personality are of the appropriate sign, all are statistically significant, and all are substantial. We learn something additional from the distinction made in the Polish survey between "pure" and "unemployed" housewives: The correlations between complexity of housework and all three dimensions of personality are much stronger for the "pure" housewives than for the "unemployed" housewives—as strong as, or stronger than, the corresponding correlations for employed Polish women. Even for the "unemployed" housewives, though, the correlations of the complexity of household work and personality are entirely consistent with my hypothesis.

For Ukrainian housewives, the correlations of the complexity of housework with all three facets of personality are distinctly stronger than are the corresponding correlations for the substantive complexity of employed Ukrainian women's work.

Thus, there can hardly be any doubt that the complexity of people's activities is substantially related to their self-directedness of orientation and to their intellectual flexibility for all segments of the Polish and Ukrainian populations for which we have the requisite information. We find this relationship again and again, in both countries, for both men and women. Many of the correlations for the nonemployed are as strong as the corresponding correlations for employed people of the same nation and gender, or stronger.

The evidence is not quite as uniform with respect to the relationship between the complexity of activities and the sense of well-being or distress. The major exception is that the complexity of male Polish pensioners' activities is related only weakly and nonsignificantly to distress. However, even for the male Polish pensioners, complexity of activities is significantly related to dimensions of orientation that connote a sense of being in control of one's life. And there is *nothing* in these findings reminiscent of the *positive* relationship between the substantive complexity of work and distress found for employed Polish men under socialism—not for the pensioners, nor for people in any other segment of the Polish or Ukrainian populations.

Does the Complexity of Activities Merely Reflect Educational Attainment or the Complexity of Prior Jobs?

One might reasonably ask whether the correlations between complexity of activities and personality reflect the undoubtable connection between people's attained educational levels and the complexity of their activities. Our data confirm that educational attainment is correlated substantially and significantly with the complexity of activities for people in all segments of both the Polish and the Ukrainian populations. Yet even strong correlations between educational attainment and complexity of activities do not necessarily mean that the relationships between complexity of activities and personality merely mirror the effect of educational attainment on personality. To the contrary, Schooler's and my longitudinal assessments of the interrelationships of educational attainment, the substantive complexity of work, and personality for employed U.S. men (Kohn and Schooler 1983) showed that fully half of the total over-time effect of educational attainment on personality is the product of education affecting job complexity, and job complexity then affecting personality.

With only cross-sectional data at my disposal, I cannot do true longitudinal analyses and I am again reluctant to do simulated longitudinal analyses during times of radical social change.[10] I am thus forced to adopt the expedient of statistically controlling educational attainment, *as if* any reduction in the magnitudes of relationships between complexity of activities and personality meant that those relationships were to that degree artifactual. I deliberately overcontrol to learn whether there is any residual relationship between complexity and personality that cannot possibly be attributed to educational attainment.

I find (Table 5.4) that statistically controlling educational level reduces the magnitudes of many of the pertinent correlations, sometimes substantially. Still, all but three of the correlations that had been statistically significant remain so, while two that had not been significant become so. (Both of the newly significant correlations involve the complexity of job search for unemployed Polish women—thus erasing what had seemed to be an important exception to the general pattern of complexity, in whatever realm and however measured, being significantly related to self-directedness of orientation and intellectual flexibility whenever the N is tolerably large.) Education certainly does affect the complexity of people's activities, whether in paid employment or outside of paid employment, but the psychological concomitants of complexity of activity can, at most, be ascribed only in part to educational attainment.

One might also ask whether the correlations between complexity of activities and personality reflect the undoubtable connection between the complexity of people's *past* work in paid employment and their current activities. I can test this possibility only for the Poles for we lack pertinent data about the Ukrainians' past jobs. For the Poles, the expectation of positive correlations between past job complexity and current complexity of activities is valid for all segments of the population, but these

---

10. The issue, once again, is that in simulated longitudinal analyses, one must borrow from actual longitudinal analyses information about over-time changes in the magnitudes of relationship between the endogenous variable whose earlier state is being simulated and all exogenous variables. But one cannot assume that information obtained in studies conducted during relatively stable times provides a valid basis for inferences about rates of over-time change during periods of radical social change. (For detailed explanations of what is required for simulated longitudinal analyses of cross-sectional data, see Kohn and Słomczynski 1990, pp. 194–195; Kohn et al. 1986; K. Miller et al. 1985 or 1986.)

Table 5.4. Partial Correlations of Complexity of Activities with Personality, Statistically Controlling Educational Attainment and the Substantive Complexity of Past Jobs: Poland (1992) and Ukraine (1992–1993).

	(N)	Self-Directedness of Orientation	Distress	Intellectual Flexibility
Partial Correlations, Controlling Educational Attainment				
Polish Men				
Employed: Substantive Complexity of Work	(769)	.16*	−.15*	.42*
Unemployed:				
Complexity of Activities	(84)	.36*	−.23*	.47*
Complexity of Job Search	(84)	.29*	−.29*	.77*
Pensioners: Complexity of Activities	(165)	.09	.07	.20*
Polish Women				
Employed: Substantive Complexity of Work	(632)	.12*	−.14*	.28*
Unemployed:				
Complexity of Job Search	(144)	.17*	−.01	.21*
Pensioners: Complexity of Activities	(27)	−.12	−.10	.61*
Housewives: Complexity of Household Work	(475)	.27*	−.38*	.56*
Ukrainian Men				
Employed: Substantive Complexity of Work	(495)	.03	−.18*	.08*
Unemployed: Job-Search Index	(28)	.22	−.16	.09
Ukranian Women				
Employed: Substantive Complexity of Work	(492)	.10*	.04	.12*
Unemployed: Job-Search Index	(23)	.11	−.27	.21
Housewives: Complexity of Household Work	(138)	.34*	−.11	.28*
Partial Correlations, Controlling Our Appraisal of the Complexity of Immediately Past Job				
Polish Men				
Employed: Substantive Complexity of Work	(603)	.28*	−.18*	.52*
Unemployed:				
Complexity of Activities	(81)	.41*	−.28*	.69*
Complexity of Job Search	(76)	.27*	−.31*	.67*
Pensioners: Complexity of Activities	(162)	.21*	.00	.36*
Polish Women				
Employed: Substantive Complexity of Work	(450)	.30*	−.24*	.41*
Unemployed:				
Complexity of Job Search	(121)	.13	.00	.14
Pensioners: Complexity of Activities	(26)	.09	−.16	.64*
Housewives: Complexity of Household Work	(418)	.35*	−.43*	.66*

*$p < .05$.

correlations are strong only for the currently employed. Even for the employed, statistically controlling past job complexity does not greatly reduce the correlations between the substantive complexity of current work and personality (see Table 5.4). Moreover, statistically controlling past job complexity does not render nonsignificant any statistically significant correlation between complexity of current activities and personality. In general, it is the complexity of *current* activities, not of past jobs, that matters for the personalities of both the employed and the nonemployed—which is entirely consonant with past findings for employed U.S. men (Kohn and Schooler 1983, Chapters 5 and 6).

In short, the correlations between complexity of activities and personality can be ascribed only in part, if at all, to either educational attainment or past job complexity.

Discussion

My collaborators' and my earlier research, and that of others, demonstrated the importance of the substantive complexity of work, both in paid employment and in other settings, for such fundamental dimensions of personality as self-directedness of orientation, feelings of well-being or distress, and intellectual flexibility. The evidence was particularly strong for employed men in the United States, where analyses had been based on longitudinal data, but it held as well for employed men in other countries, for employed women, and for housework (at least for women) and schoolwork (for both high school and college students).

The research discussed in Chapter 4, based on data collected in Poland and Ukraine during a period of radical social change attendant on the transformation of those countries' economies, provides evidence that the findings for employed men and women hold true not only under conditions of apparent social stability, but also under conditions of radical social change.

The analyses presented in this chapter, based on the same surveys as those of Chapter 4, show that the complexity of *nonemployed* men's and women's activities bears relationships to personality similar to those for the employed—not only for housewives, but also for the unemployed and pensioners—thus, for people in all sizable segments of the adult population. Moreover, these analyses demonstrate that the complexity of nonemployed people's activities is of considerable importance for personality even during a period of radical social change, when one might expect the psychological effects of complexity of activities to be overridden by those of social conditions that engender uncertainty and financial duress.

Limits of Generalizability

I certainly do not mean to imply that the complexity of *all* activities, under any conditions, affects personality in the same ways, and to the same degree, as does the complexity of work in paid employment. My guiding hypothesis was limited to activities in psychologically salient realms of life. The distinction between the "pure" housewives and the "unemployed" housewives made in the current Polish study may provide a good indication of what is a sufficiently "salient" realm of life to meet such expectations. Although the correlations between the complexity of housework and all three dimensions of personality are substantial and statistically significant for both types of housewives, the correlations are decidedly larger for the "pure" than for the "unemployed" housewives. The implication is that the centrality of activities in people's lives may be crucial not only in determining *whether* the complexity of those activities affects their personalities, but also in determining the *magnitudes* of relationship between complexity of activities and personality. The magnitudes of correlation appear to be roughly commensurate with the centrality of the activities in people's lives.

Directionality of Effects

My thesis is that the relationships between complexity of activities and personality are reciprocal—that the complexity of psychologically salient activities both affects and is affected by personality. Yet, although this thesis refers to reciprocal *effects,* my empirical analyses have assessed only *relationships.* Because the data are cross-sectional, I have no way of doing longitudinal analyses that would permit me to assess empirically the directionality of effects. Nor (as stated previously) can I do simulated longitudinal analyses, because the very fact of radical social change precludes my extrapolating from what we learned in longitudinal studies conducted in more stable times about rates of change in the magnitudes of relationship among the variables in the model. I can, however, compare the present findings with those of past longitudinal and simulated longitudinal analyses to see what inferences can logically be drawn.

The basis for such a comparison is the remarkable similarity, not only in the *patterns* of correlations between the complexity of activities and personality for almost all segments of the Polish and Ukrainian populations and for those of employed men and women in these and other countries, but also in the *magnitudes* of those correlations, even when studied under conditions of radical social change. It seems a reasonable inference that the processes that produced the correlations between complexity of activities and personality in the present research cannot be wholly dissimilar from those that produced the correlations between the substantive complexity of work and personality in earlier studies.

The central conclusion of past longitudinal and simulated longitudinal analyses (admittedly always of data collected at times of relative social stability) is that the substantive complexity of work *is not only correlated with many dimensions of personality, including all three fundamental dimensions that are at issue in the present analyses, but also affects them.* Simulated longitudinal analyses of housework for U.S. women (Schooler et al. 1983) and of schoolwork for U.S. high school and college students (K. Miller et al. 1985; 1986) have shown that the complexity of work in these realms, too, not only reflects but decidedly affects personality. These findings are particularly pertinent to my extension of the hypothesis to the complexity of activities beyond the realm of paid employment.

Thus, there is extraordinarily consistent evidence in study after study, both of men and of women, in diverse countries and under diverse circumstances, that the substantive complexity of work is not only *affected by* personality but *affects* it as well, even if the work is performed outside paid employment. Could it be that the strikingly similar findings for complexity of activities for all segments of the population, including the employed, result *entirely* from personality affecting the complexity of activities? That scenario seems to me to be exceedingly unlikely.

There will be longitudinal evidence in Chapter 7 for Ukraine during a period of radical social change that bears on this very issue.

Social Structure

Where does social structure enter into the picture? In all pertinent studies of the employed, including the study of employed Poles and Ukrainians under conditions of radical social change (Chapter 4), the uniform finding has been that position in the class structure and in the social-stratificational hierarchy are highly correlated with the substantive complexity of people's work. Moreover, these facets of social structure affect personality largely because position in the class structure and in the social-stratificational hierarchy is closely linked to the substantive complexity of work. Crucial to this depiction is the fact that the effects of the substantive complexity of work on personality are much the same throughout the social structure.

In extending the analysis beyond the employed to encompass people in the nonemployed segments of the population, I have dealt with only half of the causal model: I have shown that the psychological concomitants of engaging in complex activities transcend social-structural position not only for all social classes of employed people, but also for all segments of the nonemployed. Engaging in complex activities, whether or not these activities are called work, even when these activities are performed under conditions of radical social change, is associated with holding a self-directed orientation, having a sense of well-being, and being intellectually flexible. I have not yet assessed whether complexity of activities is related to social-structural position for the nonemployed, and—if it is—what the consequences are for the relationships between social structure and personality. I shall attempt to deal with this challenging task in the next chapter.

Suggestion to increase complexity of activities?

Chapter 6

Extending the Analysis to the Nonemployed

Part 2. Structural Location and Personality during the Transformation of Poland and Ukraine

This chapter is based almost entirely on a paper coauthored with Wojciech Zaborowski, Krystyna Janicka, Valeriy Khmelko, Bogdan W. Mach, Vladimir Paniotto, Kazimierz M. Słomczynski, Cory Heyman, and Bruce Podobnik, published in the *Social Psychology Quarterly* (*SPQ*) (Kohn et al. 2002). The original paper was dedicated "to our beloved collaborator and coauthor, Wojtek Zaborowski, whose tragic death is a huge loss to his family, to us, to his many other collaborators and friends, and to world sociology." I dedicate this chapter to Wojtek as well. He played a pivotal role in developing the measurement models and the ideas used throughout the analyses.

Since this chapter and the preceding chapter were originally conceived as one (much too long and complex) paper, and the analyses were carried out nearly simultaneously, the intellectual debts that I acknowledged in the prefatory note to the previous chapter also apply to this chapter—most of all to my collaborators in the research. I am also indebted to Michael Hout, Ho-fung Hung, Krzysztof Zagorski, and the editor, Cecilia Ridgeway, as well as anonymous referees of *SPQ* for their critical readings of earlier versions of the paper.

My intent in this chapter is to enlarge the scope of analysis in research on social structure and personality to encompass not only the employed, but also those segments of the population who are not gainfully employed, whom I collectively term the *nonemployed*. I do this in a comparative analysis of Poland and Ukraine during an early period in the transformation of their economic and social structures. This transformation presented both the need and the opportunity (unfortunately, at considerable cost to the people involved) to expand the study of social structure from the class positions and social-stratificational levels of the employed to include the social-structural positions of the nonemployed. The transformation was so radical that major categories of nonemployment, although not entirely new, were greatly expanded and substantially altered in social composition. This was particularly true for the *un*employed (those who are actively seeking paid employment) and for the housewives, especially in Poland. Equally far-reaching have been changes in the conditions of life of both new (or newly expanding) and existing segments of the population, in particular the economic adversity experienced by the unemployed, many housewives, and the pensioners.

Including the nonemployed in a comprehensive assessment of the psychological ramifications of social structure takes us into new territory. Previous analyses of social structure, including my own, generally focused on the employed portion of the population. They did so for a perfectly sensible reason: The most prominent conceptualizations of socioeconomic structure—social stratification and social class—are based primarily on occupational placement. Social stratification is generally conceptualized as some combination of the educational qualifications or credentials for occupational placement, the status of the occupation (whether thought of as occupational prestige, as the socioeconomic status of the occupation, or as any other variant of occupational ranking), and the income derived from the particular job or occupation. At its core, social class, although variously conceptualized, always concerns conditions of employment, be they ownership of the means of production, control over the labor power of others, supervision, manual versus nonmanual work, or exploitation of or by others. The nonemployed generally have been treated as an annoying classificatory problem or even (as in depictions of the *lumpenproletariat*) as a reserve army of potential strikebreakers, as threats to the employed.

During times of high employment, the nonemployed are mainly ignored. For studies of men conducted during such times, omitting the relatively small number of the nonemployed probably had little serious consequence, so long as the authors did not generalize their findings and interpretations to populations younger or older than most employed men or to the institutionalized and the disabled. For studies of women, omitting the nonemployed meant ignoring larger portions of the population, notably housewives.

Alternatively, many investigators have attempted to assign ranks or positions to the nonemployed equivalent to those of comparable employed people. This is sometimes done on the basis of thoughtful appraisal of their circumstances, as in Erik Wright's (1978, pp. 91–96) discussion of the "class location of positions not directly determined by production relations." In other studies, the *un*employed are assigned the class position or stratification rank of their last job; or are treated as a separate category; and in at least one instance (Wright 1978, p. 94) are considered to be a "marginalized segment of the working class."

Students present an even thornier classification problem. Some investigators (e.g., Wright 1978, p. 92, borrowing from Bertaux's notion of class trajectories) have placed them in the class or stratification position into which they will move when they complete their studies. Others (e.g., Rosenberg and Pearlin 1978) have assigned them the status of their parents.

Housewives—and sometimes employed women as well—have often been placed in their husbands' class or stratification positions (see the debate among Goldthorpe 1983, Wright 1989, and Baxter 1994). Other investigators have assigned statuses to housewives equivalent to those of comparable employed people, an ingenious example being Michiko Naoi's (1992) classification of housewives' occupational status in terms of the complexity of their housework. The underlying rationale of nearly all these procedures has been to force the nonemployed into a procrustean framework of categories based on the socioeconomic differentiation of the employed.

In the present study of Poland and Ukraine during the early period of transformation, I have had to recognize that neither ignoring the nonemployed, nor treating them as if they were employed but happened to be jobless at the moment, is conceptually appropriate. I had to deal with the major nonemployed segments of the population as distinct social categories. Once I realized this, conceptualizing what I call "structural location" was straightforward.

In the analyses of this chapter, I use the term *structural location* to distinguish the same five segments of the adult population that formed the basis of my analyses in the preceding chapter: those men and women who are employed, whether as employees or self-employed, for at least 15 hours per week; those who are out of work and seeking employment (the *un*employed); those who are pensioners, whether because they had retired for reasons of age, had willingly or otherwise taken early retirement, or suffered some disability; those who consider themselves to be housewives, whether or not they are seeking paid employment; and—to make the classification comprehensive—the small portion of the adult population who are full-time students.[1]

---

1. A comprehensive depiction of structural location would not treat all the employed as a single category but would differentiate them according to their relationship to the means of production: that is, their social-class positions. To do this in the present analysis, however, would merely repeat the analysis of class and personality already reported in Chapter 4. It would also make it difficult to pursue one of the primary objectives of the present analysis—to see whether the various segments of the nonemployed differ in personality from the "employed," however heterogeneous the employed may be. In the next chapter, though, it will no longer be appropriate to treat all the employed as a single category. I shall then utilize a comprehensive classification of structural location that differentiates the several social classes into which I divide the employed and the four segments of the unemployed. Thus, the index of structural location that I use in this chapter can be regarded as a *truncated* version of the comprehensive classification that I shall employ in the following chapter.

Thus, rather than ignoring the nonemployed or treating them as if they were employed, I take seriously what in everyday discourse are regarded as the main categories of nonemployment, recognizing that each segment occupies a distinctive place in the socioeconomic structure. I ask, as studies of social structure and personality have always asked of social-stratificational levels and of social classes, "What are the personality concomitants of each—and why?"

There is a rich research literature on the effects of *un*employment on personality (for reviews, see Jahoda 1982; Warr 1987, pp. 59–60, 194–236). Some date back or pertain to the Great Depression (Eisenberg and Lazarsfeld 1938; Jahoda 1982, pp. 15–32), one of these being a study of Poland (Zawadski and Lazarsfeld 1935). There are also directly pertinent studies of the psychological effects of *housework* and of being a *housekeeper* (see, in particular, Schooler et al. 1983 and the references cited there), and of *retirees* (although these studies generally focus on retirement rather than on pensioners as a distinct social category). Far from being a pioneer in the study of the psychological concomitants of membership in any of these social categories, my intended contribution is to systematically compare *all* these segments of the population with the employed and with each other. I assess the same fundamental dimensions of personality that my collaborators and I previously studied for the employed.

That I do so during the transformation of the socioeconomic structures of Poland and Ukraine is doubly motivated. The *inflow* of people into the ranks of the nonemployed, occasioned by the transformation, highlights the importance and makes possible the systematic comparative analysis of the nonemployed—just as the Great Depression did the study of the unemployed, mainly (but not exclusively) in western Europe and the United States. The *outflow* of people from the ranks of the employed makes evident that it is no longer sufficient, if it ever was, to limit the study of social structure and personality to the employed. Using the same body of data as I used in the earlier analysis of the employed segment of the Polish and Ukrainian populations (in Chapter 4), I now attempt to assess the relationships between structural location and personality for nonemployed segments of the urban portions of these countries, comparing them to the employed segment (treated as a single entity) and to each other.

Hypotheses

At the most basic, descriptive level, I ask whether people variously located in the nonemployed segments of the Polish and Ukrainian populations differed from the employed and from each other in the same fundamental aspects of personality as my collaborators and I assessed in earlier studies of the employed: self-directedness of orientation, distress, and intellectual flexibility. My first two hypotheses are little more than general expectations, but they flow from my collaborators' and my knowledge of the ongoing transformations:

First, the nonemployed segments of the population differ not only from the employed but also among themselves, in all three fundamental dimensions of personality.

Second, there are substantial differences between Poland and Ukraine in the ②
patterns of relationship between structural location and personality. These differences reflect, at least in part, differences in the extent of job loss and the resulting
social compositions of the nonemployed segments of the populations of the two
countries at the time of our surveys.

I further hypothesize that personality differences among the nonemployed segments, and between the nonemployed and the employed, are not solely a function of
these and other processes of social selection, but result as well from the differential
conditions of life experienced by people in the various segments of the population.
My third and fourth hypotheses specify two differentially experienced conditions
that may have had important consequences for the relationships between structural
location and personality.

Many observers of events in eastern Europe and the former Soviet Union have
noted that the initial period of transformation brought prosperity for a few and a
considerable deterioration in economic circumstances for many. Economic deprivation was particularly pronounced for those who had lost their jobs or were living
on pensions, which failed to keep up with inflation. I thought it a self-evident and
appealing third hypothesis, certainly consonant with past research (Feather 1997;
Jahoda 1982, pp. 58–59), that real or perceived economic adversity would result ③
in feelings of distress. I could not predict confidently, however, whether economic
adversity would also affect people's self-directedness of orientation and their
intellectual flexibility.

An equally appealing fourth hypothesis is the logical extension of the analyses
of complexity of activity and personality in Chapter 5. Just as past studies of
the employed have repeatedly demonstrated that the relationships of social class
and of social stratification to personality are in substantial part a function of the
close link between social-structural position and the substantive complexity of
people's work, I hypothesized that the relationships of the structural locations
of the nonemployed to personality might similarly be a function, in perhaps ④
substantial part, of a link between structural location and the complexity of
their activities.

Specifically, I speculated that the lives of many of the nonemployed, particularly
the unemployed and the pensioners, are not as conducive to, or requiring of, complex
activity as are the resources provided and the demands made by gainful employment.
These speculations are supported by past research on the unemployed (Eisenberg
and Lazarsfeld 1938, pp. 364–365; Jahoda 1981, pp. 188–189). I therefore expected
that the unemployed and the pensioners were not likely to engage in activities as
complex as those of most employed men and women. I saw no reason, though, to
suppose that housework is any less complex than the work done by most gainfully
employed people (Schooler et al. 1983). Nor is there any reason to believe that the
schoolwork done by young adults is any less complex than the work done by most
gainfully employed people.

Not only speculative, but also firmly rooted in past analyses, was my further
expectation that complexity of activities, even outside the realm of paid employment,
would affect all three fundamental dimensions of personality. The most directly

pertinent evidence, of course, comes from the analyses of Chapter 5, which demonstrate that the complexity of activities of all segments of the nonemployed bears relationships to personality similar to those of the substantive complexity of work in paid employment. In fact, the correlations between the complexity of nonemployed people's activities and their self-directedness of orientation, intellectual flexibility, and sense of well-being or distress are generally as strong as (or stronger than) the correlations between the substantive complexity of employed men's and women's paid work and the corresponding facets of personality.

Two questions remain unanswered: *Are the activities of the unemployed and the pensioners any less complex than those of the employed? If they are, does this help explain differences in personality among these three segments of the population?* I hypothesize that the answers to both questions are positive.

Structural Location and Personality

I use the same conceptualization and measurement of personality as in the two preceding chapters. For my examination of the relationships between structural location and personality, I rely primarily on analysis of variance.[2] The "independent" variable is the truncated version of "structural location"; the "dependent" variables are self-directedness of orientation, distress, and intellectual flexibility. I also use analysis of covariance: the "covariates" are variables that might help explain the relationships between structural location and personality.

The first hypothesis—that the several segments of the nonemployed population differ in personality not only from the employed but also among themselves—is readily tested. Analyses of variance yield a correlational statistic, *eta*, that is appropriate for assessing the magnitude of relationship when one of the variables (in this case, structural location) is nominal. As is evident in Table 6.1, all the correlations (*etas*) of structural location and personality are statistically significant and nontrivial in magnitude. This is true for both men and women in both Poland and Ukraine. Structural location does matter for personality, even though I am treating all the employed as a single category. The magnitudes of correlation are roughly similar for Poles and for Ukrainians of each gender and for men and for women of each country.[3] Moreover, for self-directedness of orientation and for intellectual

2. Analysis of variance is mathematically equivalent to a multiple-regression analysis that uses dummy variables for each of the nonemployed segments of the population and treats the employed as a reference category. I present analyses of variance because standardized deviations from population means are much easier to comprehend than are beta weights, and they make it much easier to compare the nonemployed segments of the population with each other rather than only with the employed. Admittedly, though, I gain these advantages at the cost of not having simple tests to determine whether any particular segment of the population differs significantly from the employed with respect to any particular dimension of personality.

3. The Polish sample had an age cutoff of sixty-five years, the Ukrainian sample had no such cutoff. For cross-national comparability, I impose an age limit on the Ukrainian data to match that of the Polish data. Analyses of the full Ukrainian sample yield entirely consonant

Table 6.1. Structural Location and Personality, by Country and Gender: Poland (1992) and Ukraine (1992–1993).

	(N)	Standardized Differences from the Mean for All People of the Particular Country and Gender		
		Self-Directedness of Orientation	Distress	Intellectual Flexibility
Polish Men				
Employed	(785)	.06	−.10	.07
Unemployed	(86)	−.06	.35	−.14
Pensioner	(165)	−.34	.27	−.31
Student	(17)	.89	.32	.87
Correlation (*eta*) =		0.21*	0.22*	0.27*
Correlation (*eta*), excluding employed =		0.33*	0.04	0.42*
Polish Women				
Employed	(654)	.17	−.10	.16
Unemployed, not a housewife	(10)	—	—	—
Unemployed, housewife	(134)	−.27	.25	−.23
"Pure" housewife	(341)	−.25	.07	−.26
Pensioner	(27)	−.21	.20	−.08
Student	(16)	.86	−.02	1.09
Correlation (*eta*) =		0.24*	0.17*	0.37*
Correlation (*eta*), excluding employed =		0.23*	0.12	0.37*
Ukrainian Men				
Employed	(535)	.04	−.09	−.02
Unemployed	(37)	.14	.41	.11
Pensioner	(116)	−.48	.37	−.26
Student	(56)	.51	−.14	.60
Correlation (*eta*) =		0.28*	0.23*	0.26*
Correlation (*eta*), excluding employed =		0.48*	0.27*	0.45*
Ukrainian Women				
Employed	(554)	.08	−.05	.04
Maternity/Child-care leave	(52)	−.01	−.04	−.02
Unemployed	(31)	.08	.08	.33
Housewife	(133)	.17	−.18	.17
Pensioner	(179)	−.45	.31	−.35
Student	(31)	.30	−.12	.26
Correlation (*eta*) =		0.24*	0.20*	0.22*
Correlation (*eta*), excluding employed =		0.32*	0.27*	0.31*

*$p < .05$.

findings except that magnitudes of relationship are consistently larger when respondents older than sixty-five are included in the Ukrainian analyses. This difference disappears when age is statistically controlled.

flexibility, the magnitudes of correlation are at least as large (and in some instances are much larger) when I exclude the employed from the analyses as when I include them. This implies that the distinctions among the nonemployed are at least as important as that between the employed and the nonemployed. For Ukraine this is true for distress as well. For Poland, however, particularly for Polish men, the fundamental finding with respect to distress is that *all* segments of the nonemployed are more distressed than are the employed. hmm   interesting

 The second hypothesis—that the *patterns* of relationship between structural location and personality will differ cross-nationally—requires an examination of the means on each dimension of personality for each segment of the population,[4] as well as analyses statistically controlling pertinent social characteristics.

The Employed

The analyses of data from the employed portions of these same samples (in Chapter 4) have shown considerable variation in personality associated with social-class position: Experts and managers rank especially high in self-directness of orientation and in intellectual flexibility, and especially low in distress; manual workers, just the opposite. In now treating the employed as a baseline by which to assess the several segments of the nonemployed, my focus of interest shifts from internal variability among employed men or women to the average levels of each of the dimensions of personality for all employed men or women. For both countries and both genders, the employed are somewhat more self-directed in their orientations and somewhat less distressed than the mean for their nation and gender (see Table 6.1). In Poland, the employed also are somewhat more intellectually flexible than the mean for their nation and gender; in Ukraine, the employed hover close to the mean for nation and gender. Even so, the employed are not the most self-directed in their orientations nor the most intellectually flexible of all segments of either the Polish or the Ukrainian population; they are surpassed by the (relatively few) students, the difference being especially great for Poland. Moreover, although employed Polish men and women are less distressed than are men and women in any other segment of the population, this may not be true for Ukraine, where housewives and students appear to be somewhat less distressed than the employed. These findings further refute any expectation that the single important distinction would be that between the employed and all segments of the nonemployed.

Ukrainian women on maternity or child-care leave from their jobs may be a little less self-directed in their orientations and perhaps a little less intellectually flexible than are employed women actively at work; in their feelings of well-being

---

4. In the tables, I present not the actual means for each of the segments but the standardized deviations from the mean for everyone of the particular country and gender. Because my measurement models of personality are specific to people of a particular country and gender, it would not be appropriate to compare the actual means of (for example) unemployed Polish and Ukrainian men with respect to some dimension of personality, or even to compare the means of unemployed Polish men and women.

or distress, though, they are no different from women who are actively employed. Thus, although their conditions of life differ decidedly from those of women actively working outside the home, it seems that, on average, their personalities are not much different from those of actively employed women. This finding may be deceptive, however, for the women on maternity or child-care leave are much younger than are other employed women. If I statistically control age, as I do in Table 6.2, it would seem that, were they not younger than other employed women, they would be less self-directed, less intellectually flexible, and more distressed than actively employed women or than Ukrainian women generally.

The Nonemployed

The *unemployed*—those who do not work as many as 15 hours per week and are seeking employment—differ for Poland and Ukraine in both self-directedness of orientation and intellectual flexibility (again see Table 6.1). Unemployed *Polish* men are less self-directed in their orientations and less intellectually flexible than most other Polish men, particularly employed Polish men. Our sample contains only ten unemployed Polish women who do not consider themselves to be housewives (in itself an interesting social fact); thus, I can make no reliable assessment of their personalities. Those unemployed Polish women who *do* consider themselves to be housewives (who constitute the overwhelmingly largest portion of the unemployed Polish women) are even less self-directed in orientation and less intellectually flexible, relative to their own gender, than the unemployed Polish men. The unemployed *Ukrainians,* by contrast, are at least as self-directed in their orientations as most other Ukrainian men and women, including the employed, and are somewhat *more* intellectually flexible.

These differences between unemployed Poles and Ukrainians may be ascribed, at least in part, to the differential extent of unemployment and the resulting differences in the social composition of the unemployed segments of the two countries' populations. Formal unemployment is a largely new phenomenon in both countries, because it had been the practice under socialism to keep people on the payrolls of the state industries even when there was no work for them to do. By the time of our surveys, though, there was substantial and growing unemployment in Poland; in Ukraine, employment patterns in state industries had been little affected. (Even the numbers for the unemployed shown in Table 6.1 reflect the larger proportions of unemployed men and women in Poland.) In consequence, a sizable cohort of older, less educated Polish workers had lost their jobs; a somewhat younger, more educated cohort of Ukrainian workers was feeling the initial brunt of unemployment. The cross-national differences in the personalities of the unemployed may well reflect the differences in the age and educational compositions of those being drawn into the ranks of the unemployed.

Consistent with this interpretation is the finding (in Table 6.2) that statistically controlling age at least partially, and in some comparisons largely, explains why unemployed Ukrainians are at least as self-directed and as intellectually flexible as are employed Ukrainians. It may also be that educational attainment at least

Table 6.2. Structural Location and Personality—Statistically Controlling Age and Educational Attainment, by Country and Gender: Poland (1992) and Ukraine (1992–1993).

| | | Standardized Differences from the Mean for All People of the Particular Country and Gender | | |
| | | | Adjusted by Covarying: | | |
	(N)	Unadjusted	Age	Educational Attainment	Both
Self-directedness of Orientation					
A. Polish Men					
Employed	(785)	.06	.02	.02	−.01
Unemployed	(86)	−.06	−.14	.02	−.06
Pensioner	(165)	−.34	−.11	−.19	.10
Student	(17)	.89	.59	.55	.19
B. Polish Women					
Employed	(654)	.17	.13	.05	.04
Unemployed, not a housewife	(10)	—	—	—	—
Unemployed, housewife	(134)	−.27	−.33	−.13	−.17
"Pure" housewife	(341)	−.25	−.17	−.05	.00
Pensioner	(27)	−.21	.02	−.23	−.08
Student	(16)	.86	.59	.47	.30
C. Ukrainian Men					
Employed	(535)	.04	.01	.01	.00
Unemployed	(37)	.14	.01	.13	.01
Pensioner	(116)	−.48	−.20	−.33	−.11
Student	(56)	.51	.21	.48	.23
D. Ukrainian Women					
Employed	(554)	.08	.05	.02	.00
On leave	(52)	−.01	−.26	−.06	−.25
Unemployed	(31)	.08	−.09	.04	−.07
Housewife	(133)	.17	.06	.12	.05
Pensioner	(179)	−.45	−.12	−.20	.02
Student	(31)	.30	−.05	.27	.01
Distress					
A. Polish Men					
Employed	(785)	−.10	−.10	−.08	−.08
Unemployed	(86)	.35	.35	.31	.33
Pensioner	(165)	.27	.27	.21	.18
Student	(17)	.32	.31	.45	.45
B. Polish Women					
Employed	(654)	−.10	−.09	−.05	−.03
Unemployed, not a housewife	(10)	—	—	—	—
Unemployed, housewife	(134)	.25	.30	.19	.21
"Pure" housewife	(341)	.07	.02	−.02	−.05

Table 6.2. *(continued)*

	(N)	Standardized Differences from the Mean for All People of the Particular Country and Gender		
			Adjusted by Covarying:	
		Unadjusted	Age	Educational Attainment	Both

	(N)	Unadjusted	Age	Educational Attainment	Both
Pensioner	(27)	.20	.07	.21	.12
Student	(16)	−.02	.12	.16	.26
C. Ukrainian Men					
Employed	(535)	−.09	−.10	−.08	−.08
Unemployed	(37)	.41	.38	.42	.38
Pensioner	(116)	.37	.44	.29	.40
Student	(56)	−.14	−.23	−.13	−.23
D. Ukrainian Women					
Employed	(554)	−.05	−.03	−.02	.00
On leave	(52)	−.04	.17	.00	.17
Unemployed	(31)	.08	.20	.10	.20
Housewife	(133)	−.18	−.10	−.15	−.08
Pensioner	(179)	.31	.05	.15	−.05
Student	(31)	−.12	.17	−.10	.12
Intellectual Flexibility					
A. Polish Men					
Employed	(785)	.07	.07	.22	.02
Unemployed	(86)	−.14	−.15	−.04	−.07
Pensioner	(165)	−.31	−.31	−.15	−.11
Student	(17)	.87	.85	.53	.46
B. Polish Women					
Employed	(654)	.16	.15	.05	.03
Unemployed, not a housewife	(10)	—	—	—	—
Unemployed, housewife	(134)	−.23	−.28	−.08	−.10
"Pure" housewife	(341)	−.26	−.20	−.08	−.05
Pensioner	(27)	−.08	.08	−.10	−.03
Student	(16)	1.09	.88	.68	.61
C. Ukrainian Men					
Employed	(535)	−.02	−.04	−.04	−.04
Unemployed	(37)	.11	.04	.13	.08
Pensioner	(116)	−.26	−.13	−.13	−.04
Student	(56)	.60	.47	.59	.51
D. Ukrainian Women					
Employed	(554)	.04	.04	.00	.00
On leave	(52)	−.02	−.13	−.04	−.13
Unemployed	(31)	.33	.25	.29	.25
Housewife	(133)	.17	.13	.13	.08
Pensioner	(179)	−.35	−.17	−.17	−.08
Student	(31)	.26	.08	.21	.13

partially explains why unemployed Poles are less self-directed and less intellectually flexible than employed Poles; on this issue, though, I shall later present an
alternative interpretation.[5]

In contrast to the cross-national differences in how the unemployed compare
with other men and women in their self-directedness of orientation and intellectual flexibility, the findings for *distress* are cross-nationally consistent (see Table
6.1). In both countries, the unemployed are more distressed (in three of the four
comparisons, decidedly more distressed) than are employed people of their country and gender, a finding entirely consistent with past studies (Warr 1987). This
cross-nationally consistent finding cannot be a function of the social compositions
of the unemployed segments of the Polish and Ukrainian populations, which are
dissimilar. Hence statistically controlling age and educational attainment (as I do
in Table 6.2) does little to explain the distress of the unemployed. The explanation
for the high levels of distress of the unemployed is to be found, not in the cross-
national differences in their social characteristics, but in cross-national similarities
in the conditions of life they experience—an issue to which I shall return.

The *housewives* differ markedly for Poland and Ukraine on all three dimensions
of personality (Table 6.1). By comparison with other Polish women, and particularly with employed Polish women, the Polish housewives are relatively low in
self-directedness of orientation and in intellectual flexibility, and the "unemployed
housewives" (but not the "pure housewives") are relatively high in their degree of
distress. The Ukrainian housewives are relatively *high* in self-directedness of orientation and intellectual flexibility, and are *less* distressed than any other segment
of Ukrainian women. These cross-national differences must be understood in light
of the equally great differences in the social and economic conditions that induced
women to be housewives in the two countries at the time of our surveys.

In Poland, being a housewife, if not a new phenomenon, was certainly much
more prevalent than it had been during socialist times. Women, even mothers of
young children, previously had been pressured to work outside the home, and the
state-provided child-care facilities and services at their places of employment were
generally quite good. By 1992, however, many women were being laid off, and the
provision of child-care facilities and services had greatly deteriorated as the large
state enterprises floundered. Although a similar process may have begun in Ukraine,

---

5. Throughout this chapter I statistically control other variables in an attempt to assess
the effects of "selection" and "experience" in accounting for the relationships between structural location and personality. Insofar as personality differences between various segments
of the population can be attributed to differences in age, we are probably seeing the results
of "selection." The same may (arguably) be the case for educational attainment, because
educational attainment usually precedes adult structural location; except for currently enrolled
students, educational attainment cannot be affected by current structural location. (Later
I consider whether educational attainment actually may be a proxy for the complexity of
activities, which certainly can be affected by structural location.) Insofar as differences in
personality can be attributed to economic adversity or to conditions of life that are more or
less conducive to engaging in complex activities, however, we are probably witnessing the
experiential effects of structural location.

it was much less far along—witness the much smaller proportion of housewives among Ukrainian than among Polish women in our samples.

The Polish housewives were older and less educated than the Ukrainian housewives, both absolutely and relative to the age and educational levels of employed women in their respective countries. It follows that statistically controlling age and educational attainment diminishes differences between housewives and other women of the particular country with respect to self-directedness of orientation and intellectual flexibility (Table 6.2). Moreover, age and educational attainment completely account for why the "pure" Polish housewives are slightly more distressed than are other Polish women, and at least partly for why the Ukrainian housewives are less distressed than are other Ukrainian women.

The segment that stands out is the Polish women who considered themselves to be housewives but were seeking paid employment: they were the most distressed of all Polish women. Age and educational attainment do not account for their distress. More detailed analysis shows that those Polish housewives who *strongly* preferred to be employed—a sizable group—entirely account for the high level of distress of the unemployed Polish housewives. What about the Ukrainian housewives? The basic fact is that few of them would have preferred to work full-time; almost all were housewives by choice. Something in the conditions then prevailing in Poland but not in Ukraine was causing many of the Polish housewives to strongly prefer to be employed—and also to be distressed. That "something" was the economic adversity faced by Polish women who were forced to become housewives.

The *pensioners* are mainly people who retired at the mandatory retirement ages for their country and gender; they also include some people who became disabled or (particularly in Poland) were retired at an earlier age as state industries released redundant workers. Of all segments of the nonemployed, the pensioners are the most consistent cross-nationally and across gender (Table 6.1). They are less self-directed in orientation, less intellectually flexible, and more distressed than the mean for people of their nation and gender, in decided contrast to the employed. Likely explanations come readily to mind, the most obvious being that the pensioners are older and less educated than are people in other segments of the population. In fact, statistically controlling age and educational attainment largely accounts for the pensioners' relatively low levels of self-directedness of orientation and intellectual flexibility (Table 6.2)—this for both men and women in both countries. With regard to distress, there is an apparent gender difference: Age seems to account for female pensioners' but not for male pensioners' distress. (I shall later present a more powerful explanation for the female pensioners' distress.)

These adult samples contain only small numbers of students (more in the Ukrainian than in the Polish sample, but only because the minimum age in the Ukrainian survey was lower). The students are by far the most self-directed in their orientations and among the most intellectually flexible of all segments of the Polish and Ukrainian populations. These findings leave unanswered the question of whether the students are self-directed and intellectually flexible because of selection, because of the influence of higher education, or both. More puzzling are the cross-national and cross-gender differences with respect to distress: The male *distress mystery for Students?*

Polish students are decidedly distressed; the female Polish students are close to the mean for their gender and nation; and the Ukrainian students, male and female, appear to be somewhat less distressed than most other Ukrainian adults. I have no explanation for either the cross-national or (within Poland) the cross-gender differences in students' levels of distress, and my further analyses (see note 6) only increase my puzzlement.

Summary

① + ②

Notwithstanding my inability to explain the cross-national and gender differences in students' levels of distress, we have gained some understanding of personality differences among the nonemployed segments of the Polish and Ukrainian adult populations. I have found that these segments differ in all three fundamental dimensions of personality, not only from the employed, but also from one another. Some of these differences are cross-nationally consistent; others are not.

Consistently, for both countries and genders, the unemployed and the pensioners are more distressed than the employed; the pensioners are also consistently less self-directed and less intellectually flexible than the employed; and the students are the most self-directed in their orientations and the most intellectually flexible of all segments of the adult population. The principal cross-national *inconsistencies* are that the Polish unemployed and housewives are less self-directed and less intellectually flexible than are the employed, while the Ukrainian unemployed and housewives are at least as self-directed and intellectually flexible as are the employed.

My tentative and incomplete interpretation of the cross-national *inconsistencies* is that they appear to reflect (at least in part) the considerably greater dismantling of state enterprises in Poland than in Ukraine at the time of our 1992–1993 surveys. This process greatly increased the size, and thereby affected the social compositions, of some nonemployed segments of the Polish population. I have presented prima facie evidence that such cross-national differences in the social compositions of nonemployed segments of the Polish and Ukrainian populations underlie cross-national differences in the personalities of members of these segments. Despite this evidence, however, we must consider an alternative explanation: that some of what appears to be the effect of social composition may in reality result from different conditions of life.

It is also possible that some of the cross-national *consistencies,* notably the pensioners' relatively low levels of self-directedness of orientation and intellectual flexibility, may result from cross-national similarities in the social compositions of these segments. Social composition, however, can do little to explicate other cross-national consistencies in personality, such as the consistently high levels of distress of the unemployed (including the unemployed Polish housewives who would strongly prefer to be employed), because the social compositions of these segments are different in Poland and in Ukraine. These similarities in personality almost undoubtedly result from cross-national similarities in the conditions of life experienced by people in these segments.

Structural Location and Distress: The Effects of Economic Adversity

Which conditions of life might help explain the cross-national similarities (and perhaps also some of the cross-national differences) in the relationships of structural location to personality? One distinct possibility (my third hypothesis) is that the early period of transformation resulted in serious economic adversity for the unemployed (including the "unemployed housewives") and the pensioners, which would adversely affect their sense of well-being or distress.

The index of economic adversity that I use is based on confirmatory factor-analytic measurement models of perceived economic well-being (or lack thereof), which I think of as the subjective face of economic adversity. Both the Polish and the Ukrainian measurement models are based on four indicators of the concept (see Table 6.3). Three are the same for both countries: the log of per capita household income (which ties perceptions to economic reality); the respondents' reports about whether their households had experienced difficulties during the past year in buying food, paying bills, providing for entertainment, or having funds for taking a vacation; and their assessments of whether their financial situations had improved or grown worse during the past three years. For Poland, the fourth indicator is the respondents' estimates of how much money they could raise within a week to meet emergency needs. That question seemed inappropriate for Ukraine, which was then experiencing extreme inflation. Instead I use as the fourth Ukrainian indicator the respondents' degree of satisfaction with their financial situation. The overlap of indicators in the Polish and the Ukrainian models is certainly sufficient to assure comparability of measurement. Both models fit the data well: The ratio of chi-square to degrees of freedom is 0.90 for Poland and 0.51 for Ukraine, and the root mean square error of approximation is 0.00 for both countries.

Perceived economic well-being does help to explain the relationships of structural location to distress (Table 6.4), albeit not for all segments of the nonemployed. Statistically controlling perceived economic well-being reduces many of the relationships between structural location and distress, although more so for the Poles than for the Ukrainians; more so for Polish women than for Polish men; more so for the unemployed than for the pensioners; and most of all for that large and distinctive category, the "unemployed" Polish housewives. Unlike the "pure" Polish housewives, the unemployed Polish housewives considered themselves to be more economically disadvantaged than did any other segment of Polish women. The Ukrainian housewives, in sharp contrast, thought of themselves as more economically *advantaged* than did any other segment of Ukrainian women, even the employed. Therein lies the explanation of both the intranational and the cross-national differences in housewives' sense of well-being or distress.[6]

---

6. Table 6.4 also suggests that the Polish students, both male and female, would be *more* distressed were it not for their believing that they are relatively well-off financially. (This finding, although it attests to the explanatory power of perceived economic well-being even where least expected, does not help explain either the cross-national or the gender difference in students' levels of distress.)

Table 6.3. Measurement Models of Perceived Economic Well-Being for Poland (1992) and Ukraine (1992–1993).

Indicators	Standardized Paths: Concept to Indicators			
	Poland		Ukraine	
	Men	Women	Men	Women
Per capita household income (logged).	.68*	.67*	.33*	.36*
Respondent's estimate of how much money he (or she) could raise in a week.	.73*	.72*	—	—
Respondent's reports on whether his (or her) household experienced difficulties in past year in buying food, paying bills, providing for entertainment, or taking a vacation.	-.76*	-.71*	-.68*	-.61*
Respondent's assessment of whether his (or her) financial situation had improved or gotten worse during the past 3 years.	.63*	.59*	.58*	.53*
Respondent's satisfaction with his (or her) financial situation.	—	—	.46*	.51*
Ratio of chi-square to degrees of freedom	0.90		0.51	
Root mean square error of approximation	0.00		0.00	
Number of cases	1083	1205	952	1324

$*p < .05$.

Table 6.4. Structural Location and Distress—Statistically Controlling Perceived Economic Well-Being, by Country and Gender: Poland (1992) and Ukraine (1992–1993).

		Standardized Differences from the Mean for All People of the Particular Country and Gender	
	(N)	Unadjusted	Adjusted by Covarying Perceived Economic Well-Being
A. Polish Men			
Employed	(785)	−.10	−.08
Unemployed	(86)	.35	.21
Pensioner	(165)	.27	.21
Student	(17)	.32	.43
B. Polish Women			
Employed	(654)	−.10	−.05
Unemployed, not a housewife	(10)	—	—
Unemployed, housewife	(134)	.25	.09
"Pure" housewife	(341)	.07	.03
Pensioner	(27)	.20	.16
Student	(16)	−.02	.14
C. Ukrainian Men			
Employed	(535)	−.09	−.08
Unemployed	(37)	.41	.33
Pensioner	(116)	.37	.30
Student	(56)	−.14	−.08
D. Ukrainian Women			
Employed	(554)	−.05	−.03
Maternity/child-care leave	(52)	−.04	−.03
Unemployed	(31)	.08	.05
Housewife	(133)	−.18	−.16
Pensioner	(179)	.31	.24
Student	(31)	−.12	−.11

Perceived economic well-being contributes little, though, to explaining the relationships of structural location with self-directedness of orientation and intellectual flexibility (which therefore are not shown in Table 6.4). To understand these relationships, we must turn to other conditions of life, namely those that affect the complexity of people's activities.

Complexity of Activities as a Possible Explanatory Variable

I speculated above that there is little in the lives of the unemployed and the pensioners that is as conducive to complex activity, or that requires engaging in as complex activities, as the conditions encountered in gainful employment. I further hypothesized (my fourth hypothesis) that engaging in less complex activities would result in correspondingly lower levels of self-directedness of orientation and of intellectual flexibility, and in greater distress. I exempted housewives and students from this hypothesis, not because the complexity of housework and schoolwork is less strongly related to personality than the complexity of activities in other realms is—quite the contrary—but because I had no reason to expect that housework and schoolwork are less complex than work performed in paid employment.

A comprehensive test of the hypothesis that the complexity of activities helps explain the relationships between structural location and personality would require a single index of the complexity of activities valid for *all* segments of the population. The problem is that my collaborators and I also wanted to tailor our questions to fit the life circumstances of people in each segment of the population. Although our intent had been to ask *both* segment-specific and more general questions about the complexity of people's activities, in the course of pretesting my collaborators found it too difficult to do both. We ended up asking housewives only questions specific to the work that they do in cooking, sewing, cleaning, and the other major activities entailed in running a household (see Chapter 5). (Similarly, students were asked questions specific to schoolwork.) Useful as this information has been for segment-by-segment analyses of complexity of activity (Chapter 5), it does not provide a basis for testing my belief that housework and schoolwork are as complex, on average, as paid employment.

The Polish unemployed (other than unemployed housewives, who were asked the questions about housework) and pensioners, though, were asked very general questions about their activities in dealing with things, with data or ideas, and with people. This information proved to be quite comparable to the more detailed information about the complexity of work in these three realms that we obtained from the employed (Chapter 4). As a result, I can test my hypotheses about the role of complexity of activities in explaining the relationships of structural location and personality for the three segments of the Polish population crucial to my hypothesis: the employed, the unemployed (other than unemployed housewives), and the pensioners. We did not secure the requisite information to test this hypothesis for Ukraine; thus I have no way of making explicitly cross-national comparisons.

I used the information about the respondents' work or activities in dealing with things, with data, and with people to appraise the complexity of their work (in paid employment) or activities (of the unemployed and the pensioners) in each of the three domains, as well as the highest level of complexity of their work or activities in any of these realms. To assure comparability in my assessments of complexity for the employed and the nonemployed, I not only used the same classification scheme for appraising the complexity of activities of the unemployed and the pensioners as used for appraising the substantive complexity of work for the employed, but the actual appraisals were made by survey methodologists who were well versed in appraising the complexity of work in paid employment. They made every effort to use the same standards in appraising the complexity of activities of the unemployed and the pensioners as in appraising the substantive complexity of work of the employed.

**Table 6.5. Measurement Model of Complexity of Activities—
Estimated for Employed, Unemployed, and Pensioned
Polish Adults as a Single Population (1992).**

Concept and Indicators	Standardized Paths: Concept to Indicators
Complexity of Activities	
Complexity of activities with data	.64*
Complexity of activities with things	.25*
Complexity of activities with people	.87*
Hours of activities with data	.31*
Hours of activities with things	−.74*
Hours of activities with people	.24
Overall complexity	.90*
Ratio of chi-square to degrees of freedom	4.18
Root mean square error of approximation	0.04
Number of cases	1752

*$p < .05$.

The interviews with all three segments also provide information about how many hours a week the respondents spend in dealing with data, with things, and with people; thus we obtained seven comparable indicators of the complexity of work or other activities.

By pooling the data provided by the respondents from all three segments of the Polish population, I was able to estimate a single-population measurement model (see Table 6.5), which provides a common measure of complexity of activities for the three segments. The model fits the data well: The ratio of chi-square to degrees of freedom is 4.18 and the root mean square error of approximation is 0.04. The paths from concept to indicators are closer in magnitude to those for the employed than to those for the unemployed and the pensioners (compare Table 6.5 to Tables 4.6 [p. 111] and 5.1 [p. 137]). Thus, I have been able to include the unemployed men, those (few) unemployed women who did not consider themselves to be housewives, and the pensioners of both genders in a measurement model that appraises the complexity of their activities by the same criteria as we use for the employed.

Using factor scores based on this model, I can assess just how complex, on average, the activities of the unemployed and the pensioners are. My standard of comparison is the complexity of the work performed by employed members of the several social classes. The activities of both the unemployed and the pensioners are no more complex than the work performed by manual workers, the social class that does the least complex work of any employed men and women.

The crucial issue, at the heart of the fourth hypothesis, is whether their engaging in less complex activities than those of the employed helps explain why the unemployed and the pensioned *differ in personality from the employed.* (Differences from the population mean are no longer at issue because I now focus on a restricted portion of the population.) I pursue this issue by statistically controlling my common measure of complexity to see whether doing so reduces the personality differences of the unemployed and the pensioners in comparison with the

Table 6.6. Structural Location and Personality—Statistically Controlling Complexity of Activities: Limited to Polish Employed, Unemployed (Other than Unemployed Housewives), and Pensioners (1992).

		Standardized Differences from the Mean for All People of the Particular Country and Gender	
	(N)	Unadjusted	Adjusted by Covarying Complexity of Activities
Self-Directedness of Orientation			
A. *Polish men*			
Employed	(769)	.06	.01
Unemployed	(84)	−.07	.02
Pensioner	(162)	−.35	−.20
B. *Polish women*			
Employed	(632)	.17	.16
Unemployed, not a housewife	(9)	—	—
Pensioner	(26)	−.15	.11
Distress			
A. *Polish men*			
Employed	(769)	−.10	−.08
Unemployed	(84)	.36	.32
Pensioner	(162)	.27	.20
B. *Polish women*			
Employed	(632)	−.10	−.09
Unemployed, not a housewife	(9)	—	—
Pensioner	(26)	.16	.01
Intellectual Flexibility			
A. *Polish men*			
Employed	(752)	.07	.01
Unemployed	(83)	−.10	.02
Pensioner	(162)	−.30	−.09
B. *Polish women*			
Employed	(615)	.17	.15
Unemployed, not a housewife	(8)	—	—
Pensioner	(27)	−.04	.25

employed. This analysis provides impressive evidence that complexity of activities helps explain these differences (see Table 6.6).

Complexity of activities is strikingly efficacious in accounting for the lower levels of self-directedness of orientation and, to an even greater extent, in accounting for the lower levels of intellectual flexibility of the unemployed and the pensioners than of employed men and women. For example, statistically controlling complexity of activities reduces the difference in self-directedness of orientation between male pensioners (−.35) and employed males (+.06) from .41 to .21. In general, complexity of activities rivals and even surpasses educational attainment in explanatory power (compare Table 6.6 with Table 6.2 [p. 160]). Thus, statistically controlling complexity of activities explains nearly half of the male pensioners' lower level of self-directedness of orientation, which is as much as is explained by educational attainment. It completely explains the female pensioners' lower level of self-directedness of orientation, which is not explained at all by educational attainment.

Additionally, complexity of activities is more efficacious than educational attainment for explaining why both the unemployed and the pensioners are less intellectually flexible than the employed; it provides complete or nearly complete explanations for both. Some of what had appeared to be an "allocational" effect, whereby less educated people were pulled into the ranks of the nonemployed, may in reality be an "experiential" effect: that is, the lower intellectual flexibility of the unemployed and the pensioners results from their engaging in less complex activities than the employed. (By implication, the "allocational" interpretation of cross-national differences turns out to be partially allocational, partially experiential.)

Complexity of activities, however, is not very helpful for explaining the relatively high levels of distress of unemployed and pensioned Polish men. The most that can be said is that (in more detailed analyses than those of Table 6.6) statistically controlling both complexity of activities and perceived economic well-being explains a bit more of why the male pensioners are distressed than does controlling either variable alone. Insofar as one can make inferences on the basis of a relatively small N, though, the low level of complexity of *female* pensioners' activities almost completely explains their relatively high level of distress.[7] Educational attainment does not explain this phenomenon at all.

Although I have found complexity of activities to be more efficacious than education in explaining some of the relationships between structural location and personality, a major interpretive issue remains: whether complexity of activities is merely a proxy for educational attainment rather than being important in its own right. Certainly educational attainment and complexity of activities are correlated, although much less strongly for the unemployed and the pensioners than for the employed. Even so, Table 5.4 (p. 146) showed that the correlations between complexity of activities (variously measured) and all three dimensions of personality, for men and women in all segments of the Polish and Ukrainian populations, remain statistically significant and nontrivial in magnitude when educational attainment is statistically controlled. I confirm this finding for the particular segments of the Polish population and the common measure of complexity of activities that I employ here. I also find that the zero-order correlations between complexity of activities, as measured here, and all three facets of personality are as strong (or stronger) for complexity of activities as for educational attainment. These findings suggest that education affects personality for the unemployed in substantial measure through its effect on the complexity of people's activities, just as Schooler and I (Kohn and Schooler 1983, p. 306) found for the substantive complexity of work in longitudinal analyses of employed U.S. men.

---

7. The difference between male and female Polish pensioners mirrors the finding in Chapter 5 (Table 5.3 [p. 142]) of a substantial ($r = -.31$), statistically significant correlation between distress and the complexity of activities for pensioned Polish women, but only a modest ($r = -.09$), statistically nonsignificant correlation for pensioned Polish men.

Discussion

This comparative analysis of Poland and Ukraine has extended the analysis of social structure and personality to encompass not only the employed segment of the population, but the entire adult populations of the urban areas of those countries. I systematically compared each of the nonemployed segments with the employed segment and with each other. The analysis has shown that, during an early period in the transformation of the Polish and Ukrainian economic and social structures, the nonemployed segments of the populations differed in personality not only from the employed segment of their respective countries, but also from each other. This was true both for Poland and for Ukraine, and both for men and for women in each country. In neither country was the distinction between the employed and the nonemployed the only important difference; in both countries, there was also substantial variation among the nonemployed segments of the population.

There were decided differences between Poland and Ukraine in the *patterns* of relationship between structural location and personality. The most noteworthy was that the Polish unemployed and housewives were less self-directed and less intellectually flexible than the employed, while the Ukranian unemployed and housewives were at least as self-directed and intellectually flexible as the employed. These cross-national differences may be ascribed in part to differences in the extent of job loss and consequent social compositions of the nonemployed segments of the Polish and Ukrainian populations at the time of our cross-sectional surveys in 1992–1993.

The study of the nonemployed thus adds a new twist to the long-standing analytic problem of differentiating the processes by which people are "selected into" structural categories from the effects of experiencing the conditions of life encountered in those categories. For analyses of the employed, this problem has mainly been viewed as a matter of individuals choosing or being selected into jobs or other social positions. For analyses of the nonemployed, however, particularly during a period of social and economic transformation when entire industries are dismantled, movement from the ranks of the employed to the nonemployed is less a matter of individual choice or even of individual selection. These matters are not decided by or even for individuals. The issue, then, becomes the social composition of entire segments of the population. Admittedly my analysis of social composition has been only tentative and incomplete, but it marks a recognition of a perspective that has been largely missing from past analyses.

Yet, my analyses show that the relationships between structural location and personality are only partly a function of the social compositions of the nonemployed segments of the population. The relationships of structural location and personality are also, in substantial part, a function of the conditions of life experienced by people in the various segments of the population. The present analyses provide evidence that substantial segments of the nonemployed—particularly the *un*employed (including housewives who would prefer paid employment) and pensioners—were subjected to conditions of life that differ markedly from those experienced by the employed.

At least two such conditions appear to be relevant to personality. The first is economic adversity, which helps to explain the relationship of structural location with feelings of well-being or distress, particularly the distress of the unemployed (notably including the housewives who sought paid employment). Second are conditions that enhance or diminish the complexity of activities, which is pertinent for explaining the relationship of structural location with all three dimensions of personality that I have studied, especially the lower levels of intellectual flexibility of the unemployed and the pensioners. The early period of the transformation not only exposed some segments of the nonemployed to conditions of economic duress, but (at least in Poland; I lack pertinent evidence for Ukraine) also resulted in the unemployed and pensioners engaging in less complex activities than those characteristic of work in paid employment.

What general lessons can be learned from this attempt to enlarge the conceptualization of social structure to include the nonemployed? Perhaps the most basic lesson is that an interpretive model that has long been employed in the study of the psychological ramifications of the class positions and stratification levels of the employed (see Kohn 1969; House 1981; Kohn 1987; 1989a) applies as well to the structural locations of the nonemployed: Social-structural position affects personality primarily through the proximate conditions of people's lives. Although the crucial proximate conditions for the nonemployed are not *job* conditions, the two that I have found to be important—economic well-being or adversity, and complexity of activities—are closely analogous to job conditions.

The analysis of the nonemployed also reinforces the lesson previously found for managers and manual workers (in Chapter 4): that the "same" social-structural location can imply quite different conditions of life in different historical and economic contexts. In particular, the analyses of the nonemployed have shown how different are the conditions of life implied in being a housewife for women who are forced to be housewives despite their own preferences for employment, as were many Polish housewives at the time of our surveys, from conditions for women who are housewives by choice, as were most Ukrainian housewives at that time. Such a difference in life conditions has dramatic implications for one's feelings of well-being or distress. The implication is that we must always assess what actually are the proximate conditions of life attendant on particular social-structural positions in particular historical and socioeconomic contexts.

Chapter 7

Social Structure and Personality during the Process of Radical Social Change

A Study of Ukraine in Transition

This chapter is based primarily on a paper coauthored with Valeriy Khmelko, Vladimir Paniotto, and Ho-fung Hung, published in *Comparative Sociology* (Kohn et al. 2004), but it also includes a crucial causal model (Figure 7.1) that had not been ready at the time that article went to press. Insofar as the analyses depend on the baseline data of 1992–1993, I am indebted to the same people as for the Ukrainian portions of the analyses of Chapters 4–6, in particular, the people who made possible the Ukrainian survey of 1992–1993 (see the prefatory note in Chapter 4). In addition, I am hugely indebted to Khmelko and Paniotto for their initiative in carrying out (and even subsidizing the costs of) the follow-up Ukrainian survey and in re-assessing field methods and the validity of the data; and to Khmelko for helping me understand, through his published writings, our conversations, and innumerable e-mails, the conditions of life of Ukraine during the prolonged period of uncertainty and change encompassed in these analyses. We did not have the financial resources for either Khmelko or Paniotto to spend extended periods of time working with me on data analysis, as they had done when we were analyzing the cross-sectional data, but they contributed considerably to those analyses and to the interpretation of the findings, at long distance, mainly through e-mails. Hung played an immensely useful role as research assistant at the early stages of analysis, as did Bruce

Podobnik at an even earlier stage of the analysis when we were merging the baseline and follow-up data files and reassessing the data.

Our Polish collaborators—Kazimierz M. Słomczynski, Wojciech Zaborowski, Krystyna Janicka, and Bogdan W. Mach—generously provided the data, and Mach supplied the measurement models he had constructed from those data, for the information about the Polish measurement models in Table 7.2. Ronald Schoenberg helped in sleuthing problems in the creation of factor scores; and Mesfin Mulatu gave me considerable guidance in creating the latent-variable scores. I am also indebted to Carmi Schooler and Mesfin Mulatu for their incisive critiques of an earlier draft of the paper on which this chapter is based, and to the faculty and graduate students of the Department of Sociology of the Johns Hopkins University for their stimulating discussion of the theoretical implications of the paper at a departmental seminar.

The theoretical question that motivates this chapter is the same as in Chapters 4–6, namely, whether the relationships between social structure and personality previously found in both Western and non-Western capitalist and socialist societies during periods of apparent social stability continue to obtain even during periods of radical social change. This question has been provisionally answered by the cross-sectional analyses of Chapters 4–6, particularly of Chapter 4: In all those respects in which socialist Poland had shown a pattern of relationships of social class and of social stratification with personality similar to that found in studies of the capitalist United States and Japan (Chapter 1), it continued to do so after the advent of nascent capitalism (Chapter 4). Under conditions of radical social change, just as under conditions of social stability, people of more advantaged class position, and of higher social-stratificational level, enjoyed much greater opportunity to be self-directed in their work—that is, to do more substantively complex work, to be less closely supervised, and to work under less routinized conditions—than did people of less advantaged social-structural position. Occupational self direction, in turn, continued to be conducive to more self-directed orientations to self and society and to greater intellectual flexibility. Where, however, socialist Poland had differed from the United States and Japan (notably, in that people of more privileged position in the capitalist countries had a stronger sense of well-being, and people of less privileged position were more distressed, while nearly the opposite obtained in then-socialist Poland), Poland in transition now fully exemplified the capitalist pattern. Ukraine seemed to be following a similar trajectory, albeit at a slower pace: Ukraine showed the same *pattern* of relationships between social structure and personality as did Poland, but all the relationships were weaker in magnitude, with those for distress not even statistically significant.

The evidence of the cross-sectional analyses thus demonstrates that the radical social change attendant on the transformation of the social and economic structures of Poland and Ukraine had not fundamentally affected the relationships between social structure and personality, *at least for the employed segments of the population,* except insofar as the social structures of these countries had become more like those of capitalist countries. Yet, the comparative analyses of Poland and Ukraine tell us little about the dynamics of the ongoing process. Not only were the analyses necessarily cross-sectional, but the transformation of Poland had occurred so rapidly that, by the fall and early winter of 1992–1993, the relationships of social class and social stratification with personality already exemplified the capitalist pattern of the United States and Japan (compare Table 4.1 [p. 96] to Table 1.6 [p. 31]). The Ukrainian transformation had not advanced nearly so far, and the relationships between social structure and personality, while similar to those for Poland, were not nearly so sharply pronounced; Ukraine was still very much in the process of transformation to nascent capitalism.

In terms of movement away from the long-term domination of the economy by a centralized system of command, however, the Ukrainian transformation was even more profound than the Polish. For sixty years prior to the breakdown of the Soviet Union, Ukrainians had had no experience with private enterprise: even small private enterprises were forbidden. In the rural areas of Ukraine, where more than 80 percent of the population lived, private ownership was eradicated by draconian measures, beginning in the 1930s. In Poland, by contrast, small private business was never forbidden, and agriculture was never socialized. Moreover, the economy of Ukraine was an integral part of the centralized economy of the USSR. With the disintegration of the USSR, the industrial connections of the enterprises of Ukraine with tens of thousands of enterprises in fourteen newly independent countries of the former Soviet Union were abruptly broken. The result was a much sharper decline in production and in the standard of living in Ukraine than in Poland. Thus, in terms of the depth of the changes that were occurring, the early years of the transformation in Ukraine were extremely radical. The process was hardly complete in 1992–1993, and was still ongoing for some years to come. Herein lies the impetus and the opportunity for the present study.

With the realization that Ukraine had been at an early stage of a very radical transformation at the time of the cross-sectional survey in 1992–1993, my Ukrainian collaborators grasped the unique opportunity to secure the data that would make possible longitudinal analyses of the ongoing processes of radical social change. In the spring and summer of 1996 they re-interviewed all of the men and women in the original sample who had been in the labor force at the time of the initial interview. This allowed us to convert a cross-sectional survey conducted at a time when the transformation of Ukraine had barely begun into a longitudinal data set extending three to three-and-a-half years into the ongoing process of transformation.

For the analyses of this chapter, even more than for most studies of social structure and personality, context is crucial. Khmelko's (2002) analysis of macrosocial change in the first decade of Ukrainian independence documents that by 1996 (and even later), although Ukraine had left its former socialist economy far behind, it had not moved decisively to a capitalist social and economic structure. This analysis, then, is *not* a study of Ukraine *before* and *after* its transformation from socialism to capitalism, nor of Ukraine *during* and *after* the transformation, but of Ukraine *during the early stages of an ongoing transformation whose eventual outcome was still uncertain.* The strategic value of a longitudinal study of Ukraine during these years is that it enables us to study the dynamics of the relationships between social structure and personality during the ongoing process of radical social change, since our analytic lens is an examination of what happens to these relationships under such uncertain, changing conditions.

This chapter thus provides an extreme test of whether the relationships of social structure and personality found in studies conducted under conditions of apparent social stability obtain even during the ongoing process of radical social change. As will be apparent in the analyses that follow, the test is not only longitudinal, and not only conducted during the very process of radical social change, but extremely severe for a reason that my collaborators and I did not anticipate and that contrasts sharply with the findings of many studies of personality conducted during times of social stability: The over-time correlations of the dimensions of personality we study are astonishingly low. *The central questions I shall pursue in this chapter, then, are (1) whether the relationships of social structure and personality are meaningful, nontrivial in magnitude, and consistent over time even during the very process of radical social change and even in the face of instability of personality during this period of time; and (2) if they are meaningful, nontrivial, and consistent under these extraordinary circumstances, what makes this possible?*

Sample and Methods of Data Collection

The Baseline Cross-sectional Survey of 1992–1993

The initial, cross-sectional survey of Ukraine, which I now treat as the baseline for the longitudinal analyses, was conducted in the winter of 1992–1993. It was based on face-to-face interviews with representative samples of all men and women living in urban areas of the country (for information about sampling and methods of fieldwork, see Chapter 3).

The Follow-up Survey

With limited resources for fieldwork, my Ukrainian collaborators restricted the follow-up survey to those respondents in the original survey who had at that time been in the labor force–defined in Ukraine, as in the United States, either as gainfully employed or as not employed and looking for work. This was a strategic subsample for studying movement into and out of the ranks of the employed and for studying the psychological concomitants of interclass mobility. Limiting the follow-up survey to people in the labor force, though, had the corresponding disadvantage of precluding longitudinal analysis of housewives and pensioners. Still, we can compensate for much of this loss by juxtaposing the cross-sectional data about people who in 1992–1993 were housewives or pensioners to the follow-up data about people who in 1992–1993 were in the labor force but by 1996 had *become* housewives or pensioners.

Securing an adequate completion rate in the 1996 follow-up survey proved to be even more difficult than in the baseline survey of 1992–1993, in part because many Ukrainians had become disillusioned with the formal institutions of their society. This was also difficult because economic conditions were so hard that many people—even employed urbanites—spent the time when they weren't at their jobs doing what amounts to subsistence farming, in small plots in or near the cities or towns in which they live, and so were not available to be interviewed.[1] With great persistence, the Ukrainian investigators did secure interviews with approximately 75% of their intended sample—admittedly, no longer fully representative of the population to which we would like to generalize, but—interpreted cautiously—useful for the study of the dynamics of change.

The Over-time Stability of Personality

Authoritarian Conservatism

An obvious question with which to begin this analysis is how stable was personality during this period of radical change. To answer this question, and to provide crucial indices of personality for analyses to follow, I developed longitudinal measurement models of the same dimensions of personality as my collaborators and I had studied in the cross-sectional analyses of Poland and Ukraine for 1992–1993 (see Chapter 4), and had earlier studied for the United States (Chapter 1; see also Kohn and Schooler 1983, Chapter 6, and Appendices C and D), Poland when it was socialist (Chapter 1; see also Kohn and Słomczynski 1990, Chapter 4), and Japan (Chapter 1). I began with authoritarian conservatism versus open-mindedness, deliberately selecting as a well-measured dimension of orientation to self and society, one that had been shown to be highly stable in the longitudinal analyses of U.S. men (Kohn and Schooler 1983, Table C.1, pp. 327–328). An initial model showed the over-time correlation (which I shall call the stability) of this dimension of orientation to be astonishingly low (at 0.18 for men and 0.37 for women), particularly considering the relatively short interval of three to three-and-a-half years, even allowing for the tumultuous times that Ukraine was then experiencing. By contrast, for U.S. men over a ten-year period of much greater social stability, from 1964 to 1974, the over-time correlation had been 0.78 (Kohn and Schooler 1983, p. 328). What may be a more apt comparison, even though it is based on a small sample: Mach's analysis of subsamples of 99 men and 98 women representative of the southern half of Poland during approximately the same span of time as the Ukrainian analyses,

---

1. A survey of a representative sample of 4,500 Ukrainian households carried out by the Kiev International Institute of Sociology in the summer of 1996 found that approximately 62 percent of the urban population was engaged in subsistence agriculture, spending on the average twenty-four hours per week on such activities. The urban residents who engaged in these agricultural activities were not limited to manual workers, but included even some self-employed and small-scale employers.

albeit during a more advanced stage of transformation, yielded over-time correlations for both men and women about as high as that for U.S. men: 0.78 for men and 0.76 for women.[2]

My Ukrainian collaborators and I were so astonished at the extraordinarily low stability of authoritarian conservatism for Ukraine that we thought it unwise to pursue the analysis until we were confident that the finding was not an artifact of some flaw in the fieldwork, or in matching baseline respondents and follow-up respondents, or in data-processing.[3] We therefore retraced our steps, beginning with the selection and locating of respondents for the follow-up survey, not only by reviewing field notes but also by conducting brief re-interviews of respondents in the follow-up survey, to be certain that they really were the same people as the original respondents. We also checked our procedures for merging the baseline and follow-up data-files to be certain that we hadn't mismatched any 1992–1993 and 1996 respondents. Since we had discovered earlier that the information provided in four respondents' initial and follow-up interviews about such identifying personal characteristics as age, gender, educational attainment, and marital and parental status had been so inconsistent as to suggest that the wrong person had been interviewed in the follow-up survey or even that one or the other interview had been fraudulent, we did a systematic analysis of the consistency of such information for all people in the longitudinal sample. We also refined the criteria that had been employed for including respondents in the follow-up sample.

We found no inconsistencies that required excluding other respondents from the sample (although we did find a few inconsistencies that seem to have resulted from miscoding, which we were able to correct). We did, however, find that twenty-eight respondents who had said they were "working" at the time of the initial interview did not provide convincing evidence that they were actually employed or on leave from their jobs or actively seeking employment. We removed them from the sample as not really being in the labor force. Neither their removal from the sample nor the correction of inconsistent information made the slightest difference in the measurement model of authoritarian conservatism. In particular, the stability of authoritarian conservatism was unchanged, both for men and for women (for the final measurement model, see Table 7.1). I count this as important evidence against the possibility that the low over-time correlations were somehow the result of methodological artifact. There is much more evidence to come.

---

2. The baseline survey for this analysis (and for other Polish analyses to be discussed below) consisted of face-to-face interviews with a representative sample of all men and women living in the urban areas of Poland (see Chapter 4). The follow-up survey was conducted with a small but representative subsample of those members of the original sample living in the southern half of the country.

3. We here followed the strategy that, before embarking on substantive interpretations of cross-national differences, one should always attempt to rule out the possibility of these differences being a methodological artifact (see the discussion of this important issue in Kohn 1987, pp. 719–721).

Table 7.1. Longitudinal Measurement Model of Authoritarian Conservatism, Ukraine (1992–1993 to 1996).

	Standardized Paths: Concept to Indicators			
	Men		Women	
Concept and Indicators	1992–1993	1996	1992–1993	1996
Authoritarian Conservatism				
The most important thing to teach children is absolute obedience to their parents.	.50*	.40*	.64*	.53*
It's wrong to do things differently than past generations did.	.67*	.49*	.62*	.47*
Any good manager should be demanding and strict with people under him in order to gain their respect.	.44*	.56*	.44*	.42*
In this complicated world, the only way to know what to do is to rely on specialists.	.41*	.46*	.47*	.31*
No decent man can respect a woman who has engaged in sexual relations before marriage.	.42*	.31*	.52*	.54*
One should always show respect to those in authority.	.48*	.31*	.41*	.42*
You should obey your superiors whether or not you think they're right.	.30*	.52*	.36*	.53*
Young people should not be allowed to read books that are likely to confuse them.	.30*	.40*	.49*	.42*
Over-time correlation of the concept =	.18*		.37*	
Ratio of chi-square to degrees of freedom			2.11	
Root mean square error of approximation			0.05	
Number of cases	380		460	

*$p < .05$.
Note: A high score on the indicator signifies strong agreement with the statement; a low score, strong disagreement.

Other Dimensions of Orientation

The logical next question is whether the low stability of authoritarian conservatism is indicative of a more general pattern of instability of orientation to self and society or is somehow unique to this particular dimension. Answering this question entails assessing the stability of all seven dimensions of orientation that we use in our analyses—anxiety, authoritarian conservatism, receptiveness or resistance to change, personally responsible standards of morality, self-confidence, self-deprecation, and trustfulness.

We developed satisfactory longitudinal measurement models for all these dimensions of orientation—satisfactory as judged by the models' fitting the data well (see the first column of Table 7.2) and the parameters being consistent with those of cross-sectional models for Ukraine and other countries and with longitudinal measurement models for the United States and Poland. These models show that, although authoritarian conservatism is one of the two least stable of the seven dimensions of orientation for men, it is of intermediate rank for women, and in any case (even for men) is not unique in having a low stability: Several dimensions of orientation had only small-to-modest stabilities for one or both genders (see the second and third columns of Table 7.2). The magnitudes of over-time correlation vary considerably, from 0.17 to 0.56 for men and from 0.16 to 0.59 for women.[4] There is, moreover, a discernible pattern to the relative stabilities of the several dimensions of orientation. For both men and women, personally responsible standards of morality and trustfulness are the most stable of these dimensions of orientation, while self-deprecation, self-confidence, and anxiety are among the least stable. In terms of a long-standing (albeit admittedly *ad hoc*) classification (Kohn 1969, pp. 78–84), self-conception is generally less stable than is social orientation, at least during this period of ongoing social change.

By comparison, the magnitudes of over-time correlation were consistently much higher for U.S. men over the ten-year period from 1964 to 1974—the range of correlations in those relatively stable times being 0.53 to 0.81 (see column 4 of Table 7.2). Still, aside from authoritarian conservatism, the *pattern* of which dimensions of orientation are more stable, and which are less stable, is much the same for U.S. men as for Ukrainian men and women. The magnitudes of the over-time correlations for *Polish* men and women during approximately the same time period as the Ukrainian study (Table 7.2, columns 5 and 6) were generally (albeit not uniformly) substantially higher than those for Ukrainians of the same gender—some of the correlations being as high for one or both genders as those for U.S. men. Mach's analyses show that, for Poland just as for the United States, the pattern of relatively

---

4. That there is considerable variability in the stability of the various dimensions of orientation, and even substantial differences between men and women in the stability of several dimensions (with men's stability being higher for receptiveness to change and personally responsible standards of morality, and women's being higher for authoritarian conservatism and trustfulness) is further evidence that low stability of personality cannot be attributed to some general methodological artifact.

Table 7.2. Over-time Correlations of First-Order Dimensions of Orientation, Ukrainian Men and Women (1992–1993 to 1996), U.S. Men (1964 to 1974), and Polish Men and Women (1992 to 1996).

		Over-Time Correlation (Stability)				
		Ukraine, 1992–1993 to 1996		United States 1964 to 1974	Poland 1992 to 1996	
	(RMSEA)	Men	Women	Men	Men	Women
Dimension of Orientation:						
Anxiety	(0.05)	.26*	.28*	.53*	.42*	.62*
Authoritarian Conservatism	(0.05)	.18*	.37*	.78*	.78*	.76*
Receptiveness to Change	(0.06)	.36*	.16	—	.56	.74*
Personally Responsible Standards of Morality	(0.04)	.56*	.38*	.65*	.52*	.63*
Self-Confidence	(0.05)	.31*	.27*	.52*	.32	.29*
Self-Deprecation		.17	.18*	.55*	.55*	.56*
Trustfulness	(0.04)	.42*	.59*	.81*	—	—
Number of Cases		379	452	687	99	98

*p < .05.

Notes: 1. RMSEA is an acronym for Root Mean Square Error of Approximation. 2. Self-confidence and self-deprecation are estimated in a single measurement model, hence there is only one measure of goodness of fit for the combined model. 3. The data for U.S. men are taken from Kohn and Schooler 1983, Table C-1, p. 328. 4. The data for Poland were provided in measurement models developed by Mach. 5. No longitudinal measurement models were created for U.S. men for receptiveness to change higher and relatively lower stabilities was much the same as that for Ukrainian men and women, the exception for Poland—just as for the United States—being the high stability of authoritarian conservatism. In short, with the notable exception of Ukraine's low stability of authoritarian conservatism, particularly for men, there is nothing unusual about the Ukrainian *pattern* concerning which are the more stable dimensions of orientation, and which are the less stable. What *is* remarkable about Ukraine during this period of radical social change is not pattern but *magnitude* of stability: Most dimensions of orientation were much less stable for Ukraine than for the United States (during a much less tumultuous decade in the United States) and, perhaps by a somewhat smaller margin, than during the same time period (but at a later stage of transformation) in Poland.

A "Second-Order" Measurement Model of Orientation

Despite the instability of these dimensions of orientation, the pattern of their inter-correlations was so similar to that found in earlier studies that I hypothesized that a "second-order" confirmatory factor analysis[5] would yield the same two *underlying* dimensions—self-directedness of orientation *versus* conformity to external author-ity, and a sense of distress *versus* a sense of well-being—as had consistently been found in earlier analyses. (These factors had been found for Ukrainian men and women in analyses of the cross-sectional data of the baseline survey of Ukraine and for Polish men and women in analyses of the comparable survey of Poland [Chapter 4, Table 4.1]; for U.S. men, women, and their late adolescent and early adult offspring [Kohn and Schooler 1983, Fig. 6.3, p. 147; Miller, Kohn, and Schooler 1986, Table 2]; for Polish men when country was socialist [Kohn and Słomczynski 1990, Fig. 4.3, p. 87], for Japanese men [Kohn, Naoi, et al. 1990], and for Japanese women [Michiko Naoi and Schooler 1990].) Indeed, the same two underlying

---

5. Since I was dealing with seven first-order dimensions of orientation, measured at two times and based on a set of 76 measured indicators, a true (full-information) second-order analysis that simultaneously estimated both the paths from first-order factors to their indicators and the paths from second-order factors to first-order factors seemed too formidable to test all at once, particularly in a two-population model for the two genders. I therefore used the cor-relations of factor scores based on the first-order factors as the input to a confirmatory factor analysis that treated these factor scores as if they were measured variables. (I have put quotation marks around "second-order" in Table 7.3 to signify that this is not a true second-order model but an approximation thereto.) Since correlations of factor scores invariably underestimate true correlations, I became concerned lest the approximate "second-order" model, based as it is on correlations of factor scores for the first-order dimensions, might underestimate the over-time correlations of the second-order concepts. To be certain that this had not occurred, I replicated the model (separately for the two genders) as full-information models, allowing the same correlations of residuals of the indicators as in the separate measurement models for the first-order factors and the same correlations of residuals of the first-order factors as in the "second-order" model. The new estimates of the over-time correlations of self-directedness of orientation and distress were very close to those of the approximate model, thus assuring that I had not underestimated those correlations.

**Table 7.3. "Second-Order" Longitudinal Measurement
Model of Orientation, Ukraine (1992–1993 to 1996).**

| | Standardized Paths: Second-Order Concepts to First-Order Concepts | | | |
| | Men | | Women | |
Second-Order and First-Order Concepts	1992–1993	1996	1992–1993	1996
Self-directedness of Orientation				
Authoritarian Conservatism	−.40*	−.48*	−.58*	−.47*
Personally Responsible Standards of Morality	.25*	.40*	.27*	.37*
Trustfulness	.36*	.38*	.19*	.34*
Receptiveness to Change	.78*	.55*	.56*	.62*
Distress				
Self-confidence	−.43*	−.45*	−.25*	−.38*
Self-deprecation	.85*	.65*	.70*	.72*
Anxiety	.46*	.51*	.58*	.54*
Correlation between Self-directedness of Orientation and Distress	−.15*	−.29*	−.40*	−.36*
Over-time correlation of:				
Self-directedness of Orientation		.28*		.18*
Distress		.22*		.32*
Ratio of chi-square to degrees of freedom		2.33		
Root mean square error of approximation		0.06		
Number of cases		379		452

*$p < .05$.

factors are readily apparent in the longitudinal Ukrainian data, both for men and for women (see Table 7.3). *Self-directedness of orientation* is reflected primarily in being receptive to change and in not having authoritarian-conservative beliefs, and secondarily in having personally responsible standards of morality and being trustful of others—all of which is in accord with our theoretical premises and with past analyses. *Distress* is reflected primarily in being self-deprecatory and anxious, secondarily in lacking self-confidence—which certainly appears to be face-valid and is consistent with past analyses. The model, which fits the data well, is quite similar for men and for women.

Of pivotal interest for the present analysis, the over-time stabilities of these underlying dimensions of orientation are, as would now be expected, very low: 0.28 and 0.22 for self-directedness of orientation and distress for men, 0.18 and 0.32 for self-directedness of orientation and distress for women. I take these figures to be as close to reality as we are able to come (see the latter half of note 5). For U.S. men, the corresponding figures are 0.78 and 0.59 (Kohn and Schooler 1983, Fig. 6.3, p. 147). Thus, a major finding of the analysis is that there has been great instability in these underlying dimensions of personality, over a period of three to three-and-a-half years of ongoing social change.

This finding flies in the face of an accumulating body of research and writing in psychology (of which Costa et al. 2000 is prototypic) that finds the stability of personality to be so invariably high that some investigators (e.g., McCrae et al. 2000; McGue et al. 1993) infer that there must be a predominantly biological (mainly genetic) basis to personality. The pertinent studies, though, were not only based on distinctly different facets of personality from those studied in research on social structure and personality, and on samples weighted to more advantaged segments of the population, but also—and crucially—even though some tangential evidence is based on studies in countries that were experiencing or had experienced radical social change, the *longitudinal* analyses were invariably carried out under conditions of much greater social stability than those experienced in Ukraine during the time of our research. Prior research does not contradict our finding of great instability in underlying dimensions of personality because, so far as I know, there had been no prior studies of the stability of these or similar dimensions of personality under conditions of radical social change, only research that generalized far beyond what was justified by the empirical evidence.

Intellectual Flexibility

There is one more dimension of personality that is essential, not only to the assessment of the stability of personality, but also to the analysis of the continuing relationship of social structure and personality: intellectual flexibility, which I again measure by assessing the respondent's intellectual performance in the interview situation itself. The longitudinal measurement model of intellectual flexibility for Ukraine (see Table 7.4) is based on our appraisals of the adequacy of the respondents' answers to the same seemingly simple but highly revealing cognitive problems that were used in the cross-sectional survey (see Table 4.3 [p. 101]); their propensity to "agree" when asked agree-disagree questions; and (for 1996) the interviewer's assessment of the respondent's intelligence, following a long session that required a great deal of thought and reflection (a rating that had inadvertently been left out of the initial interview). The full rationale for this approach, the wording of the questions asked, and cross-sectional measurement models for Ukraine and Poland are presented in Chapter 4 (see Table 4.3 [p. 101] and the accompanying text).

The longitudinal measurement model fits the data well, its ratio of chi-square to degrees of freedom being 1.76 and its root mean square error of approximation being 0.03. The over-time correlations for intellectual flexibility (at 0.52 for men and 0.55 for women) are considerably more robust than those for either self-directedness of orientation or distress, but much lower than that for the intellectual flexibility of U.S. men, which was 0.93. We have to take into account, though, that the Ukrainian model may underestimate the true over-time correlations, because the baseline survey left out the interviewer's assessment of the respondent's intelligence. In my analysis in Chapter 4 of the cross-sectional *Polish* data, comparing the full four-indicator model to a model using only the three indicators that were available for Ukraine, I found that the absence of the fourth indicator results in underestimates of the correlations of intellectual flexibility with social-structural variables by approximately one-fifth. By extrapolation, I infer that our longitudinal measurement model may underestimate the over-time correlation of intellectual

**Table 7.4. Longitudinal Measurement Model of Intellectual
Flexibility, Ukraine (1992–1993 to 1996).**

| | Standardized Paths: Concept to Indicators | | | |
| | Men | | Women | |
Indicators	1992–1993	1996	1992–1993	1996
"Commercials" Question	.44*	.23*	.45*	.49*
"Kiosk" Question	.46*	.23*	.36*	.22*
"Agree" Score	–.07	–.26*	–.22*	–.46*
Interviewer's Appraisal of Respondent's Intelligence	—	.63*	—	.51*
Ratio of chi-square to degrees of freedom		1.76		
Root mean square error of approximation		0.03		
Over-time correlation of the concept	.52*		.55*	
Number of cases	379		459	

$*p < .05.$

flexibility for Ukraine to approximately the same degree, which would imply that the true over-time stability for Ukraine would be on the order of 0.60–0.65. Thus, although intellectual flexibility was much more stable than was either self-directedness of orientation or distress during this period of ongoing radical social change, in all probability it was much less stable for Ukraine than for the United States during more stable times.

Social Structure and Personality

That self-directedness of orientation and distress were so unstable during this period of radical social change in Ukraine—and that even intellectual flexibility was in all probability decidedly less stable than it had been during a decade of apparent social stability in the United States—poses the central question of this chapter in extreme form: *Is a consistent relationship between social structure and personality possible in the face of instability of personality?*

Conceptualization and Index of Structural Location

In assessing the relationships between social structure and personality during the process of social and economic transformation, I conceptualize *social structure* in a way that encompasses not only the employed segments of the population, but also those who were not gainfully employed. To do this, I incorporate a classification of *social class* that my collaborators and I (Kohn et al. 1997; and Chapter 4 of this book) developed for the employed segments of the Polish and Ukrainian populations during the transitional period, adding appropriate categories for the *nonemployed* segments of these populations. I call the resultant classification *structural location*. In contrast to what I called the *truncated* index of structural location in the preceding chapter (where I treated all the employed as a single category), this is the *full* index (which differentiates the employed into the same seven social classes as those used in the analyses of social class in Chapter 4).

As in previous chapters (notably in the analyses of Chapters 1 and 4), I employ the term *social classes* to mean groups defined in terms of their relationship to ownership and control over the means of production, and of their control over the labor power of others (see the discussion in Chapter 1, especially the classification of social class for Poland when it was socialist). For Poland and Ukraine in transition, my collaborators and I (Chapter 4) dropped the distinction between manual workers employed in the centralized sectors of Poland's socialist economy and manual workers employed in ancillary sectors of that economy as no longer relevant to economies in transition to capitalism, and we added a distinction between those owners who employed a substantial number of nonfamily employees (the employers) and those owners who did not (the self-employed), a distinction that was becoming more relevant to Poland and Ukraine in transition than it had been for socialist Poland. We also added a distinction between experts and other nonmanual employees, which seemed to be particularly pertinent to transitional economies. The resultant set of social classes is depicted in the first seven categories of the classification below.

During the period of transformation, we must also take account of the nonemployed segments of the population: not only those who were not gainfully employed and were seeking employment (the *un*employed), but also other nonemployed people who occupy distinctive locations in the socioeconomic structure, notably housewives and pensioners (see Chapters 5 and 6). This is necessary for the analyses of this chapter, despite the follow-up sample being limited to people who were in the workforce at the time of the initial survey, because in the ensuing three to three-and-a-half years many people had *become* housewives or pensioners. The resulting classification of structural location thus combines the classification of social class that my collaborators and I had developed for the employed with the categories we later enumerated for the principal segments of the nonemployed portion of the adult population as follows:

1. *Employers:* Owners of the means of production who have at least three nonfamily employees.
2. *Self-employed:* Owners of the means of production who have no more than two nonfamily employees, and members of the owners' families who are employed in such enterprises.
3. *Managers:* Employees who direct and control the operation of a firm, organization, or major governmental unit or large subdivision thereof, as well as other employees in appropriate occupational categories who directly or indirectly supervise the activities of more than 50 people, some of whom themselves are supervisors.
4. *Supervisors:* All other employees who supervise at least two people.
5. *Experts:* Nonsupervisory employees who work in professional occupations that usually require university or polytechnic institute education.

6. *Nonmanual workers:* All nonsupervisory employees whose work includes a substantial nonmanual component other than those classified as experts.

7. *Manual workers:* Nonsupervisory employees whose work is predominantly manual in character.

8. *Unemployed:* Those who are not gainfully employed at least 15 hours per week and are seeking employment.

9. *Pensioners:* People who have retired on pension, whether they retired for reasons of age, had willingly or otherwise taken early retirement, or had suffered some disability.

10. *Housewives:* Women who were not gainfully employed for 15 or more hours per week and considered themselves to be housewives, even if they were seeking paid employment.

11. That small portion of the adult population who are full-time *students*—a category excluded from the present analysis, because none of the people who were in the labor force at the time of the initial survey became full-time students.

For pertinent analyses I shall also distinguish women who were employed but were on maternity or child-care leave from their jobs; and also people employed less than 15 hours per week (but who were not actively seeking full-time employment).

Structural Location and Personality in 1992–1993 and in 1996

Since the subsample of 1992–1993 respondents who were re-interviewed in 1996 does not include people who were housewives or pensioners at the time of the baseline survey, but some people who were in the labor force at the earlier time had moved into the ranks of the nonemployed by the time of the 1996 survey, the most appropriate baseline against which to compare the 1996 subsample is the *entire* cross-sectional sample (other than students) who were interviewed in 1992–1993 (see Table 7.5).[6] The 1996 sample is not fully representative of the urban adult

---

6. My treatment of some of the categories in the classification of structural location differs somewhat from analyses of the 1992–1993 surveys in previous chapters. The analyses of the 1992–1993 Ukrainian sample in Chapter 6 excluded respondents older than sixty-five, to make the analyses comparable to those for Poland, where the sample had an age cut-off of sixty-five; but, for an analysis limited to Ukraine, no such age cut-off is necessary, and for comparisons of the 1992–1993 sample to the 1996 respondents it is informative to include older respondents, particularly pensioners. The analyses in Chapters 5 and 6 also included adult respondents, generally younger adults, who were full-time students. Since those students were not included in the follow-up survey, and none of the respondents in that survey became full-time students in the meantime, it would make for noncomparability of the 1992–1993 and 1996 respondents to include those respondents who were then students in the 1992–1993 analyses, so I excluded them. I also combined two pairs of categories that I had kept separate in the analyses of Chapter 4. For both men and women, I combined managers and

population of Ukraine in that year, not only because follow-up samples never do completely match cross-sectional samples, but also because the pensioners and housewives in our 1996 sample are limited to previously employed women and men who *became* pensioners or housewives in the ensuing few years. This limitation on the representativeness of the 1996 sample entails a small loss but also a strategic gain, for it focuses our attention on people who *became* nonemployed during the period of radical social change.

The *pattern* of relationships between structural location and personality is much the same for 1996 as it was for 1992–1993: Men and women in more advantaged structural locations were more self-directed in their orientations, more intellectually flexible, and less distressed than were men and women in less advantaged structural locations. Specifically, as was true for men in 1992–1893 (there being too few women who were either managers or employers at that time to draw firm conclusions about them), the managers and (the few) employers, and the experts, were at one extreme in 1996, the pensioners at the other. It is notable that the pensioners of 1996 (who, as a result of the criteria employed for sample selection, were newly pensioned) were as extreme in their lack of self-direction and intellectual flexibility, and in their high degree of distress, as were the pensioners of 1992–1993 (who, as a result of the criteria for sample selection, were not included in the follow-up sample). *Stability in the relationship of structural location and personality coexisted with instability of personality.*

Insofar as there were changes in the relationship of structural location and personality from 1992–1993 to 1996, the figures for Ukraine in 1996 are closer to those for the Poland of 1992–1993 than to those for the Ukraine of that time—Poland having been further along in its transformation. (This conclusion is based on comparisons of Table 7.5 with Table 6.1 [p. 157].)

In particular, in 1992–1993 there was a decided difference between the Polish and Ukrainian *unemployed,* with unemployed Poles being somewhat *less* self-directed and less intellectually flexible than most other people of their gender—particularly the employed—while unemployed Ukrainians were somewhat *more* self-directed in their orientations and intellectually flexible than most other people of their gender, as much or more so than the average for all of the employed. In Chapter 6, I attributed the relatively higher degree of self-directedness of orientation of the Ukrainian than of the Polish unemployed of 1992–1993 to the initial brunt

---

(note 6 continued) employers, there being few respondents in either category, both categories entailing control over the labor power of others, and the respondents in the two categories being similar on our measures of personality. I also combined the small number of women on maternity or child-care leave from their jobs with the much larger number of housewives. Here, too, the respondents in the two categories differ little on our measures of personality. And I add the few people who had lost their jobs and had given up active efforts to find another to those who were still actively looking for paid employment to create a combined category, "seeking work or discouraged." None of these modifications of the basic classification distorts the findings of Table 7.5, but they do make for greater comparability between 1992–1993 and 1996.

Table 7.5. Structural Location and Personality, Ukraine (1992–1993 and 1996).

Standardized Differences from the Mean for All People of the Particular Gender in the Pertinent Sample

Structural Location	Number of Cases (1992–1993)	Number of Cases (1996)	Self-Directedness of Orientation 1992–1993	Self-Directedness of Orientation 1996	Distress 1992–1993	Distress 1996	Intellectual Flexibility 1992–1993	Intellectual Flexibility 1996
A. Men								
Structural Location								
Managers & Employers	(27)	(17)	.69	.59	–.26	–.42	.60	1.05
Self-employed	(15)	(21)	.24	.00	–.12	.12	–.14	.04
Supervisors	(116)	(69)	.16	.12	–.32	–.02	.11	.21
Experts	(31)	(20)	.77	.46	–.43	–.33	.39	.93
Nonmanual Workers	(19)	(5)	.45	—	–.20	—	.39	—
Manual Workers	(319)	(165)	.03	–.10	–.09	–.08	.00	–.27
Seeking Work or Discouraged	(37)	(23)	.27	–.04	.31	.35	.21	–.21
Pensioners	(217)	(15)	–.43	–.52	.36	.44	–.24	–.31
Employed < 15 Hours/Week	(6)	(14)	—	–.02	—	.14	—	–.07
Correlation (*eta*) =			.38*	.32*	.32*	.31*	.27*	.60*
Correlation (*eta*) Limited to the Employed =			.26*	.30*	.15	.16	.24*	.62*
B. Women								
Structural Location								
Managers & Employers	(3)	(10)	—	.63	—	–.74	—	.64
Self-employed	(10)	(15)	.31	–.11	–.13	.26	–.03	–.16
Supervisors	(102)	(72)	.27	.08	–.26	–.18	.17	.32
Experts	(74)	(48)	.67	.24	–.21	–.11	.60	.51
Nonmanual Workers	(130)	(88)	.19	–.10	–.22	–.13	.18	.08
Manual Workers	(234)	(121)	.00	–.02	–.07	.02	–.04	–.37
Seeking Work or Discouraged	(31)	(22)	.19	–.08	–.02	.35	.43	.17
Pensioners	(356)	(18)	–.42	–.10	.35	.28	–.34	–.60
Employed < 15 Hours/Week	(5)	(22)	—	.19	—	.39	—	–.11
Housewives or on Maternal or Child-Care Leave	(194)	(13)	.20	–.48	–.20	.16	.17	–.15
Correlation (*eta*) =			.35*	.37*	.31*	.24*	.33*	.47*
Correlation (*eta*), Limited to the Employed =			.25*	.33*	.14	.18	.26*	.46*

*p < .05.

of Ukrainian unemployment striking the younger and better educated. By 1996, unemployed Ukrainians (particularly the men) were relatively less self-directed and intellectually flexible than unemployed Ukrainian men had been three years earlier. And unemployed Ukrainian women, who in 1992–1993 had not been much more distressed than the mean for their gender, had joined unemployed Ukrainian men—and unemployed Poles—in being decidedly more distressed than other Ukrainians of their gender.

Housewives and women on maternal or child-care leave had also become relatively more distressed—more like the involuntary Polish housewives of 1992 than like the Ukrainian housewives of that time who were averse to full-time employment. Ukraine was past the initial brunt of unemployment.

What about class differences among the employed? Although the magnitudes of relationship of class and personality were greater for Poland than for Ukraine (see Table 4.5 [p. 106]), the *pattern* of class differences for Ukraine in 1992–1993 was very similar to that for Poland. The cross-national differences (between Poland and Ukraine) in the patterns of relationship of structural location and personality were entirely among the *non*employed.

The *magnitudes* of relationship between structural location and personality (as measured by *eta,* a correlational statistic appropriate to a nominal variable such as structural location) are roughly similar for the Ukraine of 1996 to what they had been in 1992–1993 for both self-directedness of orientation and distress[7]; and they had probably increased for intellectual flexibility (even taking into account that the figure for

---

7. I attempt to assess the "true" magnitudes of correlation (*etas*), corrected for attenuation in factor scores or latent-variable scores. The 1992–1993 figures are based on factor scores produced by the FSCORE program, which provides the exact correlation between true scores and factor scores for all three dimensions of personality; with that information I am able to correct the *etas* to take the unreliability of factor scores precisely into account. The 1996 figures are based on latent-variable scores produced by the LISREL program, which provides no information about the relationship between true scores and latent-variable scores. I have estimated the *approximate* unreliability of the latent-variable scores for self-directedness of orientation and distress by systematically comparing magnitudes of correlation of the latent-variable scores with other ordinal variables to the true correlations produced in corresponding full-information models. For intellectual flexibility, where we have created both factor scores and latent-variable scores—which correlate perfectly with each other—I use the correlations between true scores and *factor* scores as my estimate of the correlation of true scores and *latent-variable* scores. If I had made no effort to adjust the *etas* for unreliability in the factor scores or latent-variable scores for the three dimensions of personality, all the estimates of magnitude would be smaller, but the general conclusion, that magnitudes of relationship were generally as high or higher in 1996 as in 1992–1993, would still hold true.

8. The issue, once again, is that the 1992–1993 index of intellectual flexibility lacks a crucial indicator, the interviewer's assessment of the respondent's intelligence. As noted earlier, the index may underestimate the correlations of social-structural position with intellectual flexibility, thus measured, by approximately 20 percent. Even if we increased our estimate of the *eta* for the relationship of structural location with intellectual flexibility in 1992–1993 by 20 percent, the *eta* for 1992–1993 would still be considerably smaller than that for 1996, when the crucial indicator was included in the measurement model.

1992–1993 may be an underestimate).[8] Certainly, the relationships between structural location and personality had not appreciably weakened during those years.

Further insight into the relationship of social structure and personality during the ongoing transformation of Ukraine is provided by examining the magnitudes of relationship (the *etas*), not for *all* segments of the urban population, but only for the employed—i.e., for social class. Table 7.5 shows that the *etas* for the relationship of social class with intellectual flexibility are approximately as large as are those for structural location—thus, class differences among the employed are as sizeable as the differences between the employed and the nonemployed are. For self-directedness of orientation, some of the *etas* for class are substantially smaller than are those for structural location. For *distress,* the *etas* for social class are consistently *much* smaller than those for structural location and are not even statistically significant; it is the pensioners (for both years for both men and women) and the unemployed and partially employed (both years for men, only in 1996 for women, then joined by the housewives) who make the overall relationship of structural location and distress robust. Perhaps symptomatic of Ukraine's equivocal transition from socialism to capitalism, the manual workers—who in socialist Poland had enjoyed a strong sense of well-being but who in (nascent) capitalist Poland had become notably distressed—in Ukraine, both in 1992–1993 and three to three-and-a-half years later in 1996, hovered close to the mean for all urban adults of their gender, employed or nonemployed. When it comes to a sense of well-being or distress, the really sharp contrast is not of manual workers with the more advantaged social classes, but of the employed with the nonemployed.

We must therefore keep in mind that the relationships of social structure with self-directedness of orientation and intellectual flexibility are substantial in magnitude and statistically significant whether or not the nonemployed are included in the analysis, while the relationships of social structure with distress are statistically significant and substantial in magnitude *only* when the nonemployed are taken into account. We must also keep in mind that the relationships of social class with all three dimensions of personality were weaker for Ukraine in 1992–1993 than for Poland at about the same time (Chapter 4), so over-time consistency for Ukraine in magnitudes of relationship of social class with personality means that the relationships continued to be weaker for a Ukraine that had not moved rapidly toward fully developed capitalism than for a Poland that had. The ongoing process of radical social change in Ukraine may have prevented the relationships of class and stratification with personality from becoming as strong as they were in Poland.

Still, whatever accounts for the different patterns of relationship of social structure with distress in contrast to self-directedness of orientation and intellectual flexibility (an important issue to which I shall return), it is noteworthy that *all* relationships of social structure and personality remained consistent over time. This is true both for social class and for structural location, and for all three dimensions of personality. Despite the deep structural changes in the economy and society during the three years intervening between our surveys, and despite great instability of personality during that period, the pattern and even the magnitudes of relationship of social class and of structural location to personality remained remarkably consistent. One major interpretive task is to explain the stability of these relationships despite changes in all their constituent elements.

Social Stratification and Its Component Dimensions

For a finer-grained analysis of the relationship of social structure to personality *among employed men and women,* I utilize an alternative conceptualization of socioeconomic structure—social stratification. I define social stratification as the hierarchical ordering of society, a single dimension inferred from the covariation of educational attainment, occupational status, and job income. To index social-stratificational position, I developed a (true) second-order confirmatory factor-analytic model (see Table 7.6) with each of the first-order component factors having two indicators. This model closely follows the cross-sectional model developed for the Ukraine of 1992–1993 (Table 4.4 [p. 104]), now extended to be longitudinal.

The 1992–1993 portion of the longitudinal model shows that educational attainment reflects social-stratificational position most strongly, and occupational status next most strongly (they were roughly equal in the cross-sectional model), with income of decidedly lesser importance especially for men (as was also true in the

Table 7.6. Longitudinal Measurement Model of Social-Stratificational Position, Ukraine (1992–1993 to 1996).

Concepts and Indicators	Men		Women	
	1992–1993	1996	1992–1993	1996
	Standardized Paths, Concepts to Indicators			
Educational Attainment				
Years of schooling	.97*	.95*	.98*	.97*
Educational level	1.00*	.99*	1.00*	.96*
Income				
Job income (log)	.70*	.90*	.83*	.85*
Family income (log)	.94*	.89*	.48*	.74*
Occupational status				
Treiman (International) Scale	.99*	.98*	.97*	.96*
Ukranian Prestige Scale	.85*	.89*	.94*	.95*
	Standardized Paths, Social-Stratificational Position to First-Order Concepts			
Social-Stratificational Position				
Educational attainment	.94*	.95*	.96*	.92*
Income	.12*	.30*	.26*	.55*
Occupational status	.70*	.66*	.74*	.78*
Over-time correlation of social-stratificational position	.98*		.97*	
Ratio of chi-square to degrees of freedom	1.72			
Root mean square error of approximation	.041			
Number of cases	384		463	

*$p < .05$.

cross-sectional model). By 1996, income had become a stronger indicator of social-stratificational position than in 1992–1993, both for men and for women, although still not nearly as strong as educational attainment or occupational status. In other respects the 1992–1993 and 1996 portions of the model are quite similar, as they are for men and for women. The longitudinal measurement model of social-stratificational position fits the data well, the ratio of chi-square to degrees of freedom being 1.72 and the root mean square error of approximation being 0.04.

The most striking thing about the longitudinal model is the extremely high stability of employed men's and women's social-stratificational positions—the over-time correlations being 0.98 for men and 0.97 for women. At first blush, such high over-time consistency in social-stratificational position would seem to be incompatible with the considerable amount of inter*class* mobility that had occurred in Ukraine during that period (as will be shown below). The explanation lies in the component dimensions of social stratification. Educational attainment is necessarily highly stable: no one could have declined in educational attainment, nor could employed people have greatly increased their educational attainment in three or three-and-a-half years of part-time schooling. Occupational status and income, especially the latter, were more open to change. In fact, the over-time correlations of the three component dimensions of social stratification (as assessed in a first-order analogue to the second-order measurement model presented in Table 7.6) are in accord with our expectation. The over-time correlations of educational attainment were very high (0.87 for men and 0.85 for women), those for occupational status somewhat lower (0.70 for men and 0.77 for women), and those for income by far the lowest of all (0.25 for men and 0.33 for women). Since social-stratificational position can be inferred from the covariance of these three dimensions, it can be highly stable even when there is considerable interclass mobility.

Social Stratification and Personality in 1992–1993 and 1996

The extremely high stability of social-stratificational position does not necessarily mean that its relationships to personality would necessarily be similar in 1996 to what they were in 1992–1993.[9] On the contrary, the very instability of personality might suggest that social-stratificational position must have lost some or even most of its relevance for personality during those years, or else a high stability of social position would have resulted in a correspondingly high stability of personality. I find, though (in Table 7.7), that social stratification was of *greater* importance for

---

9. Since social stratification, self-directedness of orientation, and distress are ordinal variables, I was able to precisely assess the magnitudes of their intercorrelations by creating a combined measurement model of all three concepts, fixing the paths from concepts to indicators (the *lambdas*) at the unstandardized values achieved in the separate measurement models, allowing the same correlations of residuals, and leaving the unexplained residuals free. I limited the analyses of social stratification and personality to men and women who were employed both in 1992–1993 and in 1996, thus eliminating the possibility that any differences I might find in the patterns of relationship for the two years might be confounded by movement into or out of the ranks of the employed (an issue that I shall take up shortly).

**Table 7.7. Social-Stratificational Position and
Personality, Ukraine (1992–1993 and 1996).**

	Zero-Order Correlations of Social-Stratificational Position with Personality, for Men or Women Employed Both in 1992–93 and in 1996			
	Employed Men		Employed Women	
	1992–1993	1996	1992–1993	1996
Correlations of Social-Stratificational Position with:				
Self-directedness of orientation	.23*	.43*	.36*	.35*
Distress	−.15*	−.10	−.03	−.14
Intellectual flexibility	.47*	.87*	.57*	.74*
Number of cases	352		412	

*p < .05.

the self-directedness of orientation and intellectual flexibility of employed men in 1996 than it was in 1992–1993, and was of at least as great importance for the self-directedness of orientation and intellectual flexibility of employed women in 1996 as it was in 1992–1993. For *distress,* though, the safest conclusion one can draw is that social stratification was only weakly and generally not significantly related to distress for either men or women in either year. As we learned from the analyses of the relationships of structural location with distress, what mattered most for distress during these times of radical social change was not social-structural variations among the employed, but whether or not people were employed at all.

Explaining the Consistent Relationships of Social Structure and Personality Despite Instability of Personality

The foregoing analyses have answered the question of *whether* social structure can have a consistent and meaningful relationship to personality even in the face of instability of personality: It certainly did in Ukraine during a prolonged period of extremely radical social change. I have yet to answer the more fundamental question, what accounts for *stability* in the relationship of social structure and personality despite *instability* of personality? Nor have I broached the related question, what accounts for the instability of personality?

A sociologically appealing hypothesis that, *if valid,* would simultaneously answer both questions is that the considerable social mobility that must have resulted from the transformation of the Ukrainian economy would have led to changes in the personalities of those who were mobile, consonant with their new positions in the social structure. Such changes in personality could be described at an individual level as instability of personality and at a social level as sustaining a consistent relationship of social-structural position and personality. We do not have the data to trace every step of the implied processes, but we certainly can assess whether social mobility has been meaningfully related to changes in personality.

Social Mobility and Changes in Personality

Are the consistent relationships of social structure and personality that we have found meaningfully related to changes in social-structural position? Certainly, there was a great deal of social mobility in Ukraine from 1992–1993 to 1996. One hundred thirty-nine of the 337 men and 262 of the 459 women in the longitudinal sample were in different structural locations in 1996 than in 1992–1993. Movement had taken place in both directions—from more to less advantaged structural locations and from less to more advantaged locations. For example (to take a crucial segment, and one that is clearly less advantaged than most), only two of the 21 men who were not gainfully employed and were looking for work in 1992–1993 were still (or again) unemployed in 1996. And only one had dropped out of the labor force and stopped looking for employment. All 18 others were employed at least 15 hours per week, most of them as manual workers, but some as nonmanual workers, supervisors, or self-employed. Conversely, of the 21 men who were not gainfully employed and were looking for work in 1996, all but four had been working at least 15 hours per week in 1992–1993. The figures are similar for women, with only four of the 20 women who were unemployed in 1992–1993 still (or again) unemployed in 1996. All this is consistent with (but by no means proof of) the possibility that changes in structural location attendant on the transformation of the Ukrainian economy might provide the key to understanding consistent relationships between social-structural position and personality despite widespread change in personality. If people's personalities changed consonantly with changes in their social-structural positions, then instability in personality would be fully in accord with stability in the relationships of social structure and personality.

Movement to and from the ranks of the employed. I look first at changes in self-directedness of orientation and in distress associated with movement from the ranks of the full-time employed in 1992–1993 to the various categories of nonemployment in 1996, and from unemployment in 1992–1993 to employment in 1996 (see Table 7.8).[10] The numbers are small, but the changes are dramatic, and despite the small

---

10. For the analyses of change in personality, I make use of a new component of LISREL, which produces a type of factor score (which Karl Jöreskog and colleagues call latent-variable scores) that correlates perfectly with ordinary factor scores but has a feature that is extremely valuable for my purposes: The intercorrelations of latent-variable scores for factors derived from the same measurement model perfectly reproduce the correlations among the latent variables in that measurement model (Jöreskog 2000). This is crucial for my analyses, because correlations of ordinary factor scores derived from a longitudinal confirmatory factor-analytic measurement model underestimate the correlations between time-1 and time-2 measures of the same concept, obviating one of the principal purposes of the longitudinal analyses—to assess the relationships between *change* in social-structural position and *change* in personality.

Table 7.8. Movement to and from the Ranks of the Employed and Change in Personality, Ukraine, from 1992–1993 to 1996.

| | Change from 1992–1993 to 1996 | | | | | | |
| | Men | | | | Women | | |
	(N)	Self-Directedness of Orientation	Distress	Intellectual Flexibility	(N)	Self-Directedness of Orientation	Distress	Intellectual Flexibility
Unemployed in 1992–1993, employed in 1996.	(18)	+.50	–.44	+.28	(16)	+.26	–.17	–.14
Not employed at the time of either interview	(6)	—	—	—	(4)	—	—	—
Employed in 1992–1993, and:								
(a) not employed (either looking for work or discouraged) in 1996	(19)	–.31	+.39	+.01	(20)	–.16	+.42	+.16
(b) a pensioner in 1996	(12)	–.36	+.57	–.46	(17)	+.35	–.16	–.41
Employed in 1992–1993 and also in 1996	(283)	+.02	–.05	+.04	(308)	–.02	.04	.00
P (difference between those who changed from unemployed to employed and those who changed from employed to not employed) =		0.05	0.03	0.32		0.20	0.01	0.34

Note: Employed is defined as gainfully employed for an average of 15 or more hours per week.

numbers, three of the four comparisons of movement to and from unemployment are statistically significant. The findings are consistent for men and for women. Movement from unemployment to employment was associated with an increase in self-directedness of orientation and a decrease in distress—both for men and for women, although the magnitudes of change in orientation were more substantial for men. Conversely, movement from employment to unemployment was associated with a decrease in self-directedness of orientation and an increase in distress—this too both for men and for women. The one cross-gender inconsistency is in what happens when previously employed people become pensioned: Those *men* who changed from being employed to becoming *pensioned,* as best I can infer from an N of only 12, behaved similarly to men who changed from being employed to becoming unemployed—they showed a decrease in self-directedness of orientation and an increase in distress. Those *women* who changed from being employed to becoming pensioned (a slightly larger N of 17) behaved in precisely the opposite way: their level of self-directedness increased, their level of distress decreased. The cross-gender difference in distress, although based on small N's, is statistically significant. Becoming pensioned was a letdown for men, a boon for women.

As for intellectual flexibility, movement into and out of the ranks of the unemployed was not significantly related to change in intellectual flexibility for either men or women. But movement from employment in 1992–1993 to becoming a pensioner by 1996 was associated with a decrease in intellectual flexibility for both genders.

Hence, at the extreme—movement into and out of the ranks of the employed—change in structural location was significantly, substantially, and meaningfully related to changes in self-directedness of orientation and distress, albeit not to changes in intellectual flexibility, except in the case of the newly pensioned. But, since only a small portion of the population moved from employment to nonemployment, or the reverse, this is at most only a small part of the explanation of the consistency of the relationships of social structure and personality despite changes in personality. To pursue the hypothesis that mobility from one structural location to another contributed substantially to the consistent relationships of social structure and personality that we have found for the sample as a whole requires that we look also at mobility among that vast majority of men and women who were employed both in 1992–1993 and in 1996.

Interclass mobility. I begin this portion of the analysis by employing a theoretically derived classification of interclass mobility, the crux of which is that (in my conceptualization) social class represents the intersection of three dimensions of inequality: ownership versus nonownership; supervisory authority over others or the lack thereof; and, among nonsupervisory employees, their employment situation (as experts, nonmanual workers, or manual workers). I classified movement from more advantaged to less advantaged class position, and the reverse, along each of the three dimensions. I also combined the three types of movement from more to less advantaged class positions into an aggregate category, movement to a class position that is more advantaged along *any* of these dimensions. I similarly aggregated the three types of movement from less to more advantaged class positions into a single category. My hypothesis, of course, was that movement from a more advantaged to a less advantaged class position (along any or all of the dimensions of inequality) would result in an increase in distress and a decrease in self-directedness of orientation and perhaps also in intellectual flexibility; and that movement in the reverse direction would have opposite effects. *No such thing.* Neither the people who moved to a more advantaged class position nor those who moved to a less advantaged class position changed their levels of self-directedness of orientation, distress, or intellectual flexibility to a substantial (or statistically significant) degree. For those men and women who were employed both in 1992–1993 and in 1996, I find no evidence that movement to or from a more advantaged class position was significantly linked to change in any of the three fundamental dimensions of personality.

Since the theoretically derived approach had not yielded any evidence that interclass mobility along the more advantaged–less advantaged axes was linked to changes in personality among people employed in both years, I resorted to an empiricist approach: I examined a complete cross-classification of all class positions in 1992–1993 and 1996 to see whether there were any movements from *any* social class to any other social class that were associated with substantial change in any of the three principal dimensions of personality. Even where the numbers were small, I searched to find whether I could discern any patterns of change. I could not discern any consistent pattern. *My conclusion is that interclass mobility was not substantially linked to changes in personality.* There certainly was considerable class mobility, but—quite in contrast to the strong evidence for movement from the ranks of the employed to the unemployed and the reverse—I found no evidence that interclass movement among those who were employed both in 1992–1993 and in 1996 was linked to substantial changes in personality.

Change in social-stratificational position (and its component dimensions) and change in personality. The very strong over-time correlations of social-stratificational position for both men and women mean that change in the social-stratificational positions of those men and women who were employed at the times of both interviews could not account for more than a small portion of the change in personality, because there was little change in their social-stratificational positions. Still, it is possible that change in one or another of the three component dimensions of social stratification—educational attainment, occupational status, and particularly income, which was not nearly so stable—might bear a more substantial relationship to change in personality.

To assess these possibilities, I created change scores for social-stratificational position and each of its component dimensions, and calculated their correlations with change in self-directedness of orientation, distress, and intellectual flexibility. Change in *none* of the component dimensions of social stratification (nor in the overall index of social-stratificational position) is significantly related to change in either self-directedness of orientation or intellectual flexibility, either for men or for women. Change in social-stratificational position or in one or more of its components *is* significantly, albeit only modestly, related to change in *distress*—with an increase in educational level being significantly related to a decrease in distress for men and change in relative income significantly related to change in distress for women. Even these relationships are only modest in magnitude.

The findings for change in social-stratificational position are thus largely consistent with those for interclass mobility. The main lesson of the analyses of both interclass mobility and change in social-stratificational position (and in its component dimensions) is that—for the employed—social mobility does little to explain the consistent relationships between social structure and personality in the face of extreme social change and instability of personality. Only for movement to and from the ranks of the nonemployed does social mobility help explain the consistency of relationships between structural location and personality. By the same token, only for movement from the ranks of the employed to the nonemployed, and vice versa, does social mobility help to explain instability of personality. In fact, instability of personality is just as pronounced for the continuously employed portion of the Ukrainian population as for those who were unemployed at the time of one or the other of the surveys.

What, then, does account for instability of personality? And what accounts for the over-time consistency in the relationships of social structure and personality for that vast majority of the adult Ukrainian population who were employed at the times of both the initial and follow-up interviews? The hypothesis that would have answered both questions had it been valid having failed, I offer a pair of related hypotheses, both of them based on extrapolations from longitudinal studies done under conditions of social stability.

Stability of Social Conditions and Instability of Personality

A central finding of my collaborators' and my longitudinal analyses of U.S. men, going back to our prototypic analysis of the reciprocal effects of the substantive complexity of work and intellectual flexibility (Kohn and Schooler 1978; 1983, Chapter 5), and greatly extended in analyses of occupational structure and personality (Kohn and Schooler 1982; 1983, Chapter 6), is that stability of social conditions helps account *not only for the small amount of change in personality found in those studies, but also for the much greater amount of stability in personality.* (See the extended discussion of the implications of this finding with respect to cognitive functioning in my critique of *The Bell Curve* [Kohn 1996].) *I hypothesize that the obverse is also true: that under conditions of radical social change, unstable social conditions are conducive to instability of personality.* If so, my quest to find linkages between social mobility and changes in personality was doomed to failure, precisely because instability of personality is not linked to social mobility, nor to position in the social structure, but to pervasively unstable social conditions.

Absent any contrary evidence (and I have searched assiduously for such evidence), I infer that conditions of change and uncertainty must have been so widespread throughout Ukrainian society during the period of our study as to produce a great deal of instability in people's personalities regardless of their positions in the social structure and regardless of whether they were socially mobile or immobile. The extreme uncertainty about what would be the future of a Ukraine that was no longer socialist and no longer part of the Soviet Union, but was not firmly established as a capitalist, fully independent, and democratic society must have affected nearly everyone in the country, regardless of class position or social status. Although this pervasive uncertainty must have contributed, perhaps decisively, to the instability of personality, it must have been so widely experienced that it did not much affect the relationships between social structure and personality—except for that (small) proportion of the populace who experienced radical change in the most direct and compelling way, by moving to or from the ranks of the employed. This, I readily admit, is only inference—entirely consonant with the data but by no means demonstrated by my analyses. All I can say with certainty on this issue is that there has unequivocally been a degree of instability of personality in Ukraine during this period of social change undreamed of in past analyses—my colleagues' and my analyses or anyone else's—and, despite that, there has certainly been over-time consistency in the relationships of social structure and personality. Moreover—and crucially—the relationships of social structure and personality are more consistent in pattern (although perhaps smaller in magnitude) than those found for other countries during periods of apparent social stability.

The Role of Proximate Conditions of Life in Explaining Over-time Consistency in the Relationships of Social Structure and Personality for the Employed Segments of the Population

Another central finding of my collaborators' and my longitudinal analyses of U.S. men, and also of studies that we and others have conducted in diverse countries during periods of social stability, is that position in the larger social structure is linked to personality primarily through the proximate conditions of life, job conditions in particular, attendant on social-structural position. The cross-sectional analyses of Poland and Ukraine in transition (Chapter 4) suggest that, even at a time of radical social change, position in the larger social structure is closely linked to the same proximate conditions of life that studies conducted during times of greater social stability have consistently shown to be the principal mechanisms by which social-structural position affects personality. *My hypothesis is that stability in crucial proximate conditions of life largely accounts for continuity in the relationship of social structure and personality even during the ongoing process of radical social change.*

One proximate condition—the substantive complexity of work—has proved to be of crucial importance for explaining the relationships of both social class and social stratification with personality. This was true not only during times of apparent social stability in socialist Poland and in the capitalist United States and Japan (Chapter 1), but also in transitional Poland and, to a lesser extent, in Ukraine at a very early stage of transition (Chapter 4). By the substantive complexity of work, I refer again to the degree to which performance of the work requires thought and independent judgment. Substantively complex work by its very nature requires

Table 7.9. Longitudinal Measurement Model of the Substantive Complexity of Work in Paid Employment, Ukraine (1992–1993 to 1996).

| | Standardized Paths: Concept to Indicators | | | |
| | Men | | Women | |
Concept and Indicators	1992–1993	1996	1992–1993	1996
Substantive Complexity of Work				
Complexity of work with data	.87*	.89*	.90*	.90*
Complexity of work with things	.35*	.31*	.45*	.52*
Complexity of work with people	.81*	.86*	.75*	.88*
Hours of work with data	.58*	.66*	.56*	.54*
Hours of work with things	−.72*	−.47*	−.59*	−.47*
Hours of work with people	.33*	.37*	.25*	.21*
Overall complexity	.79*	.83*	.85*	.95*
Over-time correlation of the concept	.83*		.81*	
Ratio of chi-wquare to degrees of freedom		2.80		
Root mean square error of approximation		.07		
Number of cases	313		363	

*p < .05.

making many decisions that must take into account ill-defined or apparently conflicting contingencies.

I hypothesized that the substantive complexity of work has continued to play a key role in the relationships of class and stratification with intellectual flexibility and self-directedness of orientation during the process of radical social change. To play such a role, the substantive complexity of work would have had to *continue* to be linked both to position in the social structure and to these dimensions of personality, at least as strongly in 1996 as in 1992–1993. Moreover, to help account for the consistency in the relationships of class and stratification with self-directedness of orientation and intellectual flexibility, *the substantive complexity of work would itself have had to be highly stable, whatever changes were occurring in the economic structure of the country or in general social conditions.*

My measurement model of the substantive complexity of work in paid employment (see Table 7.9) is a longitudinal extension of the cross-sectional model developed for transitional Ukraine in Table 4.6 [p. 111]. The information about the substantive complexity of work is based on detailed questioning of the respondents about their work with data, things, and people. These questions provide the basis for seven ratings of each person's job: our appraisals of the complexity of that person's work with data, with things, and with people; our appraisal of the most complex work that the respondent ordinarily does, regardless of whether that work involves dealing primarily with data, with people, or with things; and the respondent's estimates of the time spent working at each of the three types of activity. I again treat the seven ratings as indicators of the underlying but not directly measured concept, the substantive complexity of the job. The model fits the data reasonably well, with a ratio of chi-square to degrees of freedom of 2.80 and a root mean square error of approximation of 0.07.

This measurement model demonstrates one key fact essential for the hypothesis to be valid—that the over-time correlations of the substantive complexity of work were very high (0.83 for men and 0.81 for women).[11] Another key set of conditions essential for the hypothesis to be valid is that the substantive complexity of work be strongly and meaningfully correlated with both social class and social stratification, both in 1992–1993 and in 1996. These conditions are unequivocally met (see Table 7.10). The *etas* for the relationships of social class with the substantive complexity of work for employed men and for employed women hover close to 0.80 both for 1992–1993 and for 1996. The social classes whose members rank highest in the substantive complexity of their work are the (combined category of) managers and employers, and the experts; not surprisingly, those who rank lowest are the manual workers. The correlations of social-stratificational position with the substantive complexity of work for employed men and women are of approximately the same magnitudes as those for social class. One could not imagine more consistent figures—consistent across both time and gender, and highly consistent with comparable figures for other countries during times of apparent social stability. Here, then, is a likely source of stability in the relationships of class and stratification with self-directedness of orientation and intellectual flexibility, assuming of course that the substantive complexity of work continued to bear a similar relationship to these dimensions of personality for Ukraine in 1996 as in 1992–1993—as it, in fact, did.

The definitive test of the hypothesis is to statistically control the substantive complexity of work to assess the degree to which the relationships (*etas* for social class, Pearsonian *r*'s for social stratification) are thereby reduced. Insofar as they are, it is to that extent that the relationships of class and stratification with these dimensions of personality are attributable to the effect of social-structural position on the substantive complexity of work, which in turn affects these dimensions of personality. For the hypothesis to be supported, the percentage reductions in the relationships of both class and stratification with self-directedness of orientation and intellectual flexibility must be at least as great for 1996 as for 1992–1993. If so, then combined with the very high stability of the substantive complexity of work, it would be a fair inference that the substantive complexity of work contributes substantially to the stability of the relationships of social structure and these dimensions of personality (for the employed) even under continuing conditions of radical social change and despite massive instability of personality. Given the findings to this point, I have no similar hypothesis for distress, only puzzlement as to why class and stratification were not significantly related to distress either in 1992–1993 or in 1996, as they were for Poland in 1992.

---

11. The high over-time stabilities of both social-stratificational position and the substantive complexity of work provide definitive evidence that the much lower over-time stabilities of personality cannot be the product of some general methodological artifact. Moreover, the strong correlations of both social class and social stratification with the substantive complexity of work belie any thought that the weaker correlations of social structure with personality are somehow an artifact of random measurement error.

Table 7.10. Social Structure and the Substantive Complexity of Work in Paid Employment for Ukrainian Men and Women Employed Both in 1992–1993 and in 1996.

Standardized Differences from the Mean for All People of the Particular Gender in the Pertinent Sample

	Men				Women			
	Number of Cases		Substantive Complexity of Work		Number of Cases		Substantive Complexity of Work	
	(1992–93)	(1996)	1992–93	1996	(1992–93)	(1996)	1992–93	1996
Social Class								
Managers & Employers	(16)	(15)	1.53	1.63	(2)	(11)	—	.77
Self-Employed	(7)	(16)	—	-.24	(6)	(9)	—	—
Supervisors	(66)	(66)	.73	.71	(62)	(72)	.70	.70
Experts	(16)	(19)	1.31	1.44	(45)	(41)	1.00	.92
Nonmanual Workers	(9)	(5)	—	—	(82)	(74)	.28	.31
Manual Workers	(167)	(161)	-.57	-.60	(117)	(113)	-.94	-.98
Correlation (*eta*) =			.79*	.82*			.82*	.81*
Correlation, Social-Stratificational Position and Substantive Complexity of Work =			.78*	.76*			.81*	.81*

*p < .05.

205

The findings for self-directedness of orientation and intellectual flexibility are generally consonant with the hypothesis (see Table 7.11). The percentage reductions in magnitude of correlation for 1992–1993 range from a modest 19 percent to a substantial 51 percent, with most of the percentage reductions in the twenties and thirties. The percentage reductions generally *increase* by 1996, some of them (particularly those for intellectual flexibility) to the sixties. A puzzling exception is that the percentage reduction for the correlation of *social class* with self-directedness of orientation *for women* drops from 51 percent in 1992–1993 to 15 percent in 1996; but there is no such diminution in the relationship of *social stratification* with self-directedness of orientation for women, nor is there a diminution of percentage reduction in the relationships of either class or stratification with self-directedness of orientation for men. Notwithstanding this single exception, I infer that the consistency of relationships of class and stratification with self-directedness of orientation and intellectual flexibility is partly attributable to the continuing role of the substantive complexity of work in bridging people's positions in the larger social structure and these dimensions of their personalities.[12] There is some evidence as well that the degree to which the relationships of class and stratification with intellectual flexibility are attributable to the substantive complexity of work was increasing from 1992–1993 to 1996, which would help explain the increasing magnitudes of relationship of social structure and intellectual flexibility.

The preceding argument is, of course, predicated on the assumption that the substantive complexity of work is not merely *correlated with,* but has a continuing *effect on,* intellectual flexibility and self-directedness of orientation *even during a prolonged period of radical social change.* The ultimate test of this assumption is to replicate for Ukraine the prototypic model of the reciprocal effects of social structure and personality of the longitudinal U.S. analyses—Schooler's and my causal model of the reciprocal effects of the substantive complexity of work and intellectual flexibility (Kohn and Schooler 1978; 1983, Chapter 5).

I do not have the instrumentation to separately assess the cross-lagged and contemporaneous reciprocal effects of the substantive complexity of work and intellectual flexibility for Ukraine, but I can do the next best thing, which is to assess their *total* effects on each other, whether those effects be contemporaneous, lagged, or a combination of the two. To be able to make precise comparisons of the U.S. and Ukrainian models, I shall modify the original U.S. model to do the same,[13] and

---

12. Unfortunately, I do not have the data to assess whether the finding for Poland (in Table 6.6 [p. 170]) that the relatively low levels of complexity of the activities of the *unemployed* and the *pensioners* contributed substantially to explaining their relatively low levels of self-directedness of orientation and intellectual flexibility also holds for the Ukrainian unemployed and pensioners.

13. The prototypic U.S. model (Kohn and Schooler 1978, Figures 4 and 5; Kohn and Schooler 1983, Figures 5.4 and 5.5) allowed both cross-lagged effects (of the substantive complexity of work at time-1 on intellectual flexibility at time-2, and of intellectual flexibility at time-1 on the substantive complexity of work at time-2) and contemporaneous effects (the effects of each at time-2 on the other at the same time). This model enabled us

Table 7.11. The Degree to Which the Relationships of Social Class and Social Stratification with Personality Are Attributable to the Substantive Complexity of Work, Ukraine (1992–1993 and 1996).

	Self-Directedness of Orientation		Distress		Intellectual Flexibility	
	1992–93	1996	1992–93	1996	1992–93	1996
A. Men						
Correlation (Eta) with Social-Class Position	.26*	.30*	.15	.16	.24*	.62*
Percent Reduction in Eta when the Substantive Complexity of Work Is Statistically Controlled	19%	60%	46%	5%	24%	61%
Correlation with Social-Stratificational Position	.23*	.43*	-.15*	-.10	.51*	.84*
Percent Reduction in the Correlation when the Substantive Complexity of Work Is Statistically Controlled	28%	49%	66%	11%	32%	34%
B. Women						
Correlation (Eta) with Social-Class Position	.25*	.33*	.14	.18	.26*	.46*
Percent Reduction in Eta when the Substantive Complexity of Work Is Statistically Controlled	51%	15%	27%	21%	40%	67%
Correlation with Social-Stratificational Position	.36*	.35*	-.03	-.14	.51*	.59*
Percent Reduction in the Correlation when the Substantive Complexity of Work Is Statistically Controlled	20%	42%	—	91%	38%	64%

*$p < .05$.

207

use the modified U.S. model as a baseline against which to assess the models for Ukrainian men and women.[14]

My hypothesis in this comparison stems directly from the preceding analyses—that the relationships between the substantive complexity of work and intellectual flexibility (for both men and women) would be similar to that in the U.S. model (for men), except for a much lower stability of intellectual flexibility: Thus, I hypothesized *a high stability of the substantive complexity of work, just as in the U.S. model; a much lower stability of intellectual flexibility in the Ukrainian models than in the U.S. model;* and, just as in the U.S. model, *strong reciprocal effects of the substantive complexity of work and of intellectual flexibility on each other.* The first half of this hypothesis, about the stabilities of the substantive complexity of work and of intellectual flexibility, is precisely what the models do show (see Figure 7.1). The second half of this hypothesis falls short of what the models clearly

---

(note 13 continued) not only to assess the *magnitudes* of the effects of the substantive complexity of work and intellectual flexibility on each other, but also to depict the *timing* of those effects. Although I do not have the instrumentation to separate cross-lagged from contemporaneous effects in the Ukrainian data, I can assess the *total* effects by *not* allowing the cross-lagged effects, thereby using the cross-lagged effects of the substantive complexity of work at time-1 on intellectual flexibility at time-2 and of intellectual flexibility at time-1 on the substantive complexity of work at time-2 as instruments to identify the contemporaneous effects, which are thereby converted into *total* effects. By thus modifying the U.S. model, as I do in Figure 7.1, I have converted the strong cross-lagged effect of intellectual flexibility at time-1 on the substantive complexity of work at time-2, and the strong contemporaneous effect of the substantive complexity of work at time-2 on intellectual flexibility at that same time, as depicted in the original model, into strong *total* effects of each on the other. I lose the ability to show that the effects of intellectual flexibility on the substantive complexity of work are predominantly lagged, and the effects of the substantive complexity of work on intellectual flexibility are predominantly contemporaneous, but I preserve the essential finding that the total effects of each on the other are moderately strong and statistically significant. (For a more extended discussion of the logic of using cross-lagged effects as instruments to identify total effects, see Kohn and Słomczynski 1990, pp. 127–131; see also the brief discussion in Chapter 8 of the present book.)

14. The U.S. model is only for men, since we did not have the data to estimate a comparable model for women. Since the Ukrainian data are based on representative samples of men and women, I am able to estimate models for both genders. In the U.S. model we also included as exogenous variables the substantive complexity of work at an earlier time than the baseline interview (based on retrospective accounts of earlier jobs), as well as several social characteristics, some of which we had used as instruments. In the Ukrainian model, I lack the requisite information to measure the substantive complexity of work at a time prior to the baseline interview (which is the primary reason why I cannot separately identify cross-lagged and contemporaneous effects). I do include some of the same social characteristics as in the U.S. model (e.g., age, religious background, mother's and father's educational attainment), but I substitute other social characteristics more appropriate to Ukraine (such as whether the respondent's native tongue is Ukrainian or Russian) for some of the social characteristics that were used in the model for the United States (such as region of the country in which the respondent was raised).

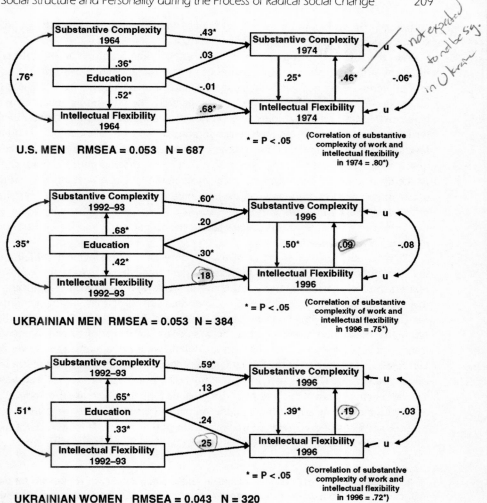

Figure 7.1. The Reciprocal Effects of the Substantive Complexity of Work and Intellectual Flexibility: U.S. Men (1964 and 1974), Ukrainian Men (1992–1993 and 1996), and Ukrainian Women (1992–1993 and 1996).

demonstrate: Contrary to my expectation, *the Ukrainian models do not show strong reciprocal effects of the substantive complexity of work and intellectual flexibility, but strong effects of the substantive complexity of work on intellectual flexibility, and only weak, statistically nonsignificant effects of intellectual flexibility on the substantive complexity of work.* My hypothesis had built on the evidence of stability in the substantive complexity of work, but had not fully taken into account that unstable facets of personality could not greatly affect job conditions. It is not that the substantive complexity of work and intellectual flexibility continue to reinforce each other even during a period of intense social change, but that the substantive complexity of work continues to affect intellectual flexibility, and thereby to link social-structural position to intellectual flexibility.

That the substantive complexity of work affects (and hardly, if at all, reflects) intellectual flexibility well into a period of radical social change confirms the essential premise on which this entire analysis of radical social change has been based, although not quite in the way that I had expected. The continuing relationships between the substantive complexity of work and intellectual flexibility are built on the base of employed men and women continuing to hold jobs of essentially similar levels of complexity even during a time of considerable change in the socioeconomic structure of the country. This is clearly a key to the continuing relationship of social structure and intellectual flexibility even in the face of instability of what under other social conditions is an exceptionally stable facet of personality. *The model thus shows how the continued stability of the substantive complexity of work sustains the relationship between social structure and personality even when personality is itself unstable.*[15]

There is one other implication of this model: It may help explain something that has puzzled me ever since my collaborators and I discovered the weaker relationships of the substantive complexity of work (and the other job conditions that facilitate or limit the exercise of occupational self-direction) with personality for Ukraine than for Poland (Kohn et al. 1997, and Chapter 4 of this book). We originally speculated about whether the weaker relationships of these job conditions with personality for Ukraine than for Poland were more likely a carryover of Ukraine's history as part of the Soviet Union or the result of the extreme conditions of uncertainty that Ukraine was experiencing at the time of the 1992–1993 survey. The present longitudinal analysis provides grounds for believing that a third possible explanation might be applicable, in addition to or in place of the two explanations we originally considered, or even in explication of the second. If the effects of the substantive complexity of work on personality are unidirectional during times of

---

15. I would like to make one last comment on the comparability of the models for the U.S. men, Ukrainian men, and Ukrainian women: As Figure 7.1 shows, the correlation of the residuals of time-2 substantive complexity and time-2 intellectual flexibility in the U.S. model is small (–0.06) and negative, but statistically significant. When a correlation of residuals of reciprocally related variables is statistically significant, that correlation should certainly be a parameter in the model, and not fixed at zero. The comparable correlations for Ukrainian men and women are also small and negative, but not statistically significant. It is my understanding that retaining nonsignificant correlations of residuals (rather than fixing them at zero) is a judgment call, but also that negative correlations should be retained if at all possible. Both because I wanted to make the Ukrainian models as precisely comparable to the U.S. model as possible, and because those correlations are negative, I think it desirable to keep those parameters open. If, *arguendo,* they were fixed at zero, the models would yield the same conclusions as above, albeit with the paths from intellectual flexibility to the substantive complexity of work even weaker than when the model includes that correlation of residuals. (They would be at 0.14 for women and -0.06 for men, the latter both theoretically implausible and statistically anomalous because it is of opposite sign to the reciprocal path from the substantive complexity of work to intellectual flexibility.)

radical social change, with the substantive complexity of work affecting but not being affected by personality (not even by intellectual flexibility), that might help account for weaker relationships. When (as in the United States and as far as we can tell from simulated longitudinal analyses of other countries during times of social stability) the effects of the substantive complexity of work and personality are reciprocal, each affecting the other, those effects cumulatively reinforce the strength of the relationship. But, perhaps when the effects are unidirectional, as appears to be the case for the substantive complexity of work and intellectual flexibility for Ukraine during a period of radical social change when personality is itself unstable, instead of mutual reinforcement the entire relationship is built upon the unidirectional effects. In any case, the evidence is strong that the substantive complexity of work plays an important role in sustaining the relationships between social structure and personality.

Perceived Economic Well-Being

What, then, explains the (consistent) *lack* of relationship of class and stratification with *distress* for the employed? The analyses of Table 7.11 shed little light on this question, for the issue is not what *explains* the relationships of class and stratification with distress, but *why the relationships of class and stratification with distress are so weak*. A partial answer may be given in the zero-order *r*'s of the substantive complexity of work with distress, which are too weak to provide much of a linkage from social structure to distress. Presumably, if the correlations of the substantive complexity of work and distress were stronger, the correlations of class and stratification with distress would be also. But this partial explanation does not explain why the nonemployed segments of the population were more distressed than the employed, thus making the relationship of structural location and distress more powerful than that between social class and distress.

On the basis of the findings from the cross-sectional analyses of the nonemployed (Chapter 6), I speculated that, during this period of economic turmoil in Ukraine, the effect of the substantive complexity of work on feelings of well-being or distress might have been overshadowed by those of another proximate condition of life, a sense of economic adversity. Admittedly, Table 6.4 [p. 167] showed that in 1992–1993, perceived economic well-being explained less of the relationship between (the truncated version of) structural location and distress for Ukraine than for Poland, and did not explain distress for all segments of the nonemployed. But these findings made all the more intriguing the question of whether after three or three-and-a-half years of continued economic turmoil it might play a larger role by 1996.

My index of perceived economic well-being (see Table 7.12) is a longitudinal extension of the cross-sectional model developed for Ukraine in Table 6.3 [p. 166]. It has the same four indicators, now for both years: the log of per capita household income; the respondents' reports about whether their households had experienced difficulties during the past year in buying food, paying bills, providing for entertainment, or having funds for taking a vacation; their assessments of whether their

Table 7.12. Longitudinal Measurement Model of Perceived Economic Well-Being, Ukraine (1992–1993 to 1996).

| | Standardized Paths: Concept to Indicators | | | |
| | Men | | Women | |
Indicators	1992–1993	1996	1992–1993	1996
Per capita household income (logged).	.35*	.49*	.29*	.44*
Respondent's reports on whether his or her household experienced difficulties in past year in buying food, paying bills, providing for entertainment, or taking a vacation.	-.63*	-.66*	-.60*	-.54*
Respondent's assessment of whether his or her financial situation had improved or gotten worse during the past 3 years.	.62*	.41*	.55*	.54*
Respondent's satisfaction with his (her) financial situation.	.53*	.63*	.56*	.58*
Over-time correlation of the concept		.43*		.40*
Ratio of chi-square to degrees of freedom		0.65		
Root mean square error of approximation		0.00		
Number of cases		368		456

*p < .05.

Table 7.13. Correlations of the Substantive Complexity of Work and of Perceived Economic Well-Being or Duress with Feelings of Distress, Ukraine (1992–1993 and 1996).

	Men		Women	
	1992–1993	1996	1992–1993	1996
Correlations of Distress with:				
Substantive Complexity of Work	–.16*	–.05	–.15*	–.18*
Perceived Economic Well-Being or Duress	–.26*	–.28*	–.33*	–.27*

*p < .05.

financial situations had improved or gotten worse during the past three years; and their degree of satisfaction or dissatisfaction with their financial situations. The model fits the data well, the ratio of chi-square to degrees of freedom being 0.65 and the root mean square error of approximation being 0.00. The over-time correlations of the concept, as one might expect in economically precarious times, are only about half as great as those for the substantive complexity of work: 0.43 for men and 0.40 for women.

Using factor scores based on this measurement model, I find that the correlations of perceived economic well-being or duress with distress were stronger than those of the substantive complexity of work with distress (see Table 7.13). These analyses also show that, although perceived economic well-being was meaningfully related to social-class position, with managers and employers having the strongest sense of economic well-being and (among the employed) manual workers having the greatest sense of economic duress, perceived economic well-being was not nearly so strongly correlated with class position and stratificational level as was the substantive complexity of work. Thus, instead of *linking* class and stratification with distress, the sense of economic well-being or adversity contributed little to those relationships and may even have weakened them, by displacing the substantive complexity of work as an influence on people's feelings of well-being or distress.

Does perceived economic well-being help explain the relationship between *structural location* and distress? To answer this question requires that we examine, not only the degree to which statistically controlling perceived economic well-being reduces the *etas* for structural location and distress, but also the degree to which controlling perceived economic well-being affects the level of distress of each of the segments of the population (see Table 7.14). This table shows that statistically controlling perceived economic well-being results in only a modest reduction in the *etas* for either men or women in the relationships of structural location and distress. Thus, one cannot conclude that perceived economic well-being explains more than a minor portion of the *overall* relationship between structural location and distress, either for men or for women. Nor does perceived economic well-being explain more than a minor portion of the variation in levels of distress among the several segments of the *nonemployed,* in contrast to all of the employed considered as a single category. It does not even explain much of the difference between the employed, treated as an entity, and the nonemployed, treated as a contrasting entity.

Table 7.14. Structural Location and Distress—Unadjusted and Statistically Controlling Perceived Economic Well-Being, for Ukrainian Men and Women in 1996.

| | Standardized Differences from the Mean for All People of That Gender | | | | | |
| | Men | | | Women | | |
	Number of Cases	Unadjusted	Controlling Perceived Economic Well-Being	Number of Cases	Unadjusted	Controlling Perceived Economic Well-Being
Social-Structural Position						
Managers & Employers	(15)	-.54	-.34	(10)	-.74	-.64
Self-Employed	(20)	.18	.27	(15)	.26	.25
Supervisors	(69)	-.02	.01	(71)	-.19	-.14
Experts	(19)	-.35	-.23	(48)	-.11	-.11
Nonmanual Workers	(5)	—	—	(86)	-.14	-.10
Manual Workers	(163)	-.08	-.11	(121)	.02	.00
Employed < 15 Hours/Week	(13)	.22	.08	(22)	.39	.35
Looking for Work or Discouraged	(23)	.35	.27	(22)	.35	.32
On Leave or Housekeeping	(8)	—	—	(13)	.16	.10
Pensioners	(15)	.44	.43	(18)	.28	.18
Correlation (*eta*), for All Segments of the Population Above =		.33*	.30*		.24*	.20
Correlation (*eta*), Treating All Who Are Employed 15 or More Hours/Week as a Single Segment of the Population =		.28*	.26*		.18*	.15
Correlation (*eta*), Dichotomizing the Population into Those Employed 15 or More Hours/Week and Those Employed Fewer Hours or Not at All =		.25*	.22*		.17*	.14*

*p < .05.

Note: The numbers for some segments of the population are smaller than in Table 7.5, and the means correspondingly different, because the analyses in this table exclude those respondents who did not provide sufficient information to classify them on the index of perceived economic well-being.

As is evident in Table 7.5, however, the really sharp contrast in people's sense of well-being or distress is not between the more and less advantaged social classes, nor even of all of the employed with all of the nonemployed, but of the *most advantaged social classes* with some of the *nonemployed* segments of the population. Table 7.14 shows (as best one can judge on the basis of small *N*'s) that perceived economic well-being does contribute to the sense of emotional well-being of the most advantaged social classes (the managers and employers of both sexes, although perhaps more so for the men than for the women, and—for males—the experts; for females, the supervisors rather than the experts). Perceived economic well-being may also help explain the distress of *some* segments of the nonemployed, albeit with another gender difference. Indeed, perceived economic well-being helps to explain the distress of unemployed or partially employed men, but not of male pensioners; but apparently contributes to the distress of female pensioners, as well as to the distress of those women who are on leave from their jobs or consider themselves to be housewives. One could hardly conclude from such findings that perceived economic well-being largely explains the relationship of structural location and distress for either men or women, or even that it consistently explains the difference between the most and least advantaged segments of the population, but it does appear to contribute to the distress or lack of distress of some particular segments of the more and the less advantaged segments of the population. I would call these findings consonant with the hypothesis that perceived economic well-being or duress contributes to the difference in subjective feelings of well-being or distress between the *most advantaged* and some of the *least advantaged* segments of the Ukrainian population, but hardly provides definitive evidence for even that circumscribed statement.

Conclusion

The longitudinal analyses of Ukraine have yielded two principal findings. One is that during a period of three to three-and-a-half years of ongoing radical social change attendant on the transformation of Ukraine, there was extreme instability in urban men's and women's self-directedness of orientation and sense of well-being or distress, and (as best I can judge) lesser but still substantial instability in intellectual flexibility—what past studies conducted in times and places of social stability found to be the most stable facet of personality. So unexpected was this instability of personality that my collaborators and I devoted considerable effort to verifying that the finding was not merely an artifact of some defect in method. I am convinced, and have presented evidence (in the text and in notes 4 and 11), that it was not. The other principal finding is that, despite radical social change and instability of personality, the relationships of social class and social stratification with personality—which at the time of the baseline survey of 1992–1993 were generally similar in pattern albeit somewhat weaker in magnitude than those for Poland at that same time, or than those for Poland when it was socialist, or than those for the capitalist United States and Japan—remained similar in pattern after three to three-and-a-half tumultuous years, and some may have increased in magnitude. The one striking exception was that the relationships of class and stratification with distress, although consistent over time, were consistently weak. But when the nonemployed segments of the population are included in the analysis, there is a substantial and significant relationship between structural location and distress, consistent for 1992–1993 and for 1996—because the nonemployed were consistently more distressed than the employed.

Much of the analysis of this chapter has been an attempt to reconcile what, on its face, would seem to be an incompatibility in these findings. If personality was so unstable, how could the relationships of social structure and personality be consistent over time? I initially hypothesized that the extraordinary instability of personality might be linked to social mobility—that people who moved from more advantaged to less advantaged structural locations might have suffered increased distress, a decline in self-directedness of orientation, perhaps even a decline in intellectual flexibility; and that people who moved from less advantaged to more advantaged structural locations might have enjoyed an increased sense of well-being, greater self-directedness of orientation, and increased intellectual flexibility. At the extreme—the extreme being mobility into and out of the ranks of the employed—I did find evidence in support of this hypothesis, in that such movement was substantially and significantly related to consonant change in self-directedness of orientation and distress, albeit not to any significant change in intellectual flexibility. But, for the great majority of urban adults who were employed both in 1992–1993 and in 1996, there was little evidence of any substantial linkage between social mobility and change in personality. Try as I might, I could not find any substantial or statistically significant relationship between interclass mobility and change in personality. As for change in social-stratificational position, the key fact is that, notwithstanding great change in the social and economic structure of the country, and notwithstanding a substantial amount of interclass mobility, there was very little change in overall social-stratificational position. The most that one can conclude is that change in social-stratificational position or in its component dimensions is significantly but only modestly related to change in feelings of well-being or distress, albeit not to change in self-directedness of orientation or in intellectual flexibility. Moreover, different components of social stratification are significantly related to change in distress for men and for women. One could hardly conclude from such findings that instability of personality is closely or consistently linked to social mobility.

What, then, does explain the consistently significant relationships of social class and social stratification with self-directedness of orientation and intellectual flexibility during a period of three to three-and-a-half years of radical social change and despite great instability of personality? My hypothesis was that the same proximate conditions of life that have been shown to link position in the larger social structure with personality in prior studies of capitalist and socialist, Western and non-Western societies and—especially pertinent here—in studies conducted during periods of apparent social stability and of radical social change continued to play a bridging role throughout this period of Ukraine's transformation. The underlying premise of this hypothesis, of course, is that massive social change as experienced during this extended period of time in Ukraine did not affect the linkages of structural location to people's immediately impinging conditions of life. In support of this premise, I found that class and stratification were as closely linked to the substantive complexity of work during this period of radical social change in Ukraine as they have been shown to be in other societies during times of apparent social stability. And the substantive complexity of work was linked to self-directedness of orientation and to intellectual flexibility just as in other countries in more stable times, although perhaps not quite as strongly.

Moreover—a crucial ingredient in explaining the stability of relationships of social structure and personality despite social change and instability of personality—I hypothesized that the crucial proximate conditions of life were themselves highly stable. My analysis examined one key condition, one that has been shown in study after study to be of pivotal importance for explaining the relationships of social class and social stratification to personality—the substantive complexity of work. Its stability even during the three to three-and-a-half years of radical social change encompassed in our study proved to be very high—both for men and for women. And since the substantive complexity of work accounts for a modest-to-substantial portion of the relationships of both social class and social stratification with intellectual flexibility and with self-directedness of orientation, I believe that an important component of the explanation for consistency in the relationship of social structure and personality, even when personality is itself unstable, lies in the stability of the proximate conditions of people's lives. At least one such condition remains strongly linked to position in the larger social structure, and continues to be the bridge from position in the larger social structure to self-directedness of orientation and intellectual flexibility, albeit not to distress. I believe that other proximate conditions of life associated with social-structural position must similarly contribute to the consistency of relationships of class and stratification with these dimensions of personality.

The ultimate test, as far as the substantive complexity of work is concerned, was to replicate the causal model of the substantive complexity of work and intellectual flexibility that Schooler and I had estimated for U.S. men as the prototypic assessment of the reciprocal effects of job conditions and personality. If the above rationale is valid, then the substantive complexity of work should affect the intellectual flexibility of Ukrainian men and women during this period of radical social change much as it had affected the intellectual flexibility of U.S. men during an extended period of social stability. My hypothesis was also premised on the assumption that the stability of the substantive complexity of work, even in a model that statistically controls the effects of intellectual flexibility, educational attainment, and pertinent social characteristics, would be strong for Ukrainian men and women, while that of intellectual flexibility would necessarily be much weaker than in the U.S. model. Thus far, the findings were precisely as hypothesized. What I did not expect, but what in retrospect seems altogether plausible, was that the reciprocal effect of intellectual flexibility on the substantive complexity of work would be small and statistically nonsignificant. But how could it be otherwise? I put the question this way not only because the mathematics of the equations so dictate, but also because the social psychology of the situation makes the outcome inevitable. If personality is unstable, how can personality (in this instance, the dimension of personality I call *intellectual flexibility*) affect the individual's ability either to modify his or her job conditions or to affect processes of promotion, retention, and job selection?

As a corollary to these considerations, I wonder also whether we have here a partial answer to the conundrum that plagued me in Chapter 4 and thereafter: Why were the correlations of the substantive complexity of work (and of other job conditions) with personality lower for Ukraine than for Poland? I think that part of the answer is that, since these correlations are an additive function of the effect of job on person and of person on job, then if only the former applies, the correlations must necessarily be weaker than if the effects had been reciprocal, as they were for U.S. men during a stable decade.

I am not nearly as confident that I have come to a valid explanation of why the relationships of class and stratification with *distress* were weak and statistically non-significant, while the relationships of structural location and distress were stronger and statistically significant. On a descriptive level, the answer is clear: The segments of the population who were most distressed were not any of the gainfully employed, not even the members of the most disadvantaged social classes, but major segments of the *non*employed, particularly the *un*employed and the pensioners. *Why* were these segments of the population so distressed? I hypothesized that it was (at least in large part) because of their feelings of economic deprivation. That hypothesis was partly verified, but it left much of the relationship unexplained. I have a strong hunch, based on the analyses of Chapters 5 and 6 for the Polish nonemployed, that another part of the explanation may be that the activities of major segments of the nonemployed were less complex than those of most employed people; but, unfortunately, I have no data about the complexity of activities of the Ukrainian nonemployed, so my hunch remains untested.

Even taking the equivocal relationship of social structure and distress fully into account, the major lesson from the longitudinal analyses of Ukraine—a lesson that could never have been gleaned from any cross-sectional study—is one of *stability despite change: stability in the relationships of social structure and personality despite ongoing massive change in the social and economic structure of the country, and despite massive instability in the personalities of its adult populace.*

We can safely conclude from this case study of Ukraine that the general pattern of relationships between social structure and fundamental dimensions of personality that has now been found in diverse countries—capitalist and socialist, Western and non-Western, during times of apparent social stability and of radical social change—has been found again *even in the midst of an extended period of profound social change and despite extreme instability of personality.* Moreover, the *explanation* for this consistency of relationship is much the same under conditions of radical social change as during times of apparent social stability—it lies in the proximate conditions of life linked to social-structural position. Even a single instance of a country continuing to show such great consistency in the relationships of social structure and personality under such extreme conditions is enough to demonstrate that these relationships are remarkably robust.

Chapter 8

Reflections

In this concluding chapter of my account of my collaborators' and my comparative studies of social structure and personality under the contrasting conditions of apparent social stability and radical social change, I want to reflect on our distinctive mode of collaborative, cross-national research, on the methods we have used in our longitudinal and simulated longitudinal analyses, and on what we have learned from these analyses.

By a serendipitous process, partly by happenstance and partly by design, we have come to embody in our own work (and lives) a mode of cross-national research rather different from either of the two principal types of research that are the mainstay of contemporaneous (by contrast to historical) cross-national studies—one exemplified by the specialist in the intensive, primary study of one country or region or culture; the other exemplified by the generalist who does secondary analyses of data from many countries.

My collaborators and I have, at first happenstancially, now deliberately, become embodiments of something in between, a distinctively *collaborative* mode of cross-national research. I have become adept at studying several countries, not all at once and not by secondary analysis, but sequentially, one or at most two countries at a time, selecting the countries (or being selected by colleagues in those countries) as advances in knowledge and changes in social conditions make it strategic to do a comparative study of a particular new country or particular new type of country. I cannot claim the expertise of the area specialist, not even of the country I have studied for more than a quarter of a century (Poland), but I am certainly more knowledgeable about each of the countries I have studied than is the comparativist who does secondary analyses of data from many countries. My collaborators are experts in the study of their own countries, but also generalists as they become involved in comparing their countries to the others in our set of comparisons. This truly exciting blend of specialist and generalist roles makes for excitement in doing the research and also, I think, a depth of understanding rarely matched in other modes of inquiry.

I would also like to reflect on what I have learned and what methodological lessons I have derived from doing longitudinal and simulated longitudinal analyses of rather different bodies of data and types of problems as we have encountered them in analyses of different countries at different times. What appear to be different methods of analysis are often, on reflection—though it was not always obvious to me at the time—really much the same methods, but adapted to very different real-world conditions. I have learned some general lessons from such analyses, lessons that I do not believe have been spelled out by anyone else, certainly not by me.

Then, finally, I shall discuss what I believe to have been the new substantive knowledge gained from the cross-national analyses that my collaborators and I have conducted, particularly in the comparison of what we have learned about social structure and personality under conditions of apparent social stability and of radical social change—the core of this book. My overriding thesis is that the cross-national analyses have provided insight into the relationships of social structure and personality that could never have been learned from studies of the United States (or any other single country) alone, and that the comparative study of those relationships under conditions of social stability and social change adds considerably to those insights.

The proof of this thesis is in the findings and enlarged interpretations stemming from this research. I shall at this point add only one comment—that it does not disturb me at all that every new addition to the body of knowledge opens up further questions to be studied. As a poignant example, what I see as the next important question, unimaginable a few years ago, is whether the findings and interpretations derived from the study of Poland and Ukraine during their transformation from socialism to nascent capitalism would apply as well to different types of transformations, such as the one now being experienced in China. I intend to spend the remainder of my already long research career investigating this very question.

My vantage point in all these reflections is, of course, the study of social structure and personality. I leave it to the reader to judge whether, and to what degree, my observations and the conclusions I draw are applicable to other types of sociological inquiry.

A Distinctive Mode of Cross-National Inquiry

In my presidential address to the American Sociological Association (subsequently published as Kohn 1987), I presented an *ad hoc* typology of cross-national research, embodying four distinguishable types of inquiry: those studies "in which nation is *object* of study, those in which nation is *context* of study, those in which nation is *unit of analysis,* and those that are *transnational* in character" (p. 714). My essay focused on the second type, which I characterized as being primarily concerned with "testing the generality of findings and interpretations about how certain social institutions operate or about how certain aspects of social structure impinge on personality." I did not contend that this type of research was inherently more valuable than the other types of cross-national inquiry, but that it was an especially strategic mode of inquiry in the present state of knowledge. In a brief review of a large and diverse body of studies, I illustrated how this mode of research had already contributed to sociological knowledge, both of historical and contemporaneous phenomena, in several domains of sociological inquiry.

Later in that essay (on p. 725), I raised the question, "How many nations are needed for rigorous cross-national analysis, and how should they be chosen?" My discussion of this question began by contrasting the secondary analysis of data from "all countries for which pertinent data can be secured" to the primary analysis of a smaller number of countries, with primary emphasis on the latter:

> We are rarely able to collect reliable data about enough nations for rigorous statistical analysis. Nor are we ordinarily able to study many countries in sufficient depth for intensive comparison. It is not necessarily true that the more nations included in the analysis, the more we learn. There is usually a tradeoff between number of countries studied and amount of information obtained. In this tradeoff, investigators can certainly disagree about the relative importance of number of countries and depth of information. And the same investigator might make different choices for different substantive problems. By and large, though, I would opt for fewer countries, more information. My own preferred strategy is the deliberate choice of a small number of nations that provide maximum leverage for testing theoretical issues.... [T]he deliberate choice of a small number of countries for *systematic, intensive study* offers maximum leverage for testing general propositions about social process. (p. 726)

Having opted for intensive studies of a small number of well-selected countries, I went on in that essay to discuss the choice of countries, the theme of my discussion being that "cross-national research is maximally useful when it can resolve a disputed question of interpretation. It follows that what is a strategic comparison at one stage of knowledge may be overly cautious or overly audacious at another."

I also commented on the central importance of the collaborative relationship in doing this type of cross-national research:

> Both the greatest benefits and the most difficult problems of cross-national research come from the collaborative relationships. If a good collaboration is like a good marriage, rewarding yet difficult, then a good cross-national collaboration is akin to a cross-cultural marriage that manages to succeed despite the spouses living much of the time in different countries, sometimes with considerable uncertainty about passports, visas, and the reliability and timeliness of mail delivery, and despite working in different institutional settings with conflicting demands and rewards. And still, it's far preferable to the alternatives. More than that, without good collaboration, many types of cross-national research are simply not possible. (p. 727)

I find these thoughts of nearly two decades ago a good preface to what I want to discuss now—for the type of research that I both advocate and pursue requires the collaboration of scholars from each of the host countries, with someone, from some country, playing the role of generalist. When Włodzimierz Wesołowski proposed that his protégé, Kazimierz Słomczynski, replicate a study that Carmi Schooler and I had done in the United States, and that I participate in that inquiry (initially as advisor, and "let's see how things develop from there"), he was unintentionally inventing a role for Słomczynski as host-country specialist and another for me as cross-national generalist. I was destined never to be the expert about any society other than my own, always dependent on my collaborators for their expert knowledge of their own countries. He was also inventing a mode of inquiry, in which the same person could play different roles, as when Słomczynski played the role of cross-national generalist in the comparative analysis of Japan and the Western countries of Poland and the United States. There are other variations on the theme, as when Schooler plays both the role of Japanologist and that of comparativist, sometimes simultaneously.

My point is simply that cross-national research that addresses itself to the intensive study of more than one country and is based on collecting and analyzing primary data is nearly always dependent on the active participation of one or more investigators from each of the host countries and usually also on the active participation of an investigator who is less the specialist in the study of any of the host countries and more the generalist. The point would be trivial, were it not for my reason for bringing it to the fore: This mode of inquiry has some very great advantages, as well as some drawbacks; and it also has marked implications for the way that the collaborators (and their families) lead their lives. My late wife once happily remarked that our lives had been transformed by Wesołowski's invitation. I would add that my ability to do cross-national collaborative research would have been greatly diminished if my wife had been less enthusiastic about having Polish and Japanese and Ukrainian and Russian friends visiting our house, sometimes for weeks on end, or who had been less enthusiastic about her own travel or less supportive of mine. This mode of research is a way of life, and either one thrives on it or it would be very painful.

In these reflections on my most recent—but, I trust, not my last such study, for I am now planning a collaborative study of China—I want to reflect on the advantages and limitations of this particular mode of research (and of this way of living one's life).

At least from the perspective of the outside generalist (me), my collaborators and I have had a tremendous advantage in designing the studies and interpreting the findings, because our knowledge of the issues is informed by our participant-observation: in my own case, as is illustrated in Chapter 2, by my limited but far from trivial exposure to the conditions of life being experienced by the people of those societies; and in the case of my collaborators, by their intensive involvement in the life of their own societies.

These advantages have been heightened by our intensive discussions about what to include in the surveys, discussions that sometimes involved all the collaborators, sometimes were limited to me and either the Polish or the Ukrainian collaborators, but always involved bringing the insights learned from the discussion with one set of collaborators back to the other set. Valuable, too, were the questions we asked of the data we collected, and perhaps worth most of all, were the critical evaluations of the interpretations that any of us drew and of my drafts of the papers that have become the basis of most of the chapters of this book. I do think that there are huge advantages to having one's principal informants be one's full-fledged collaborators, advantages that are not available even to the area specialist.

These advantages come at considerable cost: This is not easy research to do, perhaps especially for academics whose time schedules are constrained by the academic calendar, and collaboration across national boundaries entails many frustrations. What, then, motivates the host-country collaborators? I will answer this from my own perspective, not presuming to speak for my several collaborators.

First and foremost: I have long despised what Sovietologists used to call "dollars for data," whereby sociologists from rich countries employ sociologists in poor countries to collect data that they will then have no role in analyzing, nor will they gain any other professional rewards. I think that such exploitation is likely to produce data of inferior quality. Either the questionable ethics or the inferior data would be reason enough to eschew the practice. Admittedly (and also proudly), I have been fortunate in having collaborated with highly qualified and highly motivated colleagues. But my good fortune also demonstrates that such people exist. I think the conditions of our collaboration have also maximized the professional rewards for both my collaborators and me.

No question about it, I could never have done any of the cross-national studies in which I have been involved without being able to rely on the knowledge, thoughtfulness, and hard work of my collaborators. Without embarrassment, I admit that my travels, even to Poland, have been much less extensive than any area specialist would deem sufficient, and my travels to Ukraine and Japan have been even less extensive than that. My knowledge of the Polish language is rudimentary, of Ukrainian and Russian and Japanese nonexistent. My knowledge of the countries I study comes in small part from what I have observed without even knowing their languages, and in much larger part from the expertise of my collaborators, who may also be (most of them are) generalists, but who are specialists in the study of their own countries. I am dependent on them for their knowledge, and I also suffer from not having any independent source of information—other than what I read in books and journals that are published in or translated into English, and, crucially, what the analyses of our data tell me. I will never have the knowledge of Polish or Ukrainian or Japanese society and culture that an area specialist develops (and that my collaborators have). I am hugely dependent on my collaborators in doing research on their countries.

The skills that I bring complement those of my collaborators—some of them technical (teaching my collaborators and their colleagues confirmatory factor analysis and linear structural-equation modeling), and, what may be much more important for our research, a distinct theoretical perspective and a generalist's knowledge of several countries. The combination of my collaborators' knowledge and skills and mine makes for lively discussion and has certainly resulted in research designs and in inquiries different from what either they or I would have done alone, as I hope is evident in Chapter 2 and elsewhere in this book. But, our often being apart has made for instances when their knowledge or mine was missing at crucial times. I am perhaps most keenly aware that I was not present when crucial decisions about fashioning our surveys were made during and immediately after pretesting. Even if I could have been present at those times, my linguistic limitations would have precluded my playing a meaningful part in decisions that to my collaborators must have seemed to be about tactical issues (does one ask the questions about housework or the questions about unemployment to the unemployed housewives?)—but to me were strategic issues about needing to have a uniform index of complexity of activities for all segments of the population for the analyses I intended to do.

I am also aware that I have sometimes not known to ask my collaborators crucial questions about events and conditions of their own countries, which they readily explained to me later. In the main, though, I am delighted by how much I have learned from my collaborators and by how much they have enriched the studies. Still, I also suffer from knowing that I do not have firsthand expertise about the countries. I remain to this day astonished that, when I have lectured to knowledgeable audiences in any of the countries we have studied, no one has ever challenged what I said. They sometimes do, of course, offer different interpretations, and they often tell me of other research bearing on our findings and interpretations, but no one ever says that the emperor (in this rare instance, I) has no clothes. What I have learned from my collaborators and our data rings true to locally knowledgeable audiences.

And what are the professional rewards that help to motivate the parties to such collaborations? For me, they come in research that I love to do but could not have done alone, from fascinating discussions at all stages of the research, from knowing that the quality of the analyses that we publish is much better than I could do alone, from friendships with my collaborators and their families and their colleagues and friends, and from travel to their countries. For them, I trust that some of the same rewards apply. They certainly do not get the dubious rewards of dollars for their data: In fact, they have not only not received dollars for their data, but have mainly raised their own funds for conducting the surveys, and in the case of the Ukrainian follow-up study have actually paid most of the monetary expenses of the surveys themselves.

But I trust and believe that they receive the rewards that "dollars for data" most conspicuously does not pay: They (just as I) have participated in exciting research; they have learned new methods of statistical analysis; have traveled to the United States to work with me on data analysis and interpretation, and to each others' countries for conferences for planning the research, and, later, for interpreting the findings; and have received professional recognition in their own countries and internationally from being coauthors of papers published in major U.S. and international journals and from publishing from this research in their own countries.[1]

---

1. My Polish collaborators have drawn on our research in Słomczynski et al. 1996; Słomczynski et al. 1997, published also as Słomczynski et al. 1999; and Mach 1998. My Ukrainian collaborators have translated the articles of which they were coauthors into Ukrainian and Russian and published them in both languages in the principal sociological journal of their country, *Sociology*; the Poles and I have jointly published variants of two of our papers in Polish journals (Słomczynski et al. 1987; Kohn et al. 1992b). And I have

Reflections on My Collaborators' and My Longitudinal and Simulated-Longitudinal Analyses of Social Structure and Personality[2]

It may seem strange for me to reflect on our longitudinal and simulated-longitudinal analyses in a book that relies mainly on cross-sectional analyses, but as you will see, the findings of the earlier longitudinal and simulated-longitudinal analyses (on which Chapter 1 relies) are fundamental as well to the interpretations of the cross-sectional analyses (of Chapters 4, 5, and 6); and the new longitudinal analyses (of Chapter 7) are the capstone to the cross-sectional analyses.

In reflecting on how my collaborators and I have attempted to do causal analyses of social structure and personality, I would like to discuss three rather different sets of analyses.

Truly Longitudinal Analyses of Social Structure and Personality during Times of Relative Social Stability

These reflections are based on Schooler's and my longitudinal analyses of U.S. men interviewed in 1964 and reinterviewed in 1974 (reported in Kohn and Schooler 1983 and basic to the analyses of Chapters 1 and 7 of the present book). I will state the methodological and substantive lessons I draw from these analyses rather categorically.

1. The first and in some respects most fundamental thing we learned is that it is essential that you take measurement error into account in longitudinal analyses or you will be mainly interpreting noise in the system. We found, as a prime example, that the ten-year over-time correlation of our index of intellectual flexibility when assessed by doing ordinary factor analyses at two times and correlating factor scores based on those analyses is 0.57; but, when assessed in a longitudinal measurement model that takes over-time correlations of residuals into account, that correlation is actually a much higher 0.93 (Kohn and Schooler 1978; 1983, Chapter 5). If you were to do a causal analysis of the effect of social variables on intellectual flexibility based on the first estimate of stability, you would be attributing to the social variables all the variation in intellectual flexibility that really results from measurement error, and you would therefore greatly overestimate the effects of the social variables. Conversely, if you underestimated the stability of the social variables, you would greatly overestimate the effects of intellectual flexibility.

---

published a brief overview of the main themes of this book (Kohn 1999) as a chapter in a Polish *Festschrift* honoring the initiator and sponsor of the Polish research, Włodzimierz Wesołowski.

2. I was stimulated to think about these issues by Słomczynski's invitation to discuss the causal modeling we have done in an address to a symposium on social change at the Institute of Philosophy and Sociology of the Polish Academy of Sciences in Warsaw in September 2004.

2. The second lesson of our longitudinal analyses is theoretical, and we didn't fully understand it even when we published our prototypic analysis of the reciprocal effects of the substantive complexity of work and intellectual flexibility (Kohn and Schooler 1978). Many developmental psychologists still don't understand it, and those extreme reductionists, Richard Herrnstein and Charles Murray (1994), in *The Bell Curve,* didn't begin to allow for the possibility: namely, that social factors can be of immense importance in affecting personality, not only because they help account for *change* in personality, but also because they help account for the *stability* of personality. In the case of the reciprocal relationship of the substantive complexity of work and intellectual flexibility, Schooler and I found in our U.S. analyses that the effect of the substantive complexity of work on intellectual flexibility was 0.17, which is fully one-fourth as great as the effect of earlier intellectual flexibility on intellectual flexibility ten years later. From the perspective of old-fashioned (pre–Urie Bronfenbrenner) developmental psychology—and even more from the perspective of the doubly reductionist Herrnstein-Murray assumption that what they call cognitive *ability* (certainly a misnomer) is entirely a product of genetics and maybe a little bit of early life experience—that would be impossible, for with an over-time correlation of 0.93 for intellectual flexibility, there is very little change to explain. But our full causal model shows that the substantive complexity of work helps explain *stability* in intellectual flexibility. *Stable social conditions help explain stable personalities.* You will of course recognize the crucial importance of this conclusion for the hypotheses and the longitudinal analyses of the Ukrainian data (in Chapter 7).

3. The third basic lesson of our longitudinal analyses of the data for U.S. men is a vivid illustration of how methodological decisions can have serious implications for the theoretical inferences one draws from the analyses. I will state it as a dictum: You cannot validly assess the reciprocal effects of social structure and personality (or anything else) by causal models that take into account only cross-lagged effects, failing to also take into account contemporaneous effects. If you wonder what are the implications of that rather abstract statement, it means that analyses based on methods that do not permit the assessment of contemporaneous reciprocal effects, such as those based on cross-lagged correlations or on ordinary least squares or on any other method that does not allow the possibility of contemporaneous reciprocal effects, are misspecified and invalid.

From a methodological point of view, the explanation for these strong assertions is simple, and is spelled out in Kohn and Słomczynski (1990, pp. 127–131): The ideal is to assess both cross-lagged and contemporaneous effects. If you cannot do both, as is often the case, assessing only cross-lagged effects loses the contemporaneous effects—there is no indirect path in the model that picks them up. But, assessing only the contemporaneous effects permits an assessment of *total* effects, with the cross-lagged effects indirectly depicted as part of the contemporaneous effects, which become *total* effects. You lose the ability to specify the *timing* of the effects, but you don't lose the ability to assess the *overall* effects.

Let me explicate by describing Schooler's and my actual model, which will get us into the theoretical implications as well. In our full model, which depicts both the cross-lagged and contemporaneous effects of the substantive complexity of work on intellectual flexibility and of intellectual flexibility on the substantive complexity of work, we found that intellectual flexibility has only a cross-lagged effect on the substantive complexity of work: It is the intellectual flexibility of the baseline time that affects the substantive complexity of work ten years later, and that effect is very strong, on the order of 0.45. We also found that the timing of the effect of the substantive complexity of work on intellectual flexibility is just the reverse: It is *only* the effect of the complexity of the work you do now that directly affects your intellectual flexibility at the present time.

What happens if you model the processes as only cross-lagged (as is often done) or as only contemporaneous (as I advocate doing and did in Figure 7.1 [p. 181])? If you model the processes as only cross-lagged, you entirely lose the effect of the substantive complexity of work on intellectual flexibility, and will erroneously conclude that intellectual flexibility strongly affects the substantive complexity of work (as indeed it does) but that the substantive complexity of work has no effect at all on intellectual flexibility (which is not true). If, however, you model the processes as entirely contemporaneous (using the cross-lagged effects as instruments), then you find that the effects of intellectual flexibility on substantive complexity are about twice as strong as are those of substantive complexity on intellectual flexibility—*but that both are statistically significant and, over time, the cumulative effect of each on the other will be substantial.* This depiction of process doesn't tell us anything about the timing of the effects, but it does give a valid summary picture of total effects (in this instance, for U.S. men during stable times).

I think it is much better to have the full picture when you are able to do so. I think it is theoretically meaningful to learn that the effects of substantive complexity of work on intellectual flexibility are ongoing and continuous, with the work you are now doing affecting your intellectual functioning at the present time; and to learn that the effects of intellectual flexibility on substantive complexity take time—time to change jobs or to modify one's job conditions in accord with one's intellectual (and other) proclivities. But, if I cannot learn the full picture, then I will gladly settle for a valid estimate of the total effects, as I have done for the model of the reciprocal effects of the substantive complexity of work and intellectual flexibility in my comparison of U.S. men during a period of relative social stability and Ukrainian men and women during a period of radical social change (in Figure 7.1 [p. 181]). I would not settle for knowing only about cross-lagged effects, which give a partial and misleading picture.

Simulated Longitudinal Analyses Based on Cross-sectional Data

Everything I have said thus far assumes that you have truly longitudinal data. What do you do when you have only cross-sectional data? My collaborators and I have faced this situation repeatedly, in analyses of U.S. women, for whom we had collected data only at the time of the follow-up study of their husbands, and for analyses of both men and women in our study of Poland during socialist times.

Karen Miller, Joanne Miller, Carmi Schooler, Carrie Schoenbach and I, with advice from Ronald Schoenberg, developed methods of *simulated* longitudinal analysis for the study of U.S. women, and Słomczynski, Schoenbach, and I refined those methods for the analyses of Polish men and women. I want to emphasize that, although we didn't think much about it at the time, *the methods we invented make sense only for times of relative social stability.*[3] As I shall further explain below, this is why I used the method for some of the analyses of Chapter 1 (of the United States, Japan, and Poland during times of social stability), but eschewed using the method for the analyses of Chapters 4–6 (of Poland and Ukraine during times of radical social change).

The method is based essentially on using real data from a cross-sectional survey as if it were a follow-up survey, and making assumptions about the *rates of change* in correlations between social factors and personality based on findings imported from longitudinal studies of *other* populations to make estimates of what a baseline survey from an earlier time would have shown. The method also requires making assumptions about the stability of personality, which can be based on actual analyses of other populations, or on theory, or even on intuition—*provided that* you test alternative assumptions. The key to this making sense is something we thought we invented but later learned is so well established that it even has a name—*sensitivity* analysis: Whatever assumptions you make, whatever their rationale, you must test the robustness of the model by systematically altering the assumptions. If, for example, you find that the correlation between some facet of social background, for example rural versus urban residence in childhood, and intellectual flexibility increases or decreases by 10 percent over a ten-year period for U.S. men, you assume that it increases or decreases to the same extent over an equivalent period of time for Polish men. But then you must test that assumption: What if the correlation increased or decreased by somewhat less? or by much less? or by somewhat more? or by much more? What would be the consequences for the interpretations you draw? Our findings, in general, were that our simulated models were surprisingly robust when we systematically varied the assumptions.

It was from these findings that we concluded that the reciprocal effects of social structure and personality were, in general, quite similar for U.S. women as for U.S. men (J. Miller et al. 1979; Kohn and Schooler 1983, Chapter 8), for U.S. students in their schoolwork as for U.S. adults in their paid employment (K. Miller et al. 1985; 1986), for U.S. women in their housework as for U.S. women and men in their paid employment (Schooler et al. 1983, Chapter 10), and for employed Polish men and women as for employed U.S. men and women (Kohn and Słomczynski 1990). Does this mean that cross-sectional data are adequate for causal analysis, that you don't need to go to the work and expense of collecting longitudinal data?

---

3. For a somewhat more technical discussion of the nuts and bolts of simulated longitudinal analyses, see note 13 of Chapter 1 [p. 43]. See also the brief discussion of simulated longitudinal models of housework and schoolwork (in the United States) in Chapter 5. A more detailed presentation of the logic and procedures for doing simulated longitudinal analyses can be found in Kohn and Słomczynski (1990, pp. 159–162, 194–196).

Certainly not, not even in times of relative social stability. But let me pose the question from the opposite direction: Is simulated longitudinal analysis better than conventional cross-sectional analysis, which assumes unidirectionality of effects and does not make any effort to statistically control earlier measures of personality when assessing the effects of social factors on later measures of personality, and vice versa? The answer is, most decidedly, yes.

Then why haven't I used the method in my analyses of the cross-sectional data of 1992–1993 for Poland and Ukraine in Chapters 4, 5, and 6? Sadly, because it makes no sense to assume that the rates of change that obtained, say, for the United States from 1964 to 1974 can be used for estimating rates of change for Poland or for Ukraine during a period of radical social change in the years leading up to 1992. I am willing to import (and test!) assumptions about rates of change in correlations of social and psychological variables from longitudinal data for U.S. men to do analyses across culture, social system, and gender for Polish women in socialist times. But I am not willing to make assumptions about rates of change in correlations (or in anything else) based on data from U.S. men (or anyone else) during times of social stability for analyses of what happens during times of radical social change. In all the comparative analyses of Poland and Ukraine based on the cross-sectional surveys that my collaborators did of those countries in 1992–1993, we never once did a simulated longitudinal analysis.

I must admit, though, that the price of this virtue is that I have instead been forced to resort to the very type of assumption that longitudinal analysis abhors: an assumption about directionality of effects. Fortunately, I do not have to assume *uni*directionality of effects, but I do assume that at least some major portion of the relationships between social structure and job conditions, and of job conditions and personality, is the result of social structure affecting (and not only reflecting) job conditions, and of job conditions affecting (and not only reflecting) personality. On what basis can I make such an assumption? Essentially (as stated in Chapter 5) because the patterns of correlations and even the magnitudes of correlations were so similar for Poland and Ukraine in transition to those for other countries during times of social stability that I reasoned that similar social processes must have been involved. That is what lawyers would call *prima facie,* not definitive, evidence. What now gives me stronger evidence of process is the longitudinal analyses of Chapter 7, made possible by the Ukrainian longitudinal data.

Longitudinal Analysis of Data Collected during Times of Radical Social Change

To my great good fortune, my Ukrainian collaborators—Valeriy Khmelko and Vladimir Paniotto—did a follow-up study of Ukraine, on the since-confirmed premise that the process of radical social change was still ongoing in Ukraine three to three-and-a-half years after our 1992–1993 survey. So we have truly longitudinal data during an extended period of radical social change.

The interpretive problem I faced in analyzing the Ukrainian longitudinal data, though, was almost the opposite of the one that Schooler and I had faced in analyzing the U.S. data for men: For Schooler's and my analyses, the problem was the exceedingly *high* over-time correlation of intellectual flexibility and the lesser, but still very high, over-time correlations of most of the other facets of personality that we studied. For the Ukrainian analyses of data collected during an extended period of ongoing radical social change, the problem was the unprecedentedly *low* over-time correlations of *all* the facets of personality we had studied. I posed this issue (in Chapter 7) as one of trying to explain how there could be consistent relationships between social structure and personality (as indeed there were) despite huge instability of personality. For this problem, I had to use three distinct methods of analysis, only one of them being the method that Schooler and I had used for analyzing the longitudinal U.S. data.

One method I used was a very old one—the use of *change scores,* but calculated in a new way that I think makes these scores less vulnerable to the previously valid charge that change scores are notoriously unreliable (because error either in mea- surement at time-1 or in measurement at time-2 makes any calculation of their dif- ference invalid). The new type of change score is based on two fundamental aspects of confirmatory factor analysis, one old and one new. The old is that this type of analysis enables one to measure underlying latent variables devoid of measurement error, meaning devoid of idiosyncratic variance in any of the indicators. The new is that LISREL (here I refer to the particular program) now enables one to calculate something called latent-variable scores. These scores are really factor scores, but they differ from ordinary factor scores in one major way: Their intercorrelations perfectly reflect the true correlations among the latent variables in a measurement model. For a *longitudinal* measurement model, this means that the latent-variable scores accurately reflect the relationships between time-1 measurement and time-2 measurement, which correlations of ordinary factor scores invariably underestimate. Thus, it is now possible to calculate change scores—for personality, for social- stratification position, or for any other interval or ordinal variables—that are much more accurate than the older types of change scores.

I used such change scores to search for, and assess, possible social-structural sources of the massive instability of personality during these three or three-and-a-half years of radical social change in Ukraine. I have to admit that my use of the method proved useful mainly for *dis*confirming a sociologically appealing hypothesis—that the instability of personality resulted from the changes in people's social-structural positions attendant on the transformation of the economy. There was indeed a great deal of change in social-structural position, but aside from the most extreme types of change in social-structural position—change from being employed to losing one's job, or from being unemployed to gaining a job—such changes bore only small, statistically nonsignificant relationships to change in *personality.*

What, then, does explain the massive changes in personality? On this I can only speculate (as I did in Chapter 7), for none of the analyses that I have done sheds much light on this question, except to disprove hypotheses. My interpretation—en- tirely consistent with the evidence presented throughout this book, but by no means proved by these analyses—is that, just as stable social conditions contribute to stability of personality, unstable social conditions are conducive to instability of personality. When the unstable social conditions are pervasive, affecting nearly everyone in the society as they undoubtedly did in Ukraine during this period, so, too, is instability of personality.

The even more interesting—and theoretically more important—issue is to explain the finding that, during this period of three to three-and-a-half years of radical social change, and despite great instability of personality, the relationships of social class and social stratification with two fundamental dimensions of personality—intellectual flexibility and self-directedness of orientation—were largely unchanged. They were, in fact, very much the same as those relationships had been found to be in the United States, Japan, Poland when it was socialist, and Poland during its rapid transformation from socialism to nascent capitalism. How could this be?

My hypothesis was that the same proximate conditions of life that have been shown to link position in the larger social structure with personality in prior studies of capitalist and socialist, Western and non-Western societies continued to do so throughout this period of radical social change. The underlying premise of this hypothesis, of course, is that massive social change as experienced during this period in Ukraine did not affect the linkages of structural location to people's immediately impinging conditions of life. My analysis focused on one key condition, one that has been shown in study after study to be crucial for explaining the relationships of social class and social stratification to personality—the substantive complexity of work in paid employment. *This* part of the analysis was not fully longitudinal, but rather the combined use of longitudinal *measurement models* (to assess the over-time stability of such proximate conditions of life as the substantive complexity of work and perceived economic well-being) and parallel cross-sectional analyses of the data for 1992–1993 and 1996 (to show consistency of relationships and of intervening processes).

Consonant with my underlying premise, class and stratification were as strongly correlated with the substantive complexity of work during the extended period of radical social change in Ukraine as my collaborators and I have found them to be in other societies during times of apparent social stability—correlations in the high .70's and low .80's. Moreover, the stability of the substantive complexity of work also proved to be very high—approximately 0.80, for both men and women. And the substantive complexity of work was linked to self-directedness of orientation and to intellectual flexibility just as in other countries during more stable times, although perhaps not quite as strongly. Finally—the crucial test of my underlying premise—the substantive complexity of work accounts for at least a modest, and in some instances a substantial, portion of the relationships of both social class and social stratification with both intellectual flexibility and self-directedness of orientation.

I therefore concluded that an important component of the explanation for consistency in the relationship of social structure and personality even when personality is itself unstable is the stability of the proximate conditions of people's lives. At least one of these conditions remains strongly linked to position in the larger social structure, and continues to link position in the larger social structure to self-directedness of orientation and intellectual flexibility, albeit not to distress.

The linchpin to this argument rests on again using the very same methods of longitudinal analysis that Schooler and I employed in our analyses of the reciprocal effects of social structure and personality many years ago. I deliberately replicated (with necessary but minor modifications) the prototypic model of those analyses, the reciprocal effects of the substantive complexity of work and intellectual flexibility, now addressed to a quite different analytic problem but with equally incisive results. Quite in contrast to the relationship between the substantive complexity of work and intellectual flexibility being "quintessentially reciprocal," as I had so often characterized it, during a prolonged period of radical social change in Ukraine the relationship became one of the substantive complexity of work having essentially unidirectional effects on intellectual flexibility—which was quite enough to sustain the linkages between social-structural position and intellectual flexibility. Thus, I tentatively conclude that the "quintessentially reciprocal" relationship of social structure and personality that obtains at times of relative social stability appears not to obtain during times of radical social change, but that social structure continues to affect personality *unidirectionally* during such times. Therein lies the explanation of the continued relationships of social structure and personality even when personality is itself unstable. *This* conclusion could not have come from analysis of change scores, or from parallel cross-sectional analyses of time-1 and time-2 data (even when combined with longitudinal measurement models), but required truly longitudinal linear structural-equation analysis.

What Have We Learned from the Cross-National Analyses and—in Particular—from the Analyses of Poland and Ukraine during a Period of Radical Social Change?

In this final section of the chapter and this book, I want to reflect on the development and testing of the ideas developed in my four books—particularly in the two that deal with cross-national research, but going back to the earlier U.S. research as needed—in terms of the major themes that were developed in the entire body of work. I have already done this for one central theme—*the complexity of activities*—in Chapter 5, where I thought that a history of the concept, the *substantive complexity of work,* was a useful introduction to the gradual enlargement of the concept from applying only to work in paid employment to applying as well to activities in any realm that is important to the individual concerned. I now want to sketch the development of other concepts central to the overall interpretive schema. In discussing conceptual developments, I want also to at least touch on shortcomings of these developments—what I see as needed next steps, albeit not necessarily to be done by me.[4]

---

4. I refrain from again discussing a wide range of "unresolved issues in the relationship between work and personality" that I have discussed in previous publications (Kohn and Schooler 1983, Chapter 13; Kohn 1990; Kohn and Słomczynski 1990, Chapter 9), but which have not been at the forefront of attention in the cross-national studies, issues such

The history of my collaborators' and my research has been one of continual expansion of the explanatory framework. It has evolved from comparing white-collar to blue-collar workers' families (which I initially and erroneously called *middle-class* and *working-class* families), to a much enlarged conceptualization of social stratification, and then also to a conceptualization of social class; and from a singular focus on parental values, to an enlarged examination of values and orientations, to a more encompassing assessment of personality (including, crucially, cognitive functioning). It has gone from generalizing from a study of a single, largely nonindustrial city in the United States (Washington, D.C.), to a comparative study of a markedly dissimilar European city (Turin, Italy), then to studies of the entire continental United States, in comparison to Poland when it was socialist and to a non-Western capitalist country—Japan, and finally to a comparative study of Poland and Ukraine during their transformation from socialism to nascent capitalism. During these successive enlargements of perspective, there were also enlargements in how we defined the problems, what new problems we opened up, and the evidentiary basis of my interpretation.

Conceptualization of Social Structure

If one goes back to my study of what I then called *social class and parental values* (Kohn 1959, later incorporated in modified form as Chapter 2 of *Class and Conformity* [Kohn 1969], based on a small-scale survey of Washington, D.C., the comparison was of "middle-class" to "working-class" families, hardly a definitive conceptualization of social structure, but a useful beginning. Particularly because my colleague, Leonard Pearlin used much the same classification in his replication of this portion of my research in Turin, Italy (Pearlin and Kohn 1966; Kohn 1969, Chapter 3; Pearlin 1971), it served to provide *prima facie* evidence that social stratification is meaningfully related to parental values, not only in one rather atypical U.S. city, but also in a contrasting Italian city. The finding, particularly the comparative finding, broke new ground, but the conceptualization of social structure was a bit primitive.

The conceptualization in the nationwide study of employed males, as reported in *Class and Conformity* (Kohn 1969, pp. 10–15; Kohn and Schooler 1969), as a hierarchy of power, privilege, and prestige (a conceptualization taken from Williams 1951; 1970), was much better, but poorly indexed in our study. And calling this conceptualization of social structure *social class* surely confused the distinction—not much made in U.S. sociology at that time—between class and stratification. The Poles taught me better (see Wesołowski 1988), and I never afterwards said *social class* when I was really talking about *social stratification*.

In *Work and Personality* (Kohn and Schooler 1983) my collaborators and I were precise in our definitions and usages of the terms, *class* and *stratification*—the same

---

as the timing of the effects of job conditions on personality, and the conceptualization of personality in my studies. For better or worse, I have little new to say about many important topics discussed in these earlier works, not even second thoughts on positions then taken.

definitions as those employed throughout this book. In my chapter with Carrie Schoenbach (Chapter 7), I reviewed what I considered to be the most useful conceptualizations then employed in studies of the United States and modified the best of them to be consonant with my interpretive purposes (see Chapter 1 of the present book). What was dramatically new in the cross-national comparative research (Kohn and Słomczynski 1990, Chapter 3) was Słomczynski's conceptualization of social class for socialist Poland—a conceptualization that adapted Marx's definition of class to the realities of Polish social structure at that time.[5] (As you have seen in Chapter 1 of this book, my collaborators and I found the conceptualization and index of social class that I had developed for the United States to be applicable for Japan, but requiring modification in the empirical distinctions that define the boundaries of the several social classes.)

In all of these studies, which were done at times of relatively full employment (or, in the case of socialist Poland, of hidden unemployment), and in studies focused on employed men (which did not have to deal with the class positions of housewives), I conveniently ignored the nonemployed. It would have been foolhardy to ignore the nonemployed in our studies of Poland and Ukraine in transition (see Chapters 2 and 3 of the present book for our recognition of this reality, and Chapters 5–7 for its empirical implementation). I think that rejecting the usual practices in U.S. sociology of treating the nonemployed as if they were employed, or as if their class positions were based on someone else's occupational roles, was long overdue.

My provisional solution, admittedly *ad hoc,* of adding the principal segments of the nonemployed population to the class categories of the employed and giving the overall classification a new name—*structural location*—served to demonstrate that the conceptual schema I had used for class and stratification applied as well to the nonemployed segments of the populations of Poland and Ukraine. For the

---

5. I presented a preliminary version of what is now Chapter 1 in the present book to audiences in several countries, with intriguingly different reactions to my presentation of how my collaborators and I conceptualized and indexed *social class,* particularly for socialist Poland. In presentations in the United States, no one seemed to recognize that I was saying anything controversial in this conceptualization of social class for a socialist society. When I presented the paper to a specially convened meeting of the Polish Sociological Association (to celebrate my return to Poland after two years of not being able to get a visa during the time of military rule), Stefan Nowak gave the conceptualization lukewarm approval as tentatively useful, but something less than definitive, a judgment with which the rest of the audience seemed to agree, as did I. When I presented the paper to a conference of Soviet and U.S. sociologists in 1987, however, the conceptualization and I were roundly attacked by a leading Soviet sociologist, but at first I couldn't figure out why. After much discussion, I realized something that any Sovietologist would have known: Soviet sociologists eschewed the concept, *social class,* as applied to socialist society, because to them it connoted a Stalinist conceptualization, no matter what I said to the contrary (see Chapter 2 of this book). Two years later, I presented, not this paper, but the same conceptualization to an audience of midcareer Communist Party officials at the Higher Party School in Kiev, and no one raised the slightest objection. By then, Stalinist conceptualizations were no longer to be taken seriously, certainly not in Ukraine, not even by the Party officialdom.

nonemployed segments, just as for the employed social classes, position in the social structure is linked to individual personality, not only by processes of social selection, but also by the proximate conditions of life attendant on social-structural position. (I will discuss this further below.) I must acknowledge, though, that the overall rationale for the classification of structural location is hardly elegant.

I must also acknowledge that, although I have repeatedly emphasized that social class and social stratification are not the only major dimensions of social structure, I have never studied any of the other main dimensions. Even in the studies of Poland and Ukraine in transition, where I finally have representative samples of women, my treatment of gender has been limited to asking whether the relationships of class and stratification (and their attendant job conditions) to personality are the same or different for women as for men. The answer has consistently been, "the same, with the relationships often stronger for women than for men."

I think that this is a useful type of comparison, even essential in a research design in which the baseline for all comparisons of social structure and personality during a period of radical social change consists of studies of men during times of social stability. But neither I nor anyone else has tested my oft-stated hypothesis that gender matters for personality in large part because of the proximate conditions of life attendant on gender, just as do class and stratification (see Kohn and Słomczynski 1990, Chapter 9). I also hypothesize that race and national background and all other major dimensions of social structure affect personality for the same reason—because all these aspects of people's positions in the larger social structure have important consequences for their proximate conditions of life. I have the audacity to suggest, as well, that the modern-day mantra of "race, class, and gender" (which I think of as the *interaction*—in the statistical sense of that term—of three primary dimensions of social structure) should be addressed in the same way: What are the proximate conditions of life imposed by various combinations of race, class, and gender, and how do they affect personality? I do *not* contend that the proximate conditions are necessarily *job* conditions, which may be much more important for class and stratification (which are themselves based on position in the occupational structure) than for other dimensions of social structure. Discerning *which* conditions of life link other dimensions of social structure to personality is a formidable task, which I leave to others. I just hope that others will tackle this challenging task.

Similarities and Differences in the Linkages of Social-Structural Position and Proximate Conditions of Life Cross-nationally, Cross-systemically, and during Times of Social Stability and Times of Radical Social Change

My original speculations about job conditions as the primary link between personality and position in the social-stratificational hierarchy (and, later, also in the class structure) were in pursuit of an explanation of why white-collar and blue-collar U.S. workers held significantly (but not radically) different values for their children (Kohn 1959 and 1963). In retrospect, my specification of the critical job conditions was lacking in precision, but was at least on the right track, toward specifying the crucial job conditions as the substantive complexity of the work, how closely it is supervised, and how routinized it is.

Schooler and I (Kohn and Schooler 1983, especially Chapters 3, 4, and 6) later examined the psychological effects of a much wider array of job conditions, many of them closely related to social-stratificational position, but our concern in that inquiry had less to do with their possible role in linking position in the larger social structure to personality and more to do with the psychological effects of job conditions and of their place in the occupational structure. Even from this perspective, the substantive complexity of work turned out to be of central importance. It was also evident, though, that job risks, job uncertainties, and job protections were especially pertinent to a sense of well-being or distress. (That these job conditions helped mediate the relationships of class and stratification with feelings of well-being or distress became more evident with re-analyses of the U.S. data in light of our Polish findings.) In any case, the three job conditions that we saw as determinative of the opportunity, even necessity, of exercising self-direction in one's work were of central importance in our U.S. analyses for linking social stratification and social class with self-directedness of orientation and intellectual flexibility in all the countries we have studied.

The cross-national studies carried out during times of social stability did not examine as broad a range of job conditions as did the U.S. study, so they attest more to the importance of the substantive complexity of work, closeness of supervision, and routinization, than to any lack of importance of other job conditions, in linking social structure and personality. In the study of Poland and Ukraine during their transitions, however, my collaborators and I examined a host of job (and other) conditions that we thought might be especially important for the relationships of social structure and personality during a period of radical social change (Kohn et al. 1997; and Chapter 4 of this book). Many of them were, indeed, linked to personality; but such conditions as job uncertainties and changes in organizational structure were so widespread throughout the social structure that they mattered little for *the relationship of social structure to personality*.

I don't think this means that *only* the substantive complexity of work, closeness of supervision, and routinization matter for linking position in the social structure with personality, but that the opportunity to be self-directed in one's work is (so far as our studies have thus far shown) universally and unconditionally important in linking social structure to self-directedness of orientation and to intellectual flexibility, and of conditional importance for linking position in the social structure and distress.

I say "of conditional importance" because even the U.S. analyses show that job risks and uncertainties, and protections from those risks and uncertainties, rival the substantive complexity of work in explaining the relationships of social structure and distress (Kohn and Schooler 1983, Chapter 6; Kohn and Słomczynski 1990, Chapter 8; and this book, Chapter 1). They also show that the countervailing effects of the job conditions that are determinative of occupational self-direction and of the conditions of risk and uncertainty account for the rather weaker relationships of social-structural position with distress than with other facets of personality. I believe that the effects of risks and uncertainties, and protections therefrom, over-rode those of occupational self-direction in the socialist Poland of 1978 (Kohn and Słomczynski 1990, Chapter 8; this book, Chapter 1). But, admittedly, I do not have the concrete evidence to demonstrate this belief—only the remarkable finding that, whatever did account for the nearly opposite relationships of class and stratification with distress for socialist Poland and the capitalist United States, with the end of socialism Poland rapidly evidenced the same pattern as did the United States.

Thus, one conclusion that I draw from the complex of findings about the counter-vailing effects of occupational self-direction and job uncertainties vis-à-vis distress in the United States, along with the extraordinary reversal of the relationship of social structure and its attendant job conditions with distress in the transition from socialist to capitalist Poland, is that it would be invalid to conclude that the only job conditions that matter for linking social structure and personality are those crucial for occupational self-direction. Although the evidence for the importance of other job conditions is less certain and less universal, at least some of them—notably job risks, job uncertainties, and job protections—do seem to be important, perhaps not for self-directedness of orientation or for intellectual flexibility, but for distress and its component dimensions.

I would draw another conclusion as well, this one of even greater theoretical import for our understanding of social structure and personality. Whatever the job conditions attendant on being a manager, or an expert, or a manual worker in social-ist Poland, something about those three structural locations changed very quickly in the transition from socialism to capitalism—resulting in the managers and the experts having a greater sense of well-being, and the workers a greater sense of distress. Regardless of whether my speculations about these changed conditions are correct or wide of the mark, these three positions in the social structure must have entailed different conditions of life under socialism and nascent capitalism.

In Chapter 6, I also drew a parallel to a cross-national difference—between Poland and Ukraine during an early period of their transitions—in the situations of housewives. In Poland at that time, many women were being forced to leave employment to become involuntary housewives, while in Ukraine at that time most housewives wanted to be housewives. Here, too, what is nominally the same position in the social structure entailed very different conditions of life. The moral I draw is that what appears to be the *same* position may actually entail a very different set of life conditions in different systems or even in similar systems at different times. The names of the categories do not tell the whole story.

The larger implication I draw is that none of our findings—not even the oft-found linkage of advantaged social-structural position to the job conditions that I deem to be conducive to occupational self-direction, thence to self-directedness of orientation and to intellectual flexibility—can be treated as universal and uncon-ditional. What I do think is universal is that position in the larger social structure affects individual personality primarily through its effects on more proximate conditions of life. (If you think that this has become a truism, think of all the sociological inquiries that interpret the relationships of social status and one or another dimension of personality, say self-esteem, as a function of status directly influencing one's sense of self.) But it is always problematic, always something to be empirically assessed, just how any particular position in the social structure affects proximate conditions of life, and whether and how those conditions of life affect which aspects of personality. This is certainly not to say that we can draw no general interpretations, but that we must be exceedingly careful and thoughtful in assessing the conditions under which those interpretations apply.

Rather than end this book on so equivocal a note, though, I hasten to add that we have found a remarkable resilience in the relationships of class and stratification to two central dimensions of personality—self-directedness of orientation (and all its constituent dimensions of orientation) and intellectual flexibility. I began, in Chapter 1, by showing that the relationships of class and stratification with these dimensions of personality were much the same in (at least) one socialist and two capitalist societies, and in (at least) one non-Western and two Western countries and cultures. Moreover, the explanation for these relationships was very much the same in all three countries: because of the close linkage of advantaged social position to opportunities to exercise self-direction in one's work. Many analyses and several chapters later, we saw that the same relationships obtained in two countries undergoing a radical transformation from socialism to nascent capitalism; that the same interpretive schema that had been developed for understanding the relationship of social structure and personality for the employed segments of the population applied as well to the nonemployed segments of the population; and that the fundamental relationships held right through the most chaotic conditions of the transformation, even in the face of instability of personality. The specifics of which structural locations entail which proximate conditions of life with which consequences for personality may vary with changing social conditions, but the fundamental relationships have thus far remained much the same for several disparate countries under radically different sociopolitical and cultural conditions. Perhaps there are conditions under which these relationships might fail—as my empirically refuted hypotheses of Chapter 3 had proposed—but the scope of analyses done thus far suggests that those conditions would have to be extreme and, in all likelihood, impermanent.

My Two Visits to My Mother's Village

A Glimpse at Social Change in Rural Ukraine

I wrote this personal account at the suggestion of Robert Randolph, the executive director of the National Council for Soviet and East European Research, who had not only a major financial stake but also an enthusiastic intellectual interest in our research. He wanted to have this account for his State Department and diplomatic clientele. When I was later invited to contribute a paper to a *Festschrift* in honor of my colleague and friend, Aleksandra Jasinska-Kania, I offered this brief paper somewhat hesitantly, for I was not altogether sure of the appropriateness of an amateur ethnography for such a volume, and was rather surprised and very pleased when the editors included it. It was published in Piotr Chmielewski, Tadeusz Krauze, and Włodzimierz Wesołowski, eds., 2002. *Kultura, Osobowosc, Polityka* [Culture, Personality, Politics]. Warsaw: *Wydawnictwo Naukowe* [Scholar].

On my first visit to Kiev, in December 1989, I mentioned to my colleagues and hosts—they were not yet my collaborators and friends—that my mother had been born in a village not far from Kiev and that I was curious to see the place. They quickly gave me several reasons why it was impractical to go there at that time: My schedule of lectures and discussions about possible collaborative research was too full for the four days that I would be in Kiev; the roads were icy; there isn't much to see in a village in midwinter; there was no public transportation, and private transportation would be difficult to arrange on short notice. When my colleagues suggested that, if I returned next spring, they would arrange a visit then, I doubted very much that this was anything more than a polite way of putting me off. Too bad, but my curiosity was not that great, and I really was eager to discuss the possibilities for research—which, as we planned it, meant survey research.

When I returned to Kiev in early June of 1990, my colleagues told me almost immediately, to my delighted surprise, that they had arranged for the graduate-student son of a high-ranking member of the *nomenklatura* to borrow his father's car and to drive us to the village. They didn't tell me that the village was now, and had long been, a collective farm; nor that they were decidedly puzzled about what we should do when we got there. But, as it happened, one of first my lectures this trip was at the Higher Party School. After my lecture, my colleagues told the officials there of our planned trip, and—unknown to me—*they* made the arrangements for my reception.

Two days later, three of us (one of my colleagues, the student driver, and I) left early for our eighty-kilometer journey, took what appeared to be a nearly deserted superhighway, which turned into a two-lane country road immediately after we passed a walled-in community of *dachas* for the *nomenklatura,* past lovely countryside—rolling hills, forests, then, as the countryside flattened, luxuriant fields. As we approached the town that was clearly the administrative headquarters for the region, my two companions joked about where in this town they might find Communist Party headquarters. They guessed it would be on Leninsky Prospekt. They were wrong: It was on October 5th Revolution Street. The street name hardly mattered: The moment we got into the center of the town, it was evident that this was the dominant building, not only by virtue of its size (a three-story office building in a town of much smaller buildings), but also because of its huge billboard with colorful photographs and banners and slogans. We parked, walked up two flights of stairs, noticing long lines of people waiting in the corridors to see officials, to the third floor—its corridors empty—to the office of the Secretary for Ideology of the Communist Party of this region of Ukraine. The Secretary, a pleasant-looking, rather beefy man, dressed formally in a rather shabby-looking suit and tie, greeted us at the entrance to his inner office. There, under the watchful eye of the inevitable painting of Lenin, he lectured us about agricultural production for the region—not an uninteresting lecture, but why? It was only beginning to dawn on me that I was being given an official reception to the village.

In time (it seemed to me a very long time, but it was probably less than half an hour), the Secretary stood up. I eagerly reached out to shake his hand and get on with the journey to the village, when my colleague (who had been translating, and would continue to do so) pulled my arm back and told me that the Secretary would be accompanying us. Now it was fully evident that this was an officially arranged trip.

It was only a few minutes' drive to the village. The main street of the village consisted of a long row of pleasant-looking one-story cottages, built of building block, with front yards given over to flowers, vegetables, or fruit trees, and large back yards for vegetables, chickens, a few pigs. In the center of town, behind a large and imposing statue of Lenin, were the headquarters of the collective farm, and nearby buildings that I later learned were the kindergarten, three small stores, and a "cultural" building that I take it was used for movies and more or less official gatherings. We parked at the side of the headquarters building, almost abreast of what turned out to be the official welcoming committee: the director of the collective farm (a somewhat Oriental-looking man, also suited and tied), the president of the village Soviet (in our terms, the mayor), the president of the (official) trade union, and two ladies holding embroidered scarves which served as platforms for loaves of bread, salt, and a small bag of Ukrainian soil—symbolic gifts to be taken to my mother. Speeches and photos, all of this observed from a respectful distance by a small cluster of old folks, the men in shabby slacks and jackets, the women in babushkas and heavy skirts and wool blouses, this on a rather warm day. Then to the director's office (with not a single statue or picture of Lenin to be seen anywhere along the way), with all of the officialdom tagging along, for questions about my mother's family, and statistics about the farm and village: population about 650, half directly employed by the collective farm, the others working in enterprises directly or indirectly dependent on the farm. A clinic, staffed by "subdoctors," with further medical care in the town. A café (which didn't seem to be open). A kindergarten. I think he said a primary school, too, but I never saw such a building so I surmise that the older children are bussed to the nearby town for post-kindergarten schooling. Main crops: wheat, peas, corn, sugar beets, some animals—I saw chickens, dairy cows, and in people's private plots behind their houses, pigs.

Then a tour—*all of us.* (I could only imagine what the locals thought of this.) My first thought was, Potemkin Village. But it was more than that. I actually saw quite a lot, and I doubt that I could have seen it any other way. The shops, which sold only the things that people who raise and preserve their own food might need: bread (not flour), salt, cooking utensils, toiletries, vodka, clothing (and materials for making same), but no meat or vegetables, which were not needed. Then we invaded the home of the woman who runs the "cultural center," who was flustered and apologetic—her house was not in order because of recent rains, and she wasn't expecting us; but she was exceedingly gracious. Pleasant and spacious house, several rooms, all of them larger than in my colleagues' apartments in Kiev, the front yard given over to strawberries, the large back yard—I was told, a full hectare—intensively gardened, along with caged chickens, rabbits, and a single pig, another having been slaughtered last week. Furniture Soviet-nondescript. What was most striking was the formal room. No Lenin here, but icons of Jesus and Mary.

Was this the best house in town? No way to know, but on the outside it was undifferentiable from all the other houses I could see from the street, and I was assured that all the farm families have a hectare of land and produce all their own vegetables and about a quarter of their own meat (but no milk or dairy products) on the plots behind their houses. It looked that way.

Next, we piled into a Soviet equivalent of a Land Rover, and drove for perhaps two or three kilometers through deep mud, slipping and sliding all the way, past an immense shed covering tractors and other farm machinery—I could not tell what their state of repair was, since none could be used today because of the mud—a dairy barn, chickens, and endless fields, the crops mainly at an early stage, with the peas a little higher than the other crops and in blossom. All of the fields seemed well tended. Proudly, the director told me that there was no stoop labor: Everything was mechanized. He also told me that the rich black topsoil is more than a meter deep. Then back to the village center, with the director continuing to provide knowledgeable explanations and answers to my many questions.

All the while, as we encountered people, the director asked whether they knew, or knew of, my mother's family. I thought these inquiries a charade, because my grandfather had left the village in 1905, to escape being drafted into the Czar's army, which would have been a horrible fate for a Jew at that time. He somehow got across Europe, traveled steerage to New York, and saved enough money working as a harness-maker to send for his oldest daughter, who worked at a sewing machine in a sweatshop. They both saved until they could bring the next oldest daughter, and then the next, until finally, around 1911 or possibly 1913, they were able to bring his wife and the youngest child, my mother. Who was likely to remember a family that emigrated during the years 1905 to 1911 or 1913, three-quarters of a century ago?

Next, the kindergarten. The children were all seated on benches outside the building. The teacher was wearing what appeared to be her Sunday best. I asked whether I might take a photo of the children, was asked to wait, while the teacher's assistant ran into the building to get a towel, with which the teacher wiped all the children's noses; *then* it was alright to take their photos. With the children still outside, under the supervision of the assistant, the teacher then gave me a tour of the building: playrooms, a classroom, a nap room, the teacher's study. It all seemed well equipped and exceedingly pleasant, but much too neat to be real. I need not have been so suspicious. Once I had seen the building, the children were allowed in. They came in a rush, and within a minute or two there were toys all over the floor and they were having a wonderfully undisciplined time.

Some presents: a *pêpier-maché* dish and pitcher, made by the children, mainly yellow, very attractive, and much too fragile to ship or to carry to my mother. (It became a gift to a colleague's grandchild.) A bottle of vodka, for me.

As we were preparing to leave, someone brought over the oldest woman in town, who just might possibly remember my mother's family. I repeated my description, which my colleague again translated into Ukrainian—my grandfather's name was Mickenberg, he was a harness-maker, he left in 1905.... The woman responded, "There used to be Jews in the village, but they had money, so of course they left." I thought of my grandparents' desperate poverty, and also wondered at the meaning of "of course they left." Would only Jews have, of course, left? There was no opportunity to ask, for the director of the farm immediately commented, in Ukrainian, which my colleague translated to me: "I wish that what she said were true. There were still Jews in the village when the Nazis came. They were all killed at Babi Yar."

Five years later, June 1995. I had been to Kiev several times in the intervening years, although not recently. My colleagues—by now, my close collaborators and friends—and I were working intensively on assessing the findings of our research. We decided to take Saturday off. They asked me where I might like to go on a one-day jaunt. It was too short a time for any extensive traveling, but I thought it might be interesting to return to my mother's village, to see what changes might have occurred in these momentous five years. They jumped at the idea, and we planned an excursion—both of my collaborators, their wives, one grandchild, and me.

This time there was no need to get the sponsorship of the Higher Party School, there was no longer a Higher Party School. (The school had long since been converted into a school of "politology," which—as best I can infer—meant free-market economics as taught by former "scientific communists," in the same building, but with the huge marble statue of Lenin removed from its lobby. Not surprisingly, that school had soon failed.) All we needed to do was to drive to the village. How? Well, both of my collaborators now had cars. Those cars, like most of those on the now-crowded streets of Kiev, were Western European imports, cars so old and in such bad shape that there was no market for them in Western Europe or even in Eastern Europe, but they still could be sold to people in the former Soviet Union. We took both cars, partly because they were too small to hold our entire party and partly because one car could tow the other if either of them broke down—a good possibility on a round trip of 160 kilometers. (One did break down, but we didn't have to use the two strong nylon ropes we had brought along for possible towing; the car had developed a leak in its cooling system and we were able to supply it with enough water to make it back to Kiev on its own.)

The drive was as lovely as I had remembered, through largely unchanged countryside: a few building projects here and there, but no dramatic differences, other than in the road signs, which were now in Ukrainian, not Russian. (Both languages use Cyrillic script, but a few of the letters are different. Even someone who speaks neither language soon notices the differences.) As we drove through the town where we had visited Communist Party headquarters, it was evident that the same building was used for administration, but now without the billboard and its colorful posters and slogans.

The village, too, seemed much the same. This being a Saturday, there was not much activity to be seen, other than some men leading a herd of dairy cows down the main street, and a woman selling pieces of a freshly butchered pig on a little stand in front of her house. Lenin still held his place of honor in front of the administrative building for the collective farm, which was still a collective farm. One of the shops was open, selling much the same goods as before, albeit with a noticeable increase in imported toiletries; the bread, which this time we unceremoniously bought, was delicious. The external appearance of the buildings was much the same as I had remembered—the school, the barns and tractor sheds, the café (again, or still, closed), people's homes. The front yard of the house that we had invaded was again full of strawberries, the only yard thus gardened.

We did see a few signs of new construction and reconstruction: a new house being built here, a barn being rebuilt there, but—until we were almost ready to leave the village—relatively little overall. Then, on the far end of the village, I spotted what seemed to be a modernistic church tower, with its onion-shaped dome signifying that it was Orthodox. (What else could it possibly have been in this part of rural Ukraine?) Some inquiries yielded the information that it was not really a church, but a chapel, i.e., there was no regular priest in attendance, but a priest from a nearby town came to officiate at important occasions. We walked over to the church, which seemed to have been fully constructed but was still in the process of being furnished. It had been built at the edge of the village graveyard, a beautiful place because of the Ukrainian practice of growing flowering plants on the graves, so that at this time of year the graveyard was in full and lovely bloom.

And then we spotted another change in the physical appearance of the village. At the edge of the graveyard, perhaps fifty meters from the church, was a new monument. From the distance, it appeared to be typical of monuments all over the former Soviet Union, commemorating those who died in the Great Patriotic War. But why should such a monument have been constructed only recently, and not years ago? We walked over. No patriotic inscriptions. Just a long list of names, headed by the dates, 1932–1937. No Ukrainian would have to be told that these were the years when, under Stalin's orders, farmers who resisted the collectivization of agriculture were murdered, and then the rural population was systematically starved as their produce was taken to the cities in the brutal process of industrialization.

Only two apparent changes, but how much they signified. A church and a monument to Stalin's victims. Thus was social change manifested in a village of independent Ukraine.

References

Baxter, Janeen. 1994. "Is Husband's Class Enough? Class Location and Class Identity in the United States, Sweden, Norway, and Australia." *American Sociological Review* 59:220–235.

Bonjean, Charles M., Richard J. Hill, and S. Dale McLemore. 1967. *Sociological Measurement: An Inventory of Scales and Indices.* San Francisco: Chandler.

Boskoff, Alvin. 1966. "Social Change: Major Problems in the Emergence of Theoretical and Research Foci." Pp. 260–302 in *Modern Sociological Theory in Continuity and Change,* edited by Howard Becker and Alvin Boskoff. New York: Holt, Rinehart, and Winston.

Cole, Robert E. 1971. *Japanese Blue Collar: The Changing Tradition.* Berkeley: University of California Press.

Cole, Robert E., and Ken'ichi Tominaga. 1976. "Japan's Changing Occupational Structure and Its Significance." Pp. 53–95 in *Japanese Industrialization and Its Social Consequences,* edited by Hugh Patrick. Berkeley: University of California Press.

Coser, Rose Laub. 1975. "The Complexity of Roles as a Seedbed of Individual Autonomy." Pp. 237–263 in *The Idea of Social Structure: Papers in Honor of Robert K. Merton,* edited by Lewis A. Coser. New York: Harcourt Brace Jovanovich.

Costa, Paul T., Jr., Jeffrey H. Herbst, Robert R. McCrae, and Ilene C. Siegler. 2000. "Personality at Midlife: Stability, Intrinsic Maturation, and Response to Life Events." *Assessment* 7:365–378.

Cummings, William K. 1980. *Education and Equality in Japan.* Princeton, N. J.: Princeton University Press.

Cummings, William K., and Atsushi Naoi. 1974. "Social Background, Education, and Personal Advancement in a Dualistic Employment System." *Developing Economics* 12:245–274.

Daniłowicz, Pawel, and Pawel Sztabinski. 1977. *Pytania Metryczkowe.* Warsaw: Institute of Philosophy and Sociology of the Polish Academy of Sciences.

Drazkiewicz, Jerzy. 1980. "Development of Social Structure and the Concept of Interest." *Polish Sociological Bulletin* 1:23–38.

Duncan, Otis Dudley. 1961. "A Socioeconomic Index for All Occupations" and "Properties and Characteristics of the Socioeconomic Index." Pp. 109–138 and 139–161 in *Occupations and Social Status,* edited by Albert J. Reiss et al. New York: Free Press of Glencoe.

Eisenberg, Philip, and Paul F. Lazarsfeld. 1938. "The Psychological Effects of Unemployment." *Psychological Bulletin* 35:358–390.

Feather, N. T. 1997. "Economic Deprivation and the Psychological Impact of Unemployment." *Australian Psychologist* 32:37–45.

Form, William. 1976. "Field Problems in Comparative Research: The Politics of Distrust." Appendix B (pp. 277–299) in his *Blue-Collar Stratification.* Princeton, N.J.: Princeton University Press.

———. 1987. "On the Degradation of Skills." Pp. 29–47 in W. Richard Scott and James F. Short, Jr., eds., *Annual Review of Sociology.* Vol. 13. Palo Alto, CA: Annual Reviews, Inc.

Gagliani, Giorgio. 1981. "How Many Working Classes?" *American Journal of Sociology* 87:259–285.

Goldthorpe, John H. 1983. "Women and Class Analysis: In Defense of the Conventional View." *Sociology* 17:465–488.

Gutierrez, Roberto. 1995. *Unregulated Work and Its Effects on Personality: An Inquiry into the Impact of Social Structure.* PhD dissertation, Department of Sociology, Johns Hopkins University, Baltimore, MD.

Hashimoto, Kenji. 1986. "*Gendai Nihon Shakai no Kaikyu Bunseki.*" [Class Analysis of Modern Japanese Society.] *Shakaigaku Hyoron* [Japanese Sociological Review] 37:175–190.

Herrnstein, Richard J., and Charles Murray. 1994. *The Bell Curve: Intelligence and Class Structure in American Life.* New York: Free Press.

Hodge, Robert W., Paul M. Siegel, and Peter H. Rossi. 1964. "Occupational Prestige in the United States, 1925–63." *American Journal of Sociology* 70:286–302.

Hollingshead, August B., and Fredrick C. Redlich. 1958. *Social Class and Mental Illness: A Community Study.* New York: Wiley.

Horie, Masanori. 1962. *Nihon no Rodosha Kaikyu.* [The Japanese Working Class]. Tokyo: Iwanami Shoten.

House, James S. 1977. "The Three Faces of Social Psychology." *Sociometry* 40:161–177.

———. 1981. "Social Structure and Personality." Pp. 525–561 in *Social Psychology: Sociological Perspectives,* edited by Morris Rosenberg and Ralph H. Turner. New York: Basic Books.

Hryniewicz, Tadeusz. 1983. "*Metodologiczne Aspekty Analizy Struktury Klasowej w Polsce. Stosunki Produkcji, Wladza, Klasy Spoleczne.*" [Methodological Aspects of the Analysis of Class Structure in Poland. Relations of Production, Power, Social Classes.] *Studia Socjologiczne* 1:43–73.

Jahoda, Marie. 1981. "Work, Employment, and Unemployment: Values, Theories, and Approaches in Social Research." *American Psychologist* 36:184–91.

———. 1982. *Employment and Unemployment: A Social-Psychological Analysis.* Cambridge, UK: Cambridge University Press.

(Japanese) Bureau of Statistics. 1970. *Employment Structure of Japan (Summary of the Results of 1968 Employment Status Survey).* Tokyo: Office of the Prime Minister.

Johnson, Samuel. 1755. *Dictionary of the English Language.* Privately printed; reprinted in 1971 by Times Books, London.

Jöreskog, Karl G. 2000. "Latent Variable Scores and Their Uses." Accessible on the Web site, http://www.ssicentral.com/lisrel/column6.htm.

Kalleberg, Arne L., and Larry J. Griffin. 1980. "Class, Occupation, and Inequality in Job Rewards." *American Journal of Sociology* 85:731–768.

Khmelko, Valeriy. 2002. "Macrosocial Change in Ukraine: The Years of Independence." *Sisyphus: Sociological Studies* XVI:125–136.

Kishimoto, Eitaro, ed. 1962. *Nihon no White-Collar.* [Japanese White-Collar]. Tokyo: Mineruva Shobo.

Kohn, Melvin L. 1959. "Social Class and Parental Values." *American Journal of Sociology* 64:337–351.

———. 1963. "Social Class and Parent-Child Relationships: An Interpretation." *American Journal of Sociology* 68:471–480.

———. 1969. *Class and Conformity: A Study in Values.* Homewood, IL: Dorsey Press. (Second edition, University of Chicago Press, 1977.)

———. 1971. "Bureaucratic Man: A Portrait and an Interpretation." *American Sociological Review* 36:461–474.

———. 1980. "Job Complexity and Adult Personality." Pp. 193–210 in *Themes of Work and Love in Adulthood,* edited by Neil J. Smelser and Erik H. Erikson. Cambridge, MA: Harvard University Press.

———. 1983. "On the Transmission of Values in the Family: A Preliminary Formulation." Pp. 3–12 in *Research in Sociology of Education and Socialization.* Vol. 4, edited by Alan C. Kerckhoff. Greenwich, CT: JAI Press.

———. 1987. "Cross-National Research as an Analytic Strategy: American Sociological Association, 1987 Presidential Address." *American Sociological Review* 52:713–731.

———. 1989a. "Social Structure and Personality: A Quintessentially Sociological Approach to Social Psychology." *Social Forces* 68:26–33.

———, ed. 1989b. *Cross-National Research in Sociology.* Newbury Park, CA: Sage/ASA Presidential Series.

———. 1990. "Unresolved Issues in the Relationship between Work and Personality." Pp. 36–68 in *The Nature of Work: Sociological Perspectives,* edited by Kai Erikson and Steven P. Vallas. New Haven, CT: Yale Univ. Press.

———. 1993. "Doing Social Research under Conditions of Radical Social Change: The Biography of an Ongoing Research Project." [1992 Cooley-Mead Award Lecture, American Sociological Association.] *Social Psychology Quarterly* 56:4–20.

———. 1996. "Review Essay: The *'Bell Curve'* from the Perspective of Research on Social Structure and Personality." *Sociological Forum* 11: 395–411.

———. 1999. "Social Structure and Personality under Conditions of Apparent Social Stability and Radical Social Change." Pp. 50–69 in *Power and Social Structure: Essays in Honor of Włodzimierz Wesołowski,* edited by Aleksandra Jasinska-Kania, Melvin L. Kohn, and Kazimierz Słomczynski. Warsaw: University of Warsaw Press.

———. 2002. "My Two Visits to My Mother's Village: A Glimpse at Social Change in Rural Ukraine." Pp. 457–462 in *Kultura, Osobowosc, Polityka* [Culture, Personality, Politics], edited by Piotr Chmielewski, Tadeusz Krauze, and Włodzimierz Wesołowski. Warsaw: *Wydawnictwo Naukowe* [Scholar].

Kohn, Melvin L., Valeriy Khmelko, Vladimir Paniotto, and Ho-fung Hung. 2004. "Social Structure and Personality during the Process of Radical Social Change: A Study of Ukraine in Transition." *Comparative Sociology 3:3–4:1–46.*

Kohn, Melvin L., Atsushi Naoi, Carrie Schoenbach, Carmi Schooler, and Kazimierz M. Słomczynski. 1990. "Position in the Class Structure and Psychological Functioning in the United States, Japan, and Poland." *American Journal of Sociology* 95:964–1008.

Kohn, Melvin L., and Carrie Schoenbach. 1983. "Class, Stratification, and Psychological Functioning." Pp. 154–189 in *Work and Personality: An Inquiry into the Impact of Social Stratification,* by Melvin L. Kohn and Carmi Schooler. Norwood, N.J.: Ablex.

———. 1993. "Social Stratification, Parents' Values, and Children's Values." Pp. 118–151 in *New Directions in Attitude Measurement,* edited by Dagmar Krebs and Peter Schmidt. Berlin: Walter de Gruyter.

Kohn, Melvin L., and Carmi Schooler. 1969. "Class, Occupation, and Orientation." *American Sociological Review* 34:659–678.

———. 1973. "Occupational Experience and Psychological Functioning: An Assessment of Reciprocal Effects." *American Sociological Review* 38:97–118.

———. 1978. "The Reciprocal Effects of the Substantive Complexity of Work and Intellectual Flexibility: A Longitudinal Assessment." *American Journal of Sociology* 84 (July): 24–52.

———. 1982. "Job Conditions and Personality: A Longitudinal Assessment of Their Reciprocal Effects." *American Journal of Sociology* 87:1257–1286.

———. With the collaboration of Joanne Miller, Karen A. Miller, Carrie Schoenbach, and Ronald Schoenberg. 1983. *Work and Personality: An Inquiry into the Impact of Social Stratification.* Norwood, N.J.: Ablex.

———. 1986. *Praca a Osobowosc: Studium Wspolzaleznosci* [Work and Personality: A Study of Their Interrelationships], translated and edited by Bogdan Mach. *Warszawa: Panstwowe Wydawnictwo Naukowe* [Polish Scientific Publishers].

Kohn, Melvin L., and Kazimierz M. Słomczynski. With the collaboration of Carrie Schoenbach. 1990. *Social Structure and Self-Direction: A Comparative Analysis of the United States and Poland.* Oxford: Basil Blackwell.

Kohn, Melvin L., Kazimierz M. Słomczynski, Krystyna Janicka, Valeriy Khmelko, Bogdan W. Mach, Vladimir Paniotto, and Wojciech Zaborowski. 1992a. "Social Structure and Personality under Conditions of Radical Social Change: A Comparative Study of Poland and Ukraine." Pp. 97–111 in *Power Shifts and Value Changes in the Post Cold War World: Proceedings (Selected Papers) of the Joint Symposium of the International Sociological Association's Research Committees: Comparative Sociology and Sociology of Organizations,* edited by Hiroshi Mannari, Harry K. Nishio, Joji Watanuki, and Koya Azumi. Kurashiki City, Japan: Kibi International University.

Kohn, Melvin L., Kazimierz M. Słomczynski, Krystyna Janicka, Valeriy Khmelko, Bogdan W. Mach, Vladimir Paniotto, Wojciech Zaborowski, Roberto Gutierrez, and Cory Heyman. 1997. "Social Structure and Personality under Conditions of Radical Social Change: A Comparative Analysis of Poland and Ukraine." *American Sociological Review* 62:614–638.

Kohn, Melvin L., Kazimierz M. Słomczynski, Krystyna Janicka, Bogdan Mach, and Wojciech Zaborowski. 1992b. "Social Structure and Personality under Conditions of Radical Social Change: A Theoretical Approach and Research Strategy." *Sisyphus: Sociological Studies* (Polish Academy of Sciences) 2 (VIII):145–159.

Kohn, Melvin L., Kazimierz M. Słomczynski, and Carrie Schoenbach. 1986. "Social Stratification and the Transmission of Values in the Family: A Cross-National Assessment." *Sociological Forum* 1:73–102.

Kohn, Melvin L., Wojciech Zaborowski, Krystyna Janicka, Valeriy Khmelko, Bogdan W. Mach, Vladimir Paniotto, Kazimierz M. Słomczynski, Cory Heyman, and Bruce

Podobnik. 2002. "Structural Location and Personality during the Transformation of Poland and Ukraine." *Social Psychology Quarterly* 65:364–385.

Kohn, Melvin L., Wojciech Zaborowski, Krystyna Janicka, Bogdan W. Mach, Valeriy Khmelko, Kazimierz Słomczynski, Cory Heyman, and Bruce Podobnik. 2000. "Complexity of Activities and Personality under Conditions of Radical Social Change: A Comparative Analysis of Poland and Ukraine." *Social Psychology Quarterly* 63:187–208.

Ladosz, Jaroslaw. 1977. "Contradictions in the Development of Socialist Society." *Dialectics and Humanism* 4:83–93.

Lockwood, David. 1958. *The Blackcoated Worker: A Study in Class Consciousness.* London: George Allen & Unwin.

Lockwood, W. W. 1968. *The Economic Development of Japan.* Princeton: Princeton University Press.

Mach, Bogdan W. 1998. *Transformacja Ustrojowa a Mentalne Dziedzictwo Socjalizmu* [Transformation of Socioeconomic Regime and Mental Legacy of Socialism]. Warsaw: *Institut Studiow Politycznych, Polskiej Academii Nauk* [Institute of Political Studies, Polish Academy of Sciences].

Mach, Bogdan, and Włodzimierz Wesołowski. 1986. *Social Mobility and the Theory of Social Structure.* London: Routledge and Kegan Paul.

McCrae, Robert R., Paul T. Costa, Jr., Fritz Ostendorf, Alois Angleitner, Martina Hrebickova, Maria D. Avia, Jesus Sanz, Maria L. Sanchez-Bernardos, M. Ersin Kusdil, Ruth Woodfield, Peter R. Saunders, and Peter B. Smith. 2000. "Nature over Nurture: Temperament, Personality, and Life Span Development." *Journal of Personality and Social Psychology* 78:173–186.

McGue, Matt, Steven Bacon, and David T. Lykken. 1993. "Personality Stability and Change in Early Adulthood: A Behavioral Genetic Analysis." *Developmental Psychology* 29:96–109.

Miller, Joanne, Carmi Schooler, Melvin L. Kohn, and Karen A. Miller. 1979. "Women and Work: The Psychological Effects of Occupational Conditions." *American Journal of Sociology* 85:66–94.

Miller, Joanne, Kazimierz M. Słomczynski, and Melvin L. Kohn. 1985. "Continuity of Learning-Generalization: The Effect of Job on Men's Intellective Process in the United States and Poland." *American Journal of Sociology* 91:593–615.

Miller, Karen A., and Melvin L. Kohn. 1983. "The Reciprocal Effects of Job Conditions and the Intellectuality of Leisure-Time Activities." Pp. 217–241 in *Work and Personality: An Inquiry into the Impact of Social Stratification,* by Melvin L. Kohn and Carmi Schooler. Norwood, N.J.: Ablex.

Miller, Karen A., Melvin L. Kohn, and Carmi Schooler. 1985. "Educational Self-Direction and the Cognitive Functioning of Students." *Social Forces* 63:923–944.

———. 1986. "Educational Self-Direction and Personality." *American Sociological Review* 51:372–390.

Mizuno, Ichiu. 1974. "*Kaikyu Kaisokenkyu no Kadai to Hoho*" [The Problem and Method of Research on Class and Status]. *Hokkaido Rodo Kenkyu* 113:38–49.

Mortimer, Jeylan T., Jon Lorence, and Donald S. Kumka. 1986. *Work, Family, and Personality: Transition to Adulthood.* Norwood, NJ: Ablex.

Mortimer, Jeylan T., Ellen Efron Pimentel, Seongryeol Ryu, Katherine Nash, and Chaimun Lee. 1996. "Part-Time Work and Occupational Value Formation in Adolescence." *Social Forces* 74:1405–1418.

Naoi, Atsushi. 1970. "*Keizai Hatsuten to Shokugyo Kouzou no Henndou*" [Economic Development and Changes of Occupational Structure]. *Nihon Rodo Kyokai Zatsushi* [Monthly Journal of the Japan Institute of Labor] 141:14–27.

————. 1972. "*Sangyoka to Kaisou-Kouzou no Henndou*" [Industrialization and the Change of Stratification Structure]. Pp. 86–109 in *Henndou-ki no Nihon Shakai,* edited by Hiroshi Akuto, Takao Sofue, and Ken'ichi Tominaga. Tokyo: *Nihon Housou Shutsuppan Kyokai.*

————. 1979. "*Shokugyo-Teki Chiishakudo no Kosei*" [Construction of the Occupational Status Scale]. Chapter 14 in *Nihon no Kaisokozo* [Social Stratification Structure in Japan], edited by Ken'ichi Tominaga. Tokyo: Tokyo University Press.

Naoi, Atsushi, and Carmi Schooler. 1985. "Occupational Conditions and Psychological Functioning in Japan." *American Journal of Sociology* 90:729–752.

Naoi, Atsushi, and Tatsuzo Suzuki. 1977. "An Analysis of Social Evaluation of Occupational Status: Examining Japanese Occupational Prestige Score." *Contemporary Sociology* (in Japanese) 4:115–156.

Naoi, Michiko. 1992. "Women and Stratification: Frameworks and Indices." *International Journal of Japanese Sociology* 1:47–60.

Naoi, Michiko, and Carmi Schooler. 1990. "Psychological Consequences of Occupational Conditions among Japanese Wives." *Social Psychology Quarterly* 53:100–116.

Odaka, Kunio. 1966. "The Middle Class in Japan." Pp. 541–551 in *Class, Status and Power,* edited by Reinhard Bendix and Seymour M. Lipset. 2nd ed. New York: Free Press.

Ohashi, Ryuken. 1971. *Nihon no Kaikyu Kosei* [Japan's Class Composition]. Tokyo: *Iwanami Shoten.*

Pearlin, Leonard I. 1971. *Class Context and Family Relations: A Cross-National Study.* Boston: Little, Brown.

Pearlin, Leonard I., and Melvin L. Kohn. 1966. "Social Class, Occupation, and Parental Values: A Cross-National Study." *American Sociological Review* 31:466–479.

Poulantzas, Nicos. 1975. *Classes in Contemporary Capitalism.* London: New Left Books.

Robinson, Robert V., and Jonathan Kelley. 1979. "Class as Conceived by Marx and Dahrendorf: Effects on Income Inequality and Politics in the United States and Great Britain." *American Sociological Review* 44:38–58.

Rosenberg, Morris and Leonard I. Pearlin. 1978. "Social Class and Self-Esteem among Children and Adults." *American Journal of Sociology* 84:53–77.

Rychlinski, Stanislaw. 1938. "*Warstwy Spoleczne*" [Social Strata]. *Przeglad Socjologiczny* 8:153–197.

Schooler, Carmi. 1984. "Psychological Effects of Complex Environments during the Life Span: A Review and Theory." *Intelligence* 8:259–281.

Schooler, Carmi, Melvin L. Kohn, Karen A. Miller, and Joanne Miller. 1983. "Housework as Work." Pp. 242–260 in *Work and Personality: An Inquiry into the Impact of Social Stratification,* by Melvin L. Kohn and Carmi Schooler. Norwood, NJ: Ablex.

Schooler, Carmi, Mesfin Samuel Mulatu, and Gary Oates. 1999. "The Continuing Effects of Substantively Complex Work on the Intellectual Functioning of Older Workers." *Psychology and Aging* 14:483–506.

Schooler, Carmi, and Atsushi Naoi. 1988. "The Psychological Effects of Traditional and of Economically Peripheral Job Settings in Japan." *American Journal of Sociology* 94:335–355.

Siegel, Paul M. 1971. *Prestige in the American Occupational Structure.* Unpublished Ph.D. dissertation, University of Chicago.

Słomczynski, Kazimierz M., with Krystyna Janicka, Bogdan W. Mach, and Wojciech Zaborowski. 1997. "Mental Adjustment to the Post-Communist System in Poland." *International Journal of Sociology* 27:1–2 (two issues).

————. 1999. *Mental Adjustment to the Post-communist System in Poland.* Warsaw: IFiS Publishers [Institute of Philosophy and Sociology, Polish Academy of Sciences].

Słomczynski, Kazimierz M., Krystyna Janicka, Bogdan W. Mach, and Wojciech Zaborowski. 1996. *Struktura Społeczna a Osobowosc: Psychologiczne Funkcjonowanie Jednostki w Warunkach Zmiany Społecznej* [Social Structure and Personality: Psychological Functioning under Conditions of Social Change]. Warsaw: IFiS PAN [Institute of Philosophy and Sociology of the Polish Academy of Sciences].

Słomczynski, Kazimierz M., and Grazyna Kacprowicz. 1979. *Skale Zawodow* [Scales of Occupations]. Warsaw: Institute of Philosophy and Sociology of the Polish Academy of Sciences.

Słomczynski, Kazimierz M., and Melvin L. Kohn, with the collaboration of Krystyna Janicka, Jadwiga Koralewicz, Joanne Miller, Carrie Schoenbach, and Ronald Schoenberg. 1988. *Sytuacja Pracy i Jej Psychologiczne Konsekwencje: Polsko-Amerykanskie Analizy Porownawcze* [Work Conditions and Psychological Functioning: Comparative Analyses of Poland and the United States]. Wrocław: Ossolineum Publishing Co.

Słomczynski, Kazimierz M., Joanne Miller, and Melvin L. Kohn. 1981. "Stratification, Work, and Values: A Polish-United States Comparison." *American Sociological Review* 46:720–744.

————. 1987. "Stratification, Work, and Values: A Polish-United States Comparison." (Revised and expanded version) *Sisyphus: Sociological Studies* (Polish Academy of Sciences) IV:59–100.

Spenner, Kenneth I. 1983. "Deciphering Prometheus: Temporal Change in the Skill Level of Work." *American Sociological Review* 48:824–837.

————. 1988. "Social Stratification, Work, and Personality." Pp. 69–97 in *Annual Review of Sociology.* Vol. 14. Palo Alto, CA: Annual Reviews, Inc.

Steven, Rob. 1983. *Classes in Contemporary Japan.* Cambridge: Cambridge University Press.

Taira, Koji. 1970. *Economic Development and the Labor Market in Japan.* New York: Columbia University Press.

Treiman, Donald J. 1977. *Occupational Prestige in Comparative Perspective.* New York: Academic Press.

Vogel, Ezra. 1963. *Japan's New Middle Class.* Berkeley: University of California Press.

Warr, Peter. 1987. *Work, Unemployment, and Mental Health.* Oxford: Clarendon.

Wesołowski, Włodzimierz. 1975. *Teoria, Badania, Praktyka. Z Problematyki Struktury Klasowej.* Warsaw: *Ksiazka i Wiedza.*

————. 1979. *Classes, Strata and Power.* London: Routledge and Kegan Paul.

————. 1988. "Does Socialist Stratification Exist?" *The Fifth Fuller Bequest Lecture.* Dept. of Sociology, University of Essex.

————. 1994. *"Przetwarzanie sie Struktury Klasowej: Perspektywa Teoretyezna a Sytuacja Polska"* [Transformation of the Class Structure: Theoretical Perspective and the Polish Situation.] Paper presented at the Congress of the Polish Sociological Association, Lublin, June 30.

Widerszpil, Stanislaw. 1978. "Problems in the Theory of the Development of a Socialist Society." *Polish Sociological Bulletin* 2:23–36.

Williams, Robin M., Jr. 1951 [3rd ed., 1970]. *American Society: A Sociological Interpretation.* New York: Alfred A. Knopf.

Wright, Erik Olin. 1976. "Class Boundaries in Advanced Capitalist Societies." *New Left Review* 98:3–41.

————. 1978. *Class, Crisis and the State*. London: New Left Books.

————. 1985. *Classes*. London: New Left Books.

————. 1989. "Women in the Class Structure." *Politics and Society* 17:35–66.

Wright, Erik Olin, and Luca Perrone. 1977. "Marxist Class Categories and Income Inequality." *American Sociological Review* 42:32–55.

Zawadski, Bohan, and Paul F. Lazarsfeld. 1935. "The Psychological Consequences of Unemployment." *Journal of Social Psychology* 6:224–251.

Index

actually existing capitalist society, 2

actually existing socialist society, 2

advantaged social classes, 3

age of respondent, 156n, 159, 189n; *see also* social characteristics

Alexander, Karl, 2

American Sociological Association, xxi, 57–58

anxiety, as a component of distress, 27, 95, 98–99, 185; definition of, 22; measurement models of, 26, 97; *see also* distress

authoritarian conservatism (vs. open-mindedness), as a component of self-directedness of orientation, 27, 95, 99, 185; definition of, 20; measurement models of, 24, 96, 179–81; over-time stability of, 179–81; *see also* self-directedness of orientation

background characteristics: *see* social characteristics

Baxter, Janeen, 153

The Bell Curve, 201, 226

blue-collar workers: *see* manual workers

Boskoff, Alvin, 82n

bourgeoisie, 6; *see also* employers, social class

Bronfenbrenner, Urie, 226

change, receptiveness to, as a component of self-directedness of orientation, 95–99, 185; measurement models of, 98; *see also* self-directedness of orientation

change in social-structural position and personality, in transitional Ukraine, 197–201

change scores, 230

chi-square, as a measure of the goodness of fit of LISREL models, 14n, 22, 95, 181, 182–83

China, xvi, 220, 222

Chinese Academy of Social Sciences, xvi

Chinese edition of this book, xvi

Cherlin, Andrew, 2

class: *see* social class

Class and Conformity, xiii, 127, 233

closeness of supervision, as impeding the exercise of occupational self-direction, xiii-xiv, 35, 109; as an explanatory link in the relationships of social structure and personality, 37, 41–42; measurement models of, 35–36, 109–111; and personality, 116; and social class, 37–39, 112–113; and social stratification, 37–39, 112–113; *see also* occupational self-direction

cognitive functioning: *see* intellectual flexibility

Cohen, Robert A., xx

Cole, Robert E., 9, 10

collaborative mode of cross-national research, xix-xx, 219–20, 220–24; advantages and disadvantages of, 223–24

Columbia, 49n

Commission of Scientific and Technological Progress of the Cabinet Ministries of Ukraine, 68, 75

Communist Party: see Polish United Workers Party, Ukrainian Communist Party

comparability of meaning (in translations of interview questions), 20, 61–62, 63, 88

comparative analyses of the relationships of social structure and personality: for Polish men under socialism and during the transition to nascent capitalism, 119–20; for men and women in transitional Poland and Ukraine, 120; for Poles and Ukrainians during the transitions of their countries to nascent capitalism, 123

complexity, definition of, 126; development of the concepts of substantive complexity of work and complexity of activities, 126–34; of housework, 132–33, 139–40; of schoolwork, 133; see also complexity of activities, substantive complexity of work, occupational self-direction

complexity of activities, conceptualization of, 134, 147–48; and education, 144–46, 159–62, 170–71; and distress, 218; and personality, 141–44, 156; as a possible explanation of the relationships between structural location and personality, 167–71; and social structure, 73, 149, 156; measurement models of, 136–140, 168–69

complexity of prior jobs, as a possible explanation of the relationships between complexity of activities of the nonemployed and personality, 145–46

conditions of life: see job conditions, proximate conditions of life

conditions of uncertainty, 83, 117–19, 201–2; see also job conditions

confirmatory factor analysis, xiv; see also measurement models

conformist orientation: see self-directedness of orientation

contemporaneous effects in structural-equation models, 80, 206n, 226–27; see also cross-lagged effects in structural-equation models, directions of effects

contradictory locations in the class structure, 6

control over the conditions of one's own work, 4, 50; see also occupational self-direction

control over the labor power of others: see social class

control over the means of production: see social class

Coser, Rose, 128n, 140

Costa, Paul T. Jr., 185

countervailing effects (on distress) of occupational self-direction and other job conditions, 46–48

cross-lagged effects in structural-equation models, 80, 206n, 226–27; used as instruments for identifying total effects, 43, 227; see also contemporaneous effects

cross-national consistencies: see cross-national similarities and differences in findings

cross-national similarities and differences in findings, xv, 23, 46–48, 48–50, 81, 92, 105–107, 108, 159–64, 172, 176; methodological issues in interpreting, 179–84, 180n, 182n; in the relationship between self-directedness of orientation and distress, 23, 27, 95, 185

Cummings, William K., 9, 10

Czarnota-Bojarska, Joanna, 126

Daniłowicz, Pawel, xxi, 5, 68–69, 76, 89, 92

definition of: anxiety, 22; authoritarian conservatism, 20; closeness of supervision, 35; distress, 22; eta, 16n; fatalism, 22; idea-conformity, 22; intellectual flexibility, 18, 20; morality, personally responsible standards of, 20; occupational self-direction, 35; parental values, 18; radical social change, 78; second-order factor analysis, 14n;

self-confidence, 20; self-deprecation, 20; self-directedness of orientation, 22; social change, 78; social class, 2–3, 6–8; social stratification, 3; social structure, 2; substantive complexity of work, 35; trustfulness, 20

Dictionary of Occupational Titles, 127n

directions of effects (in causal modeling), xiv, 40–45, 133, 148–49; *see also* reciprocal effects (in causal modeling)

distress (versus a sense of well-being), countervailing effects of occupational self-direction and other job conditions, 46–48; definition of, 22; dimensions of, 22–23, 95, 99; and job conditions, 46–48; and job protections, 46–47; among managers, 48; among manual workers, 47; measurement models of, 27, 95, 99, 184–86; and occupational self-direction, 44–45, 46–48; over-time stability of, 184–86; and perceived economic well-being, 165–67, 211–15; and self-directedness of orientation, 23, 27, 95, 185; and social class, 30–32, 46–48, 105–106; and social stratification, 33–34, 46–48, 106, 108–109; and unemployment, 162; *see also* orientations to self and society, personality

"dollars for data," 223, 224

Drazkiewicz, Jerzy, 11

Duncan, Otis Dudley, 14n, 15

Duncan's index of occupational socio-economic status, 14n, 15; *see also* occupational status, social stratification

dynamics of the process of radical social change, 175–218

Eberhart, John C., xx

economic adversity, as a possible explanation of the relationship between structural location and distress, 165–67; *see also* perceived economic well-being

education, and complexity of activities of the nonemployed, 144–46, 159–62, 170–71; as a component of social stratification, 14–15, 104, 194–95; as a possible explanation of the relationship between complexity of activities and personality of the nonemployed,

144–46; and social class, 118n; and structural location, 162n; *see also* social stratification

educational attainment: *see* education

Eisenberg, Philip, 154

Elliott, Marta, 54

employed segments of the population (taken as a whole), 91–124, 158–59

employers, 35n, 102; *see also* ownership, social class

entrepreneur: *see* social class

error: *see* measurement error

eta, definition of, 16n, 156; adjusted for unreliability of measurement of factor and latent-variable scores, 16n, 192n

ethnicity: *see* social characteristics

experts, as a social class in transitional Poland and Ukraine, 102–103, 108

face-to-face interviews (as purportedly done in surveys conducted in the Soviet Union), 61

factor analysis: *see* confirmatory factor analysis

fatalism, as a component of self-directedness of orientation, 23, 27, 95, 99; definition of, 22; inability to develop a measurement model for socialist Poland, 26–27, 87; measurement models of, 26–27, 98; *see also* self-directedness of orientation

father's education: *see* social characteristics

father's occupational status: *see* social characteristics

Feather, N.T., 155

Finkel, Leonid, 89, 92

Firebaugh, Glenn, 92

first-order concepts: *see* measurement models; *see also* second-order confirmatory factor analyses

Form, William, 2, 54n, 83

formal grievance procedures: *see* job protections

FSCORE (a program for computing factor scores), 14n, 141n

funding the research, xxi, 58n, 60, 63–64, 65, 66–68; *see also* "the Wesołowski model"

Gagliani, Giorgio, 6, 7
gender (similarities and differences in the
    relationships of social structure and
    personality for men and women), xivn,
    120, 231
generalizability of findings and
    interpretation, xv, 2, 80–81,130, 131,
    147–48, 218, 235; *see also* cross-
    national similarities and differences in
    findings
Goldthorpe, John H., 153
goodness of fit (of LISREL models),
    181, 182–83: *see also* chi-square, as
    a measure of the goodness of fit of
    LISREL models, confirmatory factor
    analysis, root mean square error of
    approximation (RMSEA) as a measure
    of goodness of fit of LISREL models
Griffin, Larry J., 6
Grushin, Boris, 61
Gutierrez, Roberto, 49n, 54, 91–92, 131

Haney, Michael, 68, 92
Hashimoto, Kenji, 9
Hauser, Robert M., 128–29n
Herrnstein, Richard J., 226
Heyman, Cory, 91–92, 125–26, 151
hierarchical ordering of society: *see* social
    stratification
hierarchical position, 7; and occupational
    self-direction, 42; *see also* managers
Higher Party School (of the Ukrainian
    Communist Party), 63, 234n, 240
Hodge, Robert W., 14n, 15
Hodge-Siegel index of occupational
    position, 14n, 15; *see also* occupational
    status, social stratification
Hollingshead, August B., 14n, 15
Hollingshead's Index of Social Position, 14n
Hollingshead's classification of
    occupational status, 14n, 15; *see also*
    occupational status, social stratification
House, James S., 2n, 78, 173
housewives, economic duress of Polish
    housewives during the transition,
    162–63, 237; personalities of, 162–63,
    192; *see also* housework
housework, complexity of, 73, 139–40;
    and personality, 133, 142, 144

Hout, Michael, 151
Hung, Ho-fung, 151, 175–76
Hryniewicz, Tadeusz, 11

idea-conformity, as a component of
    distress, 23, 27; as a component of
    self-directedness of orientation, 23,
    27; definition of, 22; dropped from the
    second-order model of orientation in
    the comparative study of Poland and
    Ukraine in transition, 94; measurement
    models of, 26; *see also* distress, self-
    directedness of orientation
ideas, work with: *see* occupational self-
    direction; substantive complexity of
    work
ideational flexibility, as a dimension of
    intellectual flexibility, 20, 100;
used synonymously with intellectual
    flexibility, 20; *see also* intellectual
    flexibility
immediately impinging conditions of life:
    see proximate conditions of life
income, as a component of social
    stratification, 14–15, 104, 194–95;
    measurement models of, 194–95; *see
    also* social stratification
inconsistencies, cross national: *see* cross-
    national similarities and differences in
    findings
indices: *see* measurement models
industrialized societies, xvi, 79; *see
    also* non-industrialized (and partially
    industrialized) societies
initiative: *see* occupational self-direction,
    definition of
instability of personality: *see* stability of
    personality
Institute of Philosophy and Sociology of
    the Polish Academy of Sciences, 67, 75,
    225n
Institute of Political Studies of the Polish
    Academy of Sciences, 67
Institute of Sociology of the Soviet (later:
    Russian) Academy of Sciences, 58
Institute for the Study of Fundamental
    Problems in Marxism-Leninism of the
    Polish United Workers' (Communist)
    Party, 56

intellectual demandingness of leisure-time activities, 79, 129–30
intellectual flexibility, definition of, 18, 20; measurement models of, 18, 21, 95, 100–101, 186–87; and occupational self-direction, 44–45, 79; over-time stability of, 186–87; and social class, 29, 31–32, 106, 108; and social stratification, 33–34, 106, 108–109, 195–96; and substantive complexity of work, 79, 206–210; see also ideational flexibility
intellectual functioning: see intellectual flexibility
intelligentsia, 105n; see also nonmanual workers
inter-class mobility and change in personality, 199–200; see also social mobility
intergenerational transmission of values: see transmission of values in the family
International Research and Exchanges Board (IREX), 60, 61, 62
International Sociological Association, 55, 57–58, 65–66
intolerance of nonconformity: see authoritarian conservatism

Jahoda, Marie, 154, 155
Janicka, Krystyna, xix-xx, 54, 65, 77, 91, 125, 151, 176
Japan, xv, xvi, 1–51
Japan Bureau of Statistics, 10
Japanese (Occupational) Prestige Scale, 15
Jasinska-Kania, Aleksandra, 239
job complexity: see substantive complexity of work
job conditions, as a key to understanding the relationships of social class and social stratification with personality, 60; and distress, 46–48; historical changes in, 47; and personality, 80, 83; see also occupational self-direction, proximate conditions of life
job income: see income
job protections, 46–48; and distress, 46–48; indices of, 46–48; among managers, 48; among manual workers, 46–47; for Polish workers, 47; and union membership, 46–47

job-search activities of the unemployed, complexity of, 138–39, 139n
job uncertainties: see uncertainty, conditions of
job security: see job protections
Johns Hopkins University, 56, 65, 91, 125–26
Johnson, Samuel, 126
Jöreskog, Karl G., 197n

Kacprowicz, Grazyna, 5, 14n, 15
Kanto plain (Japan), 5
Kalbarczyk, Agnieszka, 126
Kalleberg, Arne, 6
Kelley, Jonathan, 6, 7
Kiev, 59–60, 90, 239
Khmelko, Valeriy, xix-xx, 54, 58, 59–60, 63–64, 67–68, 76, 77, 89, 91, 125, 151, 175, 177, 229
Kiev International Institute of Sociology, 68, 89, 179
Kohn, Janet, v, 222
Kohn, Rose Mickenberg (and family), 242
Koninklijke Brill NV (Brill Academic Publishers), xxi

Ladosz, Jaroslaw, 11
language used in the Ukrainian interviews, 61, 88–89
latent-variable scores, 197n, 230
Lazarsfeld, Paul F. 154
learning-generalization, 134
Lenin, Vladimir Illich, 56, 240, 241
Lentchovskii, Roman, 92
Liebow, Elliot, 54
life-course analyses, 79, 130, 131
linear structural-equations modeling: see confirmatory factor analysis, directions of effects (in causal modeling), LISREL, reciprocal effects (in causal modeling),
LISREL, 14n, 22, 94, 197n, 230; see also confirmatory factor analysis
location in the centralized economy (of socialist Poland), 12; as a criterion of social class in socialist Poland, 12
Lockwood, David, 7
Lockwood, W. W., 9

longitudinal analyses, of Ukraine,
175–218, 229–32; of the United States,
218–19, 225–27; *see also* confirmatory
factor analyses, LISREL, reciprocal
effects (in causal modeling)

Mach, Bogdan, xix-xx, 6, 8, 54, 64, 65, 70,
73, 77, 91, 125, 151, 176, 179, 182–84,
224n
magnitudes: of correlations between
complexity of activities and personality
for various segments of the population,
134, 141–44; of correlations between
the substantive complexity of work
and personality in Poland and Ukraine
during their transitions, 210–11, 218;
of over-time correlations of personality
in Ukraine during its transition,
179–87; of relationships of class and
stratification with personality, 105,
107–8, 109, 177; of relationships of job
conditions conducive to occupational
self-direction with personality, 116–17,
210–11, 218; of the degree to which the
psychological effects of social structure
can be attributed to occupational self-
direction, 113–116; of the relationships
of structural location and personality
during the process of radical social
change in Ukraine, 192–94
managers, as a distinct social class, 6–13;
distress among Polish, 30, 48, 105–107,
108
manual vs. nonmanual work as a criterion
of social class, 7–8, 10–11, 12
manual workers, as a social class, 7–8,
10–11, 12; distress among, 46–48,
105–107, 108; and job protections,
46–48; *see also* social class
Marx, Karl, 6, 7, 56, 59n
Marxism-Leninism Institute of the
Communist Party of the Soviet Union,
Ukrainian branch, 59–60
maternal education: *see* social
characteristics
maternal grandfather's occupational status:
see social characteristics
McCrae, Robert R., 186
McGue, Matt, 186

measurement error, 225; *see also*
confirmatory factor analysis
measurement models of: anxiety, 26, 97;
authoritarian conservatism, 24, 96,
179–81; closeness of supervision, 35–36,
109–111; complexity of activities of
the nonemployed, 136–40; distress, 27,
95, 99, 184–86; idea-conformity, 26;
intellectual flexibility, 18, 20, 95, 100–101,
186–87; morality, personally responsible
standards of, 24, 96; occupational self-
direction, 35–36, 109–110; occupational
status, 14–15; orientations to self and
society, 20–28, 94–95, 179–86; parental
values, 18–19; perceived economic well-
being, 165; receptiveness to change, 98;
routinization of work, 109–111; self-
confidence, 25, 97; self-deprecation, 25,
97; self-directedness of orientation, 27,
95, 99, 184–86; self-esteem, 25, 97; social
stratification, 14–15, 103–105, 194–95;
substantive complexity of work, 35–36,
110–111, 203–204; trustfulness, 25, 96–97
membership in unions: *see* union
membership
mental production, 7; *see also* social class
Merton, Robert K., 128n
methodological interpretations of cross-
national differences, 179–84
methodological lessons of the research,
220, 225–32
Miller, Joanne, 49n, 79, 100, 131, 228
Miller, Karen A., 79, 129, 133, 145n, 148,
184, 228
Mizuno, Ichiu, 9
mobility: *see* inter-class mobility, social
mobility
Molm, Linda, 126
Momdjan, Khatchik, 57–58
morality, personally responsible standards
of, as a component of self-directedness
of orientation, 23, 27, 95, 99, 185;
definition of, 20; measurement models
of, 24, 96; *see also* self-directedness of
orientation
Mortimer, Jeylan T., 92, 131
mother's education: *see* social
characteristics
mothers' values: *see* parental values

movement to and from the ranks of the
employed, and change in personality,
197–99
Mulatu, Mesfin Samuel, xxi, 79, 176
Murray, Charles, 226

Naoi, Atsushi, xv, 1, 6, 9, 10, 11, 14n, 15,
42, 184
Naoi, Michiko, xix, 80, 153, 184
national background: *see* social
characteristics
National Council for Soviet and East
European Research (NCSEER), xxi,
66–67, 239
National Institute of Mental Health, xx,
56, 57n
National Opinion Research Center
(NORC),
National Science Foundation (NSF), xxi,
66–67, 77
non-authoritarian: *see* authoritarian
conservatism
non-capitalist societies: *see* socialist
societies
nonemployed segments of the society, xvi,
125–49, 151–73; classifying respondents
into categories of nonemployment, 72,
135n; developing questions about the
activities of the nonemployed, 73; *see
also* housewives, pensioners, structural
location, students, unemployed
non-industrialized (and partially
industrialized) societies, 49n, 131
nonmanual workers, 7; *see also* social
class
nonproduction workers, 11, 102; *see also*
social class
non-response, rates of: *see* response, rates
of
Nowak, Stefan, 56, 234n
number of children in family of
orientation: *see* social characteristics

Oates, Gary, 79
objectivity of indices (of job conditions),
87
occupation: *see* job conditions,
occupational self-direction, occupational
status

occupational conditions: *see* job conditions
occupational prestige: *see* occupational
status
occupational recruitment: see occupational
selection
occupational self-direction, definition
of, 35, 109; and distress, 45, 46–48;
and intellectual flexibility, 45, 79; job
conditions that facilitate or limit the
exercise of, xiii-xiv, 35, 79, 109; as
an explanatory link in the relationship
of social structure and personality,
4, 37, 41–42, 46–48, 50, 79, 82n,
109, 113–115; measurement models
of, 35–36, 109–110; and parental
valuation of self-direction, 45, 79; and
personality, 42–45; and self-directedness
of orientation, 45; and social class,
37–39, 42, 79; and social stratification,
37–39, 79; and transmission of values
in the family, xv; *see also* closeness
of supervision, routinization of work,
substantive complexity of work
occupational socio-economic status: see
occupational status
occupational status, as a component of
social stratification, 14–15, 33–34, 104,
194–95; measurement models of, 33–34,
194–95; *see also* social stratification
occupational structure, 42; *see also* job
conditions
Odaka, Kunio, 11
Ohashi, Ryuken, 9, 10
open-mindedness: *see* authoritarian
conservatism
orientations to self and society,
confirmatory factor analyses of,
20–28, 94–95; measurement models of,
20–28, 94–95; *see also* distress, self-
directedness of orientation
other conditions of life (other than those
conducive to occupational self-direction)
that might explain the relationships
of social structure and personality,
117–118, 235
ownership, 6, 42, 102; differentiated
into employers and self-employed as
separate social classes, 9, 10; *see also*
social class

Paniotto, Volodia, xix-xx, 54, 58, 60, 61–64, 65, 67–68, 76, 77, 88, 89, 91, 125, 151, 175, 229

parental valuation of self-direction: *see* self-direction/conformity, parental valuation of

parental values, xv; definition of, 18; measurement models of, 18–19; and offspring's values, xv; and occupational self-direction, 44–45; and social class, 29, 31–32; and social stratification, 33–34; *see also* self-direction/conformity, parental valuation of

partially industrialized societies: *see* non-industrialized (and partially industrialized) societies

paternal education: *see* social characteristics

paternal grandfather's occupational status: *see* social characteristics

paternal occupational status: *see* social characteristics

pay: *see* income

Pearlin, Leonard I., xv, 153, 233

pensioners, complexity of activities of, 73, 136–38; complexity of activities of, and personality, 142–44, 163

people, complexity of work with: *see* substantive complexity of work

people, hours spent working with: *see* substantive complexity of work

perceived economic well-being, and distress, 165–67, 213; as an index of economic adversity, 165–67; measurement models of, 165–66, 211–13; as a possible link between social structure and distress, 118–19, 165–67, 211, 213–15

perceptual flexibility: see intellectual flexibility

perestroika, 64

Perrone, Luca, 6

personality, and complexity of activities of the nonemployed, 141–44; dimensions of (in these analyses), 18n; and job conditions, 80; and occupational self-direction, 42–45; and social class, 29–32, 44–45, 105–108, 187–94; and social stratification, 33–34. 106,

108–109, 195–96; and social structure, 187–96; stability of, under conditions of radical social change, 179–87, 215; and structural location, 156–64, 187–94; structure of, 23; and the substantive complexity of work, 202–211; *see also* distress, intellectual flexibility, parental values, self-direction/conformity (parental valuation of), self-directedness of orientation

personally responsible standards of morality: *see* morality, personally responsible standards of

petty bourgeoisie, 6; *see also* social class

physical production, 7; *see also* social class

Podobnik, Bruce, 125–26, 151, 175–76

Poland, in transition to nascent capitalism: analyses of the employed, 91–124, 177; analyses of the nonemployed, 125–49, 151–73; over-time stability of personality, 182–84

Poland, when it was socialist: xvi, 1–51; as an exemplar of actually existing socialist society, 2; but not exemplary of some ideal type of socialist society, 80

Polish Academy of Sciences, 67, 75, 89

Polish Prestige Scale, 14n, 15; *see also* occupational status

Polish United Workers (Communist) party, 48, 56

Portes, Alejandro, 2

position in the class structure: *see* social class

Poulantzas, Nicos, 7

prestige: *see* occupational status, social stratification

pretesting (of interview schedules), 68

privilege: *see* social class, social stratification

production workers, 11, 102; *see also* social class

proletariat, 6, 16; *see also* manual workers, nonmanual workers, social class

proximate conditions of life, as a bridge between position in the social structure and personality, xiii, 46–48, 78, 79, 92, 172–73, 202–211, 216–18, 235–36; job conditions as central in bridging social class and social stratification with personality, xiii; proximate conditions of life other than job conditions as possible bridges from dimensions of social structure other than class and stratification to personality, 235; same social-structural position entailing different proximate conditions of life during times of social stability and social change, 46–48, 237

psychological functioning: *see* personality; *see also* distress, intellectual flexibility, parental values, self-directedness of orientation

race: *see* social characteristics

radical social change, xv, 53–76, 64, 91–124; definition of, 78, 177; depth of, in Ukraine, 177; differences between Poland and Ukraine in their experience of, 93–94, 177–78; differences in the relationships between social structure and personality from times of apparent social stability, 123–124

Radio Liberty, Research Institute of, 68

Randolph, Robert, 66–67, 239

Reagan, Ronald, 57n

receptiveness to change: *see* change, receptiveness to

reciprocal effects (in causal modeling), xiv, 42–45, 79–80, 129, 134–35n, 206n, 207–208n; models of the reciprocal effects of the substantive complexity of work and intellectual flexibility for U.S. men and for Ukrainian men and women, 208–10, 232; *see also* directions of effects (in causal modeling)

Redlich, Fredrick C., 14n

region of origin: *see* social characteristics

reliability of measurement: *see* measurement error

religious background: *see* social characteristics

repetitiveness of work: *see* routinization of work

replications of the research, xiv, 80, 93

research design, 70–72, 84–86

response, rates of, in surveys: 90, 179

Ridgeway, Cecilia, 151

Robinson, Robert V., 6, 7

root mean square error of approximation (RMSEA), as a measure of goodness of fit of LISREL models, 95, 181, 182–83

Rosenberg, Morris, 153

Rossi, Peter H., 14n, 15

routinization of work, as impeding the exercise of occupational self-direction, xiii-xiv, 35, 109; inadequacies of and improvements to index, 35, 87, 109–111; as a link in the relationships of social structure and personality, 37, 41–42; measurement models of, 109–111; and social class, 37–39, 112–113; and social stratification, 37–39, 112–113; *see also* occupational self-direction

rurality of childhood residence: *see* social characteristics

Rutkevich, M. N., 55

salary: *see* income

sample selection: in the 1979 Japanese survey of employed men, 5; in the 1978 Polish survey of employed men, 5; in the 1992 Polish survey of men and women living in urban areas, 71–72, 89; in the 1992–93 Ukrainian survey of men and women living in urban areas, 89; in the 1996 Polish follow-up survey, 180n; in the 1996 Ukrainian follow-up survey, 178–79; in the 1964 U.S. survey of employed men, xiv, 5; in the 1974 U.S. follow-up survey of men less than 65 years of age, their wives, and selected offspring, xiv, 5

Schoenbach, Carrie, xivn, xix, 1, 8, 42, 49n, 54, 92, 234

Schoenberg, Ronald, xxi, 14n, 176

Schooler, Carmi, xiv, xv, xix, xx, xxi, 1, 5, 42, 46, 51, 54, 56, 60, 64, 77, 79, 80, 92, 126, 126n, 127, 129, 131, 132–33, 137, 148, 154, 176, 179, 185, 201, 206, 217, 222, 225, 226, 228, 230, 232, 233, 236

schoolwork, substantive complexity of, 197, 197n, 258, 258n

second-order concepts: *see* confirmatory factor analysis, measurement models, second-order confirmatory factor analyses second-order confirmatory factor analyses, 35, 95, 99, 109–111, 184–86, 194–95; approximations thereto, 22n, 184n; *see also* confirmatory factor analysis; measurement models

segments of the population, 135–36; *see also* structural location

self-conception: *see* orientations to self and society

self-confidence (or absence thereof), as a component of distress, 27, 95, 99, 185; definition of, 20; measurement models of, 25, 97; *see also* distress, self-directedness of orientation

self-deprecation (or absence thereof), as a component of distress, 27, 95, 99, 185; as a component of self-directedness of orientation, 27; definition of, 20; measurement models of, 25, 97; *see also* distress, self-directedness of orientation

self-directed work: *see* occupational self-direction

self-directedness of orientation, definition of, 22; and distress, 23, 27, 95, 185; measurement models of, 99, 184–86; and occupational self-direction, 44–45; over-time stability of, 184–86; and social class, 29, 31–32, 105–106; and social stratification, 33–34, 106, 108–109; *see also* distress, orientations to self and society, personality

self-direction: *see* occupational self-direction, self-directedness of orientation, self-direction/conformity, parental valuation of

self-direction/conformity, parental valuation of, measurement models of, 18, 19; and occupational self-direction, 44–45; and social class, 29, 31–32; and social stratification, 33–34; *see also* parental values

self-employed (as a social class), 35n, 102; *see also* social class

self-esteem, dimensions of, 25, 97; measurement models of, 25, 97; *see also* self-confidence, self-deprecation

semi-autonomous employees, 6–7; *see also* social class

sensitivity analyses, 228

Shkaratan, Ovsei, 59n

Siegel, Paul M., 14n, 15

Siegel's index of occupational status, 14n, 15; *see also* occupational status

simulated longitudinal analyses of cross-sectional data, 42–43, 42n, 227–29; inappropriateness for analyses of radical social change, 134n, 145, 145n

size of community; *see* social characteristics

Słomczynski, Kazimierz M., xiv, xv, xix-xx, 1, 5, 14n, 15, 42, 49n, 54, 56–57, 61, 64, 65, 77, 79, 80, 88, 100, 102, 125, 132, 145n, 151, 176, 184, 222, 224n, 225n, 226, 228, 232n, 234, 237

small employers: *see* employers, social class

social background: *see* social characteristics

social change, 62; definition of, 78, in rural Ukraine, 239–244; *see also* radical social change

social characteristics, 41n, 44; used as statistical controls in the causal models, 41, 44

social class, in the capitalist United States, 6–9; and closeness of supervision, 37–39, 112–113; as a component of social structure, xiii; conceptualization of, xv, 2–3, 6–14, 49, 101–102, 233–34; as distinct from social stratification, 3, 16, 49, 51, 233; and distress, 30, 31–32, 46–48, 105–106; and education, 118n; as independently (from social stratification) related to personality, 33–34, 51, 108–109; and intellectual flexibility, 29, 31–32, 106, 108; in Japan, 9–11; as a multidimensional typology, 3; as "nominal" categories, not a continuum, 3, 101; and occupational self-direction, 37–39, 42, 51, 79; and parental valuation of self-direction, 29, 31–32; and parent-child relationships, xiii; and personality, xiii, 3–4, 19–32, 105–108, 119–120; and routinization of work, 112–113; and self-directedness of orientation, 29, 31–32, 105–106; and social stratification, 14–17; in socialist Poland, xv, 11–14, 59, 234n; in the

Soviet Union, 59–80, 234n; Stalinist conceptualization of, 60, 60n; and job uncertainties, 46–48; and the substantive complexity of work, 37–39, 112–113, 231; and the transmission of values in the family, xv; in transitional Poland and Ukraine, 101–103, 105–108; in the United States, 6–9

social composition of the social classes as a possible explanation of class differences in personality, 40, 46

social factors, as contributing to the stability of personality, 226

social mobility, and changes in personality, 197–201, 215

social orientation: *see* orientations to self and society

social selection, 44, 50, 172

social stability, xiv, xvi; *see also* radical social change, social change

social stratification, 55; in the capitalist United States, 14, 14n, 15–16; and closeness of supervision, 37–39, 112–113; component dimensions of, 14–16, 104, 194–95; as a component of social structure, xiii; as a continuum, 14–16, 102, 194; definition of, 2–3, 14, 104, 194; as distinct from social class, 3, 14–16, 51, 233; and distress, 33–34, 46–48, 106, 108–109; as a fundamental feature of industrialized society, 2; as independently (from social class) related to personality, 33–34, 51, 108–109; and intellectual flexibility, 33–34, 106, 108–109, 195–96; measurement models of, 14–15, 103–105, 194–95; and occupational self-direction, 37–39, 51, 79; over-time stability in transitional Ukraine, 195–96; and parental valuation of self-direction, 33–34; and personality, xiii, 33–34. 106, 108–109; and routinization of work, 37–39, 112–113; and self-directedness of orientation, 33–34, 106, 108–109; and social class, 14–17; in socialist societies, 55; in socialist Poland, 33–34, 55; stability of, in Ukraine during the transition, 195; and the substantive complexity of work, 37–39, 112–113, 231; in transitional Poland and Ukraine, 102, 103–105, 106, 108–109, 194–95; in the Soviet Union, 55; and the transmission of values in the family, xv; and values and orientation, 33–34

social structure, conceptualization of, 2n, 233–35; dimensions of, xiii, 51, 78, 92, 235; and complexity of activities, 149; and occupational self-direction, 82–83; and personality, xiii, 78, 151–73, 187–96; and social change, 82n; social class and social stratification as alternative (complementary) conceptualizations of, 51; during times of apparent social stability, xvi, 78; during times of radical social change, xvii, 78, 187–96; and the transmission of values in the family, xv

Social Structure and Self-Direction, xv

socialist societies, xv

socio-economic status: *see* social stratification

Solidarnosc, 57, 64n, 81

Sociological Association of Ukraine, 62–63

Soviet Sociological Association, 55, 57–58

Soviet Union, xv, 57–64

specification (of causal models), 226–27

Spenner, Kenneth I., 78, 83, 92

stability of personality, xvi, 178, 179–87; in Ukraine by comparison to the U.S. and Poland, 182–84, 215

stability in the relationship of social structure and personality, in transitional Ukraine, 189–91, 195–96, 210, 215–16

stability of social-class position, in transitional Ukraine, 197

stability of social conditions and stability of personality, 201–202, 226

stability of social-stratification position, in transitional Ukraine, 194–95

standards of morality: *see* morality, personally responsible standards of

State Committee for Science and Technology of Ukraine, xxi, 75

State Committee for Scientific Research (KBN) of Poland, xxi, 67, 75

Steven, Rob, 9, 10

stratification: *see* social stratification

structural imperatives of the job, 129

structural location, and complexity of
activities, 156; conceptualization of,
135n, 153–54, 153n, 187–89, 234; and
personality, 156–64, 189–95; truncated
and full indices of, 187–88; *see also*
social class, social structure

students, 73, 162–63

subjective appraisals of the job, 8, 241–243

substance of work with things, data, and
people: *see* substantive complexity of
work

substantive complexity of work (or of
the job), as conducive to the exercise
of occupational self-direction, xiii-xiv,
35, 109; definition of, 35, 109; and
distress, 46–48, 130, 132; development
of the concept and evidence of its
relationship to personality, 127–132; and
intellectual demandingness of leisure-
time activities, 130; and intellectual
flexibility, 130, 206–10, 231–32; as an
explanatory link in the relationships
of social structure and personality, 37,
41–42, 130, 204–11; measurement
models of, 35, 109–111, 203–204; and
parental valuation of self-direction,
130; and personality, 141–42, 202–11;
and self-directedness of orientation,
130; and social class, 37–39, 204–205,
231; and social stratification, 37–39,
204–205, 231; stability of, during the
transition of Ukraine, 203–204. 231, as
uni-dimensional, 128, 129

substantive knowledge gained from the
cross-national research, 220, 232–38

surveys: of employed men in the United
States, 5; of employed men in Japan,
5; of employed men in Poland in 1978,
5; of adult men and women in the
urban areas of Poland and Ukraine in
1992–93, 178

Suzuki, Tatsuzo, 14n, 15

Swafford, Michael, 68, 92

Sztabinski, Pawel, 5

Taira, Koji, 9

things, complexity of work with: *see*
substantive complexity of work

things, amount of time spent working with:
see substantive complexity of work

timing of the studies of Poland and
Ukraine in transition, 69

Tokyo, 5

tolerance of nonconformity: *see*
authoritarian conservatism

Tominaga, Ken'ichi, xxi, 9

training of Ukrainian interviewers, 68

transmission of values in the family, xv, 70

Treiman, Donald J., 3, 14, 15

Treiman's International Prestige Scale, 14,
15; *see also* occupational status

"true scores", xx; *see also* measurement error

trustfulness (or lack thereof), as a
component of distress, 27, 95, 99; as
a component of self-directedness of
orientation, 27, 95, 99, 185; definition
of, 20; measurement models of, 25,
96–97; *see also* self-directedness of
orientation

Turin study, xv, 233

typology of cross-national research,
220–21

Ukraine, cross-sectional analyses of the
employed, 91–124; cross-sectional
analyses of the nonemployed, 125–49,
151–73; longitudinal analyses, 175–218

Ukrainian Academy of Sciences, 62–64

Ukrainian Communist Party, 62

uncertainty, conditions of, 46–48, 83, 87,
118–19, 178

unemployed, complexity of activities of,
73, 136–38; complexity of activities
of, and personality, 141–43, 154;
complexity of job-search activities
of, 138–39; personalities of the
unemployed, 159–62, 190–92

"unemployed housewives," 135, 163

union membership, and distress, 46–48;
and job protections, 46–48

United States, xvi, 1–51; as an exemplar
of actually existing capitalist society, 2;
but not exemplary of some ideal type of
capitalist society, 80

United States Employment Service, 127n

University of Chicago Press, xxi

University "Kiev-Mogila Academia", 69, 75

unreliability of measurement: *see* measurement error

unresolved interpretive issues in the relationships between work and personality, 232n

urbanness of principal place raised: *see* social characteristics

validity of indicators: *see* measurement error

valuation of conformity: *see* self-direction/ conformity, parental valuation of

valuation of self-direction for children: *see* self-direction/conformity, parental valuation of

values: *see* parental values, self-direction/ conformity, parental valuation of

values for children: *see* parental values

Verdery, Katherine, 54

Vogel, Ezra, 11

wages: *see* income

Warr, Peter, 154

Washington, D.C., xv, 233

Weber, Max, xiv

Webster, Murray, 66

Wejland, Andrzej, xxi, 68–69, 73, 76, 89, 92

Wesołowski, Włodzimierz, xiv, xxi, 6, 8, 11, 55, 56–57, 64, 103, 222, 225n, 233; "the Wesołowski model" (for funding cross-national research), 56, 60, 65, 66

white-collar workers: *see* nonmanual workers

Whyte, William Foote, 55n

Widerszpil, Stanislaw, 11

Williams, Robin M., Jr., 2n, 78

Witkin summary of Draw-a-Person test: *see* intellectual flexibility

Witkin's Embedded Figures test: *see* intellectual flexibility

work: *see* job conditions, occupational self-direction

Work and Personality, xiv, 233–34

work with things, data, and people: *see* occupational self-direction

working class: see manual workers, nonmanual workers, social class

Wright, Erik Olin, 2, 6–7, 9, 152–53

Yadov, Vladimir, xxi, 58, 66

Zaborowski, Wojciech, xix-xx, 54, 55, 65, 91, 125, 151, 176; obituary note in honor of, 151n

Zagorski, Krzysztof, 151

Zaslavskaya, Tat'iana, 59

Zawadski, Bohan, 154

About the Author

Melvin L. Kohn studied at Deep Springs Junior College and Cornell University, receiving his B.A. (in psychology) in 1948 and his Ph.D. (in sociology) in 1952. He did research in the Laboratory of Socio-environmental Studies of the National Institute of Mental Health from 1952 to 1985, serving as chief of that laboratory from 1960 until he left the National Institute to become professor of sociology at Johns Hopkins University.

Kohn's research has been almost entirely in the field of social structure and personality. In recent years, this work has been primarily cross-national and collaborative—initially comparing the United States to Italy, later and much more intensively, comparing the United States to Poland and Japan, then (in this book) comparing Poland and Ukraine under conditions of radical social change. He is now undertaking a comparative study of China in transition.

Kohn's principal publications in English are *Class and Conformity: A Study in Values* (1969), *Work and Personality: An Inquiry into the Impact of Social Stratification* (coauthored with Carmi Schooler, 1983), and *Social Structure and Self-Direction: A Comparative Analysis of the United States and Poland* (coauthored with Kazimierz M. Słomczynski, 1990), as well as an edited book, *Cross-National Research in Sociology* (1989), and numerous journal articles. He has also published books in German, Italian, and Polish, and (currently in press) in Ukrainian and Chinese. His articles have been translated into these and several other languages.

Kohn is a past-president of the American Sociological Association and a former member of the executive committee of the International Sociological Association. He is an honorary foreign member of the Polish Sociological Association, and a fellow of the American Academy of Arts and Sciences, the American Association for the Advancement of Science, and a past fellow of the Guggenheim Foundation. He has been a visiting fellow of the Institute for Social Research, Oslo, Norway, of the Institute of Advanced Studies of the Australian National University, and of the

267

Japan Society for the Advancement of Science. He was for some years a member of the Scientific Advisory Board of the Max-Planck Institut für Bildungsforschung in Berlin, and, in the dying years of the Soviet Union, was a member of the US–USSR Commission on the Humanities and Social Sciences of the American Academy of Learned Societies and the Soviet Academy of Sciences.